Street Corner Society

STREET CORNER SOCIETY

THE SOCIAL STRUCTURE OF AN ITALIAN SLUM

WILLIAM FOOTE WHYTE

THE UNIVERSITY OF CHICAGO PRESS

CHICAGO AND LONDON

Standard Book Number: 226–89538–6 (clothbound);
226–89539–4 (paperbound)

THE UNIVERSITY OF CHICAGO PRESS, CHICAGO 60637

The University of Chicago Press, Ltd., London

To

THE CORNER BOYS OF CORNERVILLE

PREFACE TO THE ENLARGED EDITION

THIS study is the product of many hands besides my own. A Junior Fellowship from Harvard University made the research possible by supporting me for a period of four years. Without the complete freedom afforded me by the Society of Fellows, I should never have been able to undertake the study of Cornerville. The University and Marshall Field fellowships at the University of Chicago supported me while I was writing up my results.

I owe a great personal debt to Conrad M. Arensberg, now of Columbia University, from whom I learned my field-work techniques. I discussed my plans with him before I began my study and had the benefit of his advice and criticism every step of the way. Dr. Eliot D. Chapple, in collaboration with Dr. Arensberg, worked out the conceptual scheme for the study of interactions which I have used throughout this book.

I am indebted both indirectly and directly to W. Lloyd Warner, of the University of Chicago, who conducted the "Yankee City" study. The techniques and the conceptual scheme of Drs. Arensberg and Chapple developed out of field-work experience beginning in Yankee City. Professor Warner also offered invaluable advice and criticism in the final preparation of the manuscript.

John Howard spent two years of field work in Cornerville. In this book I have found it wise to concentrate upon my own material, which I know best, but discussions of our separate observations were exceedingly valuable in clarifying my ideas. Mr. Howard was the first to suggest that an analysis of leadership would provide a means of integrating the study.

Lawrence J. Henderson, chairman of the Society of Fellows, helped me to develop powers of self-criticism. Elton Mayo, of the Harvard Business School, guided me in learning the techniques of interviewing used in my research. Everett C. Hughes, of the

University of Chicago, and E. B. Wilson and James Ford, of Harvard, gave me some valuable criticisms and suggestions.

Of course, the author assumes the usual responsibility for any defects which may have arisen through the misinterpretation of the ideas and criticisms furnished by others.

I am indebted to the *American Journal of Sociology* for permission to use some of my material from "Corner Boys: A Study of Clique Behavior," an article published in the March, 1941, issue. I am indebted to *Applied Anthropology* for permission to use the material contained in "The Social Role of the Settlement House," published in the October–December, 1941, issue.

Throughout the last two years of my research I was aided by Kathleen King Whyte. She also did the charts and criticized the manuscript in every step of its preparation, thus simplifying my job immeasurably.

For this edition I have written an extended account of the methods I used and of the experiences I had in making this study. This I have placed in an appendix because I feel it will mean more to the reader if he goes through the body of the study first.

For reading the Appendix and for their helpful comments, I am indebted to Everett C. Hughes and Buford Junker, of the University of Chicago; Bernard Cohen, of the Department of Sociology and Anthropology, Cornell University; Edith Lentz, of the New York State School of Industrial and Labor Relations; Stephen A. Richardson, of the Social Science Research Center; Alpheus W. Smith, of the New York State School of Industrial and Labor Relations; and Kathleen Whyte.

Those who wish to read of Cornersville or slums beyond this book may be interested in the following articles not included here:

"Social Organization in the Slums," *American Sociological Review*, Vol. VIII, No. 1 (February, 1943). An attempt to relate Cornerville to the literature on social organization and disorganization.

"A Slum Sex Code," *American Journal of Sociology*, Vol. XLIX (July, 1943). Here I point out that there are certain definitely recognized standards of behavior that the corner boys apply to sex. Also available in Reinhard Bendix and S. M. Lipset (eds.), *Class, Status, and Power* (Glencoe, Ill.: Free Press), pp. 308–16.

"A Challenge to Political Scientists," *American Political Science Review*, August, 1943. Based upon my study, I argued that it would be a good thing if political scientists gave some attention to the study of political organization. This article excited a good deal of controversy. The *Review* in August, 1944, published a rejoinder by John H. Hallowell, and in the April, 1946, issue I replied to Hallowell and also to other comments by Gabriel Almond and Lewis Dexter.

Since fictitious names are given to all characters in the book, I cannot acknowledge directly the help of local informants. The people of Cornerville had a greater part in making this book than most of them will ever realize. Their hospitality made the research possible and made my stay in Cornerville a thoroughly enjoyable experience. I count some of the people of the district among my closest friends. They gave me very active assistance in my study. They helped me, in part, because they thought my book might help Cornerville. That is perhaps too much to expect, but at least I hope that it will not bring harm to them or to any of the people of Cornerville.

WILLIAM FOOTE WHYTE

NEW YORK STATE SCHOOL OF INDUSTRIAL
AND LABOR RELATIONS
CORNELL UNIVERSITY

TABLE OF CONTENTS

PART III. CONCLUSION

APPENDIX

INDEX

LIST OF ILLUSTRATIONS

INTRODUCTION: CORNERVILLE AND ITS PEOPLE

IN THE heart of "Eastern City" there is a slum district
known as Cornerville, which is inhabited almost exclusively
by Italian immigrants and their children. To the rest of the
city it is a mysterious, dangerous, and depressing area. Cornerville is only a few minutes' walk from fashionable High Street, but
the High Street inhabitant who takes that walk passes from the
familiar to the unknown.

For years Cornerville has been known as a problem area,
and, while we were at war with Italy, outsiders became increasingly concerned with that problem. They feared that the
Italian slum dweller might be more devoted to fascism and Italy
than to democracy and the United States. They have long felt
that Cornerville was at odds with the rest of the community.
They think of it as the home of racketeers and corrupt politicians,
of poverty and crime, of subversive beliefs and activities.

Respectable people have access to a limited body of information upon Cornerville. They may learn that it is one of the most
congested areas in the United States. It is one of the chief points
of interest in any tour organized to show upper-class people the
bad housing conditions in which lower-class people live. Through
sight-seeing or statistics one may discover that bathtubs are rare,
that children overrun the narrow and neglected streets, that the
juvenile delinquency rate is high, that crime is prevalent among
adults, and that a large proportion of the population was on home
relief or W.P.A. during the depression.

In this view, Cornerville people appear as social work clients,
as defendants in criminal cases, or as undifferentiated members of
"the masses." There is one thing wrong with such a picture: no
human beings are in it. Those who are concerned with Cornerville seek through a general survey to answer questions that require the most intimate knowledge of local life. The only way to
gain such knowledge is to live in Cornerville and participate in

the activities of its people. One who does that finds that the district reveals itself to him in an entirely different light. The buildings, streets, and alleys that formerly represented dilapidation and physical congestion recede to form a familiar background for the actors upon the Cornerville scene.

One may enter Cornerville already equipped with newspaper information upon some of its racketeers and politicians, but the newspaper presents a very specialized picture. If a racketeer commits murder, that is news. If he proceeds quietly with the daily routines of his business, that is not news. If the politician is indicted for accepting graft, that is news. If he goes about doing the usual personal favors for his constituents, that is not news. The newspaper concentrates upon the crisis—the spectacular event. In a crisis the "big shot" becomes public property. He is removed from the society in which he functions and is judged by standards different from those of his own group. This may be the most effective way to prosecute the lawbreaker. It is not a good way to understand him. For that purpose, the individual must be put back into his social setting and observed in his daily activities. In order to understand the spectacular event, it is necessary to see it in relation to the everyday pattern of life—for there is a pattern to Cornerville life. The middle-class person looks upon the slum district as a formidable mass of confusion, a social chaos. The insider finds in Cornerville a highly organized and integrated social system.

It follows, therefore, that no immediate and direct solution to the problems posed for Cornerville can be given. It is only when the structure of the society and its patterns of action have been worked out that particular questions can be answered. This requires an exploration of new territory. In order to see how the present organization grew up, we may review the history of the local Italian settlement. When this is done, it will be time to go in and meet the people in order to discover from them the nature of the society in which they live.

For the Cornerville of today, history began in the 1860's, when a small group of Genoese settled together on an alley in one corner of what was then an Irish district. The stream of Italian immigration expanded slowly in the seventies and eighties and grew to a great flood in the nineties and in the first decade of the new century. The North Italians were the first to arrive, but the great wave of immigration came from the south, particularly from the vicinity of Naples and from Sicily. By the time that the southern immigration was at its height, most of the early Genoese settlers had moved to other sections of Eastern City or to suburban towns.

As early as 1915 the racial composition of Cornerville was practically the same as it is today. All but a few Irish families had moved out. The Jews, who came in at the same time as the Italians, had also been superseded, though many of them retained Cornerville business interests, particularly in the retail dry-goods line.

The Italian settlers brought over with them not only their language and customs but also a large proportion of their fellow-townsmen. The immigrants attracted relatives and friends. People from the same town, *paesani*, settled together, formed mutual aid societies, and each year celebrated the *Festa* of their patron saint as they had in Italy. The *paesani* made up little communities within a community, and even today one can mark out sections of Cornerville according to the town of origin of the immigrants, although these lines are fading with the growth of the younger generation.

First-generation immigrant society was organized primarily around the family and secondarily along the lines of *paesani*. Ties between families were cemented by the establishment of godparent-godchild relationships. Relatives by blood and ceremonial ties, as well as friends of the family, were linked together in an intricate network of reciprocal obligations. The individual who suffered misfortune was aided by his relatives and friends, and, when he had re-established himself, he shared his good fortune with those who had helped him.

The general region from which the immigrant came was also important in the organization of Cornerville life. The North Italians, who had had greater economic and educational opportunities, always looked down upon the southerners, and the Sicilians occupied the lowest position of all. Since many North and Central Italians were able to establish themselves before the southerners arrived, these distinctions were accentuated in the period of settlement, and they have not yet completely died out.

As the American-born generation has grown to maturity, the pattern of Cornerville life has undergone far-reaching changes. The ties of loyalty to *paesani* do not bind the son as they do the father. Even the Italian family has been broken into two separate generations. The Italian-born are known to the younger generation as "greasers." The children are often strongly attached to their parents, and yet they look down upon them. A few of the older people hold respected positions, but on the whole they do not have the authority that is characteristic of the older generation in most societies.

The younger generation has built up its own society relatively independent of the influence of its elders. Within the ranks of the younger men there are two main divisions: corner boys and college boys. Corner boys are groups of men who center their social activities upon particular street corners, with their adjoining barbershops, lunchrooms, poolrooms, or clubrooms. They constitute the bottom level of society within their age group, and at the same time they make up the great majority of the young men of Cornerville. During the depression most of them were unemployed or had only irregular employment. Few had completed high school, and many of them had left school before finishing the eighth grade. The college boys are a small group of young men who have risen above the corner-boy level through higher education. As they try to make places for themselves as professional men, they are still moving socially upward.

In a society such as ours, in which it is possible for men to begin life at the bottom and move up, it is important to discover who the people are who are advancing and how they are doing it. This gives perspective upon Cornerville society, and, at the same time, it shows what the world outside Cornerville has to offer to local people. The stories of Doc and his corner-boy gang and of Chick and his college-boy club present the contrast between the two groups and explain the different careers of the individual members.

While Doc and his boys and Chick and his club members are representative of a large part of local society, they are all "little guys" in Cornerville. In order to understand them, it is necessary to discover who the "big shots" are and see how they function. In Cornerville the big shots are racketeers and politicians.

With the South Side and Welport, Cornerville makes up Eastern City's Fourth Ward. Until recently the ward was dominated by the Cleveland Club, an Irish Democratic political organization located on the South Side. When the Italians first settled in Cornerville and began displacing the Irish population, there were sharp clashes between the races. As the Irish moved out, the hostilities were transferred to the political arena. Italian politicians organized Cornerville to overthrow the Irish domination of the ward.

Illegal activities during the prohibition era centered around the liquor traffic. With repeal the racketeer built his career upon the control of gambling activities. Cornerville men have played prominent roles in this field, although their Irish and Jewish colleagues share in the direction of the Eastern City rackets.

The racket and political organizations extend from the bottom to the top of Cornerville society, mesh with one another, and integrate a large part of the life of the district. They provide a general framework for the understanding of the actions of both "little guys" and "big shots."

In this exploration of Cornerville we shall be little concerned with people in general. We shall encounter particular people and observe the particular things that they do. The general pattern of life is important, but it can be constructed only through observing the individuals whose actions make up that pattern.

The "little guys" will be first on the scene (Part I). We shall see how they organize the activities of their own groups, and then, to place those groups in the social structure, we shall move up and observe the "big shots." The description of the racket and political organizations (in Part II) will give a general picture, but we are still concerned with particular people. The question is: What makes a man a big shot and by what means is he able to dominate the little guys? To answer that question, let us watch Tony Cataldo. He is a prominent racketeer, and he is concerned, among other things, with controlling the corner boys. How does he go about it? And let us watch George Ravello, Cornerville's state senator, as he organizes his political campaign. He needs the support of the corner boys. How does he get it? We know in general that the heads of political and racket organizations in Cornerville co-operate with one another. But what is the nature of that co-operation, upon what is it based, and how is it established? In order to answer that question, let us look at the particular people again and see how they act in relation to one another in the various situations that confront them in their careers.

If we can get to know these people intimately and understand the relations between little guy and little guy, big shot and little guy, and big shot and big shot, then we know how Cornerville society is organized. On the basis of that knowledge it becomes possible to explain people's loyalties and the significance of political and racket activities.

PART I

CORNER BOYS AND COLLEGE BOYS

CHAPTER I

DOC AND HIS BOYS

1. THE MEMBERS OF THE GANG

THE Nortons were Doc's gang. The group was brought together primarily by Doc, and it was built around Doc. When Doc was growing up, there was a kids' gang on Norton Street for every significant difference in age. There was a gang that averaged about three years older than Doc; there was Doc's gang, which included Nutsy, Danny, and a number of others; there was a group about three years younger, which included Joe Dodge and Frank Bonelli; and there was a still younger group, to which Carl and Tommy belonged.

Since the Nortons, as I knew them, grew out of these earlier groupings, some historical background is necessary. The story of the evolution of the Nortons can best be told as Doc's story.

Doc was born on Norton Street in 1908. His mother and father, who came from the province of Abruzzi, were the first non-Genoese Italians to settle on the street. In a large family, Doc was the youngest child and his mother's favorite. His father died when he was a small boy. When he was three years old, infantile paralysis shriveled his left arm so that it could never again be normal, but by constant exercise he managed to develop it until he was able to use it for all but heavy work.

Doc spoke of his early years in this way:

When I was a little boy, I used to dress very neatly. I always used to have a clean suit on, and when I sat down on the doorstep my mother told me always to sit on a newspaper. . . . . Other mothers would tell their sons, "Look at the way Dicky dresses. Why can't you be like Dicky?" It's only natural that they didn't like me—until I showed them they'd have to respect me. . . . .

I was about twelve when I had my first fight. I had a brother two years older than me. He got in an argument with a kid my size. He said to me, "He's too small for me, you fight him." At first I didn't want to, but finally I fought him. And I beat him up. . . . . After that I began to think maybe I was pretty good.

Nutsy was the head of our gang once. I was his lieutenant. He was bigger than me, and he had walloped me different times before I finally walloped him. When he walloped me, there weren't many people around, so I didn't mind, but the one time he broke his promise that he wouldn't hit me, there was a big crowd around. I was a proud kid. I couldn't let him get away with that. . . . . You see, I was wrestling him, and I had him down. I said, "If I let you up, will you promise not to hit me?" He promised, but when I let him up and turned away, he cracked me on the nose, and I got a bloody nose. I went after him, and I was beating him up when the big fellows stopped us. . . . . Next day I saw him leaning up against the wall. I went up to him and said, "I'll kill you," and I let him have one. He didn't fight back. He knew I was his master. And that got around. So after that I was the leader, and he was my lieutenant. . . . . That was when I was thirteen or fourteen. . . . . Nutsy was a cocky kid before I beat him up. . . . . After that, he seemed to lose his pride. I would talk to him and try to get him to buck up.

After I walloped him, I told the boys what to do. They listened to me. If they didn't, I walloped them. I walloped every kid in my gang at some time. We had one Sicilian kid on my street. When I walloped him, he told his father and the father came out looking for me. I hid up on a roof, and Nutsy told me when the father had gone. When I saw the kid next, I walloped him again—for telling his father on me. . . . . But I wasn't such a tough kid, Bill. I was always sorry after I walloped them.

They had faith in me, Bill. That's why I had to do some of these things. If one of our kids had gotten beaten up on some other street, I would go down there with him. Two or three of our boys would follow, not to help fight— just to watch. I would ask the kid, "Which one hit you?" He would point out the fellow, and I would wallop him. Then I would tell him, "Don't hit this kid any more, see!"

I was a tiger when I was a kid. I wasn't afraid of anybody. Most kids when they fight just push each other around, but I had a knockout punch in my right. I had the power. I could only use that one hand except for blocking but that commanded even more respect. They said, "What couldn't he do if he had two good hands?" And they thought the right was stronger because of it—maybe it was. . . . . It wasn't just the punch. I was the one who always thought of the things to do. I was the one with half a brain.

Doc was always sensitive about his arm, and he would not permit anyone to make allowances for his disability. He spent many hours at home shadow-boxing to develop speed and co-ordination.

Doc's most serious challenge came from Tony Fontana. As he told me:

Tony was in my gang when we were kids together. He was a good fighter. When he entered the ring as an amateur, he started off winning three fights by knockouts. When he turned pro, he was still knocking them out. . . . . At that time I was the leader of the gang. I was the tough guy. But he began to get fresh with me. One night he began pushing me around and talking big. I listened to him. I thought, "He must be tough. All those knockouts have got to mean something." So after a while I said, "I'm going up to bed." I got undressed and went to bed, but I couldn't sleep. I put on my clothes and came down again. I said, "Say that to me again!" He did and I let him have it—pow! . . . . But he wouldn't fight me. Why? Prestige, I suppose. Later we had it out with gloves on the playground. He was too good for me, Bill. I stayed with him, but he was too tough. . . . . Could he hit!

Doc told me these things only when I questioned him, and always, when he had finished telling about an incident in which he had "flattened" some rival, he would half-apologize and say that he really wasn't so much, that he could hardly understand how such things had happened.

Every now and then there was a clash with some other gang, and a "rally" resulted:

Once a couple of fellows in our gang tried to make a couple of girls on Main Street. The boy friends of these girls chased our fellows back to Norton Street. Then we got together and chased the boy friends back to where they came from. They turned around and got all Garden Street, Swift Street, and Main Street to go after us. . . . . It usually started this way. Some kid would get beaten up by one of our boys. Then he would go back to his street and get his gang. They would come over to our street, and we would rally them.

This time they carried banana stalks and milk bottles. We were armed. We used to hide our weapons in cellars so that we would have them ready in case of an emergency. But there were fifty of these fellows and only sixteen of us so we retreated into doorways and cellars to wait for them to cool off. . . . . They hung around there for a while, doing nothing, until I gave the signal to come out. Then we charged on them. I swung a banana stalk around me. I swung it through all the way to Main Street, and then I was behind the enemy lines, so I had to swing it back again. . . . . They used to have cement flowerpots standing up around the playground. We knocked them down. They would have killed anybody they hit, but we didn't want to hit anybody. We only wanted to scare them. . . . . After a while, things quieted down, and they went away.

I don't remember that we ever really lost a rally. Don't get the idea that we never ran away. We ran sometimes. We ran like hell. They would come over to our street and charge us. We might scatter, up roofs, down cellars, anywhere. We'd get our ammunition there. Then they would go back to the other end of the street and give us a chance to get together again. We would come out one after another—they would never charge us until we were all out there and ready. Then we would charge them—we had a good charge. They might break up, and then we would go back to our end of the street and wait for them to get together again. . . . . It always ended up by us chasing them back to their street. We didn't rally them there. We never went looking for trouble. We only rallied on our own street, but we always won there.

You know, the Nortons were a finer bunch. We were the best street in Cornerville. We didn't lush [steal from a drunk] or get in crap games. Sometimes we stole into shows free, but what do you expect? . . . . The Tylers were a tougher bunch. They'd steal, and they organized crap games. We used to rally the Tylers. After a while it died down, and later the Tylers and the Nortons merged. Their champion fighter was Johnny DiCausa, and their champion runner was Mike Torre. I was champion everything for our gang. When we got together, I had to race Mike around the block. They timed us. He made it in 26 seconds. Then I ran it. When I came down the street, I could hear them yelling, "Come on, Doc, come on, Doc!" I made it in 26 seconds too. So nothing was settled. They used to argue, "Johnny can lick him." "No, Doc can lick him." And we would look each other over, but we didn't fight. I guess we respected each other. . . . . Johnny went into the ring later, and he did pretty well. Mike was a champion runner on St. Patrick's College track team.

We didn't have many rallies between gangs. There was a lot of mutual respect. . . . .

We didn't go out to kill them. We didn't want to hurt anybody. It was just fun. . . . . I don't remember that anybody ever got hit on the head with a bottle. Maybe on the leg or in the back, but not on the head. The only time anybody ever got hurt was when Charlie got that tin can in his eye. We were rallying the King Streets on the playground. We charged, and Charlie got ahead of us. When he got into King Street, somebody threw this can, and the open end caught him right in the eye. The rally stopped. They were scared when they saw blood coming from his eye. . . . . We took Charlie home. I remember him screaming while the doctor worked on his eye. That made an impression on us. It never occurred to us before that somebody might be permanently injured in a rally. . . . . After that, there weren't any more rallies. I don't remember ever seeing one after that. . . . . And, then, we were getting older, around seventeen or eighteen. And I got going with the bigger fellows and didn't see my boys so much. They accepted me as one of them. That was a great honor. But when I didn't see my boys so much any more, our gang broke up.

At two stages in his career Doc participated in the activities of the Norton Street Settlement House. According to his story:

I used to go into the settlement when I was a small boy, but then I broke away. I went back in on account of the Sunset Dramatic Club. They were the pet club in there. They had been giving plays for a long time, and they had a lot of prestige. Lou Danaro used to tell me how hard it was to act and how much training you needed. Danny tried to steam me up to go in there and show them up. He had a lot of faith in me. He'll back me up in anything that requires brains. Danny and I got together, and we figured how I would get into that club. You had to have a unanimous vote. Some of the members knew me, and some of them didn't, but I managed to get around, and I was voted in. After a while I had the lead in a couple of their big plays, and all the boys from the corner came in to see them.

At that time we had two members of each club on the house council. I represented the Sunsets, and I was president of the council one year. I was very active then, and we raised money for a new amplifier for the house.

About that time, Tom Marino's crowd came in. They called themselves "the Corner Bums." There were a hundred of them, and I think they came in because they didn't have any place to meet at that time. They had it in for the Sunsets because the Sunsets were the pet club of the social workers. We could do anything we wanted to in that place. . . . . One time Joe Cardio went into Tom Marino's store to get some cream for the club's coffee. When they told him they didn't have any, he snapped his fingers and stamped his foot and said, "Aw, shucks!" All the boys were around, and, when they heard that, they couldn't get over it. They called the Sunsets the Cream Puffs from then on. I used to argue with them about it. At that time I used to hang around that corner as much as anywhere, and I fitted with the Corner Bums, so they would call us "the Cream Puffs—with one exception." I told them there were plenty of exceptions, but I couldn't make them change. . . . .

When the Bums got in there, they wanted to run the place. They started buying up votes so they could elect the president to the house council. They took girls out and bought them sodas. They really had a big campaign. Miss Baldwin wanted me to run for president again, because she thought I had done a good job, but I refused to run. The Sunsets put up Ted Riccio, and the Bums put up Fred Mantia. Ted was snowed under, but after the election they told me that if I had run again, they wouldn't have put up anybody to oppose me. . . . .

The Bums were really out to tip the joint. They had no respect for the social workers. I heard Guy Polletti talking to Mr. Ramsay in the hall one day. He was really obscene. Ramsay had to take it. What could he do? . . . . Then they were always calling up the police station and telling them, "There's a riot in the Norton Street Settlement. Send the riot squad down right away." A couple of cops would come down and joke with the boys, because they were good friends, but it looked bad for the settlement. . . . . One night the Bums put on a cabaret party, and they spiked the punch. They had two bowls of punch, one for the social workers and one for the party. But a couple of the girls got drunk, and Miss Baldwin found out about that other punch bowl. She started an argument, and Guy Polletti told her to get out. He called her a ———. I saw her going down the stairs crying. . . . .

That was pretty bad. At that time I was Kid Galahad, and I took it upon myself to defend the settlement. They were all in Marino's store one night when I went in to argue with them. There was Guy Polletti—he was a heavyweight fighter. There was Fred Mantia—he was a light-heavyweight, and he had done pretty well in the ring. They were all talking, but I interrupted them. I said, "Wait a minute, listen to me!" And then I gave it to them. They argued back, and they had a good argument. They had plenty to say about the social workers. "They're a bunch of snobs." "They're high-toned." "Who do they think they are in there that they're better than us?" They had a good argument there, and I couldn't answer that. But I said, "After all, the place does some good. In a crowded district like this, we need rooms to meet in." . . . . And they had chased plenty of people out of the settlement by acting so tough. I told them that the mothers had faith in the place, they thought it was a safe place for their daughters, and now the Bums were ruining that reputation. I told Fred, "You're only tough because nobody else in there is tough."

"Oh, no," he says, "I'm tough wherever I am."

I said, "If Terry Giovanni was in there you wouldn't be so tough." He didn't like that because Terry had knocked him out plenty of times. Well, the windup was that he agreed to apologize to Miss Baldwin. . . . .

About that time they got into another argument. In those days there was a mixed week end at the settlement camp at the beginning and end of each camp season. It was the biggest social event of the season, and the fellows and girls looked forward to those week ends from one year to the next. They were well chaperoned, and if there were ever any sexual affairs out there, I never heard of them. It was just good clean fun. But this time some of the Bums had had something to drink. Jesse Alluni was a real nice boy and not tough at all, but he couldn't hold his liquor. He came into the kitchen that night when Baldwin was in there and asked for a cup of coffee. She told him he was drunk and she made him go to bed. . . . . After that one incident, the camp was closed to men. Ever since that, it has been only a girls' camp except for the small boys. The fellows were steamed up about losing the camp, and they protested to Mr. Bacon [the headworker]. They sent around a petition, and they wanted to appeal to the board, but Mr. Bacon wouldn't let them. After a while, the excitement died down, and nothing was done. . . . .

About this time, the Sunsets broke up. They had been in the settlement ten or twelve years, and some of the fellows were getting married, so that had something to do with it, but I'm sure it was partly pressure from the Bums that drove them out of the settlement. When the Bums went after them, they wilted. I called them quitters and tried to make them keep the club going, but it broke up anyway.

After the Sunsets quit, the Bums got a clubroom outside and didn't come into the settlement any more. I don't think they were officially kicked out. They quit before they were thrown out. When Tom Marino entered politics, the name of the club didn't sound so nice, so they changed it to the Taylor A.C. after Ellen Taylor. She was a social worker that was loved and revered by all the other social workers. That name is funny when you think about the times the Bums used to have in the settlement.

Since the Bums dropped out, there has never been another crowd like them in the settlement. And that year they had their own man president of the house council was the last year that there was a house council. . . . .

When the Sunsets and the Corner Bums dropped out, I wasn't in the settlement any more myself.

Doc found school work easy. He read widely both at school and in the branch library. After the third year of high school, he left to take a job with a stained-glass firm. Art work had always been a major interest, and he did so well with the firm that he was promised rapid advancement. But then the depression came, the business failed, and Doc was unemployed. At first he went about aggressively looking for a job and continued his art work at home, but, when all his efforts brought no results, he stopped looking for work and even lost interest in art.

Doc lived with his sister and brother-in-law, so that he had food and shelter, but he hated to impose upon them. With the start of the federal relief program, he was able to go to work on the W.P.A., but, as a single man without dependents, he could not count upon steady employment. Between working days and in the long layoff periods, he spent nearly all his time on the street corner.

Danny was his closest friend. As Doc told me:

> Danny lived on Stone Street near Norton. I remember now the day when he came over to our street, when he was a small kid. He was a greaser— spoke broken English. The fellows made fun of him, but I liked the kid from the start. I told him to come along with our gang and do the things we did. He stuck with us.

When the kids' gang broke up, Doc and Danny remained together, though they were not often seen on Norton Street.

Danny left school after the eighth grade to take a factory job. He supplemented his earnings there by organizing a crap game in the washroom, and, in between jobs, he worked wherever there was labor trouble, for either side—"whoever pays me." Danny was powerfully built and well equipped by experience to fight in labor wars, but he did not relish this work. He fought for the money that was in it. In all my time in Cornerville, I never heard of Danny picking a fight with anyone.

With the passage of new labor legislation and government action against strike-breaking agencies, one of Danny's sources of income dried up. He had to fall back upon a crap game that he conducted in partnership with Mike Giovanni and Mike's brother, Terry.

Mike had been the leader of his kids' gang on King Street. He also had left school early for a factory job and was active wherever labor battles were being fought. Unlike Danny, he worked for only one side—the union. As he explained: "Unionism is like a religion. You have those beliefs, and you have to stick to them." In the last years of prohibition, factory work in his line became scarce, and Mike supported himself by running a crap game and a small speakeasy. He did not like the crap game, nor was it very profitable, for he refused the business of those who especially could not afford to lose. He thought he had "the right connections" to provide protection for the speakeasy, but police raids forced him out of business. He opened a lunchroom, but that also proved unprofitable, since too much of the business was on a credit basis. While the lunchroom operated, it provided a social center for Mike and his friends. Danny was a frequent visitor, and Doc spent some of his time there.

Long John, a young man from another part of Cornerville, took to hanging with Mike's crowd. He had been hanging with a particularly tough gang up to the time that his older brother was sentenced to life-imprisonment for murder. Prodded by his mother, Long John began to worry about his own future. Danny and Mike advised him to break away from his former associates and hang with them. For some time they took care of his spending money and let him earn small sums by serving as watchman (looking out for the police) in their crap game. Then he got himself a factory job which provided sporadic employment throughout the year.

When Doc's kids' gang broke up, Nutsy was the only member who continued to spend all his spare time on Norton Street. Since he took up with the younger boys, Doc and Danny called him "the King of the Kids." Frank Bonelli became particularly attached to Nutsy. Joe Marco, known as Joe Dodge, was a good friend of both men. Carl and Tommy, who had belonged to a still younger group, now accepted Nutsy's leadership. Alec had gone to school with a younger brother of Joe Dodge, and he first took to hanging on Norton Street in order to be with Joe.

At this time Nutsy was a part-time postal employee, Frank was trying to get started in professional baseball, and Joe had a highly paid but seasonal job in a quarry. Carl and Tommy both had steady factory jobs, and Alec had seasonal employment in the market district.

Besides Mike's crowd and Nutsy's boys, there were three other men who went to make up the Nortons as I knew them. Angelo Cucci, Fred Mackey (Macaluso), and Lou Danaro were all closely attached to Doc. Some years earlier, Fred's uncle had opened a grocery store on Norton Street and had placed Fred in charge part of the time. One day Danny got the boys to play a practical joke on him. They lined up in front of the counter and demanded protection money. Fred was panic-stricken until Doc took pity on him and explained the situation. Fred was so relieved that he looked upon Doc as his benefactor and frequently sought his company, even after the store had been sold.

For several years Lou Danaro had worked for Mr. Bacon, the headworker of the Norton Street Settlement, and had even lived in the house. The corner boys thought that he considered himself above them, and they would have nothing to do with him. Doc knew Lou's cousin very well. The cousins did not get along; Doc thought that was too bad, so, when he went out with Lou's cousin, he insisted that they get Lou to join them. In that way he struck up a friendship with Lou. When Lou finally broke with Mr. Bacon and moved out of the settlement, his friendship with Doc made it possible for him to be accepted on the street corner.

Fred and Lou both lived in the suburbs, but they drove into Eastern City for their part-time jobs and into Cornerville to join Doc and his friends.

When Doc first met him, Angelo was exceedingly shy and had no friends. He spent most of his time at home practicing the violin, which he hoped some day to play in a concert orchestra. When Doc accepted him as a friend, it was possible for Angelo to join the corner boys.

Close friendship ties already existed between certain of the men, but the Nortons, as an organization, did not begin to function until the early spring of 1937. It was at that time that Doc returned to the corner. Nutsy, Frank, Joe, Alec, Carl, and Tommy had a great respect for Doc and gathered around him. Angelo, Fred, and Lou followed Doc in making the corner their headquarters. Danny and Mike were drawn to Norton Street by their friendship for Doc and by the location of their crap game, right next to "the corner." Long John followed Danny and Mike.

The men became accustomed to acting together. They were also tied to one another by mutual obligations. In their experiences together there were innumerable occasions when one man would feel called upon to help another, and the man who was aided would want to return the favor. Strong group loyalties were supported by these reciprocal activities.

There were distinctions in rank among the Nortons. Doc, Danny, and Mike held the top positions. They were older than any others except Nutsy. They possessed a greater capacity for social movement. While the followers were restricted to the narrow sphere of one corner, Doc, Danny, and Mike had friends in many other groups and were well known and respected throughout a large part of Cornerville. It was one of their functions to accompany the follower when he had to move outside of his customary social sphere and needed such support. The leadership three were also respected for their intelligence and powers of self-expression. Doc in particular was noted for his skill in argument. On the infrequent occasions when he did become involved, he was usually able to outmaneuver his opponent without humiliating him. I never saw the leadership three exert their authority through physical force, but their past fighting reputations tended to support their positions.

Doc was the leader of the gang. The Nortons had been Doc's gang when they had been boys, and, although the membership had changed, they were still thought to be Doc's gang. The crap game and its social obligations prevented Danny and Mike from spending as much time with the Nortons as did Doc. They were not so intimate with the followers, and they expected him to lead.

Long John was in an anomalous position. Though he was five years younger than Doc, his friendship with the three top men gave him a superior standing. As Doc explained:

> It's because we've always catered to Long John. When we go somewhere, we ask Long John to go with us. We come up to him and slap him on the back. We give him so much attention that the rest of the fellows have to respect him.

Nevertheless, he had little authority over the followers. At this time he was accustomed to gamble away his week's earnings in the crap game, and this was thrown up against him.

There is an important social distinction between those who hold crap games and those who play in them. The game-holders enjoy something of the standing of businessmen; the "shooters" are thought to be suckers. The Nortons as a group considered themselves above the crap-shooters' level, and at this time Long John was trying unsuccessfully to break away from the game.

In the spring of 1937 Nutsy was recognized informally as the superior of Frank, Joe, and Alec, but his relations with a girl had

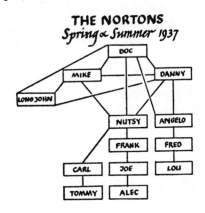

THE NORTONS
Spring & Summer 1937

☐ *Corner boy*

—— *Line of influence*

Positions of boxes indicate relative status

already begun to damage his standing. A corner boy is not expected to be chaste, but it is beneath him to marry a girl who is "no good." Nutsy was going so steadily with this girl that marriage seemed a distinct possibility, and, reacting to the criticism of his friends, he gradually withdrew from the gang. He did not again play a prominent role in the Nortons until toward the end of my stay in Cornerville, but in the spring and summer of 1937 he was still a man of moderate importance.

As the story gets under way, Doc was twenty-nine; Mike, twenty-nine; Danny, twenty-seven; Long John, twenty-four; Nutsy, twenty-nine; Frank, twenty-three; Joe, twenty-four; Alec, twenty-one; Angelo, twenty-five; Fred, twenty-five; Lou, twenty-four;

Carl, twenty-one; and Tommy, twenty. The accompanying chart presents a picture of the relations between the men as they appeared at this time. For purposes of shorthand designation, I shall refer to the top four men as the "leaders" and to the others as the "followers." If the special characteristics of Long John are borne in mind, this should not be confusing.

2. BOWLING AND SOCIAL RANKING

One evening in October, 1937, Doc scheduled a bowling match against the Italian Community Club, which was composed largely of college men who held their meetings every two weeks in the Norton Street Settlement House. The club was designed to be an organization of well-educated and superior men, although Doc was a member, and Angelo, Lou, and Fred of the Nortons had been voted in upon his recommendation. The other Nortons felt that the club was "high-toned," and around the corner it was known as the "Boys' Junior League." They were a little flattered that members of their group could mix with such a club, but their opinion was formed largely from the personalities of Chick Morelli, the president, and Tony Cardio, another prominent member, both of whom they considered snobbish and conceited. Consequently, the Nortons took this match very seriously.

Doc was captain of the Nortons. He selected Long John, Frank, Joe, and Tommy for his team. Danny and Mike were not bowling in this period. Chick and Tony led the Community Club team.

Feeling ran high. The Nortons shouted at the club bowlers and made all sorts of noises to upset their concentration. The club members were in high spirits when they gained an early lead but had little to say as the Nortons pulled ahead to win by a wide margin.

After the match I asked Frank and Joe if there was any team that they would have been more eager to beat. They said that if they could pick out their favorite victims, they would choose Chick Morelli, Tony Cardio, Joe Cardio (Tony's brother), Mario Testa, and Hector Marto. These last three had all belonged to the Sunset Dramatic Club.

Frank and Joe said that they had nothing against the other three men on the Community Club team but that the boys had been anxious to beat that team in order to put Chick and Tony "in their places." Significantly, Frank and Joe did not select their favorite victims on the basis of bowling ability. The five were good bowlers, but that was not the deciding factor in the choice. It was their social positions and ambitions that were the objects of attack, and it was that which made victory over the Community Club so satisfying.

Lou Danaro and Fred Mackey had cheered for the club. Although they were club members, the boys felt that this did not excuse them. Danny said: "You're a couple of traitors—Benedict Arnolds. . . . . You're with the boys—and then you go against them. . . . . Go on, I don't want your support."

Fred and Lou fell between the two groups and therefore had to face this problem of divided allegiance. Doc's position on the corner was so definitely established that no one even considered the possibility of his choosing to bowl for the Community Club against the Nortons.

This was the only match between the two teams that ever took place. The corner boys were satisfied with their victory, and the club did not seek a return match. Tony Cardio objected to the way in which the Nortons had tried to upset the concentration of his team and said it was no fun to bowl against such poor sports. There were, however, clashes with individual members of the club. One night in November, Doc, Frank Bonelli, Joe Dodge, and I were bowling when Chick Morelli and Lou Danaro came in together. We agreed to have two three-man teams, and Chick and Doc chose sides. Chick chose Lou and me. The match was fairly even at first, but Doc put his team far ahead with a brilliant third string. Toward the end of this string, Chick was sitting next to Joe Dodge and mumbling at him, "You're a lousy bum. . . . . You're a no-good bowler."

Joe said nothing until Chick had repeated his remarks several times. Then Joe got up and fired back at Chick, "You're a conceited ———! I feel like taking a wallop at you. I never knew anybody was as conceited as you. . . . . You're a conceited ———!"

Doc stood between them to prevent a fight. Chick said nothing, and Doc managed to get the six of us quietly into the elevator.

Joe was not satisfied, and he said to me in a loud voice: "Somebody is going to straighten him out some day. Somebody will have to wallop him to knock some of that conceit out of him."

When we were outside the building, Lou walked away with Chick, and the rest of us went into Jennings' Cafeteria for "coffee-ands." We discussed Chick:

Doc: It's lucky you didn't hit him. They'd be after you for manslaughter. You're too strong for the kid.

Joe: All right. But when somebody's too tough for me, I don't fool around..... He shouldn't fool around me..... If he's gonna say them things, he should smile when he says them. But I think he really meant it.

Doc: The poor guy, so many fellows want to wallop him—and he knows it.

Frank: I liked him all right until the other night. We went to the Metropolitan Ballroom..... He didn't mingle in at all. He just lay down on a couch like he wanted to be petted. He wasn't sociable at all.

After driving Chick home, Lou joined us in Jennings'. He said that Chick felt very bad about the incident and didn't know what it was that made people want to hit him. Lou added: "I know he didn't mean it that way. He's really a swell kid when you get to know him. There's only one thing I don't like about him." Then he told about a time when Chick had started an argument with a dance-hall attendant on some technicality involved in the regulations of the hall. Lou commented: "He was just trying to show how intelligent he was."

A few days later, when Joe's anger had subsided, Doc persuaded him to apologize.

Doc did not defend Chick for friendship's sake. Nor was it because they worked together in the Community Club. In the club Doc led a faction generally hostile to Chick, and he himself was often critical of the manner in which Chick sought to run the organization. But Doc had friends in both groups. He did not like to see the groups at odds with each other. Though friendship between the Nortons and Chick was impossible, it was Doc's function to see that diplomatic relations were maintained.

The Community Club match served to arouse enthusiasm for bowling among the Nortons. Previously the boys had bowled sporadically and often in other groups, but now for the first time bowling became a regular part of their social routine. Long John,

Alec, Joe Dodge, and Frank Bonelli bowled several nights a week throughout the winter. Others bowled on frequent occasions, and all the bowlers appeared at the alleys at least one night a week.

A high score at candlepins requires several spares or strikes. Since a strike rarely occurs except when the first ball hits the kingpin properly within a fraction of an inch, and none of the boys had such precise aim, strikes were considered matters of luck, although a good bowler was expected to score them more often than a poor one. A bowler was judged according to his ability to get spares, to "pick" the pins that remained on the alley after his first ball.

There are many mental hazards connected with bowling. In any sport there are critical moments when a player needs the steadiest nerves if he is to "come through"; but, in those that involve team play and fairly continuous action, the player can sometimes lose himself in the heat of the contest and get by the critical points before he has a chance to "tighten up." If he is competing on a five-man team, the bowler must wait a long time for his turn at the alleys, and he has plenty of time to brood over his mistakes. When a man is facing ten pins, he can throw the ball quite casually. But when only one pin remains standing, and his opponents are shouting, "He can't pick it," the pressure is on, and there is a tendency to "tighten up" and lose control.

When a bowler is confident that he can make a difficult shot, the chances are that he will make it or come exceedingly close. When he is not confident, he will miss. A bowler is confident because he has made similar shots in the past and is accustomed to making good scores. But that is not all. He is also confident because his fellows, whether for him or against him, believe that he can make the shot. If they do not believe in him, the bowler has their adverse opinion as well as his own uncertainty to fight against. When that is said, it becomes necessary to consider a man's relation to his fellows in examining his bowling record.

In the winter and spring of 1937–38 bowling was the most significant social activity for the Nortons. Saturday night's intra-clique and individual matches became the climax of the week's events. During the week the boys discussed what had happened the previous Saturday night and what would happen on the coming Saturday night. A man's performance was subject to continual evaluation and criticism. There was, therefore, a close connection between a man's bowling and his position in the group.

The team used against the Community Club had consisted of two men (Doc and Long John) who ranked high and three men (Joe Dodge, Frank Bonelli, and Tommy) who had a low standing. When bowling became a fixed group activity, the Nortons' team evolved along different lines. Danny joined the Saturday-night crowd and rapidly made a place for himself. He performed very well and picked Doc as his favorite opponent. There was a good-natured rivalry between them. In individual competition Danny usually won, although his average in the group matches was no better than that of Doc's. After the Community Club match, when Doc selected a team to represent the Nortons against other corner gangs and clubs, he chose Danny, Long John, and himself, leaving two vacancies on the five-man team. At this time, Mike, who had never been a good bowler, was just beginning to bowl regularly and had not established his reputation. Significantly enough, the vacancies were not filled from the ranks of the clique. On Saturday nights the boys had been bowling with Chris Teludo, Nutsy's older cousin, and Mark Ciampa, a man who associated with them only at the bowling alleys. Both men were popular and were first-class bowlers. They were chosen by Doc, with the agreement of Danny and Long John, to bowl for the Nortons. It was only when a member of the regular team was absent that one of the followers in the clique was called in, and on such occasions he never distinguished himself.

The followers were not content with being substitutes. They claimed that they had not been given an opportunity to prove their ability. One Saturday night in February, 1938, Mike organized an intraclique match. His team was made up of Chris Teludo, Doc, Long John, himself, and me. Danny was sick at the time, and I was put in to substitute for him. Frank, Alec, Joe, Lou, and Tommy made up the other team. Interest in this match was more intense than in the ordinary "choose-up" matches, but the followers bowled poorly and never had a chance.

After this one encounter the followers were recognized as the second team and never again challenged the team of Doc, Danny, Long John, Mark, and Chris. Instead, they took to individual efforts to better their positions.

On his athletic ability alone, Frank should have been an excellent bowler. His ball-playing had won him positions on semiprofessional teams and a promise—though unfulfilled—of a job on a minor-league team. And it was not lack of practice that held him back, for, along with Alec and Joe Dodge, he bowled more frequently than Doc, Danny, or Mike. During the winter of 1937–38 Frank occupied a particularly subordinate position in the group. He spent his time with Alec in the pastry shop owned by Alec's uncle, and, since he had little employment throughout the winter, he became dependent upon Alec for a large part of the expenses of his participation in group activities. Frank fell to the bottom of the group. His financial dependence preyed upon his mind. While he sometimes bowled well, he was never a serious threat to break into the first team.

Some events of June, 1937, cast additional light upon Frank's position. Mike organized a baseball team of some of the Nortons to play against a younger group of Norton Street corner boys. On the basis of his record, Frank was considered the best player on either team, yet he made a miserable showing. He said to me: "I can't seem to play ball when I'm playing with fellows I know, like that bunch. I do much better when I'm playing for the Stanley A.C. against some team in Dexter, Westland, or out of town." Accustomed to filling an inferior position, Frank was unable to star even in his favorite sport when he was competing against members of his own group.

One evening I heard Alec boasting to Long John that the way he was bowling he could take on every man on the first team and lick them all. Long John dismissed the challenge with these words: "You think you could beat us, but, under pressure, you die!"

Alec objected vehemently, yet he recognized the prevailing group opinion of his bowling. He made the highest single score of the season, and he frequently excelled during the week when he bowled with Frank, Long John, Joe Dodge, and me, but on Saturday nights, when the group was all assembled, his performance was quite different. Shortly after this conversation Alec had several chances to prove himself, but each time it was "an off night," and he failed.

Carl, Joe, Lou, and Fred were never good enough to gain any recognition. Tommy was recognized as a first-class bowler, but he did most of his bowling with a younger group.

One of the best guides to the bowling standing of the members was furnished by a match held toward the end of April, 1938. Doc had an idea that we should climax the season with an individual competition among the members of the clique. He persuaded the owner of the alleys to contribute ten dollars in prize money to be divided among the three highest scorers. It was decided that only those who had bowled regularly should be eligible, and on this basis Lou, Fred, and Tommy were eliminated.

Interest in this contest ran high. The probable performances of the various bowlers were widely discussed. Doc, Danny, and Long John each listed his predictions. They were unanimous in conceding the first five places to themselves, Mark Ciampa, and Chris Teludo, although they differed in predicting the order among the first five. The next two positions were generally conceded to Mike and to me. All the ratings gave Joe Dodge last position, and Alec, Frank, and Carl were ranked close to the bottom.

The followers made no such lists, but Alec let it be known that he intended to show the boys something. Joe Dodge was annoyed to discover that he was the unanimous choice to finish last and argued that he was going to win.

When Chris Teludo did not appear for the match, the field was narrowed to ten. After the first four boxes, Alec was leading by several pins. He turned to Doc and said, "I'm out to get you boys tonight." But then he began to miss, and, as mistake followed mistake, he stopped trying. Between turns, he went out for drinks, so that he became flushed and unsteady on his feet. He threw the ball carelessly, pretending that he was not interested in the competition. His collapse was sudden and complete; in the space of a few boxes he dropped from first to last place.

The bowlers finished in the following order:

1. Whyte	6. Joe
2. Danny	7. Mark
3. Doc	8. Carl
4. Long John	9. Frank
5. Mike	10. Alec

There were only two upsets in the contest, according to the predictions made by Doc, Danny, and Long John: Mark bowled very poorly and I won. However, it is important to note that neither Mark nor I fitted neatly into either part of the clique. Mark associated with the boys only at the bowling alleys and had no recognized status in the group. Although I was on good terms with all the boys, I was closer to the leaders than to the followers, since Doc was my particular friend. If Mark and I are left out of consideration, the performances were almost exactly what the leaders expected and the followers feared they would be. Danny, Doc, Long John, and Mike were bunched together at the top. Joe Dodge did better than was expected of him, but even he could not break through the solid ranks of the leadership.

Several days later Doc and Long John discussed the match with me.

LONG JOHN: I only wanted to be sure that Alec or Joe Dodge didn't win. That wouldn't have been right.

DOC: That's right. We didn't want to make it tough for you, because we all liked you, and the other fellows did too. If somebody had tried to make it tough for you, we would have protected you. . . . . If Joe Dodge or Alec had been out in front, it would have been different. We would have talked them out of it. We would have made plenty of noise. We would have been really vicious. . . . .

I asked Doc what would have happened if Alec or Joe had won.

They wouldn't have known how to take it. That's why we were out to beat them. If they had won, there would have been a lot of noise. Plenty of arguments. We would have called it lucky—things like that. We would have tried to get them in another match and then ruin them. We would have to put them in their places.

Every corner boy expects to be heckled as he bowls, but the heckling can take various forms. While I had moved ahead as early as the end of the second string, I was subjected only to good-natured kidding. The leaders watched me with mingled surprise and amusement; in a very real sense, I was permitted to win.

Even so, my victory required certain adjustments. I was hailed jocularly as "the Champ" or even as "the Cheese Champ" Rather than accept this designation, I pressed my claim for recognition. Doc arranged to have me bowl a match against Long John. If I won, I should have the right to challenge Doc or Danny. The four of us went to the alleys together. Urged on by Doc and Danny, Long John won a decisive victory. I made no further challenges.

Alec was only temporarily crushed by his defeat. For a few days he was not seen on the corner, but then he returned and sought to re-establish himself. When the boys went bowling, he challenged Long John to an individual match and defeated him. Alec began to talk once more. Again he challenged Long John to a match, and again he defeated him. When bowling was resumed in the fall, Long John became Alec's favorite opponent, and for some time Alec nearly always came out ahead. He gloated. Long John explained: "He seems to have the Indian sign on me." And that is the way these incidents were interpreted by others—simply as a queer quirk of the game.

It is significant that, in making his challenge, Alec selected Long John instead of Doc, Danny, or Mike. It was not that Long John's bowling ability was uncertain. His average was about the same as that of Doc or Danny and better than that of Mike. As a member of the top group but not a leader in his own right, it was his social position that was vulnerable.

When Long John and Alec acted outside the group situation, it became possible for Alec to win. Long John was still considered the dependable man in a team match, and that was more important in relation to a man's standing in the group. Nevertheless, the leaders felt that Alec should not be defeating Long John and tried to reverse the situation. As Doc told me:

Alec isn't so aggressive these days. I steamed up at the way he was going after Long John, and I blasted him. . . . . Then I talked to Long John. John is an introvert. He broods over things, and sometimes he feels inferior. He can't be aggressive like Alec, and when Alec tells him how he can always beat him, Long John gets to think that Alec is the better bowler. . . . . I talked to

him. I made him see that he should bowl better than Alec. I persuaded him
that he was really the better bowler. . . . . Now you watch them the next
time out. I'll bet Long John will ruin him.

The next time Long John did defeat Alec. He was not able to
do it every time, but they became so evenly matched that Alec
lost interest in such competition.

The records of the season 1937–38 show a very close correspondence between social position and bowling performance. This developed because bowling became the primary social activity of
the group. It became the main vehicle whereby the individual
could maintain, gain, or lose prestige.

Bowling scores did not fall automatically into this pattern.
There were certain customary ways of behaving which exerted
pressure upon the individuals. Chief among these were the manner of choosing sides and the verbal attacks the members directed
against one another.

Generally, two men chose sides in order to divide the group into
two five-man teams. The choosers were often, but not always,
among the best bowlers. If they were evenly matched, two poor
bowlers frequently did the choosing, but in all cases the process
was essentially the same. Each one tried to select the best bowler
among those who were still unchosen. When more than ten men
were present, choice was limited to the first ten to arrive, so that
even a poor bowler would be chosen if he came early. It was the
order of choice which was important. Sides were chosen several
times each Saturday night, and in this way a man was constantly
reminded of the value placed upon his ability by his fellows and
of the sort of performance expected of him.

Of course, personal preferences entered into the selection of
bowlers, but if a man chose a team of poor bowlers just because
they were his closest friends, he pleased no one, least of all his
team mates. It was the custom among the Nortons to have the
losing team pay for the string bowled by the winners. As a rule,
this small stake did not play an important role in the bowling, but
no one liked to pay without the compensating enjoyment of a
closely contested string. For this reason the selections by good
bowlers or by poor bowlers coincided very closely. It became gen-

erally understood which men should be among the first chosen in order to make for an interesting match.

When Doc, Danny, Long John, or Mike bowled on opposing sides, they kidded one another good-naturedly. Good scores were expected of them, and bad scores were accounted for by bad luck or temporary lapses of form. When a follower threatened to better his position, the remarks took quite a different form. The boys shouted at him that he was lucky, that he was "bowling over his head." The effort was made to persuade him that he should not be bowling as well as he was, that a good performance was abnormal for him. This type of verbal attack was very important in keeping the members "in their places." It was used particularly by the followers so that, in effect, they were trying to keep one another down. While Long John, one of the most frequent targets for such attacks, responded in kind, Doc, Danny, and Mike seldom used this weapon. However, the leaders would have met a real threat on the part of Alec or Joe by such psychological pressures.

The origination of group action is another factor in the situation. The Community Club match really inaugurated bowling as a group activity, and that match was arranged by Doc. Group activities are originated by the men with highest standing in the group, and it is natural for a man to encourage an activity in which he excels and discourage one in which he does not excel. However, this cannot explain Mike's performance, for he had never bowled well before Saturday night at the alleys became a fixture for the Nortons.

The standing of the men in the eyes of other groups also contributed toward maintaining social differentiation within the group. In the season of 1938–39 Doc began keeping the scores of each man every Saturday night so that the Nortons' team could be selected strictly according to the averages of the bowlers, and there could be no accusation of favoritism. One afternoon when we were talking about bowling performances, I asked Doc and Danny what would happen if five members of the second team should make better averages than the first team bowlers. Would they then become the first team? Danny said:

Suppose they did beat us, and the San Marcos would come up and want a match with us. We'd tell them, those fellows are really the first team, but the San Marcos would way, "We don't want to bowl them, we want to bowl you." We would say, "All right, you want to bowl Doc's team?" and we would bowl them.

Doc added:

I want you to understand, Bill, we're conducting this according to democratic principles. It's the others who won't let us be democratic.

3. THE NORTONS AND THE APHRODITE CLUB

In March, 1938, the Nortons made the acquaintance of the Aphrodite Club girls. The club had a dozen members, most of them attractive, all of them well dressed, who met once a week in the Norton Street Settlement House with one of the social workers. The girls went to plays, held socials, and each year saved up their dues for a trip to some point of interest.

In the winter of 1937–38 the Italian Community Club and the Aphrodite Club had become very friendly. They met in the settlement house on the same evening and sometimes gave their social activities together. The girls had a great respect for education and were anxious to make a good impression on the Community Club boys, although they thought some of them conceited. The men found the girls attractive, but some of the leading figures in the Community Club were anxious to make contacts with girls from the Italian Junior League and thus leave the Aphrodite girls and Cornerville behind them in their social contacts. While individual members were still mildly interested in some of the girls, by March the two clubs were slowly drifting apart.

Doc, Angelo, Lou, and Fred knew the girls through being members of the Community Club, but up to this time the Nortons as a whole had no social contacts with the Aphrodite Club. To all outward appearances their attitude was hostile. In June, 1937, I heard them discussing Carrie, one of the most attractive of the Aphrodite girls:

NUTSY: She's a good-looking girl, but I don't like her.

FRANK: If you took three hours to make up your face, you'd be good-looking too.

LONG JOHN: She has tough pins [legs]. Did you ever notice the pins on her? That's why she always wears such low dresses.

JOE DODGE: She goes for anybody with a little money. She likes you if you have a car. I like to drive by her in my car and stick my nose in the air. . . . . She's just an alley cat.

Except for the four men who belonged to the Community Club, the Nortons almost never set foot inside the settlement house. The girls moved in a different social orbit, and the Nortons considered them "high-toned" and conceited. Still, they could not help finding them attractive.

As Doc told me:

They had admired the girls for a long time, and they were always after me to fix it up with them. . . . . Friday night the Community Club was going bowling after the meeting. They wanted me to go with them, but I stalled them off. I said I would be down in a little while. . . . . Then I rounded up these boys [the Nortons] and told them we were going to bowl the girls. . . . . I think the Aphrodite Club expected they were going to bowl with the Community Club. If I had asked them to bowl with this bunch, they would probably have refused because it's a tougher bunch. . . . . But I just brought them down here and we bowled.

The evening was a great success. The two groups bowled together again on Saturday night, and on both occasions the bowling was followed by "coffee-ands" at Jennings'.

Alec discussed this beginning with me: "Before, we thought they were high-hat, and I guess they thought we were a bunch of rowdies. . . . . Now I think they like our clique. We're cutting out the Community Club."

Members of the two groups saw one another almost every night for a period of several weeks. This brought about important changes in the social life of the Nortons.

One night, only four days after the first bowling match, I was surprised to find Alec, Joe Dodge, Tommy, and Long John playing cards at a table in the game room of the Norton Street Settlement House. Doc was at a table by himself, reading a magazine. I sat down with him to demand an explanation. He told me that the boys had wanted to go bowling but that he had not, so he told them to come into the settlement house and promised to get some of the girls to play cards with them. The girls were not in the house at the time, but, once inside, the boys played among themselves.

Except for Danny and Mike, the Nortons began coming into the settlement house almost every night to play cards by themselves or with the girls. Sometimes, when they were standing on the corner, the girls invited them to come in.

The social workers made no effort to keep the Nortons in the settlement. Miss Halloran, who was in charge of the game room, tried to treat them like the younger boys and girls in her charge. Corner boys are quick to notice the slightest sign of condescension, and Miss Halloran's attitude was painfully apparent. For several days the boys seemed to be obsessed with the task of denouncing Miss Halloran to one another in the strongest language they could command.

Long John, who had traveled the greatest social distance to go into the house, was the first one to drop out. After one particularly unpleasant encounter with Miss Halloran, he told the boys that he would never go in again. Two days later I was standing on the corner with him when it began to rain. Not knowing of his resolution, I suggested that we go into the settlement. He agreed, but, as he opened the door, we met Joe Dodge, who laughed at him and said, "I thought you weren't going to come in here any more."

Long John was embarrassed. We went out into the rain again, and he remarked thoughtfully, "I think that everybody that goes in there thinks they're a little better than the next fellow."

Two weeks after their first evening in the game room, all the Nortons had deserted the settlement.

From the beginning the boys took their activities with the girls very seriously. When they went bowling for the second time, Alec brought along a box of candy from his uncle's shop. The following Saturday he brought a large supply of pastry.

Doc told the boys that the Alluni sisters and their cousins had a summer camp on a lake some miles from the city. If the boys became friendly with the girls, they might be invited to spend the day in the country sometime during the summer. The possibility of taking the girls away from the Community Club was another inducement.

In a short time the Nortons did supersede the Community

Club, but victory was achieved only by default. Tony Cardio was infatuated with Helen, the most attractive of the girls, but the other club members lost interest in the Aphrodite Club. However, since Tony was considered one of the two most conceited members, the Nortons could get almost a full measure of satisfaction from defeating him.

A week after the first meeting of the two groups, I asked Alec what he thought the association with the girls had done to the Nortons. He said: "The boys get along better. There aren't so many squabbles any more." At this time the Aphrodite girls and the Nortons met en masse. Alec commented:

If I went out with them a few times, I could tell which one I liked. . . . . But you start going with one girl, and you find you're going with a deadhead. It's tough. What are you gonna do? When they're all in a crowd, it's hard to shift around.

The boys had to proceed carefully. They could pay attention to Helen as much as they liked, because she was the prize of them all, but pairing-off with any of the others required a cautious preliminary survey of the situation.

A week later the first step in this direction was taken. Joe Dodge, Long John, Frank Bonelli, and I were standing on the corner. Angelo Cucci encountered Alec farther down the street and told him that he had just seen three of the Aphrodite girls on their way to Jennings'. They had remarked that it would be a nice evening for a ride but that they did not believe that Joe Dodge owned the big car the boys all talked about. Alec walked up to us and took Joe aside. Joe then left us and walked across the playground to King Street. Frank, who had been watching attentively, turned to me and asked if I wanted to walk down to Jennings' with him. I said that I thought it was too early. Frank started off alone. Alec asked me if I wanted to walk to Jennings' with him. Long John said, "You ain't bulling us. Why don't you tell the truth and say you're goin' for a ride?"

I asked Long John if he wanted to walk down with us. He refused but said that I should go.

As Alec and I walked down Main Street, he said that we were to meet Joe Dodge in his car, drive to Jennings', and take out the girls. "But now Frank has started down to Jennings'. . . . . He shouldn't do that." There were two reasons for excluding Frank: he was shy with girls and he had no money to entertain them.

We went into Jennings' to talk to the three girls. One of them had to be home early, but she urged that the other two go. I persuaded Joe and Alec to leave me behind. By this time Frank had come in and sat down at a table by himself. As Joe and Alec went out with the girls, I joined Frank. A few minutes later Long John and Nutsy came in and joined us. Long John asked, "What's the matter, Bill? Did they double-cross you?" I explained what had happened, but he said he did not like the way they had acted.

Frank and Alec had been the best of friends and had spent long hours together in the pastry shop. Now Alec became more friendly with Joe Dodge, and they began taking the girls out in Joe's father's car. Frank said to me:

Let them go out with the girls. They've pulled a few fast ones. They say they're going to do a certain thing, and then you find them with the girls. They've done things that I would never do. . . . . It's hard enough to make a friend. A girl you can meet any time. . . . . It takes years to make a real friend.

The rift between Alec and Frank widened rapidly. Easter was the rush time at Alec's uncle's pastry shop, and Alec had promised to give Frank some of the extra work at this time. Frank said that Alec simply decided not to give it to him. Alec said that he went to get Frank, but Frank was very gruff and unpleasant so he refused to bother with him. In any case, Frank did not get this much-needed work, and he was bitter about it. Frank and Alec told their stories to Doc at different times. Alec complained that Frank was being ungrateful after he had done so much for him. Frank complained that Alec had been double-crossing him over the girls. Doc listened sympathetically but was unable to smooth things over. Joe Dodge's car and the Aphrodite girls had created too wide a gulf between them.

The activities of Alec and Joe made them unpopular with all the other Nortons—except Carl and Tommy, who had cars. They continued to hang on the corner, but for some time they were simply tolerated.

One Saturday night the Nortons were bowling with the girls. Ten men who had been members of the Sunset Dramatic Club were bowling on two adjoining alleys.

Danny and Mike came in late, sat by themselves, refused all invitations to bowl, and watched the proceedings with evident disgust. Danny told me: "I don't like to bowl with the girls. There's no competition. . . . . Then, when you get a touch hit, you can't say nothing. You got to watch what you say."

Toward the end of the evening, Mike called Doc aside. He pointed to the Sunsets and said, "We used to call them the Cream Puffs, but now, compared to you, they're the Lumberjacks."

Doc laughed. Mike gave Danny a penny and Danny gave it to Doc, saying, "Toss this up. See if you're a man. Heads, you're a man. Tails, you ain't."

Doc took this good-naturedly. But then Danny called over Mario Testa of the Sunsets and told him to tell Doc that the Cream Puffs had now become the Lumberjacks. Mario laughed. Doc became angry. Danny said to him, "I'll spot you 20 pins and I'll beat you. I spot all the girls 20 pins."

Doc accepted the challenge. Danny bowled 104 against Doc's 84 and enjoyed himself thoroughly. Doc said he did not mind being beaten by 20 pins; the next time he might beat Danny by 20 pins. Nor did he mind being kidded about bowling with the girls. He said he became angry only when Danny brought the Sunsets into the argument. While he had once belonged to their club, he took pride in his position with the Nortons, and he was sensitive about anything that would make them appear in an un-favorable light compared with the Sunsets.

At Jennings', after the bowling, Doc left the girls and sat with Danny. Danny agreed that it had been a mistake to bring the Sunsets into the argument, and he apologized. Doc said that he did not want Mike and Danny to be left out of the bowling any more than they did.

On the following afternoon Danny and Mike stood on the corner telling Frank, Long John, and me what they thought about

our association with the Aphrodite girls. Danny wanted to know
what we were getting out of it.

If you want to go places with them, you got to have money, and none of
yuz have got a dime, so forget about it.

Alec says to me, "I'll lay them all."

I tells him, "You won't lay a one of them, and I'll bet money on it. If
you lay one of them girls, you'll marry her. That's the only way you'll ever
lay one of them."

Long John said that he never had cared much for bowling with
the girls in the first place. Frank said that he had enjoyed it at
first but that now all the fun was gone out of it. Mike said that
he and Danny would form a "grievance committee" and would
readmit some of us to membership in the Cornerville Bears (this
being the name of a championship baseball team on which he had
once played) if we would swear not to bowl with the girls any
more. Frank made his promise. Long John jokingly said that he
would never apply for membership, and Danny said that Long
John would get back only over his dead body.

Mark Ciampa came along and took Frank for a ride in his car
with Joe Dodge and Carl. Lou Danaro drove up, and Danny,
Mike, Long John, and I climbed into his car, picked up Doc at his
house, and drove out to Crighton, where we stopped at the bowling alleys. Danny and Doc chose sides. Doc chose Lou and Mike;
Danny chose Long John and me. But then Mike objected. He
wanted to be on Danny's side to defend the honor of the Cornerville Bears. I changed sides with Mike, and then Doc, Lou, and I
took two out of three strings from Danny, Mike, and Long John,
largely due to the fine bowling of Doc, who finished well ahead
of Danny and thus felt that he had gained his revenge for the
humiliation of the previous evening. When the match was over,
Doc asked if we were all readmitted to the Bears. Mike said that
we were. In a spirit of good fellowship, we drove back to Cornerville.

Later, Doc discussed these developments with me:

I enjoyed bowling with the girls at first. I hoped that Mike and Danny
would fall in. When they didn't, I didn't enjoy it so much any more. I
knew they didn't like it. They said to me, "It isn't right. The girls are taking
all the alleys." . . . . You might say that there was a little clash between us

about bowling with the girls, but you saw how it worked out. It wasn't really serious. We got together again right away.

Saturday night became men's night once more as the bowling season drew to a close. Social relations with the Aphrodite girls continued for some months but on a curtailed scale. The girls' summer camp was the main attraction which maintained interest after the peak of the group activities had passed. The boys drove out to the camp several times during July and August.

Alec was always boasting about his prowess with the women. Doc paid little attention to him, but the other boys felt that something should be done to put him in his place. One night in April they were kidding Alec, when, as Doc says, Alec challenged him:

"If you're such a great lover, I challenge you to show your stuff!"

I said, "Alec, I might not be as handsome as you are, and I don't have all the hair that you have, but I can outbull you any day."

Alec says, "No! No!"

"Well," I said, "I'm older now and I don't want to take a girl away from a man just to show I can do it."

But then Danny says, "Doc, I think you're slipping."

Maron! When Danny says that, I must do something. He only said it to steam me up, but I said, "All right, Danny, I pick Helen. Saturday night. You watch." . . . . Alec wasn't there to see it Saturday night. That was too bad. We were bowling one floor below the girls. I went up to see Helen, and I asked her to come down. I had something to tell her. In a few minutes she came down—by herself. She sat next to me all the evening, the only girl among all those fellows. Danny was impressed. Later he told me, "Doc, you're still the great lover."

Since Alec was not present, he remained unimpressed and continued to boast. A month later Danny was again urging Doc to put Alec in his place. First, Doc lectured him upon the objectionable character of his boasting. When this had no effect, he asked: "Which one of those girls do you really fit with?" Alec said he fitted best with Mildred.

"All right, you take her out twice more, so you can fit with her real good, and then I'll take her away from you."

Alec protested that it could not be done. Later Doc commented to me:

I didn't think I could do it, but I said it anyway. I was all steamed up. . . . . After, Alec called me aside, and he told me he loved Mildred and wanted to marry her, so I should lay off. . . . . I said, "All right, Alec, I just wanted to hear you say that." . . . . I don't think he really loves her, but that's the screwy code around here. If he says he loves her, I have to leave her alone.

Since Alec was more active with the girls than anyone except Joe Dodge, it required the intervention of the leader to put him in his place. Several months later he proposed to Mildred, and, when she refused him, he lost interest in the Aphrodite girls. A year later he married another girl.

When Doc took up Alec's first challenge and began to "bull" Helen, he realized that he was running some risks. It would have been easy to fall in love with her, and Doc had no money or job on which to get married.

When the girls saw Doc with Helen, the combination seemed natural. Dorothy, one of Helen's closest friends, often remarked that they were such an attractive couple. In April, Helen was sick. As Danny told the story:

Dorothy is always hinting about flowers. She says a couple of times to Doc, "Helen is sick. Why don't you send her flowers?" . . . . That steamed me up. She's stupid. Don't she know that Doc can't afford to send flowers? . . . . Last night me and Long John decided we should send her some flowers in Doc's name. He tried to tell us not to do it, but this morning we went down to Vanderwater, the florist on Silverton Street. . . . . He had orchids, three for $15—that was too expensive. We got roses; we told him it was not for a sweetheart, it was for a sick friend. So he suggests tear roses. We paid $5 for a dozen tear roses. . . . . We could get six dozen roses around here for that price, but if we sent the flowers from one of these florists they would have some greaser knock on the door to deliver them. Vanderwater has a nice truck, and they send a delivery boy around with a green uniform. . . . . But what things we couldn't do with that $5.

Doc greeted this gesture with mixed emotions. He realized that it had helped his standing, but it would make Helen think that he was serious. Finally, he told Dorothy and Helen that the boys had done it in his behalf.

Shortly after that, when the fellows were in Jennings', one of the girls was kidding Doc about his reputation as the great lover and claiming that he was afraid to go out with her. As he told the story:

Those kids get my goat. They're innocent, and they want to act as if they knew it all. . . . . All right, I said I would go out with her. But she said, "First you must come to my party."

I asked her, "Who's going to be there?"

"Tony Cardio, Chick Morelli, and Angelo Cucci," she says.

"Who else?"

"Nobody else."

That steamed me up. Danny, Long John, and Frank were at the same table with me, and she didn't invite them. . . . . I told her, "No, I'm going some place that night."

She says, "That's not true. You just don't want to come."

"All right," I said, "I don't want to come."

And she steamed up. When she went back to her table, I turned to the boys. They were very depressed. I told them, "Pay no attention to it, she's stupid. She's tactless."

Though he was unable to protect his boys from such a social slight, Doc at least showed that his interests were with them.

Association with the Aphrodite girls, combined with the bowling activity, brought about important changes in the life of Long John. In the spring of 1937 he was gambling away all his money in crap games. In the fall of 1937 he began to cut down on his gambling, and by winter he had given it up entirely. In the spring I said to him that it must have taken a lot of will-power to stay away from the crap game for so long. He shrugged his shoulders. "You know what really kept me away this winter? Bowling!"

Long John's attitude toward women began to change as he drifted away from the crap game and began associating with the Aphrodite girls. Whenever he stopped to think of it, he resented their attitude of social superiority, but at other times he found it very pleasant to be with them. Although he never thought seriously of marrying one of them, he said to me: "If I could just find some girl that I could really fall in love with, I would get married tomorrow. . . . . I really mean that."

In a short space of time Long John had moved from a tough corner to the more respectable corner of Norton Street, from the crap game to the bowling alleys, from the alleys into the company of a select group of girls, and, with them, even into the settlement house for a brief period. As Doc commented, "it was a metamorphosis."

The Nortons and the Aphrodite girls were brought together by Doc. When Danny and Mike wanted to break them apart, they concentrated particularly upon Doc. Two of the followers could have been left out without changing the group very much, but Danny and Mike held such important positions that the Nortons could not have continued to be the Nortons without them. Furthermore, they were Doc's closest friends, and, whenever he had to choose between them and the others, he chose them. Bowling with the girls had threatened to split the Nortons, and Danny and Mike acted upon Doc to re-establish the unity of the group. By fall the two groups had drifted apart so that one could hear the Nortons expressing the same attitudes toward the girls that they had held before becoming acquainted. Only Alec, Joe Dodge, and Fred Mackey chose, in effect, to remain with the girls, and their relationship to the Nortons became rather tenuous. Joe and Fred eventually married into the group.

Association with the girls was, like bowling, a means of gaining, maintaining, or losing prestige in the group. As in bowling, Alec had to be kept in his place. It was essential to the smooth functioning of the group that the prestige gradations be informally recognized and maintained.

4. DOC'S POLITICAL CAMPAIGN

To the casual observer the corner gang seems to go on for years without change, but actually changes are always taking place; and, as the men grow out of their twenties, the gang itself tends to disintegrate. Some of the members marry and have children. Even if they continue to hang on the corner, their interests are no longer confined to that social area. With marriage, some move out of Cornerville; and, even when they return to spend time with the boys, they are not the active members they once were. In this period of life the corner boy is expected to "settle down" and find the job that will support him and his family in future years. He becomes a different fellow, and his gang either falls apart or is included in some larger club organization.

Doc was now thirty and had to make some decision about his future. He had had no steady job since the stained-glass plant had failed. He had no other specialized training. His intelligence, popularity, and skill in handling the corner boys seemed naturally adapted to a political career, and many of his friends had urged

him to run for office. Mike Giovanni was particularly insistent.
He once said to me:

> You know, there is some people that can't do things themselves, but
> they can get other people to do it for them. Maybe I am like that. There is
> something lacking in me, but I can see it in others.

In the spring of 1937 Doc discussed his position with me:

> I told Mike to forget about the politics. . . . . He said, "You can't do that.
> I've been going around getting all these names. I been buzzing everybody."
> I told him to forget it. . . . . I can't do it without a job. Do you know how
> it feels not to have any money in your kick? Not to know where the next
> dollar is coming from? I hope you never experience that. I went through it
> once; I can't go through it again. . . . . But what can I do, Bill? I'm a so-so
> artist. If I was in the art racket, I wouldn't hire me. What else could I do?
> Maybe I should try for a civil service job, but I would get bored there in an
> office all day. . . . . But if I run, I've got to have a job—any job. I
> shouldn't be staying here. My sister takes care of me, and my brother-in-
> law is a good egg, but that is no good for them. Sometimes they want to
> love up, and they can't because I'm around. . . . . I should be off by myself.
> I should be thinking of getting married. If I had a job, it's likely that I
> would. I don't go for this stuff—the girls expect me to give them that line,
> so I do. And I'm egotist enough so I like to know when they fall for me. . . . .
> But then I drop them. . . . . What can I offer to a girl? I'll never get married
> unless I've got a good job. I'm not that dumb. . . . . I shouldn't be around
> here at all.

When the boys urged him to run for office, Doc would say to me,
"Pay no attention to that, Bill. They just want to have somebody
to cheer for."

A year later Doc's personal situation was not improved, yet he
yielded to the insistence of his friends and agreed to run for representative in the state legislature.

The political campaign only increased Doc's problems. Now,
more than ever, he felt that he must get a job. He was sensitive
about his lack of formal education, and unemployment was an
added burden. He needed money for the campaign, and he did
not want people to say that he was running for office just to get
himself a job.

From time to time in the spring of 1938 he heard from the
sister who lived in Dedfield that W.P.A. project supervisors had
intimated that they could find him a place on the rolls if he still
needed a job. If Doc got on the W.P.A. in Dedfield, he could not

make Cornerville his official residence, and he would be ruled out of the campaign. He once told me that he could not hold out any longer, that he had decided to make every effort to get on the Dedfield W.P.A. Later he said that he had not gone to see anyone in Dedfield because he could not disappoint the people who wanted him to run.

His Cornerville sister was thinking of moving to Dedfield. Her two youngest boys were learning the tough language of the streets and were becoming hard to manage; she wanted to get them out of Cornerville. If she moved, Doc would have to move with her, and she asked what this would do to his political ambitions. He lied to her that he was no longer interested in politics. Since she could not find what she wanted in Dedfield, the move was postponed, and Doc remained in Cornerville.

Doc believed that he would be able to get on the Eastern City W.P.A. if he asked certain local politicians to intercede for him, but the price for such an appointment would have been his withdrawal from the contest. Therefore, he made application by himself. As a single man without dependents, he knew that his chances were small, and he was not surprised when nothing came of this effort.

Mrs. Mallory, a vocational guidance worker at the Norton Street Settlement, became interested in Doc and arranged a month's work in a well-known stained-glass concern, his wages of $10 a week to be paid by the settlement house. Doc went to work with enthusiasm and hoped to win himself a permanent job. At the end of the month the head of the concern complimented him on his work and said that if he could continue for another month and get additional experience, at the expense of the settlement, they might perhaps be able to hire him. Mrs. Mallory suggested that this be done, but Mr. Bacon said, "We've done enough for Doc." While other needy cases demanded attention, he felt that Doc should not be supported unless there was a definite promise that a job would result. No promise was made, and the project was dropped. The month's work resulted only in bitter disappointment for Doc.

Mr. Bacon offered him a chance to teach stained-glass work in the settlement house one night a week during the spring and summer for $2.00 a class. Mrs. Mallory hoped to get him private school classes in the fall. Mr. Bacon thought that the evening class would give Doc a chance to show his initiative. Doc told Mrs. Mallory that he would not have the peace of mind to work on such a class until he had a real job and some security. She asked him to thank Mr. Bacon for the offer, and he said that he would. He never did. He knew that Mr. Bacon considered him shiftless and lazy. Sometimes he was tempted to go in and argue with Mr. Bacon. He did not, but at least he tried to avoid any move that might subordinate him to the social worker.

Mr. Smith, headworker of the Cornerville Settlement House, was interested in developing a recreation project outlined by Mr. Kendall, his boys' worker. He hoped to get funds to open recreation centers in vacant stores so as to reach the corner boys who would not come into the settlement house. I proposed that Doc should have the job of directing one of the centers and brought the two men together. I had hoped that Doc would make a favorable impression, but he had very little to say. When, in response to my persuasion, Doc went to see Mr. Smith again, he only stayed to say that he liked the recreation-center idea but could do nothing unless he found some means of immediate support. Mr. Smith was puzzled by Doc's attitude. I questioned Doc, and he explained that in the midst of the first meeting he had had a sudden attack of dizziness and that it was all that he could do to conceal it from us. At an earlier period, when faced by severe financial worries, he had the same trouble. He could not be in a room full of people without having a dizzy spell. When he had to go to a party, he would tell Angelo to come in ten minutes later and say that he was wanted on the corner. Then he would excuse himself and escape.

Even if he made a good impression on Mr. Smith, the project could not be launched until the fall, so it offered him no immediate prospect of support. Doc said to me:

Bill, that's all a good idea. It should be done. . . . . And if I had some money to live on, I would do that work for nothing. But now I can't even think about it. I have to have some security first. I need a job, any job—a definite job, right now! . . . . After that I can think about other things.

Meanwhile Doc's campaign got under way. Mike appointed himself campaign manager and went about his job with infectious enthusiasm. The main activity of the late spring and summer months of a campaign year is "talking it up" for the candidate. His closest friends go from corner to corner to let the boys know that their champion is "in the fight." Mike was known as a first-class "vote hustler," and his preliminary work was effective. He interested the members of his union. The leaders of a Welport club of Doc's *paesani* pledged their support. The leader of one Cornerville political club promised his support. A number of corner boys who were influential in their own Cornerville groups came to Doc and pledged themselves to his cause. Doc did nothing. Mike was continually pressing him to get into action, to "form a committee, draw up a platform, organize a dance to raise some money, get things rolling."

Finally, Mike became disgusted with Doc and said to him, "You got a beautiful chance to win this fight, but I'll tell you to your kisser—you're lazy."

Since the voters could make two choices in the contest and Representative Mike Kelly was sure to be re-elected, Doc needed to be the strongest Italian candidate in order to have a chance of winning. This would have been too much to expect in his first campaign. Still, he was considered a powerful candidate. Friends of one of the leading Italian candidates, in urging Doc to withdraw, predicted that he would not get more than fifteen hundred votes. In such a contest a thousand votes are enough to make a man an important political figure.

One day late in July, without consulting anybody, Doc withdrew from the contest. When I asked why he had done so, he said, "Too many in it, Bill. There were thirty-two candidates." But then he admitted that this was not the real reason.

The more there were in the fight, the better it was for me. . . . . It was the social demands that were too much for me. When I'm down at Jennings' with the boys, somebody comes up to me and wants me to buy a ticket for something. I'm batted out, so I have to refuse. That happens all the time,

Bill. . . . . As a politician, I'm supposed to go to dances and meetings, and I can't go because I haven't got the money. Fellows come up to me and ask for cards with my name on them and stickers and signs. I can't give them any. . . . . You can't be that way in politics. They hold it against you. If you don't buy their ticket, they call you a cheap bastard. They cut you up behind your back. . . . . I worried about it. Many nights I walked the floor until three or four in the morning. That was too much, Bill. . . . . It was tough getting out. The *paesani* in Welport were all steamed up. So many people had pledged their support to me. And I never asked anybody for his support. Not once! They all came to me. Now that it's all over, I think I could have won. I really think so. . . . . Next time I won't get in the fight unless I have $200 in my pocket. But this was really the time for me. In two years—who knows what will happen? . . . . Well, it was fun while I was in there.

In his earlier years Doc had moved freely through Cornerville and outlying districts, gathering a following wherever he went. Popularity and influence had come to him without effort on his part. The years of unemployment had sapped his confidence and steadily narrowed his sphere of social activity. As he told me:

It wasn't until a little while before you came down here that I began hanging on Norton Street again. Now I don't go anywhere else. I'm always on that corner. I'm too disgusted with myself to go any place else.

To become successful in politics, the corner boy must be able to go out from his own gang and continually widen his sphere of social influence. He must be able to meet new groups and participate in their activities. Doc was moving in precisely the opposite direction, and he knew it. His self-confidence was not completely gone. He was sure that if he had a steady job he could reverse the trend of his life. Then he would have money to spend, and he could do the things that were expected of him when he participated in group activities. When he gave up hope of getting a job, he saw that his own path split off from the path of the successful politician in an ever widening gap. Since he could not travel both roads at once, he took the only way out.

The news of Doc's withdrawal hit the Nortons with devastating effect. Mike was terribly upset. When he made Doc his champion, he was carried away by his own enthusiasm. Now his faith was shaken. Doc was still his close friend, but he began to talk about his shortcomings as he never had before. Doc was a fine fellow—that was understood—but he just did not have the push to be successful, and allowances had to be made for his lack of spirit. Mike was a "hustler." He had what Doc lacked. Doc was no longer Mike's leader.

The impact of Doc's action upon other corners was no less disturbing. When a corner-boy leader mobilizes his friends and arouses their enthusiasm in the support of a candidate and then the candidate suddenly withdraws, the group suffers a serious letdown. The leader has committed his group to the wrong man, and his prestige suffers. The candidate is suspected of having sold out his friends, of having made a bargain with another politician whereby he capitalizes upon their support in order to gain some material advantage.

Doc's position was strong enough so that he could have demanded something from rival politicians who were interested in his withdrawal, but, when he withdrew, he did so unconditionally and independently. There were the inevitable rumors, but, since no one could prove anything against Doc, his reputation was not destroyed.

At the height of his campaign Doc was the leader of a growing army of supporters. When he withdrew, there was a general realignment. The corners where he had been strong turned to other candidates. Even the boys of his own clique took an active part in the campaign of another candidate, Tom Marino, the boss of the Taylor Club. When both Tom and Doc had been in the contest, it was informally recognized that members of the two groups would vote for both men. When Doc dropped out, Tom became the biggest man on the street, and Doc became just "one of the boys."

In other years Doc had taken a leading role in political discussions among the Nortons. As this election approached, he was conspicuously silent. He was not leading anybody. He was just hanging around. Much of the time he was not even with his own group. For hours on end he sat by himself in the back of Stefani's dimly lighted barbershop.

5. DISINTEGRATION

If this were a work of fiction, the story would now be finished. Doc, who was once so active, had withdrawn from his boys, and, without his leadership, the Nortons began to disintegrate. However, life went on for Doc and for his friends, and certain things happened to them which illustrate the nature of their personal relations.

Danny and Mike withdrew from active participation in the group. A growing interest in horse-race betting made the crap game unprofitable. In the fall of 1938 Danny found a job with Spongi, a Cornerville racketeer who ran a horse room and held a crap game that catered to much bigger customers than had participated in the playground game. Danny's job kept him busy at Spongi's all afternoon and evening. He was no longer able to hang on the corner.

The end of the crap game dissolved one of Mike's main ties with Norton Street. For a while he worked on W.P.A., but then he was laid off, and he spent his time canvassing the city for odd jobs. Since he had little spending money, he was seldom able to bowl with the boys.

When some of the boys are broke, group activities can continue as long as there are some who can cover expenses for the others. When there is no money among the members, many activities must come to a standstill. That was the situation facing the Nortons in the fall of 1938. There was little that they could do except hang on the corner, and few were left to do that. Carl and Tommy spent most of their time with a younger group. Lou and Fred did not come into Cornerville as often as before. Alec was concentrating his attention upon his future wife. Nutsy again began to spend his time on Norton Street, and his cousin, Chris Teludo, who had always bowled with the gang, was occasionally with him. Of the original thirteen members, only Nutsy, Long John, Frank, Joe Dodge, and Angelo remained.

The Cornerville Settlement House received a grant to finance its recreation center project for six months. Mr. Smith had been planning to hire trained social workers, but he agreed to experiment by placing Doc in charge of one of the three centers. One of the workers at the Norton Street Settlement had spoken well of Doc in response to Mr. Smith's inquiries. When Mr. Bacon heard of Doc's appointment, he commented: "He's not the sort of man that I would choose for that job."

Starting early in January, 1939, Doc was busy at his center every afternoon and evening until ten o'clock, except on Sundays. This made it impossible for him to hang on the corner. The remaining Nortons responded by spending some of their time in the center, but this changed the nature of their activities.

Doc's new job helped to restore his self-confidence. Mr. Smith said that Doc had been so lackadaisical in the preliminary work of opening the centers that he had been afraid he would not do a good job. When the center opened, Doc put his heart into the work. He became completely dependable, and in a short time he had everything running smoothly. The first two days he had some trouble with stealing, but before the first week was over the stolen articles had been returned, and after that the stealing problem took quite a different turn. The young boys contributed to the center things which they claimed they had found or which had been given to them, but which Doc suspected they had stolen. Whatever the origin, these contributions indicated that the boys accepted the center as their own.

Doc's background gave him important advantages over the social workers. While he did not know the young boys in the area of his center, he knew some of their older brothers, cousins, or parents. He could also call upon his friends to help him. For a time, Mike Giovanni held a weekly boxing class in the center. Doc's experience also enabled him to size up each corner-boy group after brief observation. On the night after the opening of the center he could already point out to me the membership of each corner gang, name its hangout, and tell who led the group. He gave the leaders recognition by making them responsible for acting in matters involving their groups. He had no serious disciplinary problems. In a short time his center was organized to run itself and Doc simply was present to adjudicate disputes, to answer questions, and to give advice.

One of the two social workers had such difficulties with broken windows, stealing, and general unruliness that he was forced to close his center within a few weeks of its opening. The second managed with great difficulty to keep going for the six months, but it is doubtful whether he would have been able to do so without the assistance of Doc. Doc knew some of the older corner boys who hung near that center. The young boys respected them as "tough guys." Doc persuaded them to go inside and play cards in a quiet way so as to set a good example. The social worker admitted that this had been very helpful. At other times, Frank, Joe, and Long John went to the center to break up fights and help maintain order.

Everyone concerned with the project recognized that Doc's center was the only real success of the three. However, the job provided no permanent solution to his problems. When the six months' period was past, the project could not be refinanced, and Doc was again unemployed. Although Mr. Smith said he would like to help him to get a job, he did not think of him in connection with his regular program. That summer, as in summers past, the settlement camp for Cornerville boys hired exclusively college men from outside the district for its counselors.

While Doc was working in the recreation center, he continued to see Danny when both of them were through work for the evening. When Doc's job was over, he began hanging in Spongi's with Danny. When his business declined, Spongi no longer had a steady job for Danny, but he liked his company and took care of many of his personal expenses. Within a short time Spongi and Doc became close friends, and Spongi always wanted Doc with him wherever he went.

Some of the Nortons spent time in Spongi's, but they did not recognize it as their hangout. A new group grew up upon the Norton Street corner. Angelo, Nutsy, Frank, Joe, Phil Principio, and Paul DiMatia were hanging together. Phil and Paul were both college graduates who had been members of the Italian Community Club but had shifted their allegiance to the corner boys. They were particularly close to Angelo, and he was the leader of the gang, with Nutsy second in command.

The breakup of the Nortons involved considerable shifting of individual social positions. Doc told me about his relations with Spongi:

Spongi decides what's to be done. Naturally. It's his place, and he has a lot of the boys around to do his bidding. But he can't order me around. . . . . Sometimes, just to steam me up, Danny tells Spongi to send me on an errand. Spongi comes up to me, and he laughs before he even says anything, it seems so funny to him. He tries to give me a quarter, and he says, "Ho-ho-ho, Doc, go out and buy me something."

I tell him, "Go out yourself." He laughs. He thinks it's a hell of a joke. . . . . I tell him he can't buy me.

He says, "I haven't offered you a Buick yet." Of course, a Buick is a big thing. He says the only trouble is that I haven't been offered enough. I tell him he couldn't buy me for a million dollars. . . . . He knows there are things I won't do. I don't have anything to do with his business.

While Doc prided himself on maintaining his independence, he was no longer a leader.

Long John divided his time between Spongi's and the Norton Street corner. The realignment left him in a vulnerable position. There were two groups that hung around Spongi's "joint": the inner circle and the hangers-on. Spongi included his brother, Danny, Doc, and two others in the inner circle. When he went for "coffee-ands," for a drive, or to the movies, he would invite them to accompany him. He did not include Long John in his invitations, so Long John was excluded from the inner circle. Without the support of Doc, Danny, and Mike, he had no standing among the boys who remained on Norton Street, and he did not know where to go.

The course of bowling activity showed clearly what was happening to the Nortons. In the season of 1937–38 the boys went to the alleys every Saturday shortly after eight o'clock and bowled one string after another until midnight closing time. In the season of 1938–39 the bowling did not get under way until nine or later, there were long pauses between strings, and the evening came to an end around eleven. Instead of ten men bowling and others waiting their turn, only six or eight appeared at the alleys. Doc's recreation center kept him busy until ten o'clock, and Danny and Mike seldom came. Several of the boys commented to me that all the fun seemed to have gone out of bowling.

The following year the alleys were again crowded, but there

were so many new men bowling that the group did not seem to be the Nortons any more. Doc once commented:

Rico and Chick Morelli are never with us except at the alleys. . . . . I had an argument with Chick up at the alleys one night. He had the right all on his side, but I talked very unctuously and finally I made him apologize for what he said. Of course, the boys were all with me. . . . . He said that we were a clique, that we played favorites. Of course, that's right; we are a clique. But, still, I got him to say that we weren't.

Danny was up at the alleys that night we bowled the San Marcos. I asked them if they wanted to bowl the first team or my team. They said, "Your team," so I told Danny, "If you want to bowl, you're in." He said he didn't want to. He had been sick, and he didn't feel well enough. So we didn't have to put Rico or Chick out on account of him. But now Danny and Mike both want to bowl, and I want to bowl with them. With me, bowling isn't just a sport. It makes a lot of difference who I bowl with. I want to bowl with my friends. So I told Danny and Mike to come up this Saturday and look over the situation. If there's no room for them, they'll go on the next alleys or upstairs. And I told them, "If you do that, you've got me." I'll go with them, and whoever wants to follow us can come. In that way it will really be our team again.

Since Danny and Mike did not appear on the following Saturday or regularly thereafter, the decisive break did not take place. The boys continued to bowl in a miscellaneous group.

In October, 1939, Doc said to me: "Nutsy is staging a comeback. Danny and I haven't been around much recently, and he's been trying to take over. He's steaming up the boys to challenge us bowling." Nutsy got Frank, Carl, and Tommy to bowl against Doc, Danny, Chris, and Long John. Doc's team won the first match by a very narrow margin, Nutsy repeated his challenge, and his team evened the score. Nutsy's boys were satisfied; no play-off was scheduled.

In these two matches Nutsy gave a remarkable performance. Before this he had bowled very infrequently and was considered a poor bowler. In the first match he bowled well; in the second match he left all competitors far behind. He also led the cheering. He was constantly yelling encouragement to his team and badgering his opponents. From time to time, he shouted, "Who is the best bowler you ever seen?"

His team mates shouted back at him, "Nutsy!"

Several times Danny jokingly joined in the refrain. When the second match was over, Nutsy said to me, "Wasn't I an inspiring leader, Bill?"

The following Saturday, Nutsy delivered an individual challange to his cousin, Chris Teludo, who was then considered the best bowler among the Nortons. Chris won, but Nutsy repeated his challenge and beat him the next two strings.

When Doc, Long John, Chris, Chick, and Rico bowled a match against the San Marcos, which they lost by a single pin, Nutsy and Frank deserted them to bowl on adjoining alleys. The team members felt that Nutsy's yelling would have caused the San Marcos to lose enough pins to change defeat into victory, and Long John said to Frank: "You fellows are poor sports. Yuz run away when we need yuz to cheer."

Frank answered: "Why should we cheer for you when we want to bowl? Who are you—the boss?"

While the Nortons were one group, the second team never had a chance against the first team. When the group split into two, Doc, Danny, and Mike could no longer keep the followers in their places. Nutsy had a chance to seize the leadership among his group of bowlers, and, in spite of lack of practice, he came through with a performance that corresponded with his new position.

While Nutsy rose, Long John fell. As early as the spring of 1939 it was evident that Long John was slipping. His bowling declined, and in the individual prize competition closing that season he finished next to last. The first part of the 1939–40 season brought no improvement. In the matches against Nutsy's team, Long John bowled very poorly. Doc and Danny would say to him, "Well, it looks like you're not the man you used to be. This year maybe you won't be good enough to make the first team."

These remarks were made in a joking manner, but they were symptomatic of the changes in personal relations that had taken place. As if they sensed Long John's defenseless position, Nutsy's team members redoubled their verbal attacks upon him. They had always attacked him more than they attacked Doc, Danny, or Mike, but now, under Nutsy's leadership, they subjected him to an unrelenting barrage that was calculated to destroy his self-confidence. When he was bowling so poorly, there was little that Long John could say to defend himself.

One afternoon Doc came to consult me about Long John. He had confided to Doc that he had not slept well for several weeks. As Doc said:

> I talked it over with him. . . . . Whenever he gets half-asleep and the sheet comes up over his face, he wakes up thinking he's dead. . . . . I told him, "John, it must be something that happened to you when you were a kid. Maybe sometime when you were playing, somebody threw a coat over you, and you thought you were smothering." But he couldn't think of any case like that. I had him think some more about when he was a kid, and finally he got it. It was when he was about eight years old. He was very sick with pneumonia, and the doctor told his mother that he was dead. They pulled the sheet up over his face. When he came to, he heard his mother screaming and his relatives crying because he was dead. Then he moved a little, and they saw him move and pulled the sheet back, and everybody rejoiced, but that must have made a deep impression on John's mind. When he told me that story, I explained to him how foolish it was for him to let a thing like that bother him. . . . .

I told Doc I thought more than that was needed in order to effect a cure. I suggested that he might be able to dispel Long John's anxieties if he took him into Spongi's inner circle and if he and Danny began to defend Long John's bowling and encourage him when the others attacked him. Doc was doubtful but agreed to see what could be done. Within a short time he had fitted Long John into Spongi's inner circle. As he explained:

> I didn't say anything to Spongi, but I already fitted with him. I just made a lot of noise about Long John. If he wasn't around, I would ask the boys where he was. When he came in, I would say to him, "Here's Long John, the dirty bum," and I would ask him where he had been. I gave him so much attention that he moved in there right away. Spongi began asking him to go places with us. Now even when I'm not around John is right in there.

At the same time Doc and Danny began to support him at the bowling alleys. Long John's bowling began to improve. In a short time he was bowling as well as he had in the season of 1937–38. In the individual competition that climaxed the 1939–40 season, he won the first prize. He never again consulted Doc about his nightmares.

The structure of the new group that grew up on Norton Street can be represented in the manner shown in the accompanying chart.

Since Angelo did not bowl, Nutsy could assume the leadership at the bowling alleys. When the boys were on the corner, he could not compete with Angelo. Carl and Tommy followed him at the alleys, but they spent little time on the corner. Frank was the only one who was personally attached to Nutsy. Phil and Paul had become close friends of Angelo through their membership in the Italian Community Club, and Joe also attached himself to Angelo.

ANGELO'S BOYS

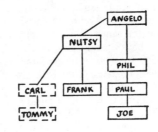

☐ *Corner boy*
- - - - *Those infrequently present*
——— *Line of influence*
Positions of boxes indicate relative status

The strength of Angelo's position on the corner depended in part upon his activities in the Cornerville Dramatic Club, to which Nutsy did not belong. In the late winter of 1939 the boys had been urging Doc to find a clubroom for his boys in order to keep the Nortons together. While he was conferring with Mr. Smith upon the recreation center project he asked if his boys might have a clubroom in the Cornerville House. Mr. Smith offered the best room in the house for one night each week. Doc got Angelo, Joe, Frank, and Long John, some of the Aphrodite girls, and some other men and girls and founded the Cornerville Dramatic Club. After that he was too busy with his recreation job to be able to attend meetings, but he placed his confidence in Angelo, who came to him for advice on matters of club policy and took the

lead in meetings whenever Doc was not present. This strengthened Angelo's position on the street corner.

Doc explained to me how things were done when Angelo was
with the boys:

One night last week I stopped in at Stefani's on the way to a party. That
whole clique was in the barbershop. I asked Angelo, "What are you doing
tonight?"

He said, "I don't know, just hanging around, I guess."

I asked him to come to the party with me. He said he couldn't, somebody
had already asked him and he had said he was busy. . . . . Then I turned to
Phil and asked him what he was doing, and he said, "I don't know. Whatever the boys do." And then he looked at Angelo. I asked Paul, and he gave
me the same answer. One by one I asked Joe, Nutsy, and Frank, and they
all said exactly the same thing: "I don't know. Whatever the boys do."
. . . . And "the boys" meant Angelo. . . . . I said, "All right, I'll see you
later." . . . . Later we went down to Jennings', and that clique was already
there at a table in the back. I sat with the fellows I came with. That's only
right. But after a while Angelo came over and sat next to me. He had
something he wanted to tell me. I guess he planned to come over for just a
few minutes, but he stayed too long. Paul pulled over a chair, and then
Phil came over. One by one, they all came over until the six of them were
with us. They had to pull up another table to sit next to us. . . . . Now suppose Paul had had something to say to me. He could have come over and
stayed as long as he wanted to, and, as long as Angelo did not come over,
none of those other fellows would have moved.

Suppose the five of them are in Stefani's one night, and Angelo hasn't
showed up. Phil might say, "Let's go up [to] a show." Nutsy will say, "All
right, but let's wait for Angelo." So they wait. If he doesn't show up after a
while, they go looking for him. They go up to his house and try to find him.
It's only after waiting for him that they feel free to go without him. Waiting
for Angelo is like a duty. . . . .

Suppose they find him and ask him to go to a show. If he says, "All
right," they go; but if he says, "No," they don't go.

Sometimes Frank and Nutsy talk against Angelo. Frank says to me,
"He's a bull-slinger. He tells me to wait for him, and I have to wait an hour
before he shows up. Me, if I'm five minutes late, they go without me." . . . .
Nutsy says, "Last night Angelo told me to meet him at Jennings' at 10:30.
I waited till twelve and he didn't show up!" . . . . The night Nutsy was
talking about, Angelo was with me. . . . . They cut up Angelo to me, and
they just hope that I'll agree with them. If I said they were right, I don't
know what would happen. But I said, "No, Angelo is a good kid."

No, Angelo doesn't know he's their leader. If you told him that, he'd be
ruined. He wouldn't know what to do.

I asked what would happen if Doc came upon the five of them
without Angelo and asked them to go somewhere.

They would have to find Angelo first. It's like a duty. You see, I'm not really a part of that clique now. I haven't been with them enough. They won't do anything unless it's all right with Angelo. . . . . Angelo and I are good friends. He always asks me what I'm doing, and I know that if I told him to come with me, he would.

The other night I saw Nutsy, Frank, Phil, and Joe Dodge on the corner. They were waiting for Angelo, and then they were going for a walk. I went up the street, and I met Angelo coming down. I said to him—not because I wanted to show I was a leader but because I wanted him to do it—I said, "Angelo, wait for me on the corner and then we'll go up to the Metropolitan Hotel together. . . . ." When I got back, they were all waiting for me. We started out together, and after we had gone a few blocks, Phil asked where we were going. I said that Angelo and I were going up to the Metropolitan. Phil said to Angelo that they had been waiting all night for him, and now he was going to leave them. I told Angelo I didn't want to take him away from the boys. He could stay with them if he wanted to. But he came with me. They left us at the corner of ———— Street. I looked back to see which way they went. They split up. Frank and Nutsy started one way. Phil and Joe went the other way.

It's Angelo that's holding that clique together now. If he went away for a month, they would break up.

In the early spring of 1941 Angelo was still leading the boys. While they often expressed dissatisfaction with his decisions, they always followed him. Doc had not been around the corner much, and Angelo felt so secure that he did not take the trouble to seek him out to consult him about plans for the group or the club. Then one night Doc appeared at a meeting of the Dramatic Club. Angelo proposed a certain line of action. Doc thought Angelo's idea was foolish, and he said so. When Doc led the opposition, Angelo's followers deserted him, and he was overridden. Angelo found it difficult to adjust to the new situation. He dropped out of the Dramatic Club. For a time he would not speak to Doc. He hoped that the boys would take his side, but they supported Doc and talked freely against Angelo. Doc defended Angelo. After a while Angelo returned to the club and made up with Doc, so that their relationship became much as it had been before Angelo became the leader of the boys on the corner. When Angelo's power in the club was destroyed, he also lost his hold upon the corner. There was no longer a leader to hold the boys together, and the last remnants of Doc's gang disappeared from Norton Street.

CHAPTER II

CHICK AND HIS CLUB

1. THE STORY OF CHICK MORELLI

SINCE Chick Morelli and some of his Italian Community Club members have appeared in the story of the Nortons, they require no special introduction. However, so far they have been seen only as they affected a group of corner boys. In order to understand who the men were and where they were going, it is necessary to step inside the club, observe their actions, and listen to the accounts they give of themselves.

Chick Morelli told his story in this way:

I was born in Italy. I didn't come over here until I was eight years old. .... I was born in Avellino, near Naples. My father was quite a powerful man over there. He started a political party, and he ran for mayor and was almost elected. I guess politics runs in the family. .... I think I get my intellectualism from my father. I realize now that the things I have done are the sort of things that he wanted to do.

My father came to Eastern City nine or ten years before my mother and I came here. He set up a fruit and vegetable store; and he also had a small bakery. We hadn't been here long before my father died and left my mother, my older sister, and me to take care of ourselves. We got a little money selling his property, but that didn't last long.

I started to work selling papers. From the beginning I used to make $5 a week on my paper business. I worked hard. I was anxious to get ahead. After a while, I was making $2 on Saturday with the papers and about $10 a week altogether. I always brought home every nickel to my mother, because I didn't know how to spend it. And she didn't know how to spend money in this country, so she saved it too. .... I used to go out for wood. I provided all the fuel for the stove, except in the coldest weather, when we would buy a little coal. .... Then I got a job after school behind an ice-cream counter. I was making $10 a week at that for a while. .... When I was in high school, I had a job with my uncle. He was in the bootlegging business. I had to take the job; I had no choice, because I needed the money. I worked there for a while, mixing the alky, selling over the counter. Once I nearly got arrested. It was just lucky that I didn't. ....

When I was working in the bootlegging business, I had plenty of money. And I was a free spender at that time. I went to plenty of dances, and whenever a couple of fellows were with me, I would invite them to have coffee or a drink. I wasted a lot of money that way, but now that I look back on it, it seems to me that it was better for me to have learned my lesson early when money didn't count for so much as it does now. . . . . One summer I was going different places with one particular friend. All summer we went out to dances and parties three times a week, and I always paid for him. At other times I would hand him a couple of bucks so that in case he met a girl, he wouldn't be embarrassed. I never thought the time would come when I would ask him for a dime and he wouldn't give it to me, but that time did come. It was just before I was going back to school. On this particular night I knew he had just gotten his pay check. He came up to me and asked me to go to a dance with him. I said I would gladly go, but I didn't have enough to buy the ticket. I needed ten cents more.

He said, "Well, I've got $30, but I need it all myself."

I said, "Don't trouble yourself, I'll get it from somebody else."

That taught me a lesson. After that I would never go so far out of my way for anybody. I would always hold back just a little. . . . . I don't know if you have found it so, but it has been my experience that I make more friends and better friendships when I act a little reserved and don't go running after the person. . . . . Probably I was influenced somewhat by my mother. She always believed that you shouldn't trust a person too far, you should keep something in reserve, and she often said that to me.

I asked him if he had found it hard to adjust when he came from Italy.

I did. I was ridiculed by my classmates because of the way I spoke. But they didn't mean anything by it. After all, we were all Italians down here. But, still, I was always sensitive about my way of speaking. I don't think I had an accent for very long, but it wasn't until recently that someone pointed out to me that I never pronounced my *th* sounds. . . . .

I did a lot of things with the boys. I played the rubber-ball game that you play with your fist. I was a champ at that. I wasn't so good at baseball or football, perhaps because I spent so much time at the other game.

I asked him if there had been a gang of fellows with whom he associated. He said there had been. Was he the leader of it?

I don't know. I wouldn't say just that. I know that they always used to call for me instead of me calling for them. I used to wait up at my house for them. It wasn't that I wanted them to come for me. It just got to be a habit. When we played cards, it was always up at my house. We would play there evenings, and sometimes I would say, "Sorry, fellows, I have to go out," and the games would break up.

I took an academic course in high school. I don't know why I did, except that I always liked those studies. At that time I didn't think I would be able to go to college, but I don't know what I would have done if I couldn't have gone. I wanted to get out in the world. I wasn't satisfied to stay just where I was. . . . . When I was working in my uncle's store, I was associating with the lowest of the low, the bums and the drunks. Sometimes I would wonder if I was going to wind up like them. . . . . We did have some good customers. One was a judge. There was another man who was very well educated. Once this man came in and wanted to buy some liquor on credit. I couldn't give it to him, not because I didn't want to, but because I had orders from my uncle. We got in an argument, and he said some things that hurted me. He said, "Chick, I like to see you in college, you'd make a jack-ass of yourself the way you talk and act." . . . . I was very sensitive about those things, and that hurted me. Right after that I went uptown and bought two books. One was a book on English, and the other was a book of etiquette. I don't know why I bought that book of etiquette, but when I got home, I read it through. I wanted to know everything I should do and not do.

The summer of my Junior year in high school, when I was at a dance down at the beach, I met a girl by the name of Edith Clark. We got along all right, and she took down my telephone number. She said she would look me up when we got back to Eastern City. A few months passed, and I didn't hear anything from her. I decided to forget about it. But then one day in my Senior year a fellow came up to me in the library and told me that a girl by the name of Edith had called in my uncle's shop. I had even forgotten who she was, but I called her, and after that we got together. I was seeing her about every other night for almost two years. She lived with a woman named Mrs. Burroughs. Mrs. Burroughs took a liking to me from the beginning. She would introduce me to people before her own sons. I learned a lot of things from her and from Edith. I began mingling in with different people. Wherever I went with Edith, I would watch what she did, and I would act the same way. Sometimes I noticed that she didn't do things just right according to the book of etiquette, but, of course, I didn't say anything. I learned a lot from her. . . . . Once I asked her if there was anything wrong with the way I talked, and she said that she had never noticed anything. I know now that I didn't pronounce my *th* sounds at that time, but probably she didn't want to hurt my feelings. . . . . After a while, I began to notice that there were other people that didn't know as much as I did. I would be in an elevator with some fellows and girls in a hotel, and I would notice that the other fellows didn't have their hats off. Or I would be sitting at a table with another fellow when a girl came up. I would get up, and he wouldn't. I began to think I wasn't so bad off. . . . .

Bill, if there is one thing I have a talent for, if I have a talent for any-thing, it is a talent for imitation. When a person says something in a certain way, I can usually imitate him, not 100 per cent but pretty well. When I was in college, I used to pay attention to everything the professor said so that I could learn from the way he said things. And when I was home at night, besides my regular studies, I used to set a book of biographies of great men before me and a dictionary beside it. I would read in the biog-raphy, and any word I didn't understand I would look up in the dictionary and write down on a piece of paper. I would review them before I went to bed. Then every night I would read aloud for ten or fifteen minutes. It didn't matter what I was reading, I wanted to make my voice come out better. . . . . I always had that desire for refinement. I was always seeking refinement. . . . .

When my mother told me that I was going to college, I was surprised. But she had some money saved, and I always worked summers. A couple of summers I couldn't find a job, so I set up a pushcart with Lou Danaro. Once a friend of mine asked me if I wasn't ashamed to be working on a pushcart. I told him, "Why should I be? This is my bread and butter."

In grammar school we were all Italians. In high school [in Welport] the races were mixed. At St. Patrick's College there were only about a hundred Italians out of 1,400 students. About 1,200 were Irish, and the other hundred were different races. I noticed the difference when I got in college. We felt discriminated against. In the beginning I was very timid. Sometimes even when I knew the right answer I wouldn't raise my hand because I was afraid people would laugh at the way I expressed myself. But in my Sophomore year, I began coming out. I talked more in class. I remember one English class when we were discussing *Macbeth*. I said something about the play, and the professor disagreed with me; but I stuck to my point, and he gave me a lot of credit for that. He referred to "Mr. Morelli's theory." That gave me a lot of confidence.

In my Junior year some Italian students came over from Italy to visit different colleges. I was appointed head of a committee of thirty at St. Patrick's to show them around. . . . . At that time there was no Italian taught there. It wasn't right. To think that they should teach Spanish instead of Italian. What have the Spaniards contributed to literature to compare with the Italian contributions? . . . . I organized an Italian Academy at St. Patrick's, and I was its first president. At my own expense I got up petitions for the Italian language. I talked with Father Donnelly, the dean of the college. He wasn't so sympathetic. I argued with him. I asked him if he could name a greater poet than Dante. He said he couldn't. I said that, for every Irishman in any field that he could name; I could name an Italian who was a greater man. He argued that there might not be enough students to take the course. I told him that there would be at least twenty students, and if there weren't, he could drop it. . . . . That fall there was an Italian course, and Professor Salerno came to the college. . . . . There were thirty students taking the course. I couldn't take it myself because I was a Senior, but the Italian Academy expanded and put on plays and many other activities.

Concerning his personal contacts, Chick told me that he valued especially his friendship with Thomas L. Brown, a prominent Eastern City lawyer. He said that Brown had a strong influence on him, often correcting his mistakes and giving him advice. Once he asked Brown if he thought the Italian people were discriminated against. The lawyer answered: "Don't be an ass,

Chick; it's only the jackasses that discriminate against the Italian people. No intelligent people would do that."

Chick said that this impressed him. He began to think that the Italians themselves were at fault.

The Italian boys down here have that feeling of inferiority. I have it myself. I really mean that. When I hear that some people think I'm pretty good, I wonder what it is that I have. I can't see it. I'm not just pretending when I say that I feel inferior. That's the truth. . . . . I think the only way to overcome that inferiority is to go out and mingle with other people. Until you can mingle in, you will never overcome that feeling.

I asked Chick how he happened to go to Ivy University Law School.

I took a law course with Professor Martini at St. Patrick's. I was proud that an Italian was teaching the law course. I asked him where I should go for my law studies. He suggested St. Patrick's Law School. So I made my applications, and I was going there when I met a lawyer named Marino. He asked me why I didn't go to Ivy Law School, instead. I said: "I know my own limitations. I couldn't get into a place like that. I'll be content to stay in my own station."

He told me: "Chick, don't be a jackass. If you've got the marks, you can get into Ivy, and a degree from Ivy will mean much more to you than one from St. Patrick's."

I thought it over. I went home and talked with my mother. It would cost me $420 to go to Ivy, not counting books, or carfare. It would cost only $250 at St. Patrick's. I made a bargain with my mother. If she would pay my tuition, I would pay for everything else. She asked me how she could be sure that I would keep to my bargain. I told her that if I didn't, I would just drop out. So she agreed. And that's the bargain we've been keeping to ever since. . . . . I was anxious to be the first Italian boy from Cornerville to go to Ivy Law School. I made my application and sent in my marks along with a letter from Mr. Brown. He boosted me to the skies. A few days later I heard that I was accepted.

Chick's entrance into Ivy University Law School constituted an important step forward in his social and professional career. There was still a hard struggle ahead of him. The next few years would be decisive in determining his position in society. Against that background we can understand what the Italian Community Club meant to Chick Morelli.

2. ORGANIZING THE CLUB

The roots of Chick's Italian Community Club can be traced as far back as junior high school. The ninth-grade home-room teacher had a system of seating her pupils according to her estimate of their scholastic performance. The special recognition they received led to the development of a clique among the boys of the first row and the front of the second row. They even formed a short-lived club. The ninth-grade clique included Chick Morelli, Pat Russo, Tony Cardio, Joe Gennusi, Paul DiMatia, Leo Marto, and Jerry Merluzzo, with Phil Principio upon its periphery. Eight and a half years later Chick called upon these men to form the nucleus of the Community Club. He invited five other Cornerville men, Tom Scala, Mike Ferrara, Frank and Al Perino, and Jim Filippo, to be charter members.

Pat Russo, Chick's closest friend, had begun a social work course at St. Patrick's. Tony Cardio had an office job and was going to law school at night. Joe Gennusi was selling insurance and also studying law at night school. Paul DiMatia was completing a business course at Eastern College. Leo Marto and Jerry Merluzzo were studying medicine at the recently organized Meridian Medical School.

Tom Scala was a Junior at Ivy College, where he was majoring in English literature. Mike Ferrara was in his last year at St. Patrick's. Frank Perino, a graduate of St. Patrick's, was taking a medical course at Sheldon University, which ranked next to Ivy University in this field in the Eastern City region. His younger brother, Al, was in his Junior year at St. Patrick's. Jim Filippo was a Senior at Eastern College, where he was majoring in accounting.

The club's organization meeting was held at the Norton Street Settlement House early in January, 1937. Chick Morelli was elected president; Leo Marto, vice-president; Tom Scala, secretary; and Frank Perino, treasurer.

Tom Scala gave this description of the meeting in his minutes:

Mr. Morelli roughly outlined to the assembled group the purpose of the assembly. He stated that Italians have made a brilliant reputation in the civilization of the world; hence we should consider ourselves a vital element of the American race.

We must create social bonds, principally with our intellectual equals, for chiefly among these can the influence of the Italian mind in the fields of Arts and Sciences be fully realized.

Our next aim is to instruct our community as to their duty concerning amelioration of their own educational and sectional interests.

The president [in the second meeting] presented his outline of the year's activities. The outline proposed points that were social as well as intellectual in nature.

I. Weekly talks by the members in their respective fields preferably.
II. Monthly articles for the ———— [local newspaper], one article a month by every individual member.
III. A monthly forum for Italian parents.
IV. Production of a play.
V. A debate.
VI. Oratorical contests for nonmembers.

Social Program

I. Monthly socials for the members.
II. Smokers for intellectuals of Italian extraction.
III. Dance for benefit of Italian Orphan's Home.
IV. Bi-monthly stag parties.
V. Fraternity pin.

The second meeting also approved a constitution that had been drawn up by Chick Morelli and Tony Cardio. Provision was made or an annual election of officers, initiation fees, dues, penalties, and the appointment of committees, but no clear statement was made upon the necessary qualifications of an applicant for membership. It was understood that the club was to be made up of a superior class of young men, but exactly what should constitute this superiority remained to be decided.

The club had a dual purpose: the social betterment of the members and the improvement of Cornerville. There seemed to be no necessary conflict between these aims when the club was organized, but it proved impossible to pursue both at the same time. Consequently, almost every issue implied a decision as to which aim was to be emphasized. When new men were admitted and when new activities were planned, the members were deciding in effect what kind of club they were to have; and, while they did not express it in these terms, they knew what was involved.

The first issue arose over the question of whether the club should admit men who had had no college or professional education. While some of the members were afraid of lowering the standing of the club, they nevertheless had friends among the noncollege men. Joe Gennusi argued that it was undemocratic to exclude them, and, after the issue had been discussed at several meetings, it was finally agreed that the membership committee should have discretion in such cases.

When the way was opened to noncollege men, Doc and Angelo Cucci were admitted to membership, and in the course of the next several months Lou Danaro, Fred Mackey, Art Testa, and Patsy Donato were voted in. Art and Patsy had both been members of the Sunset Dramatic Club. Art had an office job, and Patsy had a small contracting business.

In this same period a number of college men were added. Mike Ferrara introduced a friend, who was also a Senior at St. Patrick's. Chick brought in Vincent Pelosi, a Westland man who, like himself, was going to Ivy University Law School. Tony Cardio brought in Ernest Daddio, who had spent two years at St. Pattrick's and had left to take a white-collar job.

In April, Doc invited me to a meeting of the club and asked me to join. He told me that it would be necessary to change the constitution in order to get me in, since membership was limited to Italian-Americans. Actually there was no such provision, but the written constitution was rarely referred to, and everyone believed that an amendment was necessary. Doc submitted my name to the membership committee of Tony Cardio, Tom Scala, and Phil Principio. He told me that when he entered the club most of the members were new to him, but now he looked forward with confidence to the political maneuvers necessary in my behalf. I said that I did not want to make an issue out of my application, but Doc said that he did.

At a much later time Doc reviewed for me the progress of my case. Tony Cardio had been against me, but Tom Scala and Phil Principio gave me a majority on the membership committee. However, since several others were also against me, Tony's vote was necessary to pass the amendment. He was finally persuaded to pledge his vote to me. As Doc told me:

I had it all arranged, Bill. The vice-president of the club [Leo Marto] was against you, so if we needed the vote, I was going to have Chick stay away so he would have to take the chair. But there were only three at the meeting that told me they were against you, so I told Chick to come up. Then when we voted—by the Australian ballot—there were five votes against you. They double-crossed me, Bill. I was sore. I accused two of them of voting against you, but they swore they didn't. . . . . It didn't make any difference, Bill. I was only sore because they double-crossed me. . . . .

Doc and Chick thought that Tony Cardio had broken his word by voting against me, and, although Tony denied it, Chick said after the meeting that he would never trust Tony again. In the same meeting I was elected to the newly created status of guest membership. In the next meeting Tom Scala said that it was stupid to have a special status for me and moved that I be made a regular member. This time the motion carried.

My application for membership brought about the first sharp division of opinion in the club, but it did not give rise to the college and noncollege division. The corner boys wanted to get me in, but so did some of the college boys.

3. SOCIAL ACTIVITIES

The program outlined by President Morelli was ambitious enough to occupy the attention of a dozen clubs. It soon became evident that only a small part of his plan could be put into effect. No action was taken upon the monthly articles, the forum for parents, the debate, the smokers for intellectuals, the benefit dance, the stage parties, or the fraternity pin. An oratorical contest for nonmembers was planned and announced, but interest in this project was insufficient to carry it through. The college men took turns in giving talks, which were held with some degree of regularity upon meeting nights. In the first season the production of a play became the center of interest.

Chick Morelli took it upon himself to select the play to be given. His choice was *Night of Horror*, which, he explained, was amusing and exciting and had the additional advantage that it could be had for a ten-dollar royalty. Doc was voted into the club after the choice had been made, but he confided to me his opinion that *Night of Horror* was a bad play which Chick liked simply because he saw a good part for himself in it.

One of the members suggested that Doc be asked to direct the play, but Chick said, "No, Doc would play favorites." Chick recommended a man by the name of Felix DiCarlo, who lived next door to him. None of the other members knew DiCarlo, but they accepted Chick's suggestion.

When the tryouts were held, Frank Perino, who had starred in amateur theatricals at St. Patrick's, sat in the back of the hall and refused to participate. He said to Doc, "What's the use of trying out? Chick will get the lead anyway." A short time later Frank resigned from the club, and his brother followed him.

Doc and Chick both tried for the leading role, and DiCarlo selected Chick. Some of the members were so outspoken in their opinion that Doc deserved the part that Chick finally suggested that Doc take his place. However, neither Doc nor DiCarlo would stand for a change.

There were four feminine roles to be filled. Doc told me that there was a great interest in dramatics in Cornerville, and he felt that giving Cornerville girls the opportunity of learning how to express themselves on the stage was in accord with the local improvement aim of the club. Chick felt that this was an opportunity for the club to make beneficial social contacts. He proposed that he get in touch with the president of the Italian Junior League, an exclusive organization of girls outside Cornerville, to see if they could provide the necessary actresses. This was agreed upon.

The results of Chick Morelli's approach to the Italian Junior League were given in the club minutes.

President outlined events which occurred during the session with President ——— and her governing board. Final results being very favorable. They agreed to grant us their assistance in our social endeavors. We in turn are to give them our aid. This is considered by both parties as a mutual verbal agreement.

Felix DiCarlo's direction was a spectacle. As Doc commented, "He's more dramatic than any of the actors." The girls were so impressed that they asked him to direct the play to be given by the Italian Junior League. Most of the men were impressed at first, but as time went on they became tired of DiCarlo's temperament. Doc felt from the start that the director was a "phoney."

Doc and Angelo wanted to give the play in the Norton Street Settlement out of loyalty to Cornerville. Chick and Tony Cardio wanted to get a larger and more professional hall outside Cornerville. Their views prevailed.

Chick arranged to have some of the Junior League girls act as ushers. Too late it occurred to him that he should have invited girls from the Clarion Club, another exclusive Italian organization, so that his club could make contacts with both groups of girls.

The play was considered a great success by the club members. Chick, who played the hero, and Tony Cardio, who played the villain, were particularly enthusiastic. Doc and Angelo were the only ones who expressed to me privately their adverse opinions.

Whatever the merits of *Night of Horror* as drama, it opened the channels of social advancement to the Community Club. The actresses who took part in the play were working girls, but, unlike most Cornerville girls, they worked in offices instead of factories. They were attractive and well dressed, and they had social standing. There was much social activity in connection with the rehearsals. Chick and Tony set the pace in entertaining the girls, but all the members felt obligated to give them a good time.

Association with the Junior League girls brought on one minor and one major crisis in the club's affairs. As the first meeting after the production of the play was drawing to a close, Ernest Daddio rose to his feet.

ERNEST: Wait a minute. I've got something to say. . . . . That night of the play I was broke, but, when I was coming out, I saw five girls from the cast standing around, and they wanted to go somewhere, so I thought it was my duty for the club to spend some money on them. I said, "I haven't anything with me now, but if you'll come with me up to the house, I'll get some money." So I taxied home and got some money, and I went out and spent $4.35 on them.

CHICK: Well, so what? What do you want from us?

ERNEST: I want my money back. . . . . I wasn't acting as myself, Ernest Daddio, I was acting as a group. . . . . I was acting for the club. (*Laughter.*)

CHICK: Who told you you should act for the club?

TONY: He's right, Chick. He really had the interests of the club at heart.

JOE: Do you think you're the only one that spent money on the girls that night?

CHICK: That's right. We all spent money on the girls, but we're not asking the club to give it back to us.

TONY: But Mr. Daddio's case is different. The club has more responsibility there because he was spending money on members of the cast.

JOE: How many were there?

ERNEST: There were five members of the cast.

CHICK: Two of them weren't members of the cast.

ERNEST: Well, who the hell were they?

PAUL: Parasites.

The discussion was carried on amid laughter, Daddio being the only one who remained completely serious. Finally Doc said, "I think the kid is sincere. Let him have his money." He moved that Daddio be given three dollars (for which he agreed to settle) from the treasury. The motion was carried by eight votes to seven. Then Chick delivered an angry reprimand to the members and to Daddio in particular.

Tom Scala announced that the procedure had been unconstitutional. In order to give out money, the club had to have the authorization of the president and the executive committee. Chick said that he would not give his authorization. Daddio was asked to give the three dollars back. He said, "All right, but I need it for tomorrow. I've got to pay a bill."

It was agreed that he could owe it to the club until the following meeting. As the meeting broke up, Daddio remarked to Doc, "I had to have the money."

"That's a hell of a way to get it," Doc replied.

Daddio never again attended a meeting. When he had missed three consecutive meetings, he was automatically expelled. But he still had the three dollars, and all efforts to get it back proved futile.

The Daddio case cost the club one member and three dollars. Association with the girls created a much more serious disturbance. After the play, Chick was eager to continue the social contacts with the Italian Junior League. When the Community Club planned a social, he called the president of the Junior League and asked her to invite some of her members. It was the Cornerville custom for men and girls to go to dances separately. The Junior League girls were not used to this system, and the college men tended to break away from it, especially when going with girls from outside Cornerville. Chick's arrangements were a compromise. He asked that the girls come down by themselves, but if five girls were invited, he asked five of the members to see to it that they were entertained. Cornerville girls, especially members of clubs meeting in the settlement house, were also invited, but Chick was particularly anxious that the Junior League girls should have a good time. He and Tony Cardio made a point of dancing with each one. The other college men were shy and hung back, except when they were goaded by Chick and Tony. Paul DiMatia and Phil Principio were particularly backward. Doc divided his attentions between the two groups of girls and was popular with both of them, but he never danced. The other noncollege men confined their attentions largely to the local girls.

The division between college and noncollege men showed itself most clearly in the final social of the first season. We were invited to Patsy Donato's home in Dedfield. Chick Morelli, Tony Cardio, Leo Marto, Phil Principio, Joe Gennusi, and Jim Filippo were with Junior League girls. Doc, Angelo Cucci, Lou Danaro, and Fred Mackey were with Cornerville girls.

Chick had offered to get all the boys dates with Junior League girls for this social, but the noncollege men declined. Fred Mackey told me that it was all right for Chick to get girls for those that wanted them, but he would feel disloyal to the local girls if he deserted them for the Junior League.

There was a similar division between the two groups of girls. I took a girl named Mary, who had grown up in Cornerville and had moved out to Dedfield, but was not a member of the Junior League. We drove to the Donato home with Joe Gennusi, Tony Cardio and a friend of his, and three Junior League girls. During the drive to the suburbs the two girls with Tony and his friend confined their talk of prospective vacations and social events to one another and the two men. Mary tried to be sociable, but they paid no attention to her. Later she took pleasure in pointing out to me that the Junior League girls had bad manners and that they had mispronounced certain words. She said that all the local girls in the party shared her dislike for the Junior Leaguers.

Those who associated with the Junior League were moving away from Cornerville society. Some felt that the club should move faster in this direction, while others felt that the movement should be brought to a stop.

Felix DiCarlo was one of those who was most socially aggressive. Shortly after the production of *Night of Horror*, he applied for membership. After rushing through a by-law stipulating that no club member should ever be allowed to direct a play, the men voted him in. When the club social program was being discussed, DiCarlo suggested a dinner dance. This was the most expensive proposal of a social nature ever to come before the club. Even Chick Morelli opposed it, saying that the boys could not afford it. The proposal was dropped, and DiCarlo never came to another meeting.

While Chick did not think it possible to go so far so fast, he agreed with DiCarlo's aims for the club. Doc discussed Chick's attitude when I asked him to comment upon the club's aim to better the local community:

————! The purpose is to better themselves. Don't you hear Chick always talking about getting in with a better class of girls from outside of Cornerville? Sure, they may be smarter and all that, but why not help instruct the stupid ones around here? . . . . One time we had an executive committee meeting with Chick, Tony Cardio, Pat Russo, Joe Gennusi, and me. Chick proposed having a big dance and charging $2.00 to get in so that we could keep the corner boys away. I argued against that for an hour. . . . . Finally it was tabled.

While this proposal was not acted upon, there were others which had the same effect. If the members were to make an impression upon the Junior League girls, they could not allow corner boys who were not club members to drop in, partake of refreshments, and mingle with the girls. Chick insisted that only club members and their guests be allowed to attend socials. This policy was accepted by the club. Chick did not wish to antagonize the corner boys, but, since his chief interest was in the Junior League girls, he pursued a policy which could have no other effect. Thus, in the first few months of its existence, the club had drawn a line of social distinction through its own membership and had cut the college men off from the main body of Cornerville society.

4. OPPOSITION TO CHICK

Though they had become active immediately after being voted into the club, Chick Morelli planned an initiation for all non-charter members. Doc's case raised special difficulties. He said to me, "Don't you think that is a lot of foolishness, Bill? Why do they have to have that stuff?" He had a date with a girl on the night of the initiation, but he dropped in at the settlement at 7:30 to tell Chick that he had a half-hour free so that the boys could take him if they wanted to hurry. Chick said he would be damned if he would make any concessions to Doc.

The initiation proceeded in Doc's absence. Chick tried to give us his conception of a college fraternity initiation, but he could not put his heart into it, and, when the ritual was over, he was very gloomy.

At the next meeting Doc was sent out of the room while the members discussed what should be done to penalize him. A motion to levy a dollar fine was finally carried by a one-vote margin. Lou Danaro and Fred Mackey sought to vote against the fine, but Chick ruled that, since they had not been members of the club at the time of the initiation, they were not eligible to vote.

Doc accepted the decision without comment until he heard that Lou and Fred had not been allowed to vote. He then told Chick that this was just a private feud between them and that Chick would not get away with the imposition of the penalty. Chick replied that he was only acting in the best interests of the club.

The penalty question was reopened by Doc at the following meeting. The discussion revealed that there was no one still in favor of the fine. Someone moved that there be no penalty, and this was defeated only after Chick had broken the tie vote. He then suggested that there be a severer initiation at some future date. This was voted unanimously. Chick explained to Doc that a penalty was necessary in order to uphold the prestige of the club. Chick was satisfied and so was Doc. There never was another initiation.

Shortly after the initiation question was settled, Chick faced the most serious challenge to his leadership. Not even his best friends could claim that Chick was tactful. As a matter of fact, he did not approve of tact. He once told me that it was all right in dealing with children but that when he was with mature men he told them just what he thought of them and expected them to take it in the spirit of constructive criticism. Several times toward the end of the first season he told the members that he was doing all the work for the club and accused them of laziness and lack of spirit. In meetings he laid down the law. Once he tried to end an argument by saying, "After all, I'm president, and what I say goes."

Doc and his noncollege men had never cared for Chick's leadership, but his position would have been secure if he had had the united support of the college men. In various ways he alienated that support.

In a match against another club Chick bowled well and Joe Gennusi bowled poorly. Chick said that in future matches someone else should take Joe's place. Doc protested. He said to me that he thought Joe was just as good a bowler as Chick and, furthermore, that Chick had no authority to decide who should bowl. Chick never raised the issue again, so there was no open break, although Joe felt very bad about the incident.

Several meetings after the production of *Night of Horror*, Chick asked Tony Cardio if he had paid the club what he owed for the sale of tickets. Tony said that he was submitting a report to Joe Gennusi, the chairman of the play committee. Chick said, "I submitted my report long ago. Why can't you be forthright about this?" The remark created a furor in the meeting. Tony objected angrily and then added, in a judicial tone, "I think the president has been indulging in too many personalities. If this goes on, it will be the downfall of the club."

"Oh, forget it," Chick said. Joe Gennusi also reprimanded Chick.

In the beginning Tom Scala was a loyal supporter of Chick, but their friendship gradually cooled. Tom, who was majoring in English, had a passion for rare and archaic words. He began writing the minutes in a simple, business-like manner, but very shortly the meetings "supervened" or "came to a focus." The secretary

was to achieve his masterpiece in describing the last meeting before the summer vacation of 1937:

> The sun had passed the Meridian eight times when the last official pre-
> aestival eisteddfod of the Italian Community Club acervated at the Norton
> Street Settlement at 8:30 P.M. sharp!

Chick had said to me sometime earlier:

> When a man uses a string of big words, the fellows think he is a genius. I
> can name for you five members of the club that think Tom Scala is a genius
> just because he uses words they never heard of before. By encouraging him,
> they really spoil him for our club. . . . . I don't go for that, Bill, I tell you
> frankly. I don't think that is art. I think it is putrid. . . . . Real art is
> simple. I read Homer's *Odyssey* in the original—at St. Patrick's—and I
> want to tell you, there weren't a lot of big words in that. Everything was
> told in a very simple manner, deep and moving, of course, but the words
> were simple. . . . .

Chick did not hesitate to express this opinion in the meetings.
Tom liked to amuse the members, yet at the same time he took
pride in his writing. When Chick tried to discourage him, he
stubbornly persisted, and he was naturally drawn toward the noncollege men who were most appreciative of his efforts.

Chick had antagonized Jerry Merluzzo, Leo Marto, and Jim
Filippo with his handling of Jerry's initiation case. Jerry had been
invited to be a charter member but had been unable because of
illness to attend the organization meeting. Chick proposed that
Jerry be excused from paying the initiation fee but that he should
not be considered a charter member and therefore should submit
to an initiation. In several meetings Jerry pressed his claim to
charter membership, vigorously supported by Leo and Jim.
Though the majority of the members voted against him, Jerry
and his friends continued to protest.

Chick provoked an open clash with Jim when he announced
that he was removing him from the judiciary committee. Jim demanded an explanation. Chick said: "I don't have to give you
an answer, see. But since you ask for it, I'll tell you." The charges
were that Jim was disorderly in meetings and destroyed the so-
lemnity of the initiation by calling out, "Cut out the ———!"
Tom Scala protested against the repetition of such language in
the meeting. Jim got very angry and demanded a chance to de-

fend himself. In a voice barely under control, he held that he had not acted differently from many other members. When Chick tried to argue with him, Jim shouted, "I move the president be impeached!" Tom Scala seconded the motion. Chick was calm. He called for discussion. Tony Cardio said that there was no provision in the constitution for impeachment and suggested that one be put in. Chick said that serious charges should be made. Jim said that he objected to the personalities the president brought into the meeting and to his attitude toward the members. Doc asked Jim to withdraw his motion so that a constitutional amendment on impeachment could be put through. He refused, saying that a straight majority vote should be sufficient to remove an officer. Tom Scala said that his second to the motion had been a joke, which he now wished to withdraw. Doc moved that a three-quarters vote of the members should oust any officer. Paul Di-Matia objected, saying this meant anyone could move for impeachment at any time. He suggested that charges should be presented to the judiciary committee, which would present them to the club. Doc accepted the amendment. Tony Cardio objected, saying that any member should be able to bring up such a motion at any time. The motion was passed as made by Doc and amended by Paul.

The idea of impeaching Chick Morelli was not a new one. Tony Cardio had been privately sounding out some of the members, although he had not planned any action for that meeting. If Doc had been willing to swing his noncollege men in favor of impeachment, the move might have carried through in short order, but he took the opposite stand. He told me that, while he had no love for Chick Morelli, he was unwilling to subject him to such humiliation.

Tony Cardio had his chance to oust Chick, and he missed it. When once the impeachment motion had been made, it was necessary for Tony to act energetically to push through a vote. Instead, he was occupied with thoughts of legalism when the crisis came. If he was determined that everything should be done legally, he might have substituted a motion that the president be requested to resign. Chick could not have withstood an adverse vote on such a question. When Tony suggested the cumbersome procedure of amending the constitution, he defeated himself. When Doc and Paul had framed the amendment, Chick's position was again secure. Between meetings the proponents of impeachment tried to mobilize support, but without Doc and the non-college men they fell far short of the necessary three-quarters vote.

For a time Chick was chastened. Instead of laying down the law, he would say, "After all, it's up to you fellows to decide. Whatever you decide you want to do. . . . ." However, it did not take him long to regain his old aggressiveness.

In June the club was suspended for the summer months, to reconvene again in September. In view of the stormy sessions which closed the first season, many of the members wondered whether there would be a second season.

Doc told me about an incident which occurred toward the end of the summer:

We had a game of La Mora [a game played with fingers], with three men on a side. I was anchor man on my side, against Chick. The game was to twelve points, and when I came up, the score was eleven to three against us. I took nine points in a row and won the game for us. Chick was sore. He was calling me all kinds of names. But I only laughed. I thought it was a big joke. . . . . After a while I went over and sat down in a doorstep on Norton Street. Chick came up and slapped me in the face. I told him, "You do that again, and I'll let you have it." Then he slapped me again. . . . . The first time I didn't mind so much, but the second time I saw red. I chased him across the street. He backed up against the wall. I cracked him with a right to the shoulder. Maybe, if he had been out in the street, I would have let him have it on the jaw, but when he was backed up against the wall, I saw I might crack the back of his head open if I let him have it there. . . . . He had a black-and-blue spot below his shoulder for a long time. He couldn't go to work for two days because he couldn't move his arm. I was worried. I thought I might have crippled him. I was sorry I lost my temper, but he really got my goat. . . . . After that he didn't speak to me for three weeks.

5. THE SECOND SEASON

When the club reconvened in September, interest was at a low ebb. Only Chick Morelli, Pat Russo, Joe Gennusi, Phil Principio, Tom Scala, and Lou Danaro attended meetings regularly. Paul DiMatia had an evening job and was given a leave of absence.

Tony Cardio missed three meetings in succession and then received a leave of absence because he was "too busy" to come to meetings. Angelo Cucci began skipping meetings because he could not afford to pay dues. The other members had various excuses which all meant that the club was not very important to them.

One night Chick encountered Doc in Jennings' after a club meeting which Doc had missed.

CHICK: Where were you tonight?

DOC: I had important business.

CHICK: That's what you always say. . . . . You better come to the club meetings or you'll get thrown out.

DOC: I'll skip two meetings and come to the third. And you won't be able to do anything about it.

CHICK: That's what you think.

DOC: All right. If you don't believe me, put a little side bet on it, and we'll see what happens. You can't put me out without changing the constitution, and if you try to do it, you won't have a leg to stand on.

CHICK: You'll see.

DOC: Want to bet on it?

CHICK: No. . . . . But you better come to meetings.

Shortly after this Doc deliberately missed three successive meetings and dropped out of the club. Lou Danaro and Fred Mackey continued as members, but they were critical. Lou predicted that the club would turn into a political organization when one of the young lawyer-members wanted to run for public office. Fred said. "As long as the club has strictly a charitable purpose, it will be a good club. I don't like this mercenary stuff."

Chick bent all his efforts toward reinjecting life into the club. He opened the first fall meeting with this statement:

I know I am not diplomatic all the time. I know I have lots of enemies in the club. [Paul DiMatia said under his breath, "They are legion."] I'm glad I have enemies in the club; it makes it more interesting. . . . . Even the greatest diplomats have enemies. Who am I to be without enemies? . . . . But one thing I want to tell you fellows, my interests are always for the good of the Italian Community Club. I don't want you to forget that.

He then proposed that the club sponsor an oratorical contest for high-school students and offer a prize, to be raised by donations, which would be given to the winner when (and only when) he went to college. "After all, fellows, it is part of the purpose of our club to do something for the community. And I think this would

be a good thing because it stimulates education, and that is one
of our purposes."

The members listened without enthusiasm, but, since they had
no counterproposals, the contest was agreed upon. Three titles
were given as "preferred subjects" for the speakers: "The Rise
of the Italian-American Youth," "The Italian Contribution to
American Civic Life," and "A Famous Italian-American."

Chick named Patsy Donato chairman of the contest committee
and appointed Joe Gennusi and Phil Principio to work with him.
Shortly thereafter Patsy resigned with the excuse that his business did not leave him enough time to devote to the committee,
and Joe took his place as chairman.

Only Chick and Joe did any work toward raising money and
publicizing the contest, and finally Chick had to announce that it
was called off. He launched a tirade against the members for
their lack of spirit and unco-operative attitude. Paul DiMatia
interrupted to charge that Chick himself was responsible for the
failure of the contest, since he tried to be a dictator instead of a
leader.

This was the first time that Paul had come out with a direct
attack upon the president. Doc told me that he and his friends
had been working on Paul.

> When we would be together, I would say to him, "Look at this thing
> that Chick has done. Now, that isn't right." And he would admit it. Then
> I would say—or one of the boys would say—"Look at that thing Chick did.
> Now, that isn't right." And Paul would admit it. . . . . If he does all these
> things wrong, he must not be a good man to lead the club. After a while
> Paul would have to admit that. . . . . A man naturally wants the things
> that are right—that he thinks are right. If you point out to him these things
> that he has to think are right—or wrong—he has to agree with you. . . . .
> No, I didn't want to impeach Chick. A blow like that might blight a man's
> entire life. It just steamed me up to see the way he was tossing the fellows
> around. I didn't want to see him get away with it.

Chick had been particularly severe with Tom Scala, and Doc
and his boys had been talking to him as well. Angelo and Doc
became Phil Principio's closest friends. In this way Paul, Tom,
and Phil were won over to the noncollege faction. Since Doc was
out of the club, the opposition was unorganized, but it was evidence of growing dissatisfaction with Chick's leadership.

Whenever Chick seemed to be slipping, he came forward with a new idea. In the meeting following cancellation of the oratorical contest, he began in this way:

I don't know what is wrong with this club, but if it is the president, I'll gladly resign. I really mean that, gentlemen. I have been giving the matter very serious thought. I'll resign tonight from the presidency, if that's what you want. Not from the club, unless you want me to do that.

Tom Scala asked Chick to say what was wrong with himself. Chick said, "I can't answer that. You know, the law of self-preservation. No man condemns himself." When he saw that no one was prepared to act upon his resignation proposal, Chick proceeded with the routine business of the meeting. That concluded, he stood up, took off his coat, and announced that he was going to say things that would surprise the members. "As educated men, I think it is our duty to take some interest in the affairs of the state. Not that I think we should participate in politics, but I think that as educated men we should discuss the qualifications of the candidates in our meetings."

Tom Scala objected, saying, "I thought our discussions were supposed to be purely intellectual, and now you are bringing politics in."

"Well," Chick countered, "it is part of the purpose of our club to work for the betterment of our community. We should want to see that Cornerville is well represented at city hall and at the Capitol."

The members who were studying law were unanimous in supporting Chick.

Chick suggested that the club should write open letters to the the candidates, demanding that they take a stand on certain issues. The club could put pressure upon politicians to obtain a new public bathhouse and improved park facilities for the district.

Leo objected: "I think we should keep out of politics, because everybody in the club has different ideas on politics. They have different men they want to support, and if we once begin to talk politics we'll never get anywhere with this club."

"I don't see why we can't agree on some of the issues without indorsing candidates," Joe replied.

Tom Scala first opposed the plan, but he was won over when Chick promised that the club would not be asked to indorse any candidate. Chick added: "But if a politician is deceiving the people, it is our duty to inform them."

Only Leo Marto, Jim Filippo, and Art Testa voted against Chick.

When the boys were gathered in Jennings' after the meeting, Leo cornered Tony:

LEO: Suppose a friend of yours is running for office and you are supporting him, and he promises he will help you out if he gets in. . . . . Now I come around and show you that my friend is a better man and should win the election. Will you change your vote?

TONY (*hesitating*): . . . . No. . . . . Of course not.

LEO: Well?

In the next meeting it was Vincent Pelosi's turn to give a talk upon his field. He was planning to run for public office in his home district of Westland, and he devoted his time to presenting the case for political talks in the club. When he had finished, Chick called for discussion. After a brief silence, he took the floor himself and went over all the arguments he had given in the previous meeting. Once under way, he would allow no interruptions, and when he had finished it was time to adjourn. Lou Danaro and Angelo Cucci told me that Chick had talked his own plan to death. After this no more was heard about political discussions. In a short time Vincent Pelosi stopped attending meetings.

As the club election of January, 1938, approached, there was a revival of interest. Perhaps the prospect of electing a different president proved stimulating to the members. In December, Doc returned to the club. As he explained to me:

One night I was out riding in a car with Pat Russo, Joe Gennusi, and Chick. Pat and Joe kept trying to persuade me to come back into the club. Chick asked me to come back too. I don't know whether he wanted to say it or not. When the other fellows asked me, he had to ask me too. . . . . Sure, Fred Mackey and Lou Danaro wanted me to come back. . . . . Well, I decided that I was making too much of Chick to stay out of the club on account of him. I decided to come back.

Doc was readmitted only after it had been voted, on Leo Marto's motion, that he must attend eight consecutive meetings on pain of expulsion and that he should not be eligible to hold any office until the eight-week period expired. This regulation prevented him from seeking any office in the January elections.

As early as the preceding October the maneuvers leading up to the election were inaugurated. Doc told me that Tony Cardio was trying to persuade the members that Chick Morelli should be re-elected. Since the previous spring, when he had tried to impeach Chick, Tony had executed a sharp about-face. I do not know what passed between them. Whatever his reasons, Tony soon realized that there was no chance of re-electing the president.

In December, Doc told me that Joe Gennusi, who expected to run for political office the following year, wanted to be president of the club and had Chick's support. Lou, Fred, Art, Patsy, and Tom had told Doc that they wanted to delay the election until he became eligible to hold office, but he refused to let them do so.

One week before the election some of the members were in Jennings'. Chick, Pat Russo, and Joe Gennusi sat at one table. Doc, Angelo Cucci, and Fred Mackey sat at another. As Doc said:

For the first time the cliques in the club were recognized openly. Chick called me over. He asked me, "Who do you want for president of the club?" I told him, "We don't care, but we want Art Testa for vice-president. . . . . We shook on it. Chick pledged his vote. . . . . We figured Joe Gennusi will be busy with his campaign in the fall, and he'll have to be absent many times, so we would have Art in the chair often. Maybe they figured that too.

On election night all the members except Tom Scala were present, and there was one new member, Al Marotta, a close friend of Joe Gennusi. Leo Marto nominated Joe for president, and immediately it was moved that the nominations be closed. Doc's faction made no protest.

Chick called for nominations for vice-president. Pat Russo nominated Tony Cardio. Doc and the other members of his faction were surprised. There was a brief pause. Then Fred Mackey nominated Art Testa. Art said something about being too busy for the job, but Fred talked to him, and he did not withdraw. Ballots were passed out, marked, and collected. President Morelli counted them as several others watched him. Chick announced that the vote was an eight-to-eight tie. He hesitated. He said that it might be a good idea to have another vote. Doc and his friends insisted that it was the duty of the president to cast the deciding vote. Finally, Chick rose. He announced that he would first give his reasons for his decision. He said that the boys had put him on the spot but that he would always act in the best interests of the club and not choose a man for any personal reasons. He would give his vote to the man who was best qualified for the position, who had done most for the club and would do most in the future—Tony Cardio. Doc and his friends were stunned. Pat Russo was unanimously re-elected treasurer. I was elected secretary.

From talks with several of the members, I feel confident that the following record of the vice-presidential election is correct:

For Tony Cardio:	*For Art Testa:*
Chick Morelli	Doc
Tony Cardio	Fred Mackey
Art Testa	Lou Danaro
Pat Russo	Angelo Cucci
Joe Gennusi	Patsy Donato
Leo Marto	Phil Principio
Jerry Merluzzo	Paul DiMatia
Jim Filippo	Bill Whyte
Al Marotta	

Art Testa made the gesture of voting for his opponent and so created the tie which led to his defeat. If Art's name is placed on the other side, the actual division within the club is fully represented.

Several months later Chick discussed with me his choice between Tony and Art. He said:

I don't like Tony. I hate him. But I couldn't let my personal feelings influence my judgment. I think he is better educated and more intelligent, and he had done more for the club.

I asked Chick if he had not said that he would support Art Testa.

No, I never said that. Once I did say that I would never vote for Tony Cardio for any office, but I changed my mind during the course of the meeting. . . . . I saw that there was one member that was urging Art to run to beat Tony because Tony had once taken a girl away from this member. Now that's not right, Bill. And, another thing, Mr. Testa tried to decline the nomination, he didn't think he could do the work. I took that into consideration. . . . . When I saw they were all so anxious to beat Tony, that roused my sporting blood. I voted for Tony just so they would not be successful in their plans.

Yes, I've known Tony since we were kids. . . . . Tony has proved himself to be untrustworthy. He wanted to be friends with me. I told him, "You'll have to come to me." . . . . But then I didn't want to let my personal feelings influence me when I voted. I was looking out for the best interests of the club.

I asked Doc why Chick had said he did not trust Tony. He explained:

Tony was one of the members that held out against you when I was trying to get you into the club. One night Chick and I had him in Jennings', and we argued with him for a couple of hours. . . . . Finally, he said, "Well, if you fellows feel that way about it, maybe I'm wrong." So he agreed to vote for you. . . . . Then when the meeting came, Tony started to make the report of the membership committee, and he was ruining you. I told him he was out of order, all he had to do was tell the members how the committee ruled in your case. I don't know if I was right legally, but Chick backed me up, so we made him shut up. He just said that the membership committee was in favor of you. . . . . But then he voted against you, and that one vote was enough to keep you out at first. Afterward he denied that he voted "No," but he was lying. I thought of everything, Bill. I had one of my men sitting next to Tony to see how he voted. When I told him that, he said first he put down "No," and then he crossed it out and wrote "Yes"—but he's not kidding me. . . . . After that, Chick was sore. He said, "Cardio didn't keep his word. He's not to be trusted." . . . . I reminded Chick of that after the election.

I asked Doc if he was sure that Chick had pledged his vote to Art Testa. He said:

Chick broke his word. That's all I want to know. . . . . I checked up with Angelo Cucci yesterday to see if he remembered what happened at Jennings'. He had the same story that I did. . . . . Chick pledged his word that he would never vote for Tony only a week before the election.

Since Pat Russo put Tony's name in nomination, Chick must have known that Tony was to be a candidate. Pat was Chick's closest friend and always supported him in whatever he did. It seems likely that Chick committed himself to both sides with the expectation that he would not be called upon to show his hand. The reasons he gave for the decision that was demanded of him are very significant. First, he discounted arguments which he characterized as personal: that he hated Tony and that Tony was untrustworthy. These arguments might have been used in a different way, to indicate that it was poor policy to select a vice-president who was hated and mistrusted by half the members in preference to one who was more or less popular with all the members. As impersonal reasons, Chick cited Tony's superior intelligence and his past and future services to the club. Art had not been a member as long as Tony, but from the start of the second season until shortly before the election Tony had had so little interest in the club that he did not attend meetings. Art's friends had a high regard for his intelligence, and none of them would concede that Tony was superior in this respect. But Tony was a college man and Art was not.

Doc expressed it to me in this way:

> Don't you remember that speech Chick gave? He thought the office should go to the more intelligent man, to the college man. . . . . When two men aspire to the same office around here, and one of them is a college man and the other is a corner boy, the college man will vote for the college man every time. . . . . If he didn't, he might think he was admitting that a college education didn't do him any good.

6. DISINTEGRATION

The election of Tony Cardio had devastating repercussions in the club. According to Doc's story:

> After that speech Chick made when he voted for Tony, Art wanted an open apology. Chick told me he didn't see why he should give one because he only said what he really thought. Now Art doesn't speak to him any more.
>
> I got hold of Chick after the meeting and told him what I thought of him. He just said, "I was in a tough spot." . . . . I told him, from then on he would never have my confidences. We'll bowl together, we'll say "Hello" and "Goodbye," but we'll never be friends. . . . . The man went back on his word, Bill. That's all I want to know.

Doc's friends were equally disturbed. Patsy Donato, who was Art Testa's closest friend, dropped out of the club a short time after the election.

At the next meeting Tony Cardio surprised the members by seeking to resign from office. When he was pressed for an explanation, he said that Chick had been telling everybody, including the Junior League girls, that he had made Tony vice-president, and he had made Tony feel very cheap. Chick said he had been joking and apologized to Tony. Tony was persuaded to withdraw his resignation, but the incident revealed that the two men were once again at odds.

While President Gennusi was a college man, his attitude toward the corner boys was quite different from that of Chick or Tony. In discussing the friction between the two groups, he once said to me:

> In Cornerville the noncollege man has an inferiority complex. He hasn't had much education, and he has that feeling of inferiority. . . . . Now the college man felt that way before he went to college, but when he is in college, he tries to throw it off. He tries to break away from the inferiority complex by talking big, by impressing people with what he has learned from his education. Naturally, the noncollege man resents that. . . . . You want to know why I can get along with both groups? Because when I'm with the noncollege man, I never speak about my schooling or say that a man must have a college education in order to be qualified for a certain position. . . . . There are some smart fellows on the corner, and there are some nut-heads in college.

President Gennusi's first official acts were designed to conciliate Doc's faction. It had been rumored that Chick was to be made chairman of the judiciary committee in return for supporting Joe for president. Joe appointed Chick and Tony to the judiciary committee, but he selected Doc as chairman. He appointed Art Testa chairman of the membership committee, and chose Fred Mackey, Tom Scala, and Angelo Cucci to serve with the officers on the executive committee. Doc and his friends were favorably impressed.

Since *Night of Horror* had been the outstanding feature of the club's first season, Joe decided that the members should prepare to give another play. He appointed Doc, Fred Mackey, and Art Testa to choose a play and plan the production.

Joe questioned each member and found that only Doc, Phil Principio, Pat Russo, Fred Mackey, and Tony Cardio were willing to participate and that Paul DiMatia might be able to take a small part. Chick said that he was too busy.

When the men were discussing the feminine roles for the Community Club play, Chick argued:

We shouldn't get just any young lady. We want one with presence—by that I mean stage presence. This may not be liked by some, but I think we should get a young lady who is socially prominent. It will add to the prestige of our club. Before we had girls from A and B [outlying sections of Eastern City]. Now let's invade X and Y [suburban towns]. . . . . Mr. Cardio knows Miss Masucci. He could have her bring two girls from the Clarion Club.

It had already been decided, upon Doc's initiative, that each girls' club known to the members should be invited to send members interested in trying out. Chick was unable to persuade the club to change this plan. This was probably one of the main reasons that Chick, Tony, and some of the other college men displayed so little interest in the play.

At the same time, the Junior League girls started work on a play, with Felix DiCarlo directing. They asked for volunteers from the Community Club, but the men declined in order to concentrate upon their own play. In the following meeting Tony Cardio sought to withdraw from the Community Club play.

TONY: I've just been talking with Felix DiCarlo, and he told me he had a small part in the first act of the Junior League play that would fit me perfectly. At least that is what Felix thought. They just need one man. . . . . I'm bringing up the question because the club decided that we should not go into the play, and I don't want to go against the decision of the club.

CHICK: It is unnecessary for Mr. Cardio to bring up the question. That's a question of a man's free will. We can't dictate to the conscience of a man.

DOC: The club decided that we should stay out of the play, and therefore I think it was a fine gesture on Mr. Cardio's part to bring up the matter before us. I think it would a good idea to send one man, and I think Tony should go.

PAUL: The Junior League helped us a lot with our play, and we're making ourselves look like heels by not helping them.

PRESIDENT GENNUSI: I object to that statement.

ART: I think it would be all right to send Mr. Cardio, because that wouldn't conflict with our play.

PHIL: I think we should reciprocate in some way.

CHICK: Probably I was misunderstood. I don't object to having Mr. Cardio take the part. But don't say we sent him. I mean, we can't dictate to a man's conscience. That's up to Mr. Cardio.

PRESIDENT GENNUSI: I don't think any motion is necessary. We just want to get the sentiment of the members.

CHICK: I'm not against Mr. Cardio's going. I was only trying to avoid dictation.

TONY: That's all right, then. I'm glad to have the matter cleared up, because rumors have been going around that because I watched the first

Junior League tryout I was going to take part in the play in spite of the club's decision.

PRESIDENT GENNUSI: I don't think you should mention rumors in the club meeting, Mr. Cardio.

As Doc was unable to find a director, several weeks passed without any progress. In a late February meeting Tony Cardio suggested that, since few members were interested, the project should be dropped.

TONY: What I want to know is, can the club stand any more deficits? How many tickets to this play can we sell?

PRESIDENT GENNUSI: You take the wrong attitude. It's not how many can we sell. It's how many are we going to get out and sell.

FRED: I think each member should be able to tell ten tickets.

TONY: We'll be lucky if half our members sell that many.

PRESIDENT GENNUSI: You take the wrong attitude. According to you, we shouldn't give any affairs.

TONY: That's right. Not right now.

PRESIDENT GENNUSI: What I want to know is, why should we make a poorer showing this year than we did last year? . . . . I don't like the way Mr. Cardio is talking. He's objecting to everything the club tries to do.

TONY: That isn't fair. You know I have always been a progressive member of this club.

PAUL: That's right. He has been progressive, but in this case you showed him where he was wrong.

CHICK (*rising to his feet*): In this club we always have a big ballyhoo before every event, but unless we hammer down on the members and assess them ten tickets each, we won't succeed. I don't doubt that we will succeed, but that's the way I look at it. . . . . In this club there are a few members that are aggressive, and, in all deference, I'm one. But you can't get away from the principles of human nature. If the others slump, the aggressive ones finally won't work either.

For several more meetings the play was discussed, but only Joe Gennusi and Doc's faction were interested. In March, when the committee was still unable to find a director, Doc suggested that the project be dropped. No one protested.

In the next meeting President Gennusi announced that the Junior League girls had extended invitations to Community Club members for their dinner dance. Tickets were to cost $4.50 per couple. When the price was mentioned, some laughed and others shook their heads. Since the members could not afford to carry out the reciprocal activities planned in the "mutual verbal agreement," the club drifted away from the Italian Junior League and all that it represented.

Chick Morelli could not remain inactive while this trend continued. Ever since the election of the new president, he had been restless in meetings. Once in the middle of a lengthy discussion in which he took no part, he turned to me and said, "I'm going crazy here."

When the play question was finally settled, Chick rose to his feet and began to talk:

Fellows, I'm very serious. We have been organized one year now, and we haven't progressed too rapidly. . . . . We've been ———! Pardon me, gentlemen. . . . . When I go to school every day, I learn something. But here it is always the same thing. We want to advance. We don't want to be like the ordinary man, the $20-a-week laborer, that has no ambition. We want to turn our will into force. We need to advance. So, gentlemen, I am proposing something radical, and I want to ask you to let me handle it.

He proposed a raffle to finance elaborate socials for girls and Italian students from near-by colleges.

If we give these people functions, they'll be obligated to us. . . . . We won't be accused of being cheap pikers like before. . . . . Don't misunderstand me, gentlemen, I think the girls that said that just showed their ignorance, but we don't want to let it happen again.

After the meeting he told me what he had been talking about. The previous summer the club had given an outing to which some of the Junior League girls had been invited. Some of the girls had thought that the men were "cheap pikers" because the outing had been such a simple affair.

Can you imagine that? . . . . I was just saying that we should keep on the good side of them for diplomatic reasons. Personally, I don't think those girls have much intelligence. They don't realize that we don't have much money.

When the new project was accepted, Pat Russo called for the members to clap hands for Chick Morelli's interest in advancing the club. Chick was named head of the raffle committee, and he chose Doc, Tony Cardio, Fred Mackey, and Pat Russo to serve with him.

Chick and some of the men worked hard enough to make the raffle a success, although the receipts fell short of the original estimate. Doc told me his story of the raffle.

I went to that meeting when the drawing was to be held. I didn't want to attend the meeting, but I followed every move they made all over the settlement house just to see that the drawing was on the level. Chick wanted to put the unsold tickets into the drawing so as to weight the chances against the people that really bought our tickets. I steamed up. I said, "The people that bought those tickets are your friends. You can't cheat them like that."

Chick said, "Oh, honest guys!"

I said, "Yes, honest guys." I really steamed up. I was so eloquent that nobody dared talk against me.

Fred Mackey had been handling the regular club socials, but Chick felt that, as the initiator of the raffle project, he should also have the social arrangements in his hands. Joe agreed to the substitution. Chick organized two socials to which Italian college students, Junior League girls, and Aphrodite Club girls were invited. The socials brought out most of the members, but they did not revive interest in the club.

Encouraged by his success with the raffle project, Chick became more and more active in club meetings, until he completely dominated President Gennusi. On one occasion he delivered a lecture to Joe. He said that all the constructive action in Congress was initiated by the President and argued that Joe should be more of a leader. Joe made no reply.

When Paul DiMatia wanted to propose some new candidates for membership, Chick pointed out that Art Testa, chairman of the membership committee, was not present, and added that President Gennusi had used bad judgment in appointing a man whose attendance was so irregular. The president responded by appointing Chick head of the membership committee.

Still Chick was not satisfied. After adjournment he called me aside and suggested that we organize a caucus before the meetings. Then, when he proposed something in a meeting, Tony Cardio, Pat Russo, and I would support him, and the measure would go through. Curiously enough, he also broached this idea to Doc. When Doc and I remained noncommittal, we heard nothing more of the caucus, but Chick continued to push his own ideas as actively as ever.

Joe Gennusi knew what was happening, and he was worried. As Doc said to me:

Joe is a weakling. He's no leader. . . . . A couple of days ago Joe came to me and asked me, "Why don't you boys impeach Chick? He's taking too much power." . . . . Can you imagine that, Bill? I told him, "You put Chick in yourself. You throw him out if you want to." . . . . He wants us to do the dirty work for him. . . . . What kind of a leader is he? Chick flatters him and gets his own way. . . . . What kind of a leader is he if even Chick can toss him around?

Joe Gennusi was well liked by the corner boys. It had seemed that he might be able to pull the club together and repair some of the damage inflicted by Tony Cardio's election, but he failed because he was not accustomed to acting with decision and leading a group of men. He was unable to handle Chick and Tony Cardio. When Chick had proposals to make and he did not, Joe was at a disadvantage. Even when Chick and Tony had nothing to propose, they talked volubly. In one meeting Doc allowed Tony and Chick to go on until all the members became restive, and then pointed out that they were simply going over matters that had already been decided. Taking up Doc's lead, Joe said that they were "making technicalities." Chick admitted it. "All right, I'm making technicalities, but if everybody else is making technicalities, I'm going to make them too." Joe shut off the discussion.

Similar incidents occurred several times. When Doc made the first move against Chick or Tony, Joe was able to follow him and get them under control. He was unable to take the initiative himself, so, when Doc was not present, Chick had his way.

What was happening to the club could be largely explained in terms of three men—Chick Morelli, Joe Gennusi, and Doc. Joe's efforts to cater to Doc's faction were displeasing to Chick. When Doc was chairman of the play committee, the college men could be sure that no special concessions would be made to further relations with socially superior girls. On the other hand, Joe disgusted Doc and his friends by his inability to stand up against Chick. Doc did not try to take the lead in the club because he realized that it was intended to be a college men's club. Chick Morelli was as unpopular as ever, but he had a clear policy, and he was always stepping into action. When spring came, only a remnant of the Italian Community Club was left, but Chick dominated that remnant.

By the middle of April, Chick Morelli, Joe Gennusi, Phil Principio, Paul DiMatia, Pat Russo, and I were the only active members. The Italian Community Club was dead, but Chick would not admit it. He said to me:

This is the best thing that could ever happen to the club. We were better off in the beginning. We'll be better off with ten or twelve good members. We got in the wrong kind of members. . . . . You remember when we were having the talks every meeting, well when it came the turn of some of our members to give their talks, they would come up to me and ask me not to call on them for speeches. . . . . Now that's bad, Bill, but what could I do? If I exposed them, they wouldn't believe I did it for the best interests of the club. They look at everything from a personal viewpoint.

Reluctantly, Joe Gennusi accepted Chick's diagnosis. A year later he said:

I think we had the wrong men in it. . . . . In the beginning, I fought against having only college men. I hate discrimination of any kind. But maybe I was wrong. I think that the trouble with that club was that we had two kinds of members. There was one group that was aggressive and always wanted to do things. There was the other group that was always hanging back and never seemed to have the ambition. . . . .

You know who was the best member of that club? Chick Morelli. He always was aggressive. Of course, there is one fault that Chick has, he isn't tactful. He will tell a man right to his face what he thinks of him. Tony Cardio was a good member too, even if he wasn't well liked. . . . . In the other group there were fellows like Lou Danaro, Fred Mackey, Angelo Cucci, and Art Testa. Angelo seems to be disgusted with life. It seemed that none of these fellows wanted the club to go ahead and do things. . . . . Doc was a good member.

When the Community Club broke up, the members had to dedecide whether their allegiance was with the college boys or with the corner boys. For men like Chick Morelli and Tony Cardio, on one side, and Doc and Angelo Cucci, on the other, no real decision was involved. Joe Gennusi identified himself with the college boys, and Paul DiMatia and Phil Principio went over to the corner boys.

Paul explained to me: "I didn't have anything to do in the summer, and Phil Principio was unemployed, so we hung around together. And through Phil I was with Doc and Angelo and the rest of the boys." Later, when Doc moved over to Spongi's, Paul and Phil remained with the Nortons under the leadership of Angelo Cucci.

Since Doc and Chick were two of his closest friends, Lou Danaro had to make a decision. While the process of disintegration was still going on, he said to me:

I think the two cliques are separating. The college fellows are supposed to be smarter than us, they're better than us—so let them go their own way.

I think they're stupid in many ways. . . . . Chick is still my friend. You know, we once had a fruit stand together. We worked together for two summers. I've always defended Chick. He has got many faults, but still I like him. . . . . We used to go out a lot together, but now it's different. When I'm on the corner with Doc and Fred Mackey, he comes along and wants to go some place with me. I want Doc and Mackey to come along too, but he tells me, first we'll go this place, and then we'll come back for them. So we go, but we don't come back. After a while, I got wise to myself. Whenever Chick wants to go to a dance, Doc wants to go to a show, so I would rather go to a show with Doc. . . . . I had to make my choice. Now Chick don't come after me no more. He just says, "Hello," and that's all. . . . .

I think Chick liked to go with me because he could tell me what to do. Whenever we would get into an argument, I would stick with him for a while, and then he would begin quoting from books, and I wouldn't know what he was talking about after that. So what can I do, Bill? I always have to agree with him. . . . . That's the way Chick is. He was always trying to mold me. With Doc, it's different. When he argues with me, he wants to make sure that I understand every point. He goes slow for me. Then maybe a week later we're in the library and he comes across that point, he shows it to me: "See, Lou, remember that point we were talking about? Here it is in black and white." . . . . Chick don't do that. He don't want to explain things to me. He only wants to get the best of the argument.

7. REPUBLICAN POLITICS

At one of the last Community Club meetings Joe Gennusi told us that John Carrideo, a young Cornerville lawyer, was organizing a Republican club in the district. The Women's Republican Club of Eastern City had pledged its financial support and had invited the members to attend a meeting. Joe added:

A Republican governor will probably be elected this fall, and, in that case, if the Republicans in Cornerville make a good showing, the workers will get taken care of. . . . . After all, you've got to consider, most of the Italian judges in this state have been appointed by Republicans. . . . . I have to consider my own political aspirations, but if this new group will help the district, I'll join it instead of running for representative this fall.

Forty young men from Cornerville, with representatives of other racial groups, attended "All-American Night" at the Women's Republican Club. Joe Gennusi, Paul DiMatia, Chick Morelli, and Pat Russo were present.

The evening program began with a supper served by the ladies of the club. Mrs. Dillingham, who had once employed an Italian gardener, was in charge of entertaining the visitors from Cornerville. After supper she showed us around the luxurious clubrooms. "You can use this hall any time for your meetings. . . . . This can be your smoking-room. . . . . Just make this your home."

There was music, a speech by the chairman of the state committee, and another by the gubernatorial candidate, Percival Wickham. As the meeting broke up, Wickham shook hands with each of the Cornerville men.

The Community Club members accepted this hospitality with certain reservations. During supper Chick poured his impressions into my ear:

I don't like this, Bill. . . . . It looks like I'm being bought off. Let them convince me by argument, not by food. After all, I have my own political ambitions to think of. . . . . It's all very nice and friendly here, but how would I be received if I went to call at the home of one of these ladies? I'll tell you how. She would come to the door and tell me, "I'm afraid you have the wrong address."

While Mrs. Dillingham was showing us around, Paul DiMatia pointed at a picture of a buffalo hanging on the wall, and said to me, "They should have a bull there."

As we walked home, I asked him to sum up his impressions. He smiled and said, "It was a little patronizing."

Nevertheless, the meeting served its purpose. Afterward the Cornerville group gathered on the sidewalk to decide what should be done next. Tony Cardio joined us here. John Carrideo asked Paul DiMatia to be chairman of the next meeting of the local unit. Paul agreed. He said to me, "I have nothing to lose."

"I'm convinced," said Joe Gennusi.

Tony Cardio said, "I've always been a Republican at heart."

Chick Morelli said that he was reserving his judgment, and Pat Russo followed Chick, as he always did.

Republican money flowed into Cornerville as soon as the campaign got under way. A local headquarters was opened for committee meetings and political rallies.

College men made up the nucleus of the local Republican club. There were some corner boys active at the start, but many of them dropped out later. Although a college man, Paul DiMatia was now hanging on Norton Street, and he withdrew with the other corner boys. He told me that the new organization was entirely made up of men who wanted to be leaders. They were all prepared to give orders but not to execute them. Instead of doing the spade work of canvassing the district for votes, they preferred to stay at headquarters, where they could discuss what should be done. When men prominent in the state organization appeared in Cornerville, the members of the local club tried to outjockey one another so as to gain recognition.

In the midst of the campaign Tony Cardio won the Eastern City Young Republican's Oratorical Contest with an address on "The Constitution as Guardian of Our Liberties." On the strength of this he was chosen chairman of the largest rally held in Cornerville. Tony gained prominence as a speaker, but his personal limitations were recognized in the Republican Club as well as upon the street corner. As Joe Gennusi told me:

> We were having a committee meeting to discuss getting men for certain positions. During the meeting Tony Cardio made that speech that he always likes to make. He said we must get a man with a college education. He doesn't think that a man without a college education is qualified. . . . . A couple of days later, I was talking with one of the boys that was at the meeting. He had never met Tony before, but from that one time, he hated him. He said, "Who does he think he is anyway?" . . . . Now that man wouldn't even give Tony the right time.
>
> When we had election of officers in the Republican Club, Tony was nominated for president. John Carrideo was elected, and Tony got only two votes, his own and one other. The man who seconded the nomination didn't even vote for him. I turned in a blank ballot. I figured, they're both my friends. I knew John would get it anyway. . . . . After the meeting, I told Tony that the blank ballot was mine. He began to get mad. I told him, "Why didn't you decline the nomination?"
>
> He asked, "Why should I?"
>
> I said, "Because you're not well liked." . . . . That burned him up.
>
> He said, "Now I know who my real friends are." He hasn't spoken to me since that meeting. . . . . It must be annoying to Tony to know that he has all the qualifications, and yet he can't be elected to anything.

Wickham was elected governor that fall, but Murphy carried Cornerville for the Democrats by almost six to one. The Republicans did poll a somewhat larger vote in Cornerville than they had in 1936, but the gain was not nearly so great as had been expected, and there was no way of telling what proportion of the gain was accounted for by the efforts of the college men. Some of the most prominent racketeers in Cornerville were also working for Percival Wickham.

8. CHICK MORELLI'S CAREER

One evening in the spring of 1938, as we were walking through the market district, Chick discussed his political ambitions. He said that he could already count on five hundred votes if he ran for the board of aldermen but that he wanted to build up more support before he entered such a contest. As we passed a line of fruit stands, he stopped to pick up a couple of apples, said a few words to the dealer, and walked on without offering payment. As we munched our apples, he explained that these men all rented their stands from his uncle and that if he, Chick Morelli, ran for office, they would have to work for him or else lose their stands. He added, reflectively:

If I got a good job, maybe I wouldn't get in the fight, but politics seems to be in my blood. . . . .

Pat Russo says that charity is important. That's all right, but after all, self-preservation is the first law of man. . . . . If I get in office, I'll try to help the district, but I'll advance myself first.

In the fall of 1938 Chick was not yet prepared to join in the Republican campaign. That would have meant sacrificing his ambitions in ward politics, which could only be realized through the Democratic party. Chick looked for another outlet for his political activity and found it in the campaign of Charles Madden, candidate for the Democratic nomination for district attorney. Michael Flaherty, the incumbent, had the support of all the local political organizations. If Madden proved to be a strong candidate, organizing his local campaign might give a Cornerville man who had no place in the existing organizations a favorable opportunity for the launching of his own political career.

By the time Chick decided to support Madden, a one-time

member of the Sunset Dramatic Club was already in charge of the candidate's Cornerville organization. Chick set about forming an organization of his own and made himself district co-chairman. He had small boys distributing handbills, he had a group of young men and girls canvassing the district, and he made a number of political speeches.

Charles Madden was defeated, but in Cornerville he polled nearly as many votes as his opponent. Encouraged by this "moral victory," Chick formed the Alexander Hamilton Club, with fifteen young men and girls that had worked for Madden and several former members of the Community Club. Doc, Phil Principio, Paul DiMatia, and Angelo Cucci accepted Chick's invitation to join the new club. Doc explained his membership in this way:

Last summer, when I was going to run for representative, Chick came up to me and pledged his support. . . . . I told him that he should think of his own political ambitions. It wouldn't do him any good to support me when I wasn't going to win. . . . . But he said, "No, you're my friend, and I'm going to support you." . . . . It really meant something for him to do a thing like that. I felt obligated to him, so when he came around and asked me to join his club, I let him put my name down.

I never go to the club meetings. Chick is lucky that I don't. If I was an active member of the club, I couldn't let Chick get away with the things he does. I don't know why they stand for it.

I think Chick is doing the right thing for himself politically. He's got a bunch of young kids in that club. Those are the people he has to count on. With fellows my age, he's ruined himself already. We know him too well.

In January, 1939, Chick, Doc, Phil, Angelo, and some of the other members of the Hamilton Club attended a meeting in honor of Charles Madden. Doc had this to say about it:

They announced a dance to be given in honor of Madden, and they asked all those in the audience who thought they could sell tickets to come up on the stage and get them. . . . . Chick was on and off the stage seven times. Some others came back more than once, but—seven times—that's too much. . . . . Chick just wanted to get into the limelight. All the boys noticed that.

Later, Phil told me:

I've dropped out of the club. . . . . You know, Chick invited us to come up to that meeting for Madden. When we got there, he didn't pay any attention to us. He was too busy getting in with the important people to have anything to do with his own club members. That's bad, Bill.

This was Angelo's story:

I'm out of the club too. After the last meeting I talked to Chick out in the hall. I think he is just out for himself, and I told him that right to his face. . . . . Well, he said he had to look out for himself so that when he got in a good position, he could help out all the members. . . . . That's what he said, but I don't believe him. If he gets himself a good job, I don't think he'll try to help us. I really don't.

By the summer of 1939 the Alexander Hamilton Club was dead.

Chick had not yet hit upon the right combination. That fall he told me, "If I have the right fellows with me, we'll go places." Thereupon he set about reviving the Italian Community Club. This time the membership was limited to college men. Joe Gennusi and several other former members joined, but the membership was largely recruited from among those that had not previously belonged.

The main feature of the Community Club program for the 1939–40 season was to be the production of a play written by Ed Preziosa, who, I was told, was one of the outstanding members of the club.

Rehearsals began with Chick in the leading role and Ed directing, but the play did not proceed smoothly. Doc told me that several members of the Community Club reported serious friction between Chick and Ed: "It seems they don't get along. Ed thinks Chick is trying to toss him around. Ed is a strong-minded kid himself. If anybody is going to be tossed around, he'll do the tossing."

In the early stages of rehearsals Chick had another idea. He proposed that the club sponsor a scholarship drive to send needy and deserving Italian students to college. The drive was to be launched with a banquet in the ballroom of one of Eastern City's largest hotels. The members voted to support the scholarship project, and Chick busied himself with making arrangements for it. He became so preoccupied with the scholarship drive that he decided to drop his part in the play.

The conflict between the drive and the play split the club into two parts. Those who were more interested in Ed Preziosa and the play withdrew from the Community Club and formed the

Buskin Players. They filled Chick's part with one of their members and brought in Doc to substitute for one of Chick's adherents. Angelo Cucci wrote the music for a dance that was used in the play. Ed became very friendly with Doc, and after his own play had been produced he suggested that the Buskin Players merge with Doc's dramatic club. Doc was noncommittal, but the proposal showed the wide breach that separated Ed and his friends from Chick and his friends.

Chick delivered the first invitation to the banquet to Governor Percival Wickham. The governor's secretary told Chick that His Excellency was very much interested in the project but would not be able to find time to attend. Undaunted, Chick conferred with Attilio Volpe, a Cornerville banker who had been active in Republican politics and knew the governor's secretary. Volpe went in person and managed to get a pledge of the governor's personal appearance. This made it obviously a function which all prominent Italian-Americans should attend. Over five hundred people paid two dollars each to launch the scholarship drive.

Percival Wickham was present at the start and was called upon to say a few words. He shook hands with some of the people at the head table, gave his official blessing to the scholarship drive, and excused himself. Following the governor, there was an extended speaking program. Supreme Court Judge Gennelli and various others prominent in the Eastern City Italian colony spoke words of praise for the scholarship drive and its organizers and pledged their support. Attilio Volpe spoke for the scholarship fund trustees, who were to handle the money and select the scholarship winners. First he ran over the names of the trustees. They were Maynard H. Atwater, chairman of the board of trustees of Ivy University and a member of the board of the Norton Street Settlement; Mrs. J. Harrison Dunbar, also a member of the settlement board; Thomas L. Brown, the prominent attorney who wrote Chick's letter of recommendation for admission to Ivy University Law School; John Ramsay, boys' worker at the Norton Street Settlement; and Attilio Volpe.

Toward the end of the program, Alfred Martini, the master of ceremonies who had also been one of Chick's professors at St.

Patrick's, called upon Chick Morelli. Clearly, this was the big moment in Chick's life, and he outdid himself. He spoke of the Italians who had made great contributions to civilization. He spoke of the difficulties faced by immigrant Italians in their struggle for recognition, and he proposed more education as the solution of the problems of his people. Chick received an ovation from his audience, and the following day the Italian news commentator characterized his speech as "un' orazione veramente maravigliosa."

The Italian Community Club did not inaugurate the fund-raising campaign immediately after the banquet. Summer was coming on, and the members voted to postpone it until fall.

When fall came, politics held the center of the stage. Chick worked hard for the election of Willkie for president, Wickham for governor, Bingham for attorney-general, and the other Republican candidates. Cornerville remained overwhelmingly Democratic in the state election, but the Republicans swept all the offices.

The following winter Chick revived the scholarship campaign. He enlarged the committee to include some men and women who were prominent in Italian-American society.

The second scholarship banquet was an even more impressive affair than the first. This time the mayor attended as well as the governor. It was announced that the drive had brought in something over a thousand dollars. While this fell far short of the ten-thousand-dollar goal, the drive was expected to continue from year to year so that more funds would be available.

In the midst of the fund-raising campaign, it was announced that Attorney-General Bingham had appointed Chick Morelli to his staff. It was a small position, but it was a start in politics. Chick had come a long way since he had first organized the Italian Community Club.

CHAPTER III

SOCIAL STRUCTURE AND SOCIAL MOBILITY

1. THE NATURE OF THE GROUPS

THE Nortons and the Italian Community Club functioned at different social levels, and they were organized upon fundamentally different bases. At the same time they were representative of a large part of Cornerville society. Most of the generalizations to be made about the Nortons could be applied equally well to a great number of other corner gangs, although Doc considered his boys "a finer group." The college men in the Community Club did not have so many local counterparts, but they filled the social position that had been held earlier by the Sunset Dramatic Club. Socially, the correspondence was close enough so that some of the corner boys used the names of the two clubs interchangeably. In other words, there was a continuous change in the individuals who held particular social positions, but the positions themselves remained constant, and the people who participated at a given level of society over an extended period of time bore close resemblances to one another.

Three social levels were represented in the Nortons and the Italian Community Club in the early period of their history. At the bottom were the corner boys, at the top were the college boys, and between them were intermediaries, who could participate in either group. These distinctions were informally recognized even in the early history of the two organizations. One evening in the fall of 1937 I was standing on Norton Street talking with Chick Morelli, Phil Principio, Fred Mackey, and Lou Danaro, when Frank Bonelli and Nutsy came along and took up a position next to us. I was standing between the two groups. I talked with Chick, Phil, Fred, and Lou, and I turned to talk with Frank and Nutsy. There was no general conversation. Then Lou and Fred stepped forward and turned so that they were facing the others and standing directly in front of me. I now had two members of each group on either side of me. At this point the course of the conversation changed, so that, for example, Nutsy said something to Fred, and Fred continued the conversation with Chick and Phil; Chick said something to Lou, and Lou continued the conversation with Nutsy and Frank. At no time did Chick or Phil

STREET CORNER CONVERSATION

□ Corner boy
▨ College boy
◪ Intermediary
△ Observer
— Path of interaction
Positions of boxes indicate spatial relations

communicate directly with Frank or Nutsy. After a short time, Lou issued a general invitation to sit in his car. Chick, Phil, and Fred accepted. Nutsy walked over to the car and talked with Lou for a while through the window. Then he returned to Frank and me, and we walked away.

Although they had frequently seen one another on Norton Street, Chick and Phil and Nutsy and Frank belonged to social groups having no intimate contact with one another. Lou, Fred, and I "fitted" with both groups and could therefore serve as intermediaries. Had they been present, Doc or Angelo Cucci could have taken our roles. A year later, Phil and Paul DiMatia could have served as intermediaries. The situation can be represented diagrammatically in the accompanying illustration.

The intermediaries could function only when the gap separating the two groups was sufficiently narrow. When the gap widened beyond a certain point, there were no longer men capable of bridging it. That was what happened to the Italian Community Club.

The corner gang came together on Norton Street. The daily activities of the corner boys determined the relative positions of members and allocated responsibilities and obligations within the group. They judged a man's capacities according to the way he acted in his personal relations.

The informal gang has, of course, neither constitution nor by-laws. When the corner boys form clubs, they sometimes have constitutions, but they do not rely upon parliamentary procedure in making their decisions. Decisions are formed through informal association, and, unless the club contains more than one corner group, its meetings simply ratify what has already been agreed upon. Doc commented:

> It's better not to have a constitution and vote on all these things. As soon as you begin deciding questions by taking a vote, you'll see that some fellows are for you and some are against you, and in that way factions develop. It's best to get everybody to agree first, and then you don't have to vote.

In contrast to the corner gang, the nucleus of the Italian Community Club was formed by the teacher who ranked her pupils according to her evaluation of their scholastic performance. At an early age the Community Club members were encouraged to look upon themselves as superior individuals. Membership in this group depended not so much upon group action as upon the individual's intellectual accomplishments and upon his ability to please outside authorities. In college the emphasis was again upon individual intellectual performance.

The college boys were taught that a college education was the main qualification for leadership. Consequently, they all felt qualified for leadership positions.

Outside club meetings the members seldom associated together except in pairs. Since there was no informal organization to bind the men together, there was also no common understanding upon matters of authority, responsibility, and obligation. Those who had belonged to the junior high school clique acknowledged certain loyalties to one another, but there were members like Ernest Daddio and Felix DiCarlo who did not share even these attenuated ties.

To organize these individuals, Chick relied upon parliamentarianism. In settling controversial issues, he first argued and then called for a vote. When the vote went his way, he felt that he had won his objective. If the members failed to carry out the mandate of the vote, he chided them for their unco-operative attitude.

The college boys learned in school and settlement house that parliamentary procedure provides the framework through which groups of people should govern their behavior. When applied literally, this formal procedure provides the machinery for destroying a club. When important questions are actually decided by the argument and voting process, the club has already begun to disintegrate. Parliamentary procedure may well be used to formalize decisions which have already been informally made. However, such agreements can be reached only if the formally organized club also has a smoothly functioning informal organization. Instead of trying to build up the personal ties necessary for an effective informal organization, Chick was continually raising issues which required the club's formal decision. In this way he brought to the surface and accentuated all the latent differences that separated the members.

The history of the club demonstrated that its two aims, the social advancement of the members and the improvement of conditions in Cornerville, could not be realized by the same people at the same time. The college boys were primarily interested in social advancement. The corner boys were primarily interested in their local community. On this issue the club divided and fell.

There was, of course, a clash of personalities in the Italian Community Club, but it is only by considering personalities in relation to the social conflict that it is possible to explain the history of the organization. Chick Morelli's decision in the vice-presidential election of 1938 provides a good illustration of this point. Chick had clashed with Tony Cardio and made no effort to conceal his dislike and distrust of the man. He recognized that half the club members hated Tony, and yet, significantly enough, he felt that these considerations should not weigh with him. Tony was a college man. He was therefore qualified for the office. When Tony was being attacked, Chick recognized his kinship with the college men's candidate and forgot his pledge to the corner boys.

While the main division fell between college men and corner boys, there was also a split in the ranks of the college men. This was based primarily upon their unequal desires and capacities for social participation. When the Community Club entertained the Italian Junior League, Chick and Tony were much concerned over the failure of Paul, Phil, and some of the other college men to play active roles. Two men could not dance with all the girls at once, and when some of them were left by themselves in a corner, Chick and Tony felt that it was a reflection upon themselves as well as upon their club. They could not help asking themselves whether they might not get ahead more rapidly as individuals outside the club. Tony answered this question for himself when he accepted the part in the Junior League play and then dropped out of the Community Club. Chick preferred to base his operations upon a group, but he was prepared to shake off the group whenever he could advance himself as an individual. A club may be used as a vehicle for social advancement, but, since mobility depends so largely upon individualistic activity, such an organization is bound to have an extremely unstable existence.

2. THE SOCIAL ROLE OF THE SETTLEMENT HOUSE

To complete the picture of corner-boy–college-boy relations, we must observe the functioning of the settlement house. In the lives of the men of both groups the social workers played important roles.

The social workers whose actions defined the role of the settlement were middle-class people of non-Italian (largely Yankee) stock. The boards of directors of the Norton Street House and the Cornerville House were composed of upper-middle-class and upper-class people of Yankee racial background. The board of the Norton Street House represented the socially élite of Eastern City. Until the summer of 1940, when the Cornerville House hired a local girl for a staff position, the only Italians connected with the settlement houses had subordinate jobs, teaching special classes or doing clerical or janitorial work. Although some of the professional social workers had spend as much as twenty years in the district, there was not a single one who could speak Italian until in 1940 the Cornerville House hired a non-Italian who was proficient in the language. The workers had no systematic knowledge of the social backgrounds of the people in their Italian homeland. Furthermore, they made little effort to get to know the local social organization except as it came to them through the doors of their institutions.

The social worker's conception of his functions was quite evident. He thought in terms of a one-way adaptation. Although, in relation to the background of the community, the settlement was an alien institution, nevertheless the community was expected to adapt itself to the standards of the settlement house. Some people made this adaptation; most people did not.

None of the first-generation men met in the settlement. Each house had mothers' clubs for the first-generation women and for younger married women. The settlements got a cross-section of the population among the small boys and girls, but, as the children grew older, the selection became less diversified. A number of senior girls' clubs remained inside the institutions, but they were made up of girls who were considered superior socially to the common level of Cornerville. Among the young men the case was more striking. Only a select group continued to participate. In fact, in certain years the Norton Street House had not had a single club of boys over eighteen years old meeting in its quarters.

One night I was with Joe Gennusi, Jerry Merluzzo, and several other college men in the Norton Street Settlement when Mr. Ramsay, the head of boys' work, was talking about the policies of the institution. He said:

There's one thing about this house that no one can deny. We have always done all we could to inspire you boys that were ambitious to make your way in life. I remember when Jerry, here, wanted to be a doctor. At that time it seemed out of his reach, but I said to him, "Jerry, others have done it; why shouldn't you be able to do it too?" And now Jerry is well on his way to achieving his ambition. . . . .

Some people think we should make an effort to get the roughnecks from the street corners to come in here. Well, I wonder about that. How would you men like it if you had to associate with those fellows?

The college men agreed that they would not like it.

The "roughnecks" to whom Mr. Ramsay referred were the corner boys. Whatever one might say about them, they were the people. In their own age group they constituted the overwhelming majority of the Cornerville male population.

The gubernatorial campaign between Wickham and Murphy provides one illustration of the way in which the social workers set themselves apart from the people. Wickham was a man of inherited wealth and high social position. Murphy was also wealthy, but he had made his money in politics. Upper-class people looked upon Wickham as a man of excellent character, and they regarded Murphy as a crook. Most Cornerville people looked upon Wickham as a friend of wealth and privilege, and, while they did not defend Murphy's honesty, they regarded him as a friend of the working people.

One afternoon I was standing with Nutsy and several other corner boys when a young Italian who taught art classes in the Norton Street Settlement approached us on his way to the house. The corner boys noticed that he was wearing a Wickham button on his lapel, and they engaged him in an argument. The art teacher was distinctly on the defensive and claimed only that this was a free country, that he was not bothering the corner boys, and that he had a right to vote as he pleased. To this, Nutsy gibed, "You're just a yes-man!"

"Sure, I'm a yes-man," the man answered. "I have to be. My bread and butter depends on it."

I am sure that Mr. Bacon would have been shocked if anyone had told him that he was coercing his employees in this way. It was the general rule for the settlement to remain neutral in politics, but somehow this was thought to be different from other campaigns. It was a struggle between good and evil. In such a contest there could be no neutrality, and the social workers took their stand on the side of righteousness. Wickham stickers were pasted on the windows of the adjoining building in which some of the workers lived, and Wickham was extolled and Murphy condemned throughout the corridors of the settlement. Since those who came into the settlement were thought to be "a better class of people," they were expected to take their stand with Wickham. That was the nature of the pressure which was informally exerted. It was effective in winning over a small group of adults whom the social workers could directly influence, but otherwise it operated to isolate the settlement and those who accepted its leadership from the main body of the community.

The social cleavages were accentuated in a less obvious but equally important way through the individuals that the social workers selected as worthy of special attention and help. The story of Lou Danaro is a case in point. As Lou told me:

Mr. Bacon broke me, Bill. He really broke me. I idolized the man, and then he let me down. . . . . One day I was in church praying for a job. I needed a job in the worst way. Then when I came out, Mr. Bacon stopped me on the street and asked me if I wanted to go to work. . . . . He put me to work in his antique shop with some of the other boys from the settlement. I was making $12 a week, but I was living in the same room with him. Wherever he went, he would have me drive him. He gave me suits of clothes. He would buy two tickets to shows, and we would go together. He would give me spending money. He would take me to play tennis and golf and go riding with him. . . . . In the evenings I would sit in his office two or three hours until he was ready to go to bed. I would sit and read. I would rather do that than be with the boys on the corner. . . . . When he wanted to play bridge at night, I would go out and get some fellows for him. I would bring in Ted Costa and Frank Perino or some other fellows, and we would play. . . . . When he went some place in the evening, he would have me drive him there and then I could take the car and take the boys riding until I called for him. . . . .

I idolized the man, Bill. I had plenty of chances to get better jobs, but I didn't want to leave Mr. Bacon. I would rather be out with him than with a girl. He was always telling me things to educate me. . . . . Oh, he tried to do lots of things for me. He put me through ——— Prep, and he started me at college. But I never went for the books, Bill. . . . . I guess I wasn't ambitious enough. I was ambitious, you know, but I never wanted to stick to the job. . . . .

He tried to do a lot of things for me, but finally he did me dirt. I was playing around with Josie Cutler, a debutante that worked in our antique shop. I was petting her, but I wasn't doing anything wrong. But some of the fellows must have been jealous, and they told Mr. Bacon. He told me to let her alone. At that time it was nothing out of the way, but later I was seeing her under cover. . . . . And then one day he laid me off. That was the last thing I thought would ever happen to me, Bill. . . . . No, I don't think it was on account of the girl. I think he thought I was getting too dependent on him, so he threw me off. . . . . I went right home, packed my things, and left his room for good. I've never been back there. Every time he sees me, he asks me how things are going, and I tell him, but that's all. . . . .

He broke me, Bill. I was with him all those years with the expectation that something was going to come of it. I got to like playing golf and tennis with him. I rode with him every morning in the summer. I got to like being with him. . . . . And then he dropped me. In that time I might have learned a trade or a profession, and I would be much better off today. I know I would be better off. I could have gotten started in something. Now I don't know what to do with myself. . . . .

The only attributes that could have recommended Lou to Mr. Bacon's special consideration were his attractive personality and his docility. He idolized the social worker, and for that he was rewarded.

If Lou had been intelligent in his school work or if he had had some skill in business affairs, he might have been able to capitalize upon Mr. Bacon's support to better his social and economic position. Lacking such talents, he had no alternative but to return to the corner boys when the social worker dropped him.

Mr. Bacon took Lou away from his corner-boy associates and made it extremely difficult for him to readjust himself to them. When they deal with the corner boys, that is, in effect, what the social workers try to do. Doc told me that the Norton Street social workers had frequently tried to persuade him to stop hanging on the street corner and to break away from his old friends. If he had followed their advice, he would have subordinated himself to the social workers and lost his position in the community.

The story of Lou Danaro is a striking case, but there were a number of other cases which illustrated the same point. The condition was so general that the corner boys looked upon those who were closely identified with the settlement as "stooges" or "flunkies" for the social workers.

Even among the small group of college men, in whose activities the social workers took particular pride, there were those who were less than completely loyal. Phil Principio once said to me: "They consider us scum. . . . . Even the college men, they'll talk to us with every consideration, but behind our backs they consider us scum."

Paul DiMatia remarked that he had never felt comfortable in the settlement house. Since Phil and Paul eventually went over to the corner boys, it might be expected that they should share corner-boy attitudes, but one night Chick Morelli confided to me that he did not like the social workers because he thought they looked down upon all Italians, whether they were corner boys or college boys. There were others who expressed similar sentiments. Even the college men are lower-class people until they have advanced upon their careers, and they are always Italians. The social workers may have sincerely believed that they had no prejudices against lower-class Italians, but their actions betrayed them.

Doc's account of the history of the Corner Bums in the Norton Street House shows that the social workers were completely unable to deal with corner boys. The obscene language directed by the Corner Bums at Mr. Ramsay and Miss Baldwin did not indicate that they were by nature incorrigible. The men never used the same language in speaking to people who fitted into their own society and commanded their respect. The obscenity was simply a form of aggression against alien forces in Cornerville. It is significant that no corner gang became identified with the Norton Street House after the Corner Bums left it to set up their own club.

Besides the social positions and attitudes of the social workers, there were other aspects of the settlement house which the corner boys found objectionable. Most of the social workers were women, and girls predominated in the older age groups. This built up a feminine atmosphere, which was uncongenial to men accustomed to spending most of their time in exclusively male groups. Furthermore, because of limitations of space, no club could have its own room in the settlement every night in the week. This was a drawback from the standpoint of the corner boys, who were dependent upon a fixed social routine. The

settlement also imposed certain rules of conduct, involving manners and decorum, which were quite alien to the street corner.

If he is not willing to deal with the existing social organization,
the social worker has only one alternative: He can deal with
those people who do not fit into it. At present that is what the
settlement house does. It accepts those who already are maladjusted in terms of the local society, it rewards them for breaking
away from the ties of Cornerville, and it encourages them to
better their social and economic positions. To a certain extent,
this is a conscious policy. The social workers want to deal with
"the better element."

The primary function of the settlement house is to stimulate
social mobility, to hold out middle-class standards and middle-
class rewards to lower-class people. Since upward mobility almost
always involves movement out of the slum district, the settlement
is constantly dealing with people who are on their way out of
Cornerville. It does not win the loyalty of the great majority of
the people who look upon the district as their permanent home.

In stimulating social mobility, the Norton Street House
widened the gap between the Nortons and the Italian Community Club and so played a significant role in increasing the
friction between the two groups and in breaking up the club.

3. LOYALTY AND SOCIAL MOBILITY

Doc and his corner boys have not been advancing themselves,
and there seems to be little prospect that they will. On the other
hand, the college boys are moving up. When I last heard, before
the entrance of the United States into the war, Leo Marto and
Jerry Merluzzo had become doctors. Jim Filippo was a certified
public accountant. Joe Gennusi had set himself up in a law office
with a friend and was doing well. Tom Scala had obtained his
Ph.D. in English literature at Ivy University and had gone into
college teaching. Paul DiMatia and Phil Principio, the two men
who had gone over to the corner boys, had the most difficult time.
Paul was unemployed for a long period before he finally secured an
accounting job with a large industrial organization as a result of
his performance upon a competitive examination. Following grad-

uation in 1937, Phil could get nothing but temporary and poorly paid jobs that did not utilize his engineering training. His first engineering job came with the defense boom, and he had worked on it only a month when he was drafted.

Those who had made the greatest strides were the same men who had been most socially aggressive. Tony Cardio had won an executive position in a branch of one of Eastern City's largest department stores. Within a year of his graduation from Ivy University Law School, which in itself carries great prestige, Chick had drawn himself to the attention of the state's most important Republican politicians and had secured his first political job. He is following in the path of several others who began their careers in Cornerville and rose to eminence in Republican politics. Chick's performance up to the present time indicates that, unless the war interferes, his advancement has just begun. In a short time he will probably move out of Cornerville. If he remains single, he may stay there with his mother while she lives, but if he marries he will certainly move out. Chick would not want to marry a girl who would like to live in Cornerville.

As he moves up the social ladder, Chick Morelli will be cited by upper-class people as an example of what an able man of humble background can accomplish. His story will be related as proof of the vitality of our democratic society. And, as Chick moves up, he will report to upper-class people, as others have reported who have gone before him, that the corner boys are lazy and unco-operative and, as a group, not worth dealing with. Upper-class people will believe him, because they have heard the same story from social workers and because, after all, Chick Morelli has learned from experience.

One of the most cherished democratic beliefs is that our society operates so as to bring intelligence and ability to the top. Clearly, the difference in intelligence and ability does not explain the different careers of Chick and Doc. There must be some other way of explaining why some Cornerville men rise while others remain stationary.

The most obvious explanation is that, in Cornerville, a college education is tremendously important for social and economic advancement. However, that is only a part of the story. Most of the college men were set apart from their fellows as early as the ninth grade. When they were still children, they fitted into a pattern of activity leading toward social mobility. College education was simply a part of that pattern.

The pattern of social mobility in Cornerville can best be understood when it is contrasted with the pattern of corner-boy activity. One of the most important divergences arises in matters involving the expenditure of money. The college boys fit in with an economy of savings and investment. The corner boys fit in with a spending economy. The college boy must save his money in order to finance his education and launch his business or professional career. He therefore cultivates the middle-class virtue of thrift. In order to participate in group activities, the corner boy must share his money with others. If he has money and his friend does not, he is expected to do the spending for both of them. It is possible to be thrifty and still be a corner boy, but it is not possible to be thrifty and yet hold a high position in the corner gang. Prestige and influence depend in part upon free spending. As a rule, the corner boy does not consciously spend money for the purpose of acquiring influence over his fellows. He fits into the pattern of action of his group, and his behavior has the effect of increasing his influence.

Chick and Doc exemplify the two conflicting attitudes toward money. In his life-story Chick said that he had once been a free spender but had learned his lesson when a friend refused to reciprocate. Doc told me:

Bill, I owe money now, but if I was paid all the money owed me, I would have a gang of money. I never saved. I never had a bank account. . . . . If the boys are going to a show and this man can't go because he is batted out, I say to myself, "Why should he be deprived of that luxury?" And I give him the money. . . . . And I never talk about it.

Both Doc and Chick recognized that the free spender does not receive an equal financial return, but they drew different conclusions from that observation. While Doc sometimes wished that he could have back a portion of the money he had spent and lent, he thought of spending in terms of personal relations and not in terms of profits, losses, and savings.

Chick needed to save in order to advance himself. Doc needed to spend if he was to maintain his position in Cornerville. If Doc had had a hundred or two hundred dollars saved in the summer of 1938, he would not have needed to withdraw from the political campaign; but, in order to accumulate such funds, he would have had to alienate his friends and destroy his political support.

Chick and Doc also had conflicting attitudes toward social mobility. Chick judged men according to their capacity for advancing themselves. Doc judged them according to their loyalty to their friends and their behavior in their personal relations.

In discussing the difference between the college boys and the corner boys, Doc had this to say about Chick:

> Chick says that self-preservation is the first law of nature. Now that's right to a certain extent. You have to look out for yourself first. But Chick would step on the neck of his best friend if he could get a better job by doing it. . . . . We were talking one night on the corner about that, and I was sucking him in. I got him to admit it—that he would turn against his best friend if he could profit by it. . . . . I would never do that, Bill. I would never step on Danny even if I could get myself a $50-a-week job by doing it. None of my boys would do that.

Both the college boy and the corner boy want to get ahead. The difference between them is that the college boy either does not tie himself to a group of close friends or else is willing to sacrifice his friendship with those who do not advance as fast as he does. The corner boy is tied to his group by a network of reciprocal obligations from which he is either unwilling or unable to break away.

Sometimes the corner-boy leader complains and threatens to abandon his role. Once, when Doc was bending under the strain of his political campaign, he said to me with considerable feeling: "Now I'm out for the buck. . . . . Before it was all idealism. Now to hell with that! To hell with it! . . . . Why should I always look out for others? Nobody looks out for me."

Nevertheless, he continued to act for other people just as he had before. He was powerless to change.

It is misleading to contrast Chick with Doc in terms of egotism versus altruism, for that implies that each man was free to decide what course of action he would take. Doc would not have been Doc if he had acted solely to satisfy his material interests, and Chick would not have been Chick if he had looked out for others before taking care of himself. Consistent patterns of action cannot be changed by a mere act of will.

Doc realized what means could be most effectively used in order to advance himself, and he could even point them out to others, but he could not use them himself. He once said to me:

I suppose my boys have kept me from getting ahead. . . . . But if I were to start over again—if God said to me, "Look here, Doc, you're going to start over again, and you can pick out your friends in advance," still I would make sure that my boys were among them—even if I could pick Rockefeller and Carnegie. . . . . Many times people in the settlement and some of the Sunsets have said to me, "Why do you hang around those fellows?" I would tell them, "Why not? They're my friends."

Bill, last night at home my brother-in-law was listening to his favorite Italian program when my nephew comes in. He wants to listen to something else, so he goes up and switches the dial—without asking anybody. . . . . I'm in a tough spot here, Bill. They want to do everything for these kids, and if I try to discipline the kids, they jump on me. . . . . But that was too raw. I got the kid aside, and I gave him a lecture. Bill, I was really eloquent. But then at the end of it, I said, "But don't change too much, kid. Stay the way you are, and you'll get ahead in the world."

PART II
RACKETEERS AND POLITICIANS

CHAPTER IV

THE SOCIAL STRUCTURE OF RACKETEERING

1. HISTORY OF THE RACKETS

T HE liquor traffic of prohibition provided many of the prominent racketeers of today with their business experience and financial resources. In the early years of prohibition there were a large number of small liquor dealers in active competition. Prices fluctuated, and spheres of operation were not clearly defined. Competition often led to violence.

As time went on, some of the more skilful, energetic, and daring of the dealers gained in financial status and power, so that they were able to push a number of the smaller independents out of business and extend their control over others. This combination movement continued steadily and, in Eastern City, reached its height shortly before repeal under the leadership of a man who became known as "the Boss."

The depression fell heavily upon the liquor industry. With improvements in production and distribution, a constantly increasing supply was becoming available just when the demand fell off. Many of the bootleggers became insolvent and defaulted on their debts to the producers. This provided the Boss with his opportunity. He organized a combination of about ten of the leading wholesalers (gang leaders) for the purpose of controlling all the imports of Canadian liquor into this section of the country. The Boss signed an agreement to pay the debts incurred by the delinquent bootleggers and in return was granted exclusive control over all the liquor produced by the distilleries for the American trade in the section where the combination was operating. The monopolists also operated their own stills. Toward the end of 1932 the combine held complete control over the distribution of liquor in the Eastern City region.

Then the Boss was murdered. His killing, accomplished by

some relatively unimportant gangsters, seems to have grown out
of a dispute unconnected with the monopoly; but, even with the
Boss alive, it would have been difficult to maintain unified control
over illegal activities in such an unsettled time as that which came
with repeal in 1933. The members of the combine were unable to
agree upon a successor. Instead, they divided the field that the
Boss had controlled.

The lessons in working together that had been learned by the
combine members were to have a strong influence upon the subsequent organization of illegal activities in the vicinity of Cornerville. As the end of prohibition approached, the racketeers needed
to find an alternative field into which to expand their activities.
The policy racket seemed to provide this opportunity. Since bets
of a dime, a nickel, and even a cent were taken, the racket appealed particularly to the poor man. At the height of prohibition
profits, few of the top racketeers had paid attention to the ex-
ploitation of the numbers, but now many were beginning to see
that small change would be worth collecting if it came in fast
enough.

A conference of all the leading racketeers in the territory was
called one evening in a hotel in Eastern City. At this meeting the
syndicate for the control of the policy racket was formed, and
means of conducting the business were agreed upon.

This was a historic conference. Some say that even a high
police official was present. I understand from one who attended
the conference that this was not true. It is said that he sent a representative. The official had certain financial interests in common
with a business partner of T. S., who controlled the rackets in
Cornerville. Besides, the police would naturally be interested in
such proceedings. If the goal of the conference—the elimination
of competition and violence—were attained, the task of the police
department would be considerably simplified.

The reorganized business prospered in the following years. The
numbers and other forms of gambling replaced liquor as the back-
bone and main support of racketeering activities in Eastern City.

Before prohibition illegal activities in Cornerville were relatively unorganized. There were small gangs of extortionists (local

adaptations of the Italian Mafia and Camorra) who preyed upon workingmen, spying out those who had accumulated savings and claiming the money under threat of force. They were eliminated in the early twenties by a combination of police action and the vengeance of friends of the victims. There were small bands of holdup men and thieves, as are to be found in any city. Larger-scale organization of illegal activities came in with the liquor traffic.

The story of Mario Serrechia casts light upon this prohibition period. Mario was born in Cornerville of hard-working Sicilian parents shortly after the turn of the century. He grew up to be the tough boy of his gang. As a young man he was considered one of the best street fighters in a district which produced many competitors for this honor. Tales of his generosity have become almost legendary in Cornerville.

Mario began his career as a holdup man. He once held up a large crap game and wounded a man in making his getaway. On a later occasion he was arrested for an armed pay-roll robbery. He was arrested many times, on charges ranging from traffic violations to murder, but he served only six months in jail. Mario found various illegal means of making a living, and he always had money and connections.

After his early beginnings Mario was not primarily a holdup man. He dealt in bootleg liquor, was in on the development of the policy racket, and extorted "protection" money from other racketeers. He had a small gang of loyal followers, and he had some powerful enemies. He did not have the business capacity for building an organization. He was the rugged individualist of the rackets. As long as he was alive, he was a threat to any comprehensive organization that was attempted.

In 1930 Mario tried to cut himself in on a big crap game in a near-by city. In the shooting which resulted, he killed the man who was protecting the game and was shot six times himself. He was not expected to live, but he recovered, stood trial, and was acquitted. By now it was clear that Mario's undisciplined actions made him a menace to too many people. Within a few months of the crap-game shooting, one of his gang was killed, and another was fired upon. Mario was shot dead one day as he walked out of a friend's store.

He was the last of his kind in Cornerville. A new era of racket organization came in with his death. The story of the new era can well be told through the career of a man who came to be known in Cornerville as "T. S."

T. S. did not grow up in Cornerville. According to one familiar with his career,

T. S. came up from ———— to take care of the Italian lottery [based on the weekly tax receipts of various Italian provinces]. That was just beginning to go big in the city, and this X Gang that was handling it needed somebody up here to take care of their end. So T. S. come in and done a big business right from the start. . . . . But the men running the other rackets wanted to get their cuts. He says to them, "What the hell, you got the numbers, the horses, and the liquor racket." He wouldn't give them no cut, so there was plenty of action around here—shooting all up and down the street, men riding in cars, standing on the running board, shooting. It got pretty hot.

There was no indication at this time that T. S. was a different type from Mario Serrechia. However, he displayed superior organizing ability and business sense and within a few years had established himself as the leader of a powerful Cornerville gang dealing in liquor and other rackets. When Mario Serrechia was killed early in 1931, T. S. became the most powerful underworld figure in Cornerville, although he still had some competition within the district.

It was the O'Malley shooting which made T. S. his reputation. The O'Malleys were a tough Irish gang from another part of the city. For some time they had been seeking to expand their operations, and they had been "hijacking" T. S.'s liquor trucks. Once when T. S. needed liquor badly, they stopped one of his trucks with a cargo valued at several thousand dollars. The driver pleaded with the O'Malleys that if they would not hijack the truck but would see T. S., he would make it financially worth their while to lay off. O'Malley phoned T. S. and made an appointment to talk things over in T. S.'s office. When the O'Malleys arrived, they were mowed down with machine-gun fire.

For a short time after the O'Malley shooting, T. S. was a fugitive from justice. While the police were conducting what the chief termed "the greatest man-hunt in the history of Eastern

City," he remained at his home in a neighboring town. When he surrendered and was held for the grand jury, the state's star witness changed his story, and T. S. was not held for trial.

It seems unlikely that any compromise with the O'Malleys would have been possible. They belonged to the reckless and undisciplined school of crime exemplified by Mario Serrechia. When they were disposed of, T. S. established without question his dominance in Cornerville and a prominent position in racket circles in the city. He was one of the ten men who, under the leadership of the Boss, organized the liquor monopoly a year later.

Shortly after he was cleared of the O'Malley shooting, T. S. enlarged his field of operations in Cornerville. Tony Cataldo and Sully Defeo, two Cornerville men who had been backing the numbers themselves, were unable to pay off on large "hits" (winnings), and they agreed to give T. S. 50 per cent of the profits if he would put his financial resources behind the business. As others fell into line in the same manner, T. S. took control of the policy racket in most of Cornerville, and he became one of the members of the syndicate when it was formed to control the business throughout the city and in other towns and cities.

The organization brought about a reign of peace and order in the Cornerville rackets, which has lasted to the present day. While there have been outbreaks of violence in other sections, the Cornerville business has run smoothly for a decade.

The contrast between Mario Serrechia and T. S. illustrates the development of the rackets. Mario was a colorful and romantic figure; to Cornerville he was "the Great Gangster." T. S. works quietly in the background so that few Cornerville people can present a very definite picture of his personality. Mario was powerfully built and, using fists or a gun, did his own fighting. T. S. fought when he had to, but he built up an organization which cut violence to a minimum. Mario was the pirate; T. S. is a businessman.

2. ORGANIZATION OF THE POLICY RACKET

Doc once commented:

I'm batted out. I'm so batted out that I didn't have a nickel to put on the number today. When a Cornerville fellow doesn't have the money to put on a number, then you know he's really batted out. Put that in your book.

Women as well as men play the numbers. When a mother sends her small child to the corner store for a bottle of milk, she tells her to put the change on a number. The racketeers themselves play the numbers. Tony Cataldo once told me:

I play a dollar every day on a three-number play and a quarter on four numbers. If the four numbers come out, I get a thousand dollars. Then, once a month, I put twenty dollars on a number. I figure if that comes out, I'll really have some money.

When the horse races which determine the day's number have been run, people lean out of the windows of their houses to look for the agent who can tell them what it is. The corner boys gather around and ask one another, "What's the number?"

If the Cornerville man does not obtain the information from his friends, he can get it in the newspapers. Every evening a local tabloid appears on the streets with a "Pay-off Edition," which contains not only the results of the races but also a convenient table, like the one in the following example. The morning papers also print this table on their sports pages.

1–2–7 races	$145.20
1–2–3–5–7 races	$209.80
[All] 7 races	$323.60

The table is made up from the prices paid on two-dollar bets on winning, second-, and third-place horses in the designated races at a particular track. The digits in the table have no meaning except to the person interested in the number pool. The number is discovered by reading the first digit to the left of the decimal point, from the top down, on the table. In this case, it would be 5–9–3. The winning "four-number play" is determined in the same way, with the addition of the second digit to the left of the decimal in the bottom figure. While all important racketeers have interests in certain legal and illegal business activities besides the numbers, I shall concentrate upon describing the policy-racket organization, for that seems to provide a framework for the other activities and to give in most complete detail the relations among the men involved at various levels in the structure.

Cornerville men who seek to explain the policy racket always begin by saying, "It's run just like a business." The analogy serves to point out certain distinctive features of the racket. It runs from day to day in smoothly organized routines. Violence is held to a minimum, and other controls, including financial pressure, are used to regulate it. The syndicate in control of the numbers makes agreements to regulate competition among its members and to eliminate competition from outsiders. The leading figures in the rackets maintain efficient organizations with good discipline over their subordinates. They have fixed arrangements which enable them to deal smoothly with their legal problems.

At the bottom level of the racket organization are the agents who take the bets. Some have regular rounds of customers to be solicited, others are storekeepers or employees who "write numbers" for customers who come into the store. The agent writes the bets on a pad, gives a carbon slip to the customer, and turns the other over to his employer with his day's collections. He may accept bets of any amount from one cent up. The customer who "hits" receives odds of 600 to 1 on a three-number play, 4,000 to 1 on a four-number play, 80 to 1 on two digits, and 8 to 1 on one digit.

The agent is paid a percentage of the amount by which his total collections exceed the amount of the winnings to be paid to his customers. His share may run anywhere from 10 to 40 per cent, depending upon the amount of his daily collections and also upon his relations with his employer. In addition, whenever one of his customers makes a hit on a three-number play (the most popular type of play), the agent receives from the company (through his employer) 10 per cent of the amount of the customer's winnings.

Some of the larger agents have smaller agents working for them. If an agent's collections are large enough ($50 or more a day), he can turn in his numbers directly to "the office" and become a "50 per cent man."

All numbers collected by the agent are turned in to his 50 per cent man (except in the case of the small agent working for the larger agent, when the collections pass through an intermediate step before they reach the 50 per cent man). If both employer and employee are working in the same district, the agent personally turns in his collections, but if the 50 per cent man has a number of agents operating far away from his office, he sends out a collector (or "pickup man") to bring in the numbers written by these agents. The collector is paid a small salary. Some 50 per cent men write numbers themselves and have only a few agents working for them. Others have scores of men under them and never write a number.

The 50 per cent man turns over all his collections to "the office" or "the company," as it is variously known. The company backs the numbers. After all the collections are in and the number has "come out," the company office force calculates the amount of winnings to be paid on the numbers turned in by each 50 per cent man. This sum is turned over to the 50 per cent man, who passes it to his agents, and the agents pay off their customers.

The agent's earnings are subject to wide fluctuations, since they depend primarily upon the profits from his particular collections. When the winnings to be paid out exceed the collections, the agent becomes indebted to his employer. It is understood in Cornerville that an agent may go out of business at any time, and a number of small agents have retired rather than face the prospect of working for months without receiving a commission. Under these circumstances it is important for the organization to provide the agent with some consolation for a large hit and to create in so far as possible the illusion that the agent benefits from the hits. From the standpoint of the agent, who has to wait until the end of the month for his regular commission, it is very pleasant to receive the 10 per cent on his customers' winnings in cash at the time that the hits are made.

Since the earnings of most 50 per cent men depend upon the collections of a number of agents, their earnings are not subject to such wide fluctuations. Since the company has a much greater volume of collections, its earnings, on the average, will be even less subject to wide fluctuations. Of course, there are times when a particularly heavily played number comes out that the entire organization will be hard hit, and the company will temporarily run a deficit, dip into its reserves, or borrow money.

There are bound to be times when the luck goes against the agent and when his income from the numbers temporarily stops.

Frequently, he goes to his employer for a loan, or the employer offers help. In this way the agent becomes dependent upon the employer in a personal as well as in a business sense. The fluctuations of the business operate to increase the control of the employer over his employees. If the agent is dissatisfied with the treatment he receives from his 50 per cent man and wishes to change employers, he must receive permission from the head of the company for which his 50 per cent man works. Such changes are exceptional. The head of the company cannot usually allow a change without offending the 50 per cent man for whom the agent has been working. Generally, the relations between agent and 50 per cent man are such that the agent does not consider any other arrangement.

At an earlier period the agent had a greater degree of independence. The first two digits of the three-number play were then based on the totals of the earlier races and only the third digit was based upon figures including the totals of the seventh race. Under this system the first and second digits came out before the third. While agents were supposed to turn in all their numbers before the first digit came out, they could risk holding certain bets themselves. Then, for example, if the first two digits came out 1–6, the agent would go through his slips to see whether he had kept any which had 1–6 as the first digits. If he had one bet on 1–6–5, he would immediately place on 5 for the third digit a bet sufficiently large to meet the sum he would have to pay if 1–6–5 came out. If 1–6–5 did not come out, he would lose the amount he had bet on 5 but he would have protected himself against insolvency, and on some days he would find that none of his slips contained the first two digits, in which case he would make a clear profit. As Tony Cataldo explained to me:

That's one reason they changed the system. Too many small books were keeping the numbers. They all [the syndicate leaders] got together and decided to have the number come from the total of the different races the way it is today. Now you can't do that. The new system made it impossible for these fellows to keep the numbers the way they had been doing.

By such financial arrangements and personal influences, the superiors have established and maintained control over their subordinates.

The racket syndicate also determines spheres of operation and broad lines of policy. The head of each numbers company belongs to the syndicate, and there is one man who serves as president or chairman of the syndicate. His functions and even his identity are unknown to all but a few Cornerville people. The ten or twelve syndicate members each have particular areas in which to operate their businesses and agree not to infringe upon one another's territories.

The syndicate determines the odds paid on the numbers, as Tony Cataldo explained:

It used to be 730 to 1, but we had to bring it down. When the odds change, all these different big organizations get together and make an agreement. Now some of the numbers pay only half-price. That was agreed on because so many people would play the same number that if it ever came out, we wouldn't be able to pay off. Now we pay 600 to 1. In X they only pay 500 to 1, and they pay 500 to 1 in Y. We really should pay only 500 to 1, but the people in Eastern City are too smart. The way it is now, when you take out commissions to the agents and the overhead, we only make 3 or 4 per cent profit. It's like any other business.

All changes in odds paid are effected simultaneously throughout Eastern City and in the surrounding territory. The customers are notified through printed slips distributed to the agents when certain numbers pay only half-price. In this way a serious element of instability has been removed from the business.

The syndicate operates to stifle outside competition. According to one man who watched the monopoly grow,

they got the numbers organized like a big business. They set up the office in Eastern City, and they control the racket all over the ———— states. They got their representative in every city, and you can't write numbers unless you belong to the organization. The racket is organized just like a big business. Everybody has his own job to do. They got the con men, smart talkers—they can convince you that black is white. Then there's the muscle men. They muscle in to take over a business. There ain't much work for them now. There's the strong-arm men, they protect the business when it gets going. There's the killers. And then there's the bookkeepers, because they got plenty of accounts to figure every day. All them men get paid every week, and maybe for some of them there won't be no work for fifty-one weeks out of the year, but for that other week, there's plenty they got to do. You see, it's not like you see in the movies. Only a few of them are killers.

Suppose you start to write numbers and back them up yourself. When the office finds out about it, they will send a con man around to see you. He's a man that can make you believe that black is white, the way he talks. He says it would be a good thing for you to join the protective association and become a 50 per cent man if your collections are large enough. They would protect you in case of a shakedown. You would handle your own police protection, but if you can't reach the cop on your beat, the office will handle that for you. He tells you about the advantages of belonging to the organization and impresses on your mind that you better join. If you don't listen to reason, you get a warning, and if you still don't come in, you get beaten up. But nobody is going to hold out on them anyway. Now suppose you belong to the protective association, and I come up to you and ask you for money. You get in touch with the office and tell them, "——— is trying to shake me down." They send a man around to see me. He says, "Whadda you mean trying to shake down Billy Whyte? You better lay off." So I lay off.

Illegal businesses do not inspire men with respect for property rights, nor do they have the same legal protection which serves the legitimate businessman. Some feel that the fruits of illegal businesses belong to the man who is smart enough or tough enough to get them. Unless they were well defended, the rackets would fall a prey to such irresponsible people. Yet, while it is necessary to have force at one's command, it is the policy of the syndicate to use it as sparingly as possible.

As one prominent in the organization explained to me, physical coercion is not the only means used to control the business:

Before, the numbers used to be controlled by the bootleggers. Then it was a real tough racket. Now it's all in the hands of businessmen—some of them people have pieces of ——— and ——— [two race tracks]. They got plenty of money, so you can be sure that everything is on the up and up. . . . . Was you here when 1–2–3 come out? That was a very popular number. It must have come out about two years ago. I know my own office was hit for $150,000. At that time there was a lot of people in the game without much money behind them. When this number came up, it really straightened things out. They couldn't pay off, so it put them right out of business. In many cases, the big people would pay off their hits and take over the business. It's just like any other business. If a man goes bankrupt, you can take over his debts and carry on his business. That's the way it happened. Now everything runs more smoothly.

While there are 50 per cent men of a younger generation who began their careers in the gambling rackets, T. S. and most of his powerful colleagues were bootleggers and gang leaders before they took to the numbers. Businessmen did not supplant the gang leaders. Gang leaders became businessmen, although there were some who were unable to make the transition and lost their positions in the reorganized rackets.

Like legitimate businesses, the numbers companies meet their obligations to the customers. I have never heard of a Cornerville man who hit the number in recent years and was not paid in full. Customers have been paid even when agents have proved untrustworthy. As one agent told me:

Once a certain fellow hit for $4,000. The agent went up to the office and got the money to pay off with. Then he skipped town. When this fellow didn't get paid, he went to see T. S. T. S. says, "Wait awhile, maybe he'll be around later." After a couple of days this fellow goes up to T. S. again, and he's crying about that $4,000. So now T. S. knows the agent really skipped town, and he pays out the $4,000 himself. If they ever find that man that skipped town, his life won't be worth a nickel.

In maintaining their own positions, it is clearly in the interests of the companies to co-operate with one another—and they do. Perhaps the most common form of such co-operation is known as "edging off." When the agents turn in their number-pool slips, they write on the outside of the envelopes on what numbers they have bets totaling a dollar or more. The bookkeepers can then tell at a glance whether some numbers have been played so heavily that the company could not afford to pay the possible winnings. Then, as Tony Cataldo explained,

the big companies get together. I'll give you five dollars on 6-4-3. You might ask me if I can take five on 4-1-1, and I'd say, "I can't afford it; I already have too much on that number." That way, we have a chance to trade around before the number comes out.

This manner of spreading the risks is an important factor in the stability of the business.

One of the most important functions of the heads of the companies is the establishment and maintenance of close relations with politicians and high police officials. It is particularly important for them to have "connections" in the district attorney's office, and in this respect they have at times been very fortunate. The chief of police is obviously a key man for the operation of their business, and in the past they have had connections with at least one man who filled that office. Even if no such connection is available, the business may thrive on the basis of connections with the police captains, who are in charge of their districts. If the numbers business is flourishing in any district, it is safe to assume that the captain is "getting paid off." Political connections are important for the influence that may be brought to bear through them upon all the agencies of law enforcement. The chief of police is a political appointee. If he cannot be "reached" directly, pressure may be brought upon the man who appointed him.

A connection does not always mean bribery in the strict financial sense of the word. For example, there is one prominent law-enforcement official who does not take any money from the racketeers but who likes to bet on the horses himself. Crusades against gambling do not appeal to him. The racketeers have always given this man their political support and have been able to secure a number of favors from him.

Horse-race betting is controlled by the same organization which operates the policy racket. While the largest horse rooms are operated by the heads of the syndicate, some of the 50 per cent men have their own betting establishments. They turn in all bets to the company and receive 50 per cent of the profits. Protection is organized according to the policy-racket system.

3. RELATIONS WITH THE POLICE

It is the function of the 50 per cent men to provide police protection for their agents. As a 25 per cent man explained to me:

The cops are paid off. They call it the "union wage." The patrolman gets five dollars a month for every store on his beat that sells numbers. The plain-clothes men get the same, but they can go anywhere in Cornerville. They divide up the territory between themselves. They get on different pay rolls, and they divide up the graft, but even so a plain-clothes man can make more than a patrolman. The sergeant gets ten dollars [on every store]. The men in the cruising car get two-fifty each—some men sell themselves cheap. Of course, they got a lot of territory to cover.

The lieutenants and the captain in the local station are said to receive correspondingly larger payments, but these are handled above the level of the 50 per cent man by "the office." According to local accounts, the captain does not receive his money directly. It is placed in the hands of a patrolman or sergeant whom he trusts. Then, in case of some slip, the captain is protected as long as his subordinate does not testify against him, and, if the subordinate is accused of taking graft, the captain does all in his power to clear him of the charge.

The policeman's graft is not limited to money payments, as the 25 per cent man explained.

There's plenty of extras. Every Christmas and Easter my boss makes up a big bundle of groceries from his store for all the cops he pays off, and I deliver it for him to their houses. And then the cop never pays for nothing. They'll go in to my boss and ask for groceries and walk right out without even offering the money. That's the bad thing about having a grocery store. A man that don't have no business like that is better off in some ways. If a cop does pay, he gets a discount that you and I couldn't get. I give the cops cigarettes for ten cents. I lose two cents a pack on that. The cops get all their groceries free on market days—and other times. Some of them do it pretty raw. You come down some Saturday, and I'll show you one cop. He parks his car—it's a big Packard—on King Street, and then he loads up. And I mean he really loads up. He fills the back of that car from the floor to the roof. One family couldn't eat all that stuff. He must take care of all his relatives on that.

Not all this goods is provided by people in the racket. There are all sorts of city ordinances that can be invoked against the push-cart peddler and the small shopkeeper, if the policeman cares to take such action. Ordinances passed to meet conditions in other parts of the city can be used as weapons to force the Cornerville man to "take care of" the police. If a man were thoroughly conversant with his legal rights, he might find that he could safely refuse to give the officers anything, but few know the law well enough to take the risk. There are many small businessmen who feel secure in their legal positions but nevertheless provide the officers with free goods. They explain that it is always advantageous to have a friend on the force and that there might come a time when he could do them a favor. Graft is given as a matter of course by men connected with the racket, but even outside the racket it is not always provided reluctantly.

It is not necessary to have connections with all the members of the police department. One officer in a district who is intent upon cleaning up the racket can cause considerable trouble, but in such cases the racketeers bring pressure upon politicians and police

superiors to have him transferred to another section. One sometimes hears remarks such as this:

> John Doe was one cop that caused a lot of trouble when he was down
> here, but they had him shifted. Now he's out patrolling the cemetery in
> ———, and don't he wish he could get back in Cornerville. It's lonely out
> by the cemetery. Nothing ever happens out there.

There are other weapons with which police superiors can discipline their subordinates. The captain may assign the officer to
extra duty without financial compensation. It is understood in
the department that there are two sorts of extra duty. When
there is a parade, convention, band concert, or something of that
nature which obviously requires a larger number of officers than
are ordinarily in the area at one time, the officers detailed do not
consider it punishment. At other times assignments to extra duty
are recognized by the captain and his subordinates to be disciplinary measures. This is entirely unofficial. If the captain announces
that the extra duty is a punishment, the subordinate has a right
to appeal the decision to a trial board of the department. Naturally, most such penalty assignments are simply made "for the
good of the service," and the captain is required to give no other
explanation.

Some officers hate night work; others prefer it. Some dislike
traffic duty; others like it. The captain who is familiar with the
tastes of his men can penalize his subordinates by assigning them
to jobs that they do not like. This, again, is not officially recognized as discipline, but it is so understood by the men concerned
and thus serves its purpose.

The offering or withholding of promotions can be used as a re-
ward or penalty. For several years recently, the police chief could
promote to fill vacancies any officers who had passed the civil
service examinations for the positions. Such discretionary powers
were in his hands that there was a widespread belief that the jobs
could be bought by anyone who passed and had the right political
connections. The political requirements were a strong incentive
to aspirants to refrain from bothering racketeers who had influential political friends. Now the chief is restricted to the top three
men on the list when he has a vacancy to fill, to the top four when

he has two vacancies, etc., but still it is commonly believed that a policeman's career is aided by his connections.

The threat of transfer is particularly effective with those officers who become attached to the district in which they are assigned, and this is true of many of the Cornerville officers. One agent said to me:

You know, Bill, I've known cops that have cried when they got transferred out of Cornerville. They all want to stay here. There's plenty of graft, and then they don't have to work around here. There's one cop comes into my store as soon as I open up in the morning, and he stays there until I go away at noon. He sits in the back and reads the morning paper, and we play cards. He goes out when he has to punch the box, but outside of that he's in taking it easy all the time. In some other sections you couldn't get away with that. I know one Cornerville cop that used to be in ————. Out there he wouldn't be in a store five minutes before somebody would call up the station-house, and they would have to send for him and tell him to keep out of there. A cop in a district like that really has to pound the pavement. He can't sit around all day like he does here. Down here there is so much numbers and horses going on that the less the people see of the cops the better they like it. Then, in other districts, the people have got telephones in their houses, they call up the station-house right from there to complain about a cop. Down here, how many people have telephones in their houses? Not one out of twenty families—less than that. And how many people are going to walk out and put a nickel in a pay phone to call the station-house? Besides, the people down here don't complain. The people that have made good, most of them have moved out. The people that are left—they just don't care. They let it ride.

Cornerville people look upon the local officers as parasites and feel that the dregs of the department have been foisted upon them. It is not exceptional to hear of an officer drunk or asleep while on duty. While this does not engender respect, it is convenient for the racketeers, who find the local force easier to deal with than officers of other sections.

When he reads in the newspapers that the police have raided a gambling place, the uninitiated person may have the impression that, after a diligent search of the hidden recesses of the city, the officers have discovered and swooped down upon the lawbreakers. A crap-game operator commented:

Don't you think that a cop on the beat knows just about everything that is going on on his beat? Take our joint, now They's men going in and out of that building at all times of the night. When a cop sees that, he knows it must be one of three things—a speakeasy, a cat house, or a gambling joint. So right away he comes up to investigate, and he wants to find out who's behind it. Then he either shuts up the place or does business with the men that run it. Sure, that's the way it is. But you couldn't let people know that. The citizens would say, if you knew that joint was there a year ago, why didn't you raid it before now?

Of course, if the raiding officers are from another part of the city, the gambling place may be new to them.

Since the officers could make arrests almost any time but act only at particular times and in particular situations, it is important to distinguish among various types of arrests in terms of the objectives sought and the conditions which impel the action.

A certain number of arrests is expected by the racketeers as part of the routine of their business. Some raids are made directly from the Cornerville station-house. Occasionally, a wife whose husband has lost his week's wages gambling makes a complaint, and then the police must at least make some show of acting. While the relations between local police and racketeers are such that the racketeers are likely to be informed in advance of the raid, this does not always happen. When the complaint comes in, there may be no one present who is on the pay roll of that particular gambling place. Although the Cornerville captain has friendly and business relations with the organization, it is against his interest to have the racketeer "tipped off" on every raid. Fruitless raids can be taken as evidence of inefficiency, if not corruption. The larger establishments and the more important racketeers, who have direct connections with the captain, will be spared and the small fry will be sacrificed when raids must be made.

The complainant who knows the nature of local police-racketeer relations will take his complaint directly to headquarters of the Eastern City police. Some raids are conducted straight from headquarters, and the local captain is not aware of the raid until it has taken place. This method can be used very effectively to embarrass the captain and to show that he has not been doing his job. Headquarters raids are unpopular with the local captains, and a police chief who has regard for their feelings does not order them too frequently.

Some arrests are made on the initiative of individual policemen for the purpose of securing themselves more favorable financial relations with the racketeers. Recently a plain-clothes man in Cornerville arrested two number-pool agents the same day. From one who knew the agents well I heard the following explanation of the officer's unusual conduct. He had previously been a plain-clothes man and had been on the pay roll of a 50 per cent man. Then he had been "put back in uniform," which meant that his income from the racket was considerably curtailed. Later he was shifted again into plain clothes but was not immediately able to secure his former position on the pay roll. His arrests of agents were designed to persuade the 50 per cent man to reinstate him. The plain-clothes man was put back on the pay roll, whereupon he ceased making arrests. In the language of the corner the policeman was trying to "shake down" the racketeer.

The following story indicates the nature of the police-racketeer shakedown problem, although it arises from the parallel experiences of a crap-game operator.

On this game there's the cop on X Street and the cop on Y Street, the two cruising cops, and the sergeant to take care of. Then there's a cop that used to be on this beat. He would come around whenever I had the game, and I would always give him something. By rights I shouldn't have given him a nickel all summer, because he wasn't on this beat, but when he was here, he was a good fellow, and he treated me right. But this time he come down with a few drinks in him. He says, "I want ten dollars." Ten dollars!

I says, "Listen George, you had a couple of drinks. Come back and see me later." But he won't go away.

He says, "What's the matter? You're paying them others. Ain't I as good a fellow as them?"

I says, "Sure, you're a good fellow. Maybe you're even a better fellow than them, but you ain't on this beat, and I shouldn't give you even a nickel." So he threatens, if I won't give him the sawbuck, he'll pinch the game. I felt like kicking him in the ass. I says, "Go ahead, you ——— ——— ———, see if you got the nerve. Go ahead and break up the game, but you'll be sorry you done it." He was already starting toward the game when I says he'll be sorry he done it. He stops, because he knows what I mean. Then he turns and goes away. After he went away, I told one of the cops on the beat about it. He says, "I'll speak to that bastard when I see him."

I asked what would have happened if the officer had "pinched the game."

The cops on this beat could make it plenty tough for him. They could bust up the places where he is getting protection. And then one of the cops here is a sergeant. He could go to the captain, and maybe the captain would have the man transferred.

The racketeer has more serious difficulties in areas where he is not so firmly intrenched in his relations with the police. For example, there are certain Cornerville 50 per cent men who have agents in outlying towns. They pay the police in the particular territories where their agents operate, but every day they send out collectors who, in order to reach the agents, must drive through areas where they have not paid for protection. Even in the territories in which the agents operate, they may not do a sizable-enough business to enable the 50 per cent man to establish the far-reaching police connections existing in Cornerville. In such areas there are a number of policemen who learn to recognize racketeers' cars and stop them to demand protection money. An agent who covers a large territory in soliciting his numbers may have the same difficulty. His boss cannot pay off all the policemen with whom each agent might come into contact.

In such a situation the boss complains to some of the officers on his pay roll, perhaps threatening to withdraw his business from their section unless the shakedowns cease. The officers attempt to persuade their colleagues to "lay off," and, if persuasion is not effective, they retaliate by arresting or shaking down the sources of graft for the offending officers. In Cornerville it is well established that one policeman does not interfere with the graft of another. In other sections, I am told, these financial and personal relations have not been worked out so systematically. The racketeers still must deal with the problem of the avaricious officer who will not abide by the rules of the business.

Certain arrests are made at the behest of the companies themselves, as the following story indicates:

I know a fellow that had some money and put up a gambling joint on ———— Street. He spent plenty of money on that joint. After a while one of the big shots comes up to him and tells him, "You better close this joint."
So the man says, "I won't close this joint for you or nobody else."
The big shot says, "I'm only warning you, you better close up the joint. If you don't you'll be sorry." The man refused, so in a few days there was a

raid from headquarters. They come down and smash up all the furniture and even break in the walls. That man lost plenty of money on the raid. After that he wasn't in the business no more.

Calling in the police to force out competition has become common in recent years. It has obvious advantages. The competition is disposed of in a legal manner, and the organization need not use violence. In the earlier days of the rackets it was considered the rankest treachery to "squeal" to the police even on one's enemies. That this is being done with increasing frequency today is another indication that business methods are supplanting the old code of gangland.

The racketeers have well-established procedures for dealing with the arrests which come about in the routine course of business. The law provides for penalties up to $500 or a year of imprisonment for defendants in numbers cases. The usual penalty for a first offender is a $50 fine. The recurrent offender tends to be somewhat more severely punished, but suspended sentences are common.

The racketeers frequently find it possible to get their cases before judges who are noted for their leniency. Even a suspended sentence is to be avoided whenever possible, for upon the next conviction the defendant is sent to jail to serve the suspended term, no matter how slight a penalty is imposed in the second case. Many small agents retire from the business when they are given suspended sentences, but some take a chance, and a few go to jail.

There is one convenient way of protecting the previous offender. When he is arrested and booked, he gives a false name. For a ten-dollar fee the employer hires a substitute to answer to that name in court. It is also convenient to have substitutes for men who consider themselves such respectable citizens that they do not wish to appear in court or have their names in the police records. Of course, it would be impossible to use a false name if the police cared to investigate.

When a number-pool agent is arrested, he sends word to his employer. The 50 per cent man appears at the police station with a bail commissioner and posts bail. When the case is called in court, the 50 per cent man furnishes a lawyer. In nearly all cases the defendants plead guilty. It is considered bad business to do otherwise, even when there might be a chance of "beating the case." Charges that do not stand up in court are black marks against the record of the arresting officer, and he may determine to get even by making things difficult for the racketeer in the future. The racketeers realize that the police must make some arrests, and they try to be co-operative when they are dealing with officers with whom some basis of co-operation is possible.

While the system is organized to adjust itself to a certain quota of arrests, periodic crises of law enforcement involve serious dislocations to the racket organization. Crises arise when some spectacular event, such as an act of violence, draws public attention to conditions which have existed all the time. As an agent commented: "You remember that shooting in Maxton? After that the horse rooms and gambling places were closed up all over the county. And after that killing in Crighton, Crighton was all closed up for a few weeks." In such a time of crisis few places are actually raided, but the racketeers are told by their friends in the department that they must close their establishments, and they do—for the duration.

The possibility of such police action has important effects upon the operation of the rackets, as the following story indicates:

You know what happened a few months ago in Tony Cataldo's horse rooms? These three fellows came up and knocked on the door. They gave some name of a fellow that was known there. When they got in, they worked the holdup. They wore masks, and they had three guns. They took over $1,500.

They couldn't get away with a thing like that now. The place is well guarded.

A thing like that is really a shame. Of course, the business is against the law, but still it's honest, and we aren't bothering nobody. Tony always pays what he's supposed to pay. He takes care of his customers. He don't want to harm nobody. But what can you do in a case like that? You can't call the cops. We kept this quiet. Even today nobody knows about it. It would kill the business if a thing like this got around. You know what happened after that killing in Crighton. The police clamped down tight on all the gambling places. We can't afford to have that. That's why Tony didn't shoot when the men were making their getaway. He leaned out the window, and he seen them running up the street. He could of shot at them easy, but if he had done that, the whole of Cornerville would have been closed up overnight. Shooting don't pay in a case like that.

Following the holdup, Tony Cataldo and his men gave chase in a vain effort to catch the holdup men outside Cornerville.

It is in the interests of both racketeers and policemen that the rackets be conducted as peacefully as possible. When there is an outbreak of violence, the newspapers and the "good people" of the city demand that the police chief take vigorous measures against the lawbreakers. In such a situation the chief feels impelled to call upon a type of officer who is known in the newspapers as an "untouchable" and in Cornerville as a "100 per cent copper." This type presents special problems for both the racket and the police organizations.

Recently the chief gave evidence of the difficulty of finding available untouchables when he appointed a racket squad headed by a lieutenant but otherwise completely manned by "rookies"—patrolmen who had just been appointed to the force. It was freely stated in the newspapers at the time that the chief considered lack of experience their most important asset. I am told by those with experience in police relations that his estimate of the situation was sound. The racketeers fear the rookies. It is hard to do business with them. Their actions are unpredictable. Of course, as time goes on, they become familiar with the system by which the department operates, and most of them take their places in it.

The best known of the untouchables in Eastern City is Captain O'Leary. At one time he and certain subordinates were given a free hand to clean up in Cornerville. As Tony Cataldo told me: "When O'Leary was around here, we didn't make no money for six months. What a hell of a six months that was. No profits at all. We had to pay out all the profits to take care of the pinches." Finally, O'Leary was transferred, and for a time nothing was heard from him in connection with racket arrests. Then a prominent racketeer in the neighboring city of Crighton was murdered, and a scandal involving large-scale bribery of Crighton politicians and policemen broke into the newspapers. The state police were sent in. District Attorney Flaherty asked that Captain O'Leary be sent to Crighton with a squad of untouchables to aid him in carrying out an investigation for the county. While the captain's squad was working on this assignment, a newspaper published the following paragraphs:

One ironic note is attached to the operations of these noted Eastern City police officers as "untouchables." Following their activities in Eastern City some months ago, when they cleaned up this city, these men were returned to their stations and instead of being received as heroes, more or less, were actually penalized, according to reports.

It has been claimed that they have been "stigmatized" by certain officials under whom they were obliged to continue their work as ordinary policemen, and in some cases they were delegated to night patrol work.

When the Crighton cleanup is completed they will probably find themselves back in their old police stations, treated the same way, certain police officials admitted guardedly last night.

Within a short time, Captain O'Leary and his squad were withdrawn from Crighton and returned to their former assignments. The last I heard, the captain was in charge of the city's traffic division. The position is an important one, so it cannot be said that he has been "stigmatized." On the other hand, O'Leary is not in a position to disturb racketeer-police relations.

An agent who worked in a store discussed with me the case of a Cornerville untouchable:

There's only one honest cop down here, one man they can't pay off. That's Sergeant Clancy. I know. They've offered him hundreds, even thousands, and he won't take the money. It's a funny thing about that man, they tell me he'll take a bunch of bananas, groceries, things like that, but he won't take money.

We have to watch out for Clancy. When he's assigned to the station-house, the cops will tell us, "It's all right, boys, you can do what youse want." When he gets out, they come and tell us, "Watch out, boys, Clancy is on the loose again." The word spreads like wildfire. When Clancy makes a pinch, we hear of it. We hear, "Clancy just made a pinch in ——— Square," "Clancy just made a pinch on ——— Street." The word spreads along the grapevine.

The other cops try to keep him in the station-house as much as they can. When the captain was out sick, the lieutenant was in charge, and when he would go out, he would put Clancy in charge of the desk. He would keep him there as much of the day as he could. But when Clancy would go out on his lunch hour, he would make a raid. Can you imagine that? I think the man makes pinches in his sleep.

I don't think Clancy is very smart. Sometimes he does the dirty work for the other cops. If one cop don't think he's being treated right on the pay roll, he'll tip Clancy off to make a raid. That way the cop won't make a bad fellow out of himself, but still he'll get even. And I don't think Clancy knows what's going on.

A few weeks back, he walked into the grocery store, and he started to go behind the counter. My boss wouldn't let him.

He says, "You can't come behind without a search warrant." Clancy was sore, but there wasn't nothing he could do.

He says, "I'll get a search warrant, and I'll get you yet."

If he had ever got behind that counter, he would have found plenty. If he catches you in the act of writing a number, he don't need no search warrant, but, outside of that, he's got to get it. Of course, if he goes and gets the warrant, the place will be tipped off before he can pull the raid.

Clancy don't walk into your store like another cop. When he's gonna raid you, he starts three blocks away, and he runs. He runs right in your store before you got a chance to do anything about it.

Clancy nearly always goes around by himself. The other cops duck when they see him. Suppose you're getting paid off by me. Clancy might come along to you and say, "You're a cop, let's go in and raid ————." Naturally you wouldn't like that. Once Sergeant Kelly was out with Clancy. Clancy tells the captain he's gonna make some raids and he wants another sergeant with him. The captain assigns Kelly. Before they started out, Kelly phones all the places, and when they get there, of course they don't find nothing. Clancy says, "I know, you was tipped, but I'll get yuz next time." It's funny that the man don't catch on to what is going on. He must know something, but he don't seem to wise up.

Clancy was walking along with a patrolman one day past X's store. There's a big window in that store by the sidewalk. You can look right in. As they were walking by, the cop looks in the window, and he sees X writing a number in plain sight. The cop tries to keep Clancy from seeing by pointing out something across the street, but Clancy looks in the window, and he sees. He grabs the cop, and he says, "Come on, we're gonna make a raid." So the cop had to follow him. They ran in and made the pinch. Do you think the cop liked to do that? But what could he say? He couldn't tell Clancy he was getting paid off by the place.

The cops down here all hate Clancy. They don't want to have nothing to do with him. He makes it tough for them. It wouldn't look right up at headquarters if Clancy was the only sergeant making pinches. Headquarters is paid off too, but there are some honest cops there, and you have to watch out for them. On account of Clancy the other sergeants have to make some pinches too.

A sergeant will come up to my boss and say, "I got to pinch one of your men."

So my boss says, "All right," and he comes to see me.

He tells me, "You'll have to take a pinch for me. I'll give you a finif for it [$5.00]. You just give a false name, and you won't have to appear in court."

The cops don't care what name you give. They just want to make a pinch. Even if we pay them off, we have to take the pinches too. About once every two months a sergeant has to make a pinch for the numbers.

Everybody wants to get Clancy out of here in the worst way, but somehow they can't do it. He got on the force through Matt Kelliher [once boss of Ward 4]. Kelliher made more policemen than any man in the city. Sure, he's dead now, but there must still be somebody behind Clancy, because he's been down here four years now, and they haven't been able to move him.

Although it is necessary to pay off the police, their toleration of the rackets does not depend exclusively upon bribery. Even so single-minded an officer as Clancy is influenced by his personal relations, and those who establish closer ties find their actions still more influenced by social considerations. A Cornerville barber commented to me:

Sergeant Clancy is all right if you talk to him nice, but if you answer him back, he's always out to get you. My boss [in the numbers and horse-race bets] always answers him back, and he's made my boss move his horse room a few times.

One day Clancy came in when five of the boys were sitting in the front of the shop. He told me that he didn't like the looks of things, and he was going to report me to the Board of Health. I answered him right back. I says, "You can't do that. I got a license from the state and I'm not doing nothing out of the way. These are my customers." I give him an argument, and I was right, too, but just the same I was foolish to say anything, because after that he comes into my store every day to look around and bother me. That was pretty bad, so one afternoon I went into the station-house and asked for Sergeant Clancy. When he heard I wanted to see him, he got sore.

He says, "Whadda ya want with me?"

I says, "Sergeant, I come here to apologize. That time I give you the argument, I wasn't feeling right. I had an argument at home before I come to work, and I didn't really know what I was saying." He talked to me nice after that.

I says to him, "You understand, Sergeant, I do a little something in the back room, but I got a wife and kids. We couldn't live off what I make in the barbershop."

He says, "I understand, but of course that's against the law, and I'm 100 per cent for the law. If I come in there and catch you, I'll have to pull you in."

I says, "Sure, Sergeant, you can come in any time you want, but I just want to ask you one favor. Please don't come in on Saturdays because that is my busy day in the barbershop. It would look bad." He gives me his word he won't come in on Saturdays. . . . . Now I haven't seen him for two months at all. He says he'll come in some time, but I ain't seen him. That's why I'm glad we had the argument. It gave me a chance to get around him. I heard later from the station-house that he says after I come in, "I always did like that fellow. That's why I couldn't understand the way he talked to me in the barbershop because I always thought he was a gentleman. I'm glad he was man enough to apologize."

You have to keep on the right side of the cops. Now you take Sergeant Kelly. He would take graft and all that, but he was a good fellow. I never had any trouble with him. When he came here for the first time, I gave him a haircut. Ever since then we've been friendly. He knows what's going on here, but he never bothers me. I don't have to pay him off either. He never asks for money.

You know, Bill, these cops have their favorites. They play favorites. Sergeant Kelly raids plenty of other places in Cornerville, but he'll even stop in and tell me when I might be raided. And then there are other cops that I have to watch out for, but I know a couple of places in Cornerville that they won't touch. They play favorites.

Another Cornerville man discussed with me a related aspect of police protection in this way:

You and me, we could buy a patrolman and maybe a sergeant, but we couldn't buy a lieutenant or captain, not even if we had the money to do it. Suppose some punk paid money to the captain. He might go around boasting about it, telling everybody, "I bought the captain." That would sound bad. They can't allow that. They only want to deal with people that they can depend on to do things in the right way.

In dealing effectively with the police, money is important, but so are position and personal relations. Neither is effective without the other.

There are prevalent in society two general conceptions of the duties of the police officer. Middle-class people feel that he should enforce the law without fear or favor. Cornerville people and many of the officers themselves believe that the policeman should have the confidence of the people in his area so that he can settle many difficulties in a personal manner without making arrests. These two conceptions are in a large measure contradictory. The policeman who takes a strictly legalistic view of his duties cuts himself off from the personal relations necessary to enable him to serve as a mediator of disputes in his area. The policeman who develops close ties with local people is unable to act against them with the vigor prescribed by the law.

Local people do not know what to make of a 100 per cent copper like Sergeant Clancy. His unorthodox behavior impels some to consider him crazy and others to admire him. One racketeer said to me: "You know, Bill, I respect a man like that even though he hurts my business. If all cops were like him, we would have law and order in every city in the country."

However, this respect does not lead to friendship. In spite of the prevailing hostile attitude toward the police, all the other officers can count at least a few friends in the district. But not Clancy. Since he does not conform to the prevailing pattern of behavior, he has become socially isolated from his colleagues and from the people of Cornerville. At the same time, because he does his duty according to the *legal* requirements of his position, Sergeant Clancy forces the other officers to simulate conformity with his behavior.

It is not only the officers who are in the pay of racketeers who stress the importance of using discretion in enforcing the law. A police captain who was well known for his incorruptability once said to me:

We don't judge the efficiency of an officer by the number of arrests he makes. There are so many arrestable offenses committed even by the law-abiding citizen that if the officer made all the arrests that he could, he would be a very, very busy man. If a man makes too many arrests, he isn't doing his job right. Of course, if he doesn't make any arrests at all, we know something is wrong. We rate the efficiency of the man as a variable considering the character of his route and how quiet he keeps it. If a man has a difficult section and he keeps it quiet so that there isn't much violence, places aren't being robbed, and the women aren't being bothered, then we know he is doing a good job.

I commented that, according to such a rating, an officer could be doing a good job while numbers were being sold all over his beat as long as the business was carried on in an orderly fashion.

That's right. There are so many millions of people in this country, and about half of them play the number pool. We all know it's going on. Why, one of those three men at the desk outside my office can play a number for you any time. He just calls up the office. The number pool isn't considered such a serious thing. The only bad thing is that it's run by men who don't want to work. As long as it is kept quiet, the cop can't complain. We might say, "For God's sake, don't write them under my nose. Go in the back street." The police have to see that it doesn't become too open. Of course, if an officer accepts money to let them do business, that's a very serious thing .

The captain's remarks are representative of the police attitude toward gambling. Many policemen have grown up in the same environment as the racketeers, where gambling is taken for granted. Some like to gamble themselves. At one time numbers were written in police headquarters, and, I am told, an officer handled the business. Gambling involves personal relations quite different from those to be found in other illegal activities. As long as the gambler feels that he is being fairly and honestly treated, he does not think of complaining to the police when he loses money. He participates of his own volition. But when a man is held up or has his home or store broken into, he complains to the police. Holdup men and burglars do not develop the routine day-to-day relations with the police that characterize the racket organization; their more spectacular breaches of the law receive more publicity and necessitate more energetic police action.

Observation of the situation in Cornerville indicates that the primary function of the police department is not the enforcement of the law but the regulation of illegal activities. The policeman is subject to sharply conflicting social pressures. On one side are the "good people" of Eastern City, who have written their moral judgments into the law and demand through their newspapers that the law be enforced. On the other side are the people of Cornerville, who have different standards and have built up an organization whose perpetuation depends upon freedom to violate the law. Socially, the local officer has more in common with Cornerville people than with those who demand law enforcement, and the financial incentives offered by the racketeers have an influence which is of obvious importance.

Law enforcement has a direct effect upon Cornerville people, whereas it only indirectly affects the "good people" of the city. Under these circumstances the smoothest course for the officer is to conform to the social organization with which he is in direct contact and at the same time to try to give the impression to the outside world that he is enforcing the law. He must play an elaborate role of make-believe, and, in so doing, he serves as a buffer between divergent social organizations with their conflicting standards of conduct.

In times of crisis it becomes difficult for the policeman to play his dual role. An outbreak of violence arouses the "good people" to make demands for law enforcement which must be carried out to a certain extent, even when they disturb police-racketeer relations. Therefore, it is in the interest of the department to help maintain a peaceful racket organization. Since competition in illegal activities leads to violence, it is also in the interest of the department to co-operate with the racket organization in eliminating competition. By regulating the racket and keeping the peace, the officer can satisfy the demands for law enforcement with a number of token arrests and be free to make his adjustment to the local situation.

Periodic crises in law enforcement require a high degree of flexibility on the part of the police department. In order to play the dual role, the organization must be able to move in opposite directions according to the requirements of the situation. The 100 per cent copper helps to maintain the necessary flexibility. When a racket scandal breaks, he is let loose upon the case. His reputation for incorruptability is accepted by the public as a sign that the police are in earnest. When the furore dies down, he is shifted into the background. A man so prominent as Captain O'Leary cannot be too obviously penalized or shelved, but, if he is kept within certain bounds, his actions serve to strengthen the police organization. If there were no untouchables on the force, police-racketeer relations known as corruption would develop to such an extent that, when finally a crisis arose to bring this condition to public notice, the department would lack the men necessary to bring about an apparent reversal of policy. The resulting scandal might assume such proportions as to threaten the prevailing system of police organization with destruction. Then, presumably, a period of confusion would follow while a new (or similar) social system was developing. The untouchable officer therefore helps to keep the police organization in a state of equilibrium between the pressures which are exerted upon it from both sides.

These generalizations do not mean that the police department and the racket organization enter into a great conspiracy and agree upon a common policy. The relations between them are established not in the mass but between individuals of both groups, and the actions on both sides become a matter of habit and custom just as they do between other people and other groups. While a study reveals certain consistent patterns in the actions of men, it is not correct to assume that anyone planned them to be such as they are.

4. THE RACKETEER IN HIS SOCIAL SETTING

The strength of the racketeer rests primarily upon his control of gambling activities. In our middle-class society gambling is a disreputable activity. In Italy, as in many European countries, gambling is taken for granted, and the state promotes its own lotteries. Protestants tend to identify law and morality and therefore to consider illegal acts as immoral. The Catholic church makes no such identification. Gambling is a temporal matter. The state has the right to forbid it, but the legal prohibition does not make it immoral. According to the church, gambling is immoral only when the gambler cheats, uses money which is not his own, or deprives his dependents of what is needed for their maintenance. Recognizing that it often involves such deprivation and that it tends to be associated with immoral activities, the church looks with suspicion upon gambling; but that is quite different from an outright moral ban.

The common Cornerville attitude toward gambling was expressed to me in this way by a corner boy:

Suppose I'm a rich man, and I like to follow the horses. When they're running in Crighton, I can go out there and bet my money. When they're in Florida in the winter, I can go down there and play them. That's all legal. That's all right. But suppose I'm a poor man. In the summer I go out to Crighton. In the winter I can't afford to go to Florida, but I still want to play them. I don't lose interest just because they're in Florida. Is it immoral for me to bet them in a horse room? Why should it be immoral for me if it ain't for the rich man?

Cornerville people have quite a different attitude toward robbery and murder. They draw a sharp line between respectable and nonrespectable illegal activities. Gambling is respectable.

Gambling plays an important role in the lives of Cornerville people. Whatever game the corner boys play, they nearly always bet on the outcome. When there is nothing at stake, the game is not considered a real contest. This does not mean that the financial element is all-important. I have frequently heard men say that the honor of winning was much more important than the money at stake. The corner boys consider playing for money the real test of skill, and, unless a man performs well when money is at stake, he is not considered a good competitor. This helps to fix the positions of individuals and groups in relation to one another.

Suppose that Team X challenges Team Y, which is generally considered to be the superior team. Team Y accepts on condition that a designated sum of money is wagered. If the sum is large and the members of Team X are not confident of the outcome, they may refuse to put up the stakes. In this case, the contest will not take place, and Team Y will continue to be regarded as the superior team.

In individual and team competitions the corner boys organize their own gambling. If they wish to play the horse or dog races or the numbers, they cannot handle the situation in the same informal way. It is here that the racketeer comes in. He organizes gambling as a business.

The corner boy knows very well that, in playing the number pool or betting on the horses, he will lose on the average. For him the financial incentive is not the only one. He enjoys studying the horse-racing lore and matching his skill at selecting winners against that of his friends. There is no skill involved in playing the numbers, yet people develop attachments to their "steady numbers," and they enjoy discussing their experiences with the numbers.

A corner boy who saved his nickels and dimes would have more money in the long run than if he bet them on the numbers, but he could not pursue this course without disagreeable social consequences. The corner boy who has money is expected to help his friends. The free spender is popular and respected. Saving, therefore, is not a real alternative to gambling on the numbers. The small change would be dissipated in one way or another, whereas the large amounts occasionally won have real meaning for the corner boy. The sixty dollars that comes from a ten-cent three-number hit is used to pay off debts, to buy an outfit of clothes, to treat his friends, to give some money to his parents, and to gamble again.

The racketeer conducts activities which lend themselves particularly to the extension of his social influence. In retail trade, price and quality of goods have some influence upon sales, but the odds paid on winning numbers and horses are exactly the same throughout Cornerville. Personal ties and personal trust are, then, the only factors which influence the customers to place their bets with one agent instead of another. The corner boy wants to give his business to a friend, and close ties are established between the agent and his customers. Those on a higher level in the organization have risen to their positions through forming the same sort of relations of friendship and trust with the Cornerville people. These relations continue to exist, though in somewhat modified form. T. S., for example, cannot have close relations with all those who do business with his organization, but he spends much of his time in Cornerville, and, when he is there, he hangs on a certain corner, or in a certain barbershop, and has his "coffee-and" in a certain restaurant like any of the corner boys. Although he lives outside the district, he has not cut himself off socially from the corner boys as have most successful business and professional men.

Organized gambling activities tend to place a number of the corner boys in a position of dependence upon the racketeers. It is part of the code of the man who makes a profession of gambling that he give back some of his winnings to the losers who are "cleaned out." I know one crap-game holder who used to take home all his days' earnings to his mother. He came to be regarded as "a cheap no-good" fellow, and, had his associates in promoting the game not abided by the code in quite a liberal manner, he would have lost his customers.

In Cornerville the racketeers are known as free spenders and liberal patrons of local enterprises. They spend money in local stores. They patronize the activities of the corner boys with purchases of blocks of tickets to dances and with other contributions.

One young man in a legitimate business said of T. S. and his associates:

These gangsters are the finest fellows you want to meet. They'll do a lot for you, Bill. You go up to them and say, "I haven't eaten for four days, and I haven't got a place to sleep," and they'll give you something. Now you go up to a businessman, one of the respected members of the community, and ask him. He throws you right out of the office.

This pattern of action is substantially the same for all racketeers. While the generosity of outlaws is a theme as old as time, it is important to understand it in this case not as a peculiar personality trait but as an important aspect of the racketeer's adjustment to his society.

Generosity creates obligations which are recognized by its recipients. Beyond the group of "parasites" who are completely dependent upon his support, there are a large number of corner boys who are at some time or other beholden to the racketeer for money lent to them or spent upon them.

The racketeer's power is seen in clearer perspective when he is compared with some of his possible competitors for influence. Legitimate business and professional men are usually considered the leading members of the community. There are a number of prosperous business and professional men who grew up in the district and still have their stores or offices in Cornerville, but most of them have made their homes in less congested and more socially desirable sections. They spend many of their working hours in Cornerville, but they have little time and usually little inclination to "hang with the boys." Even those few who have continued to live in Cornerville tend to be limited socially by the nature of their activities. A storekeeper must remain in his store and wait for the customers to come to him. He must rely upon the steady trade of his circle of friends and acquaintances, and yet he cannot afford to become too intimate with the corner boys. In fact, sometimes one hears it said that a man failed in business because he had too many friends—because too much of the business of these friends was on a credit basis. If a man is too closely tied to the corner boys, he will have difficulty in refusing them credit, whereas if he avoids becoming involved with them he may still have their business if his products are good, his prices reasonable, and his location central to their activities. However, in the latter case, he will not have the influence of the man who is "one of the boys."

Many stores are dependent upon the numbers business, and the storekeepers thus become a part of the racket organization. Numbers are sold in all kinds of stores, but they are most commonly found in small variety stores, barbershops, lunchrooms, and poolrooms. It is significant that these are places which are used as hangouts by the corner boys. The boys are friendly with the owner of the store, and the owner depends for much of his income upon his numbers business. In such circumstances the influence of the racketeer needs no further explanation.

While the Cornerville rackets are organized around gambling, local racketeers have a number of other interests. Some still deal in bootleg liquor, underselling the legal product by evading the government tax. However, this business is insignificant compared with the prohibition traffic, and there are many racketeers who have nothing to do with it. At times certain men in the organization have furnished strike-breakers to industry, but this work has been sporadic. At present there are no houses of prostitution in Cornerville. The dope traffic is little in evidence in the district, though some local men have been arrested and sentenced on dope charges. There may be a tie-up between the racket syndicate and these businesses. "The Boss" who organized the liquor monopoly also controlled the Eastern City dope traffic. However, there is no evidence that any Cornerville racketeers up to and including the 50 per cent men have business interests in prostitution or dope.

There are in Cornerville some small gangs indulging in holdups and burglaries. While some prominent racketeers began their careers in this line, they have discontinued such activities since becoming established in the more secure and respectable field of gambling. Some agents occasionally participate in holdups, but this is discouraged by those prominent in the organization. It is bad business for the racketeers to have their subordinates get in trouble with the police any more than is necessary in the operation of the rackets. The holdup men usually operate independently with a few associates. Some of them are friendly with racketeers and seek their help when in trouble with the law. While the racketeers look down upon holdup men, there are informal relations existing between them.

If they exist at all, protection rackets preying upon legitimate Eastern City businesses have certainly not been organized to the extent found in other cities. Some years ago in Cornerville the racketeers forced all the bakeries to pay them protection, but the racket was short lived. On another occasion in a near-by city, racketeers attempted to set up control of the poultry market, but the murder of a well-known local businessman and member of the American Legion upset their plans at the outset.

In all their activities, legal or illegal, the racketeers perform the important function of providing employment for a large number of men. Most of the employees have no background of experience and skill to prepare them for jobs in private industry. Furthermore, it is widely believed in Cornerville, and not without considerable evidence, that a Cornerville Italian is discriminated against when he applies for a job. The corner boys do not fit into the socially approved economic organization, and in the depression the rackets provided them with jobs which were difficult to find by other means.

The racketeers also provide investment capital for new enterprises. One story will serve as an example. Tom Leonardi was a young Cornerville man who worked for a large corporation. Tom learned the business well and saw opportunities for profits if he started out for himself. Without any capital to back him, he began selling the product among his friends. He built up a small trade, but he needed capital to expand his operations. City investment bankers would hardly be interested in backing an unknown young Italian who was entering into competition with firmly intrenched corporations. Tom approached several Italian racketeers, and they agreed to invest. With their capital, he was able to buy the plant and equipment necessary for the expansion of his business. At the same time his board of directors pushed sales with enthusiasm—which sometimes led to coercion. Today the business is firmly established, and certain "tough" sales methods of earlier years are less in evidence. The company produces a product of excellent quality and seems likely to enjoy a long and prosperous existence. The evidence indicates that Tom Leonardi had superior business ability, and yet, had it not been for the support of his racketeer friends, he would still be struggling to get ahead. This is not an isolated example. The support of racket capital has helped a number of able men to rise to positions otherwise unattainable.

Racket capital in Eastern City has been invested in a large number of legitimate enterprises. It is most in evidence in the production and sale of liquor, in finance companies, in night clubs and restaurants, in race tracks, and in sports promotion.

From the racketeer's standpoint there are several advantages to having legitimate business interests. Profitable investments are welcomed for obvious reasons. Even unprofitable interests serve as convenient "fronts" for the illegal activities.

The promotion of prize fights is an uncertain and frequently unprofitable business. I understand that the racketeer most prominent in this line cleared a profit of less than a hundred dollars on the operations of a recent year. Nevertheless, he and his associates considered it well worth the trouble.

They pass out the tickets to certain police officers and businessmen. Suppose they send ten tickets to a certain officer every time there is a fight. He uses them and passes them out among his friends. Sometime if they need a favor from him, he is supposed to do it for them. That's why it's good business. . . . . And then they pass out tickets to all their numbers writers—to show their appreciation.

It appears that one of the chief incentives for entering legitimate business is the hope of becoming "respectable," as the following story indicates. Joe the Wolf started out as a bodyguard for a prominent gang leader. He had frequent clashes with the law. Once, when a gangster was shot, Joe the Wolf was caught running away from the scene of the crime. He was tried for murder and acquitted. For some time after that Joe was picked up by the police whenever a gang murder had been committed. He complained that he was being hounded. His activities were changing. He made money in the numbers and acquired some legitimate business interests. He played up the respectable side of his career and discouraged the use of his nickname. He refused to allow his daughter to go out with racketeers. She married a man of a respectable family who was engaged in a legitimate business. The elaborate wedding reception attracted a large gathering, including many local businessmen and prominent politicians. Newspaper accounts of the affair described the bride's father as a "well-known sportsman." Although Joseph Lupo is still known to the corner boys as Joe the Wolf, he has traveled far toward respectability since his early days.

The rackets function in Cornerville as legitimate business functions elsewhere. The racketeer patterns his activity after the businessman and even strives to gain respectability so that he may become accepted by society at large as he is accepted in Cornerville.

CHAPTER V

THE RACKETEER IN THE CORNERVILLE
S. AND A. CLUB

1. TONY CATALDO AND THE SHELBY STREET BOYS

THIS is the story of the struggle between Tony Cataldo, the racketeer, and Carlo Tedesco, the corner boy, for control of the Cornerville Social and Athletic Club. The conflict came out into the open on only two occasions, but each man was aware of what was at stake, and between crises they played for position and influence over their fellow-members. The power of Tony and of Carlo depended upon the nature of their personal relations. Therefore, in order to understand the struggle, it is necessary to see each man in action with his fellow-members throughout the history of club activities.

Tony Cataldo and his partner, Sully Defeo, were the biggest men on Shelby Street. In the division of labor between the partners it was Tony's function to handle personal relations in that area.

Tony was born in 1912, the youngest son in his family. His father had immigrated to Cornerville ten years earlier. In their early years here the Cataldos were poverty-stricken, but by the time Tony was born his father had got a start in the itinerant dry-goods business that he had practiced in rural Sicily. The war boom enabled the family to live comfortably and to invest savings in local real estate so that Tony faced few hardships in his early years.

Tony was intelligent and popular with his classmates, but he had no academic ambitions. After three years of high school, he dropped out to join with Sully Defeo in selling tickets in the treasury lottery. From that they moved into the policy racket, which was then developing in Cornerville. They were in business for themselves at first, but, when they were unable to pay off a hit of

$23,000, they were forced to call upon the T. S. bankroll and subordinate themselves, as 50 per cent men, to Cornerville's leading racketeer. In this position they developed a thriving business, with about three hundred agents working for them in Cornerville and other parts of the state. Besides the numbers, Tony and Sully conducted a large horse room and an out-of-town Beano game. Their gambling activities at times took them into the promotional field in other states. They also had certain legitimate and nongambling interests.

Tony was exceedingly talented in his personal relations. As he was growing up, he learned many of the Italian dialects then current in Cornerville so that he could mix readily into any social group. His future father-in-law was from Abruzzi and "dead set against Sicilians," but Tony talked that dialect so that his origin was not discovered until he had become the daughter's leading suitor.

Tony and his wife lived in one of the family-owned buildings in an apartment he had modernized. He said they would have moved out of Cornerville but remained in deference to the wishes of his mother and father.

Tony had a small son, of whom he was very proud. He did not allow the boy to play with the neighbors' children for fear that he would learn "bad language." In his devotion to his wife and child and to his parents, Tony Cataldo was an estimable family man.

Carlo Tedesco moved from Naples to Cornerville in 1927 at the age of seventeen. Having established himself in the trade practiced by his father, he married and settled down in a flat on Shelby Street. Throughout a part of the early depression period Carlo had to rely upon the W.P.A. to support his family, but, as the depression lifted, he was able to get at least seasonal employment in private industry.

Carlo told me he regretted very much that he had been unable to go to school in this country. While he could read and write English more fluently than many native-born corner boys, he still spoke with a marked Italian accent, and he felt that this had been a handicap to him in employment and social contacts. However, this would have been much more serious in certain other parts of

Cornerville than it was along Shelby Street, where accents were common. Quick-witted and high-spirited, Carlo did not allow his accent to make him diffident. He was extremely active in the social life of Shelby Street and was well known to all the corner boys.

Carlo and his closest friends hung in the shop of a middle-aged barber by the name of Joe Palermo. At the time of the founding of the Cornerville S. and A., Carlo shared the primary influence in this group with Mike Costa, a man in his forties who did some part-time barbering in Joe Palermo's shop.

On Shelby Street there were three other groups that play a part in this story. There was a group that centered its activities around the lunchroom run by Dom Romano and his partner, Jim Rizzo. Dom was born in Cornerville in 1914 of North Italian parents. He was graduated from a technical high school, where he took up automobile mechanics. Finding no future in this line, he went into the lunchroom. After an early struggle, he was able to build up the business to a point where it provided him and his partner with a comfortable living, according to Cornerville standards. Next to Dom, Salvy Bellino was the most prominent member of the clique. He was a high-school graduate who had a part-time job in a near-by warehouse, and he could express himself in writing better than any of the other members. Salvy was an all-around athlete.

The Ten Friends Club, under the leadership of Tom Reppucci, included a group of men in their early and middle twenties, most of whom had part-time warehouse jobs. Since their organization had been founded two years before the Cornerville S. and A. and none of their members spoke with an accent, they considered themselves superior to other Shelby Street groups.

Matteo Firrera, a jovial fat man in his forties, who spoke with a marked accent, ran the small Marconi Club as his personal organization. Matteo supported his club by selling wine to the members and taking "cuts" on their card games. Most of the men spoke English with some difficulty and were known to the corner boys as "greasers."

While Tony Cataldo's influence extended throughout the Shelby Street area, he had particularly close relations with some of the members of the barbershop and lunchroom gangs. The proprietors of both hangouts turned their numbers in to him, Dom being a 20 per cent man and Joe the Barber receiving 25 per cent. Chichi and Lefty of the barbershop gang also wrote numbers, Chichi turning his in directly to Tony and Lefty being a subagent to Joe Palermo. While Tony was accustomed to dealing with most of the men on Shelby Street, at the time the Cornerville S. and A. was founded he did not know Carlo Tedesco.

2. ORGANIZING THE CLUB

The Cornerville Social and Athletic Club grew out of the barbershop gang. One morning Mike, Joe, Dick, Guy, and Chichi came up to Carlo's house to have coffee with him. Feeling that frequent visits of this nature would add too much to his wife's housekeeping responsibilities, Carlo suggested that the boys rent a room and start a club. They agreed to hold a meeting that evening in the barbershop to discuss plans. At that time Mike proposed his plan of organization. He wanted to have ten original and regular members who would pay a three-dollar initiation fee and twenty-five cents a week dues and have complete control of the club. All others were to be associate members, paying a dollar a year and having no powers. The original members would handle the sale of wine and beer in the clubrooms and would collect a small fee for card games played by the associate members. As Mike later explained to me: "I wanted to get about two hundred members to that club. Then we can approach some politician and get something—maybe favors or he give us money. That was all my idea."

Carlo protested that the boys should not try to make a profit on their friends and argued that all members should have equal rights. When he had to leave to go to work, he understood that all the boys agreed with him. The next day he found that Mike had continued his argument and had brought them all around to support his plan. Carlo thereupon called them "a bunch of dirty double-crossers," said that the club could never be successful under such a plan of organization, and refused to have anything to do with it.

Mike got Joe, Chichi, Dick, and Dodo of the barbershop gang with him for a start, and they got five others, including Salvy of the lunchroom gang and Tony Cataldo. With this nucleus, Mike rented a vacant store next to the barbershop and persuaded a large number of others, including Dom Romano and Jim Rizzo, to join as associate members.

There was sharp dissension in the club almost from the beginning. The lunchroom boys protested that Mike wanted to be a dictator. Dom Romano took no part in the arguments, but Salvy clashed with Mike at the start and continued to oppose him. Even some of the members of the barbershop clique were not pleased with Mike's leadership. Guy told Carlo that the boys wanted him to come back and straighten things out, but Carlo refused to join until the club was reorganized with all members having equal rights.

Tony Cataldo did not take sides. His attitude was that it was a good idea for the boys to form an organization. They could conduct it as they saw fit, and he would try to help them, although he could not spare much time.

When there was factional strife, the boys seemed to expect Tony to take action. He also did other things for the club. Once that spring he bought two kegs of beer and some sandwiches and gave the boys a party. When the members were considering getting a charter for the club, Tony contributed the twenty-five-dollar fee out of his own pocket.

As Chichi explained to me:

When you can hang up a charter in your club, people that pass by will see that you got a chartered club. They'll see that it's more like an organized club. They'll know it's a real organization. . . . . Then when you got a charter, you can keep liquor in the club. Yes, you're supposed to keep it in individual lockers, but who bothers with that? When you got a chartered club, the cops can't come in without a search warrant. If they try to come in, you got a perfect right to throw them out. Without no charter, the cops can come in and snoop around any time. It's not so easy to get a charter. You got to pay $25 for the charter, that's the regular fee, and then you got to pay a lawyer another $25 to get it for you. That man has to make connections in order to get the charter. They're very strict, you know. They ask what you're gonna use that charter for. You got to have somebody with real good connections to shove it through for you.

Tony gave Mike twenty-five dollars with which to procure the charter, and Mike got into a crap game and lost the money. Several members of each clique later told me this story, and it is clear that this was a telling blow to the club.

In the late spring the Cornerville S. and A. fell apart. The associate members and even some of the original members dropped out, until only Mike, Joe, Dick, Chichi, and Tony Cataldo were left.

In order to make the club a success, Mike would have had to draw the lunchroom and barbershop cliques together. The two cliques differed in several significant characteristics. The lunchroom clique was considered more Americanized, and, on the average, its members had gone further in school. Only one of the lunchroom boys spoke English with an accent, and he stood at the bottom of his group. On the other hand, Carlo, Mike, and Joe—the three most prominent of the barbershop boys—all spoke with pronounced accents. The lunchroom boys were more active in sports; the only baseball players and the best bowlers were in their group. Neither clique was prosperous, but the lunchroom boys had a slight advantage in regularity of employment. The only cars owned by club members belonged to Dom, Mac, Mario, and one other member of the clique.

Under Mike's leadership, these distinctions became accentuated until the organization broke down. In a last effort to save the club, Mike urged Carlo to become a member. Carlo refused unless it was reorganized. The remaining members, with the exception of Tony Cataldo, who was not present, agreed that they would reorganize the club according to Carlo's plan if he would come back. He agreed, but the next day he found that Tony had persuaded the boys to turn the club over to him for the summer. Tony was to pay the rent and light bills in return for running card games and taking bets on the dog races. When Carlo heard of this agreement, he once again called the boys a "bunch of dirty double-crossers."

Tony Cataldo set up his business in the back room. His brother Joe was in charge when he was not there, two of his employees helped with the dog-race bets and card games, and three others spent much of their time in the club.

The opening of the gambling place in the clubrooms brought the corner boys into closer contact with Tony Cataldo and his organization. Before, Tony spent a large part of the day driving about Eastern City and near-by towns and had little time for hanging in the club. With his business operating there, he became, in effect, the boss of the club. He was much more in evidence, and, when he was not present, other members of his organization mingled with the corner boys.

This new arrangement increased the dependence of the corner boys upon the racketeers. While Mike Costa and many others accepted handouts when they had gambled away all their money, most of the influential members of corner-boy groups considered such acceptance beneath them. The effect of this behavior was to increase the influence of the racketeers over the followers in the corner gangs and thus to divide the influence of the corner-boy leaders.

Carlo did not even play the numbers. During the summer he gambled in the back room only two or three times, and, as he said,

I never ask them for nothing. If I go in there and lose fifteen or twenty dollars, what good is a half a dollar or a dollar going to do me? I wouldn't be that cheap.

Sometimes during the summer they would make $100 in a night, and they would send out for a couple of cases of beer—that costs them $3, so they're still winning $97, but that way they make themselves good fellows—on our money. That's what I tell the boys. I even say that to Tony Cataldo. Of course, Tony is a good sport. You meet him uptown, and he'll buy you a drink or something like that. He's a good sport—on our money.

3. REORGANIZING THE CLUB

When the dog-racing season was over and Tony Cataldo had relinquished the clubrooms, Mike again appealed for Carlo's support. On the understanding that this was to be the same club, except that all men were to have equal rights in it, Carlo proceeded to re-enlist the former members.

At the first meeting of the reorganized club, Dick, Chichi, and Joe of the barbershop clique were elected president, assistant secretary, and treasurer. Mario, a member of the lunchroom gang who was attending Meridian Medical School, became vice-president, and Salvy was elected recording secretary.

Carlo explained to me that some of his friends had wanted him to run for president but that he had declined, since he was working nights and could not attend most meetings. Dom was not playing an active part in club affairs. He told me that in his business he could not afford to get into arguments.

In this meeting I was voted into the club, which enabled me to follow developments at first hand.

The first controversy to arise following reorganization clearly showed the strength of the informal organizations within the club. Mike proposed that the club pay a janitor a small sum for cleaning its rooms. Salvy moved that the members take turns in performing this service. Carlo arrived midway in the meeting and sided with Mike. There was a lengthy and heated argument and then a vote which split the club neatly into two cliques. The barbershop boys all supported Carlo and Mike, while the lunchroom boys all supported Salvy. The barbershop had a two-vote margin on this occasion.

This meeting revealed clearly the standing of the president. Dick was popular with all the members, but he was unable to keep them in order. The usual parliamentary rules of procedure were not enforced. Any member was allowed to make a motion even when another motion was already on the floor. In some meetings as many as three motions were on the floor simultaneously. This put the president in the difficult position of having to decide how the motions were to be voted upon. Dick was indecisive in such situations, generally following the advice of Salvy or of Carlo. His indecision was an important factor in disorganizing the meetings. When an argument started, both sides carried it through without waiting for recognition from the chair. At times Dick rapped on the table for order, but this had little effect unless men of higher standing supported him.

At the height of the janitorial argument, when the meeting had got entirely out of his hands, he got up and said: "I'm resigning from president. I'm still with the club, but whoever wants to run the meeting can have it." He walked away from the table.

Carlo called out in a loud voice, "Mr. President, take your chair!" Immediately Dick turned around, went back to his chair, and continued the meeting.

The accompanying chart presents a picture of the informal organization of the club at this time. The names of members who do not figure in the story have been omitted. While it is not necessary for the reader to keep in mind all the names that appear here, comparison of this chart with the two which follow may help him to visualize the evolution of personal relations within the club.

A much more serious controversy arose in the meeting following the decision on the janitorial issue. Salvy was reading his version of the proposed constitution. When he reached the clause which stated that the club had been founded in August, Mike broke in. He claimed that it had been founded in January and that therefore the names of the ten original members should appear in the constitution. Other members of the lunchroom gang objected to this, saying that politicians who saw the names would think that "the originals" were the only members that counted. Carlo led the barbershop boys in supporting Mike.

The argument became more heated. The lunchroom boys concentrated their fire upon Mike, who, with his poor command of English, was unable to reply effectively. Suddenly, Mike lost his temper and said that the landlord had rented the rooms to him and that he owned most of the club furniture and could take it out if he wanted. Actually, the folding chairs, table, couch, easy chair, and radio belonged equally to Tony, Joe, Chichi, Dick, and Mike, who were the only paid-up members when the club was turned over to Tony. Mike often spoke as if he had owned the original club.

When Mike made his threat, he lost Carlo's support. The lunchroom boys demanded that the club decide to buy the furniture or to throw it out. Joe and Chichi indicated that they had no desire to sell, but they did not openly repudiate Mike. The argument continued. Dick shook his head and said, "You know what the trouble is with this club? There are cliques in here."

Finally, Mike called Joe and Chichi into the back room for a

INFORMAL ORGANIZATION OF THE CORNERVILLE S&A CLUB
Early September 1939

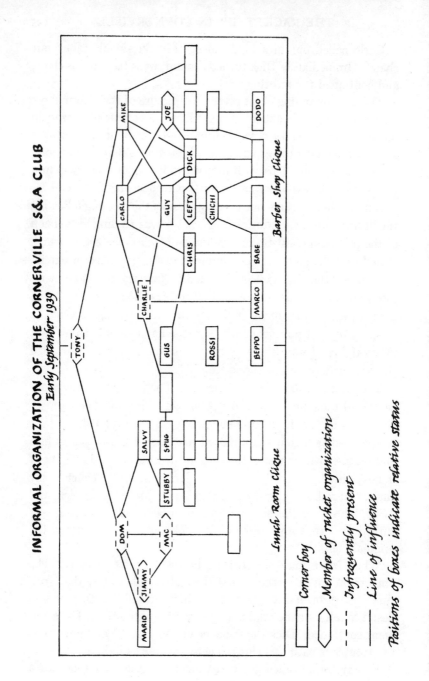

Lunch Room Clique

Barber Shop Clique

☐ Corner boy

⬡ Member of racket organization

┆ Infrequently present

── Line of influence

Positions of boxes indicate relative status

conference. When they emerged a moment later, he announced that they would take forty dollars for the furniture and also claimed fifteen dollars, which was in the treasury when they turned it over to the new club. The lunchroom boys argued that the price was ridiculously high and that the furniture should be thrown out. The meeting broke up in confusion.

The following morning I discussed the situation with Carlo, Joe, and Dodo. Carlo said:

That was too bad. Mike got excited. He didn't really mean what he said. I know him. I know what he is thinkin' better than himself. He didn't want them names in the constitution. He just wanted them stuck on the wall someplace.

Dodo said that Mike did want the names in the constitution. Carlo replied:

Well, then he was wrong. It would be different to put them on the wall. That would be all right. I was with Mike 100 per cent in the beginning, because when we reorganized it was agreed that this was the same club. That agreement was broken. I can't deny that. But when Mike started talking about the furniture, I had to go against him because he was wrong. He didn't know what he was talking about.

Joe agreed.

Now the members did not know who had a right to remain in the clubrooms. Several evenings later Mr. Baccala, the landlord, was invited in to settle that question. He was plainly confused by the situation and did not want to commit himself, but Mike finally persuaded him to say that he had rented the rooms directly to Mike and that, therefore, Mike was in charge.

The immediate issue seemed to be settled, but still it was not. There were some men who felt that such a question could not be decided without the intervention of a man who had not yet entered the controversy. Chichi told me:

I seen that other party that controls the furniture—Tony Cataldo. I told him the story. He was burned up that we would let one man break up the club. He told me that he would come down some night and straighten things out. It's only one man that's making the trouble. The three of us are willing to leave our furniture in. Now Mike can take out his share if wants to—we'll let him take three or four chairs—and the rest of us will stay in. I think Tony Cataldo will straighten everything out. He told me, "Mike still owes me the $25 I give him for the charter." He's got that on Mike, so if he comes around, Mike wouldn't be able to say nothing. Christ, we got to get going in that club. It's nearly election time, and we ain't had no politicians down. We better get busy.

Following a meeting with Tony, Mike told me that the financial arrangements had been worked out to the satisfaction of himself and the other furniture owners. Carlo told me of an incident which took place the same evening. He had been playing cards when Mike asked him to pay a nickel for the privilege, since the club was under Mike's management. Carlo refused, saying that such rulings could be made only at a special meeting of the club. Finally, he took it upon himself to straighten matters out. He had each of the furniture owners (except Tony, who was not present) state his individual demands before witnesses, and he scheduled a special meeting when he could be present to bring about a final decision.

Dick opened the meeting by calling on Mike to explain his stand. Mike started to say something for himself but then said that Carlo could explain everything better. Chichi and Joe agreed to let Carlo speak for them too.

Carlo stood in the center of the room and took over the meeting. He called Mike one of his best friends but said that he had nearly got into a fight with him on the furniture issue. The main trouble, he said, was that Chichi and Joe the Barber would say one thing when they were with Mike and another thing when somebody else talked to them, and therefore Carlo had made them commit themselves before witnesses. Now Tony Cataldo was willing to do anything for the benefit of the club to which the majority of the furniture owners would agree. That was very nice of him. Mike would get $7.50 in cash, and Tony, Joe, and Chichi would have their share deducted from their dues. This would be a good arrangement for the club. It would not take much out of the treasury, and it would "keep Mike's trap shut."

No one questioned the accuracy of Carlo's statement. Salvy said this was all very well, but the question of the names of the original members had not been settled. Carlo said that the furniture question should be settled first, and then Mike would have no authority. Mike became excited and said that Chichi and Joe had double-crossed him by settling the furniture issue without an agreement on the names. In the course of this argument, Carlo stepped forward to the president's table and placed himself in a position to answer questions and arguments from all sides: Mario asked the president why he permitted Carlo to do all the talking. Dick replied, "Because he is the smartest man here."

Carlo finally brought his furniture agreement to a vote, and it was accepted without opposition. Mike obtained some of the money that he had asked, but in so doing he surrendered to Carlo the leadership of the barbershop clique.

When I saw Tony Cataldo the following morning, he said:

Yeah, I straightened them out. That club was supposed to be going places, but I don't know. I could control the club, but I would rather let the members take care of it. In the beginning there was ten men controlling the club, but then we let the members do what they wanted [when the club was reorganized]. It's all right with me whatever they do.

Carlo also claimed the credit for the final agreement. It is difficult to say which man performed the greater service. They each acted independently but along parallel lines.

4. THE POLITICAL ISSUE

In the fall of 1939 there was a split in the Cleveland Club, and Representative Michael Kelly entered the contest for alderman against Boss Joseph Maloney. Five Italian candidates filed nomination papers, but four of them were persuaded to withdraw in favor of Angelo Fiumara, who in the previous contest had polled more votes than any other candidate opposing Maloney. At last the tables were turned on the Cleveland Club: one Italian was running against two Irishmen.

In Cornerville the field appeared to be divided. Fiumara had the backing of Andy Cotillo, who had built up a strong club, but Cotillo was the only major Italian politician to support him. All the prominent racketeers in Cornerville, with one exception, were with Kelly. Fiumara's most important asset was that he was the only Italian candidate. And, since he was of Sicilian extraction, he was particularly popular in the Shelby Street section.

Early in the fall, before the other Italian candidates had with-

drawn in favor of Fiumara, I heard several Cornerville Social and
Athletic Club members discuss the club's political aims. Carlo
said to me:

It's no use trying to get favors from a politician when he gets in. He'll
promise you anything before, but you can't get no favors from him after, so
forget about the favors. If we had a hundred members to the club and we
could get two dollars each member to support some candidate, that would
be different. We don't care if he wins or loses, so long we get the money.
But we don't spend that money. We put it in the treasury, and we save so
next time we can back up some member from our own club.

The corner boys agreed that, as a general rule, cash in advance
was preferable to favors promised.

The club's political stand was discussed in the first September
meeting, but no action was taken. Politics was then pushed into
the background by the furniture issue.

Finally, eight days before the election, posters advertising "Angelo Fiumara for Alderman" appeared in the windows of the club.
They had been placed there by Mike, who told me that two nights
later there was to be a Fiumara rally in the club. He had himself
secured the politician's promise to make an appearance, and his
special friends had chipped in to buy cases of beer for the occasion. I was told that, while no meeting had been held to indorse
Fiumara, he was "the logical candidate" and that all the boys
were for him.

On the evening of the rally, Mike was all activity. He handled
the beer orders. When Andy Cotillo came into the club to make
final arrangements for the rally, he talked to Mike. Meanwhile
Carlo was talking to Dick to give him courage to conduct the
rally.

Tony Cataldo came in, followed by Bozo, one of his employees.
This was the first time that he had entered the club since summer,
except for the furniture conference. Tony went straight to Mike,
who was standing with Carlo. Dom Romano and Salvy Bellino
joined in the conversation which followed.

TONY: What's goin' on here? I thought you fellows wasn't interested
in politics. If I had known yuz wanted to indorse a man, I could of got yuz
a couple of hundred dollars or a year's rent anyway. Now yuz come out for
Fiumara, and what do yuz get out of it? Why don't yuz do things right?

There are dictators in this club. How can you indorse a man if yuz don't call a meeting and put it to a vote?

CARLO: You're right, Tony. It wasn't done the right way, but now it's done. It's too late to change.

Mike explained that it had got late in the campaign and nothing had been done, so the previous Sunday morning, when a lot of members were in the club, he asked them if it would be all right to go up to Fiumara and promise him the indorsement. The members agreed, so Mike took Dick and a couple of others and drove to Fiumara's headquarters in Mario's car.

TONY: The trouble is, you're tryin' to run this club and you're gonna ruin it.

DOM: Tony, all the boys are for Fiumara. When I go into the booth, I put a cross by the names of all the Wops. Why not give a Wop a chance?

TONY: I don't care who yuz vote for, but why don't yuz get something out of it?

DOM: It's enough for me that the Wop gets in.

TONY: What'll he do for you after he gets in? Listen, I've had experience with politicians, and I know more about politics than all the rest of yuz put together. They promise you some favors, but after they get in, it's goodbye, they shut the door on yuz. So why not get something before they get in? That's the only time. Why take the baloney when you can get the cash?

DOM: Money isn't everything, Tony.

TONY: You can say that because you have your own business. You're makin' a good living. But how about the other members of the club?

DOM: What good is the money going to do us? [Tony smiled and did not answer.]

BOZO: This is the only club in the city that ain't gettin' a quarter to indorse a candidate. Take that club on ——— Street. They're gettin' paid by Fiumara for their indorsement.

SALVY: I don't care what candidate the club indorses. I'm for Fiumara myself, but this was all done the wrong way. What right has Mike got to speak for the club?

DOM: That's right, but nobody protested before.

SALVY: You're a liar. I protested.

DOM: All right, but that's not Tony's point. Tony Cataldo is a Kelly man. Tony wants to run the club. [Tony had been looking about the room. Now he turned his attention to Dom.]

TONY: You know that's not true. Have I ever interfered with this club?

DOM: No.

TONY: I always let the club alone so that yuz could do anything yuz wanted to. But I'm a member myself. I got some right to see that things are done in the right way. I had one politician in the satchel. I know him good. I could have brought him down here and you listen to him, and he'll give us the cash. Yuz don't even have to indorse him or vote for him. I don't believe in indorsing candidates. Suppose your candidate loses, how are you going to get any favors? Don't indorse nobody, but tell all the candidates you're with them. That's what I believe in. Then after you can go up to them and get a favor done. [Tony turned to me to elaborate upon his views.] I didn't have all this experience with politics for nothing. I learned a few things. How many favors can a politician do when he gets in office? He can't do them for everybody. So you might as well get the cash on the line in advance, and you know you're gettin' something. I don't go for this racial politics. I go for the best man, no matter what his race is. I'll pick out the man that I think will do the best for the district. But I won't come out for him openly. It don't pay. I'll tell you privately, I'm for Kelly. He's a smart fellow, and I know him good. I've known him for years. He can really do something for you. [He turned his attention back to the group and continued.] I know who is gonna win this fight. If yuz want to be with the winner, I can put yuz on the right side. If you're with the loser, how can I do anything for you after election?

Tony turned to Carlo and Mike and said that he wanted to bring a candidate in to address the club the following evening.

MIKE: That's our club meeting tomorra night, Tony.

CARLO: It's too late now.

TONY: It ain't too late. The club can keep open house up to the last night. Yuz can listen to all the candidates and yuz don't indorse nobody. . . . . I'll bring him down on my own responsibility, and if yuz don't let him in—all right.

CARLO: Suppose we don't let him in?

TONY: All right, then I'm a heel and you're great guys.

When Andy Cotillo came in again, bringing some of the Fiumara speakers with him, Tony retired to a chair in the corner, lit a cigar, leaned his chair against the wall and waited for the rally to begin. Andy told Mike that Candidate Fiumara would be along soon enough so that the preliminary speakers should begin at once. By this time the room was packed, and there was a crowd outside to listen to the speeches as they were amplified from a sound truck.

Mike told Dick to open the meeting, and Dick stood before the crowd and tried to say something, but the words did not come. He retired and let the first speaker assume the chairmanship. Several speakers, who were more or less prominent in local politics, preceded Candidate Fiumara in addressing the club. The following samples will give an idea of the nature of the appeal:

They say we raise the racial issue. It is they who have made the racial issue, and we have had to fight them in self-defense. They made this issue fifty years ago. They called us an inferior race. They spat in our faces. Now at last we have a change to give them our answer by electing Angelo Fiumara. We must elect Fiumara or lose face forever in our district. . . . .

We here in Cornerville have some young men with intelligence and background equal to any, but still they do not receive a condescending handshake from the political powers. By electing Angelo Fiumara to the Board of Aldermen, we can secure ourselves the honor, dignity, and respect, and—let's be practical—the political patronage that is rightfully ours. . . . .

Now they are going to show you plenty of finifs, sawbucks, and double sawbucks [$5, $10, and $20]. I say to you, don't be chumps. Take their dough. You can use it. But then go in and vote for Fiumara. (*Laughter and cheers.*) If you do that, we will bury and smother the Cleveland Club and elect the first Italian alderman from this ward.

The speeches were received with great enthusiasm.

As the meeting broke up, Carlo told Mike that he had done wrong in taking things into his own hands and that he would throw it up against him in the meeting although he was Mike's best friend. Nevertheless, he thought that the club must stick by Fiumara. He told me that he did not agree with Tony Cataldo and would talk right back to him in the meeting the following evening.

Sharp at eight o'clock the following night, Tony Cataldo appeared in the club. The members were sitting around, playing cards. Tony called out, "Whadda ya say, let's get goin'. Let's get the meeting started."

Dick was not present, so Vice-President Mario took the chair. Dom Romano was also absent.

After Mario had called the meeting to order, Salvy read the minutes of the previous meeting. When he had finished, Tony asked him to read one sentence over again. It was this: "The question of selecting the best candidate with the most chances of winning was discussed, but no action was taken."

Salvy asked, "Do you have some comment to make on it?"

Tony shrugged his shoulders and said: "I don't want to bring it up. If it's all right with the members, I don't want to interfere."

One of the lunchroom boys kept the discussion going: "I want to know what right a few members have to indorse Fiumara and bring him here. What's the story on that?"

Mike said that he would explain, and he told substantially the same story that he had told Tony the previous night.

Tony said: "All right, he done the wrong thing, and he's taking the responsibility for it. The thing is done. That's all."

Salvy spoke hotly to Mike: "Are you a majority of the club? What right do you have to decide what we do?"

Another member said he had heard that Mike had received a letter from Fiumara and that the club knew nothing of it. Salvy said this was true. Carlo explained that the letter, written in Italian, had come to Mike some time ago and that he, Carlo, had read it and translated it to the boys before one of the meetings. Tony said, "That don't count. If it wasn't done in the meeting, it wasn't official."

When Carlo continued, he tried to cut him off. Salvy said that we should stick to things that were done in the meeting. Thereupon Carlo dropped discussion of the letter and said that he agreed that Mike had been completely in the wrong, but now it was too late, and the club would have to accept responsibility for his actions.

Mike became excited and said that the members were just as much to blame. Why didn't they take the Fiumara posters down after he put them up? Tony answered him sharply.

You're 100 per cent wrong, and now you're trying to make the members responsible for what you done. Why should the members take them signs down? They have to wait until a regular meeting to find out why the signs are up, and then they can go through the regular procedure and take them down.

At another time Mike started to defend himself, and Carlo shouted an Italian oath which cut him off. Tony grinned.

Carlo said that nearly all the members were for Fiumara, so the club might as well support him. Tony countered, "I'm not saying you shouldn't vote for Fiumara. You can vote for the man you want to—but Mr. Sekatary, read that sentence again."

Salvy re-read the sentence from the minutes. Tony had him do this four or five times in the course of the meeting. Tony continued:

You fellows are too bullheaded. Did you hear what that says? You should pick out the best candidate. Best means best for your community—the man that will do most for your club. It don't mean that you must pick out an Italian candidate. This is America. We got a new generation here. We're all supposed to be equal. If the best candidate is an Irishman, a German, a Jew, or a Chinaman, you should vote for him. That is the man that is going to do you the most good. And the winning candidate—did youse make some calculation so that yuz knew who was gonna be the winner?

Carlo said that he was with Fiumara, win or lose; that he would rather see Fiumara win and get nothing out of it than get some personal benefit from another candidate. Tony answered:

I see there is gonna be some hard feelings from things I says. I want to make it clear, I didn't say yuz shouldn't vote for Fiumara. Yuz can do whatever yuz want. I'm just bringing out the point that yuz should try to pick out the best candidate and the most likely winner.

A moment later he was on his feet again. He said that the previous spring he had been given to understand that the club was not interested in politics. He called upon Chichi to say if this was not the truth, and Chichi nodded. Mario said that he could explain the change. This was a new club, and the decisions of last spring did not hold. Tony continued:

All right, if yuz are gonna mix in politics, yuz should go about it in the right way. Now I know from experience how they do it in all the clubs in the city. Either they make it a business proposition or else they keep open house for all candidates, and the night before election they take a sceret ballot of the members. Then they go up to the candidate that wins the secret ballot and they let him know they guarantee him so many votes. You just tell him, "We're sorry, we can't indorse anybody because we don't want to make no enemies, but we're guaranteeing you so many votes." Then the candidate knows that he is getting the votes, but you don't make no enemies. In politics you should try to be mutual with all the candidates.

One of the lunchroom boys said this was a good idea. Wouldn't Tony make it a motion? Tony did.

Carlo then moved that the club indorse Fiumara openly. Tony was annoyed. He said, "There is already a motion on this question, and I consider that bringing up a second motion is an insult to the man that made the first motion."

Carlo said that he meant no insult. Two motions could be considered at the same time, and the members could decide which one they preferred. Salvy said that the members could vote on Tony's motion first. Carlo said that the two motions did not conflict because Tony's motion could apply to future procedure while his applied to the present. Mario said that there was no point in deciding on future procedure now because we could always change our policies when the time came. He asked if Tony's motion did not apply to the present. Tony said that it did.

At this point I stood up. Tony said, "Let Bill Whyte say something. He's really an outsider so he can be neutral on this point."

I said that I knew we were nearly all for Fiumara. I was going to vote for him myself. But I saw no harm in listening to what other politicians had to say. The open house seemed a good idea.

Shortly after I spoke, the issue was brought to a vote. Tony won, eleven to seven. He had all the lunchroom boys, with one exception, on his side, and he had split the barbershop clique.

After the vote, Carlo got up and said, "So long, boys, I'm going to the Fiumara rally at the school hall."

One of the barbershop boys went with him. Carlo told me later that he thought he had made a mistake in walking out of the club this way. "I done the wrong thing. It was a personal insult [to Tony]. I realized it when I got outside, but then it was too late."

As the meeting broke up, Tony addressed the members once more:

If any of yuz want to stay around tonight and meet Mike Kelly, I'll bring him down between 9:00 and 9:30. This is the only time he can come down, he told me. I don't care if there is only four or five members here. He knows that this district is 90–95 per cent Fiumara, and he'll be glad to get even a few votes down here. I'm saying this not because I'm for Mike Kelly, but because it will be good for the club to meet the man. At least he'll know who yuz are, and if he gets in, possibly I can get some favors for yuz.

Now Tony went into action. He pulled out a thick roll of bills, passed some of them to Dodo of the barbershop gang, and told him to go out and get five cases of beer. Dodo hurried out on his errand. When one of his employees came in, Tony peeled off more bills with the order that he bring back eight loaves of bread, some ham, and other provisions. Tony turned to Beppo, a member who occasionally attended meetings, and asked him if his sound truck was available. Beppo said that he was working for Candidate Ciampa in Ward 5 and that he was afraid that Ciampa would not pay him if he found out that he was working for somebody else when he should be driving about the streets of Ward 5. Tony said:

"Don't worry about that. I'll take care of you with Ciampa. I can get you some jobs for the sound truck. Will you get it out for a finif [$5.00]?"

Beppo agreed on condition that the truck should be completely covered with Kelly signs, so that it would not be recognized as his. Tony sent one of his followers out for the signs.

When the sound truck arrived, a crowd began to gather. Dick, Chichi, Dodo, Guy, Lefty, Marco, Charlie, and Babe, all members of the barbershop gang, were the only ones who remained to meet Kelly. The others had gone to the Fiumara rally. Tony's employees, his friends, and the general public filled the main room. He commented to me, "See, I told you I could have a crowd here in ten minutes."

The word came that Mike Kelly was on his way, and shortly he arrived, surrounded by a crowd of supporters that accompanied him wherever he went. Sully Defeo had Kelly by the arm and piloted him through the crowd to Tony. Tony introduced him to a number of the club members and guided him to the back room to plan what was to be done. As Kelly stood on the step between the two rooms to make his talk, Marco of the barbershop gang slipped up beside him and shouted, "Attention everybody! Our next alderman, Mike Kelly!" There were cheers. Before Marco had a chance to say anything further, one of the Kelly hangers-on called for three cheers for Kelly. They were given, and then, undaunted, Marco called for three cheers on his own account. When all the cheering was over, Kelly spoke.

I don't want to make a speech here tonight. I just want to thank the president, the officers, and the members of the Cornerville Social and Athletic Club for inviting me down to meet the boys. I appreciate that privilege very much. And I want to say to you from the bottom of my heart that if you would like to give your vote to Mike Kelly on Tuesday next, I would like to have that vote.

That was all. When Kelly went out, Tony Cataldo, Sully Defeo, and their henchmen, and all the Kelly hangers-on went with him. Suddenly the clubroom was almost empty, and the few members who had been present were left to talk over what had happened and to finish the beer. Several others who had been at the Fiumara rally drifted in later.

The discussion which followed illustrated the prevalent conflict in the corner boy's attitude toward the racketeer. Although he had voted with Tony and had gone shopping for him, Dodo commented: "He's a smart fellow, Tony Cataldo. See how he draws the crowd? We won't get nothing out of this. It's all for his benefit."

Salvy said that it was interesting to see how the racketeers "fitted" with candidates. He would rather see "an independent man" win the election, and he was going to vote for Fiumara. Still, he thought that Tony Cataldo had the right idea in holding open house.

Carlo did not return to the club that evening.

On the night before election only sixteen members appeared in the club. Carlo, Mike, and Dom were absent. The meeting began as soon as Tony finished his shave in Joe's barbershop.

Tony addressed the members. He said he had heard that certain men had dropped out of the club because Kelly had been allowed in. Since a majority of the club had voted for an open house, he thought these members were being bad sports not to accept that decision.

Dick announced that the club was to consider indorsing a candidate. Tony moved that no indorsement be made, since too few members were present. He argued that the club would look foolish if it promised a candidate a mere ten or twelve votes. He said:

I'm not thinking of myself. I'm thinking of the interests of the club. I can get a favor from Kelly, and I can get a favor from Maloney. I can go up to Fiumara and get a favor done.

Tony's motion passed without opposition.

Chichi asked who had resigned. Salvy read the names of Mike and two other barbershop boys. Some thought that Carlo had also resigned, but this was denied. Salvy said that, according to the rules on nonpayment of dues, Mike was out whether he wanted to be or not. He added that Mike was a trouble-maker and should be kept out permanently. Tony said:

Mr. Sekatary, I think you're being too severe. You should use a little leniency. After all, the man is my worst enemy, and I don't want to throw him out of the club.

Following this brief meeting, some of us accompanied Tony Cataldo to the Kelly rally at the school hall. As we walked along, Tony said that he would try to get some of the boys jobs as poll workers on election day for five dollars each. If he had known before that they were interested, he might have been able to get as many as seven of them jobs. Now he would do what he could. He added: "This is of no help to me. I can always get a favor done."

While the rally was going on, the boys alternately stood in the back of the auditorium to listen to the speeches and went outside to confer on the election-day job situation. The general opinion was that we had been foolish to let Mike commit us instead of waiting to see what sort of bargain we could make with the candidates.

On election day Guy, Chichi, Babe, Chris, and Dodo of the barbershop gang had five-dollar jobs at the two precinct polling places which were handled for Kelly by Tony Cataldo and Sully Defeo. All day they stood on the sidewalk and passed out "Vote for Kelly" cards. Mike did the same work for Fiumara but said that he was contributing his services. Carlo had to work at his regular job, and I did not see him during the day.

While Dodo wore a Kelly badge and passed out Kelly cards, I heard him telling his friends, "Don't forget. The first name on the ballot." Fiumara's name came first. Dodo told me that he needed the five dollars to pay an instalment on his furniture, and he repeated the advice given by one of the Fiumara speakers: "Don't be chumps. Take their dough."

Guy said to me: "I voted for Kelly. I really think he is the better man. I heard them both speak, and I made up my mind that Kelly was the man."

Mike said to me:

Tony make a bunch of heels out of that club. I not looking for myself.
I don't get-a one penny from Fiumara. After election, any member want to
get favor I gladly take him up and meet-a Fiumara. I'm a-lookin' out for
all the memb's.

I am sure that few of the members voted for Kelly. Tony did
not try to persuade them to do so. His actions won over Guy and
probably several others, but his main concern was to put on a good
show for Kelly. In this he was completely successful. He had
walked into a club that was committed to another candidate, had
prevented the indorsement of that candidate, and had carried the
members as far toward his own candidate as he had attempted to
do. It was an impressive victory.

5. THE CRISIS AND TONY CATALDO

Angelo Fiumara won the election by a comfortable margin of
six hundred votes over Michael Kelly. Joseph Maloney was a
poor third. Fiumara built up an overwhelming lead in Cornerville.

The morning after election, some of the boys were discussing
the results in the barbershop. Members of the Ten Friends, which
had indorsed Fiumara, were well pleased with the situation and
freely expressed their opinions that the Cornerville S. and A. boys
had "made themselves a bunch of heels" by having Kelly in the
club after committing themselves to Fiumara. Carlo was in a
sour mood. He said that many Shelby Street people had blamed
him for what had happened, and he was getting sick of it. He
added:

I know it's against the rules to talk against the club, but I'll say what I
want anyway. Let them fine me. I'll tell them what I think of them, and
then I'll quit the club. I'll tell them they should be ashamed of themselves.

I blame three men for it. And because I am not afraid to tell them, I will
say the names right out. The second man—I won't say he was the first man—
was Tony Cataldo. The first man was our secretary [Salvy]. He brought up
the whole question just out of a personal grudge. And the third man was
Bill Whyte.

I asked what I had done.

You know, Bill, when somebody gets up to speak, I strain my ears to
hear what that man says. I watch and listen, and I don't miss nothing

When you got up, Tony Cataldo says, "There's Bill Whyte, he's neutral, he can tell us something." He made you look good. And then you said you didn't see why we couldn't hear everybody; you was only too pleased to hear them yourself. Now there's a lot of members in that club that respect you and listen to what you got to say, which they think you're a smart fellow. When you said that, you influenced them to vote for Tony Cataldo.

I pleaded guilty to the accusation and made no excuse, whereupon Carlo said that there was nothing personal in his remarks, and Mike agreed that there were no hard feelings. Carlo told me later that some of his friends had been criticizing me sharply, but he had defended me, saying that I had done wrong because I did not realize what was at stake.

Carlo was standing in the back of the shop when Chichi entered. Chichi stood by the door, wearing a sheepish grin. Carlo called him a dirty double-crosser and concluded by saying that he could not think of a word low enough to express his contempt. Then Guy came in and took up his position next to Chichi. Carlo opened fire upon him. "They bought the club out for a glass of beer and five dollars on election day. Where is that five now?"

Guy said that even if the five dollars had lasted only a minute it was still money in the pocket. However, he was distinctly on the defensive. He did not say, as he had to me on election day, that Kelly was the better man.

Carlo said they were all traitors.

The first time you have only one Italian, you have to throw him down. You make a bunch of heels out of the whole club. Now if I go up to Fiumara, I won't tell him I'm a member of the Cornerville S. and A. Why should he do anything for us when we double-crossed him?

For several days Carlo continued to talk along these lines. He told me of his encounter with Spug of the lunchroom clique. Spug had come up to him in the barbershop and said that he had not been present when it was voted to have Kelly admitted to the clubrooms but that he did not see anything wrong in the club's action.

I said to him, "Do you really want to know? All right then, let's step outside." He didn't know why I wanted to get him outside. It was cold out. So we went out and we stood there in front of the barbershop. I didn't say much.

While they stood there, several men not connected with the club came up to Carlo and criticized him for the club's actions. Carlo made no defense. Finally, he said to Spug:

"Let's go inside, it's cold."

Spug says, "Sure, I told you it was cold."

And then I says to him, "Do you see what I mean now? They think we're a bunch of heels for what we done."

He says, "Jesus Christ, Carlo, I didn't look at it that way!"

One evening Carlo cornered Salvy, according to his own story.

We was playing cards, and little by little I was rubbing it in to him. Finally he says, "Why can't you lay off? I know it was a mistake. I done it because I was sore at Mike."

That was just what Carlo wanted to hear. He called Salvy down for allowing personal animosity to sway his judgment.

The effects of the political crisis showed themselves in the club on the evening following the election. I was playing fan-tan with Carlo and Charlie of the barbershop and Dom and Stubby of the lunchroom. By 8:30 we were the only ones remaining in the club. Then Matteo Firrera's son came in and told Carlo that Mike wanted to see him in the Marconi Club. Carlo told us to play without him until he returned. Shortly, Matteo's son came back and called for Charlie. Charlie left after finishing a game. Stubby remarked: "You see how Mike calls his particular friends. For Christ sake, that man should stay out of the club. We would all be better off."

A few minutes later Carlo returned and said: "I'm sorry, boys, but there is a real Fiumara celebration going on in Matteo's that is too good to miss. If you would like to come over, you are all welcome."

Stubby and Dom did not answer. I said I might be over later. We played two more games and then, at Dom's suggestion, we quit and locked up the club. It was not yet nine o'clock.

When I went in to Matteo's Marconi Club, I found Carlo, Mike, Charlie, Dodo, and Marco there as well as the middle-aged men that frequented the establishment. One of the men had contributed a large supply of wine. The boys started opening bottles of beer. Three of Matteo's friends played Italian tunes on the mandolin, guitar, and drums, while Carlo, Charlie, and Matteo led the singing. Carlo took charge of the evening.

Once I saw Carlo talking seriously with Mike and Matteo. Matteo was talking about building up his club and saying that he and Carlo could make something big out of it. Carlo said, "That's right, Matteo, we'll reach an agreement."

After the beer ran out in Matteo's club, Carlo led the crowd into a near-by barroom, which was frequented by the Ten Friends Club. There the celebration continued. Carlo ordered beer for his crowd and for the Ten Friends Club. He called for a toast to the Ten Friends Club. President Tom Reppucci responded with a toast to the Cornerville S. and A. There was a toast to Matteo's club. Charlie and Carlo sang, and we drank until the barroom closed.

When I talked with Carlo two days later, he had decided upon his course of action. He said that if he resigned from the club, a number of other members would do likewise, although he would not tell them to quit, and then the club would break up. "But I don't do things that way."

He intended to continue as an active member. He did not mention Matteo's Marconi Club. The fact that the Marconi members were "greasers" probably was a strong influence in persuading Carlo not to go in with Matteo.

Carlo felt that the Cornerville S. and A. was in serious difficulties. The barbershop boys were going over to Matteo Firrera, and the lunchroom boys were moving toward the Ten Friends Club.

Carlo said that, in order to revive the Cornerville S. and A., he could persuade Dick to resign from the presidency and then get Salvy's friends to force him to resign also. "But I don't want to do that. I don't want to hurt the man's feelings. That would really be an insult to the man."

Carlo proposed to me the appointment of a committee of five which would decide all controversial matters until the election of new officers in February and would also attempt to bring straying members back to the club. In this way bitter arguments in the meetings could be avoided, although the members would have a chance to vote upon the committee's decisions.

I would like to be on that committee, and I would like to have Tony Cataldo on the Committee. I said I don't blame him for what he done. I don't talk behind a man's back. But I want to have a good talk with him, and I'll tell him what I think of him. He is a smart fellow, but when he talks in the club, you have to watch out what he says. I want to make him into a good member of the club.

Carlo asked me to propose this plan and promised to have someone prepared to second it. I said that, since my previous actions had been partly responsible for the present difficulties, I would do what I could to help.

One of the most striking results of the Cornerville S. and A. Club's election difficulties was a change in the relations between Tony Cataldo and Carlo Tedesco. Up to the time that they clashed upon the "open-house" issue, I had not observed a single instance of direct contact between them.

Carlo told me about a conversation he had with Tony one day shortly after the election.

I went right up to him and told him what I thought of him. I'm not the type to talk behind a man's back. I says to Tony, "You may say what you done in the club was for the benefit of the boys, but you and I know it was only for your own selfish interest." He admitted it. He said I was right, and he apologized.

After, he said, "Any time you need a job, come to me, and I'll fix you up a 30–35-dollar-a-week job."

"For what?" I says.

"For your nerve," he says.

You see, the other boys don't talk back to a racketeer. But I'll talk back to him any time I think he's wrong. That night he invited me out to a night club, and he spent $25. It didn't cost me a nickel. Since then he always comes looking for me. One day he says to me, "What's the matter, Carlo, did you break your leg? Why don't you come up to the house some time?"

"Sure," I said, "I'll come."

He's always trying to get on the right side of me so everything he says in the club I'll say the same thing. But I won't do it. I'll go against him any time I think he's going against the boys. I'm just that type.

Some weeks later Carlo told me this story:

You missed some important conversations last night, Bill. Tony Cataldo was in here with some of the boys. Guy, Lefty, Chichi, Dodo, and Chris was here. We was in the back room drinking wine. While we was drinking, we got talkin' about what Tony done in the election. I says to the boys, "After all, we shouldn't blame Tony for what he done because he was in kinda little trouble, and he needed the boys to help him out. The only thing is he should have gone about it in a different way. If he had told the boys why he needed their help, then we would have been only too glad to help out."

Then the boys wanted to know what kind of trouble Tony was in.

"Well," I said, "it don't make no difference now. That's all past and forgotten." But the boys still wanted to know what kind of trouble it was, so I said, "Well, I don't like to say it myself, but why don't you tell the boys, Tony? After all, it's all over now, and there's no hard feelings."

So Tony said, "All right, I'll tell them." And then he told us. That week before election, ten of his men got pinched, and he heard that the next week there was going to be twenty pinches. That's $50 fine for each one. If that happened, he was going to be put right out of business. So he went to Mike Kelly to fix it up, and Kelly went to the D.A., so that the pinches got fixed up, and the cops didn't arrest no twenty the next week. That's why Tony had to be for Kelly. It was for himself, not for the club. When I heard that, I laughed and the boys laughed too, because when I was talking about Tony bein' in trouble, I didn't really know what it was. When Tony found out I got it out of him without me knowing all the time, he got sore, and he called me a God damn dirty double-crosser.

I says, "Tony, how can you call me a double-crosser? I don't talk behind your back. What I got to say, I say right in front of you."

After that, he calmed down, and he says, "I'm gonna buy you a sirloin steak." He took us all out to a place by —— and bought us a steak apiece. Then he took us to a night club in ——, and he must have spent fifteen dollars there.

I says to him, "Tony, if the thing is on the level, I'm with you 100 per cent, but if it's crooked, you can't buy me."

He laughs and he says, "You dirty double-crosser."

I says, "Tony, I ain't no double-crosser. I'm just telling you." He knows I'm not afraid to tell him what I think. If I wasn't in that club, they'd all do what he tells them. . . . . That's why I come every meeting. I never miss. . . . . He would like to buy me out in the worst way. You remember the time I told you he said he would give me $35 a week just on my nerve.

Carlo may have improved upon the stories for my benefit, but subsequent events gave evidence of the same sort of new relations between the two men.

The meeting at which I was to propose Carlo's plan came a week after the election (between the events of the two stories quoted above). When the meeting began, Carlo was not present. Between them Tony Cataldo and Dom Romano settled the routine matters that came up at the start of the meeting. Then Carlo came in. He told me that he still wanted his plan brought up and suggested that I speak when there was an opening.

When Carlo joined in the discussion, the course of action changed. Dom had expressed his ideas and Tony had put them into a motion, which was seconded and passed. Carlo walked over to Tony and talked with him. Thereupon Tony proposed an amendment to his motion. Carlo spoke in favor of the amendment, and it also was passed without opposition.

Dodo made a proposal concerning the sale of beer in the club. Tony persuaded Dodo to accept certain revisions, and then recommended that the plan be accepted. Carlo talked with Tony, and Tony immediately brought up a new proposition. Both Tony and Carlo spoke in favor of it, and it was unanimously accepted.

Before I had a chance to speak, someone asked the president what members were on the buying committee. Dick said that Tony and Guy were the only members at that time, since some who had been on the committee had dropped out of the club. Carlo asked if that committee was only to handle the buying. Dick said that it was. Then Carlo addressed the members:

Mr. President, I got a suggestion. Of course, everybody has the right to make a suggestion, and you might not like mine, but this is what I think. Why can't we extend that committee to take up other questions that are coming out in the club?

He went on to say that some members were dropping out and that he did not think we could afford to lose members. He thought a committee should be chosen to take care of such things and to argue out all questions concernin' the welfare of the club. This committee should consist of reasonable men that can argue always for the club and not get personal. I won't say I consider myself reasonable, but I would like to be on that committee. And I would like to see Tony Cataldo on the committee. You could have five members.

Tony got up immediately.

I think that was covered last meeting when I suggested we have someone investigate these members that are dropping out. It would be better to have five. After all, we don't want to have only fifty members. I would like to see this club with two hundred members. We can't have that if the members keep dropping out.

Salvy nodded. "That's right, we should have sort of a board of mediation to settle the arguments."

I spoke briefly in favor of the plan, and then Tony moved that the president choose the committee of five. The motion carried unanimously. Dick looked around and chose Spug, me, and Salvy —whereupon Tony said, "Mr. President, I object; I don't want no officers on that committee." Salvy nodded. Dick chose Tony and Carlo and then paused before picking the fifth man. Someone suggested Rossi, and Dick made that selection. Rossi was one of Cornerville's few Communists. He had much to say in meetings, but the boys did not take him seriously, and he fitted with neither clique.

One of the lunchroom boys said that it should be understood that this committee was not going to bring back into the club any of those members who were already out. Salvy seconded him in this. Carlo said:

You don't understand. There is nobody out of the club. According to the constitution, if you are behind four weeks in dues, you are out, but there is supposed to be consideration of your case first. Up to now, we had no committee to consider the cases of these members so how can they be out?

Salvy argued against Carlo. Carlo took a postal card from his pocket and placed it before Salvy. It was the card that Salvy had sent to him a month earlier, informing him that he was four weeks behind in his dues and that he would be expelled if he did not pay before the next week. Carlo had been irate over this. He had claimed that Salvy had no right to send him the card without "consideration" and that it was especially bad to send a postal card, which might be read by anyone who happened to look into his mailbox.

Salvy looked at the card and asked, "Well, what about it?"

Carlo repeated his arguments. Salvy had nothing further to say. Tony agreed with Carlo: "Why should we try to get rid of members? I think we have 90 per cent good members in here. That other 10 per cent will be outvoted and outtalked all the time."

With these remarks, the subject was dropped. After the meeting was adjourned, Tony bought sandwiches and beer for the boys.

A week later the regular club meeting was held. Carlo was out of town. Without him the committee of five did not meet.

Dom had begun to attend meetings more regularly, and, in the absence of Tony and Carlo, he took over the leadership of this meeting. It was announced that Mike and several other former members wanted to rejoin the club. Salvy argued that their names should first be presented to the committee. Some supported and others opposed him, until Dom closed the argument with these remarks:

This is the way they do it in other clubs. If they hear that a former member wants to come back in, they vote on him first. If they vote for him, then they go around and invite him in. There is no sense in referring this to the committee first. Suppose they should ask the man to come in, and then the club should vote him down? We should vote first if we want the man or not.

He made this a motion, and it was passed with little opposition. After Mike and the other applicants had been passed upon, Dom announced that it was up to the committee to determine the terms of their readmission.

When Carlo returned, he called Spug and me into the club for a committee meeting. He said that Tony Cataldo would be unable to confer with us.

I seen Tony, and he says to me he ain't got the time or the patience for this. He says, "Carlo, anything you decide is all right with me." Of course, he realizes I am 100 per cent for the club.

Carlo called upon Salvy for information upon the previous meeting and then, with Spug and me, went over a list of thirteen men, including Mike, who had allowed their memberships to lapse and were from seven to twelve weeks behind in dues. He proposed that the committee's policy should be lenient so as to increase the membership and suggested that all be readmitted upon payment of the fifty-cent initiation fee and fifteen cents for a week's dues. At first, Spug felt that the members would never agree to such leniency, but finally he said that they would if Carlo put it to them as he had to us.

Two days before Thanksgiving the club raffled off a turkey, a bottle of whisky, and a case of spaghetti. Each man who had belonged to the club when the raffle was planned early in the fall was obliged to sell a book of ten tickets at ten cents each. While the club made a profit on the books sold, the raffle gave rise to dissension, which came out in the first December meeting.

Carlo, Rossi, and I were the only committee members present at this meeting. Spug and Tony Cataldo were absent. So was Dom Romano.

Before the meeting Carlo acquainted Rossi with the committee's decision, and Rossi expressed his agreement. When the president called for a committee report, Carlo read the names of the former members, gave his arguments for leniency, and made the committee's proposal. Rossi said that he had just been talking to Tony Cataldo in the barbershop and Tony had suggested the same terms. Salvy said that the plan might be all right for some of the former members but not for those who had been supposed to sell raffle books and had failed to do so. Mike had been "the instigator" of the raffle, and then he had not sold his quota.

This prompted Rossi to shift his ground. After last meeting, he said, he had told Mike, "The boys want you back in the club."

Mike had replied, "Who are you?"

When Carlo objected that he was getting personal, Rossi continued, "I don't want to contradict the committee. We did agree on the fifty cents, but we didn't vote on the raffle question, because we were not supposed to take it up."

Carlo shook his head and said to me, "When I heard that Rossi was on the committee, I says, 'We're licked.' He argues first on one side and then on the other."

In spite of Carlo's efforts, the club voted that Mike be required to pay for his raffle book as well as the initiation fee and dues. Carlo commented to me that this decision was better than nothing because, while Mike would not accept such terms, the club was sure to gain back the other former members.

In subsequent weeks the membership did increase, and the club ran more smoothly. It was evident that the Cornerville S. and A. had weathered its crisis, even though the committee had not been able to put all its recommendations into effect.

6. TONY'S BEANO PARTY

Tony Cataldo and Sully Defeo were running a weekly Beano game in a suburban town. Every Saturday night they ran busses from Cornerville to the Beano establishment, but until the middle of December the boys of the Cornerville S. and A. had not attended any of the games.

One night Carlo, Salvy, and several others were at the bowling alleys when Tony joined them. After they finished bowling, Tony went with Carlo into the Marconi Club, where they joined Mike and Matteo, drank wine, and ate sandwiches and hot peppers. Tony invited Carlo, Mike, and one or two others to come with him to visit some friends in another part of the city. Carlo agreed to go. He had not been in the house long before he felt faint and sick at his stomach. Tony immediately took leave of his friends, put Carlo and the boys in his car, and spent the time from 12:30 to 2:30 A.M. driving and walking Carlo in the fresh air. Carlo commented to me upon this.

Do you think he minded it? No, he was tickled to death that he could do something for Carlo. And the next morning he came into the club looking for me, and if I didn't come down then, he was coming up to the house with the boys to see how I was and to bring me a bottle of whisky. . . . . When he seen I was all right, he says to me, "Carlo, you got to help me, I got to get rid of five hundred tickets to the Christmas Beano by Saturday night." Then I knew why he was so glad to do something for me the night before, but, never mind why, I knew if I done something for him, I could approach him next time. The boys were all in the club. It was Sunday. I says to Tony, "Sure, I'll go to the Beano. You know Carlo—anywhere there's a good time." So I took a pile of tickets and passed them out to the boys. I seen some dirty looks, but I says, "We'll make it a big time for the club. We'll have a banner advertising the Cornerville S. and A. Club on the bus, and we'll get some publicity out of it." Tony says that's all right with him. Then I seen Salvy looking at the ticket and grumbling.

He says, "What the hell is this?"

Tony started to explain to him, but I interrupted him. I says, "Tony, leave it to me. When you want something in this club, see me. Now Salvy and me, we always argue in the club, but outside the meetings, he's one of my best friends. I know he'll be the first man to pay the dollar because he's a reasonable man and a real sport." That made Salvy feel good and he paid right away.

The Callahan brothers [new members, the only Irishmen in the club] come up to me afterward and they says, "Why the hell did you do this? We have to work a year to make a dollar." I explained to them that we would have a good time, and they might win some of the prizes.

Then Tom Reppucci come in, and I gave him five tickets. He hesitated a little, but he took them. I told him that we would have a bus for the Ten Friends Club with a banner on the side. I can always get Tom to take a few raffle books or tickets and pass them out in his club. He can say to the boys, "Carlo has always been all right with us, so let's help him out on this." You see, I installed their oil burner for them in the club, and I fix it whenever anything goes wrong. I never take no money for it. They want to pay me a dollar or two, but I say, "Forget it."

I must have made Tony sell sixty tickets just that day. He wanted me to go along with him to another club, but I refused. He wanted to know how I got rid of all the tickets. He says, "I noticed a few dirty looks in there, how about that?"

I says, "All right, leave it to me; they'll kick to me, and I'll get out of it. You're only interested in selling the tickets, ain't you? Well, all right."

I asked Carlo why he had done this for Tony. He explained that I had some part in it. When I was asked by the Community Chest organization to recommend local Cornerville people capable of canvassing the district, I spoke to Carlo about handling the Shelby Street section. He agreed to do so. Now he told me:

Ever since you told me about this Community Chest, I've had it in the back of my head. Tony Cataldo knows all the clubs around here. When the time comes, I can get him to speak for it in all the clubs. The old-timers, they think a racketeer is a professor. They think that a man just out of jail graduated from Ivy College. When I go up to them, they say, "Hi, Carlo," but when he goes up to them, they say, "Hello, Mr. Cataldo." In order to raise money for this, you got to go along the way things are around here.

You can't be too honest or people won't respect you. You got to use a little trickery. You got to go along like a boat, a little to one side and a little to the other side. But then in the end you can come out and show them you was on the level all the way through—that it was for the best of them all that you done it.

The busses for the Beano party were scheduled to leave at 7:30 on Saturday, but they did not appear on time. As eight o'clock approached, Tom Reppucci came into the club to consult Carlo about the busses. Carlo went out several times to see Tony Cataldo. Tony told him that he had ordered three busses. One had already departed, the second had an accident in coming out of the garage, and the third had been sent to a near-by city by mistake.

Tony came into the club at 8:30 to talk the situation over with Carlo. He was trying to get transportation, he said, but even if he should arrange it in the next few minutes it was so late that the boys would miss a large part of the evening. If anyone wanted his money back or a ticket for the next Beano, he could have it. Carlo explained the situation to the boys and then said to Tony that he thought it would be better if we went another time. Tony agreed. He said that Carlo could collect the tickets later and that, when they were turned into him, he would exchange them or return the money.

At the following meeting Tony apologized to the members for the difficulty with the busses. He again offered to refund money on all tickets. One of the men had torn up his ticket, but Carlo spoke to Tony for him, and Tony gave him the money anyway.

While the Beano party of the Cornerville S. and A. did not take place, Carlo performed an important service for Tony in persuading the members to buy the tickets and in handling all the club arrangements. A little over a month later the Community Chest drive began. Carlo told me beforehand that Tony had agreed to do something for him, although he said that it was a difficult job. When the drive was past, I asked Carlo about Tony's activities. He said he had asked Tony for a contribution and that Tony had said he was sorry but he had given five dollars to his brother-in-law, who was also soliciting. Carlo did not say whether Tony had talked to any clubs for him—which means, of course, that Tony did not. Carlo seemed reluctant to talk about his relations with Tony in this connection.

7. THE NEW ADMINISTRATION

Toward the end of November, Tony Cataldo's cousin and three of his employees joined the club. Tony paid their initiation fees and weekly dues. A number of others had joined. While the new men increased the membership to fifty-five, the old members continued to be the most active, and, as the February election of officers approached, the contest between cliques continued.

Tony did not attend the election meeting, and only one of his employees was there. Dick now had a job which kept him busy at night, so Vice-President Mario took the chair.

When Mario called for the election of a president, one of the lunchroom boys nominated Dom Romano, and one of the barber-shop boys nominated Carlo Tedesco. The first vote resulted in a fourteen-to-fourteen tie, with one ballot being marked "neutral." Mario was undecided as to his course of action. Some said that he should cast the deciding ballot; while others called for a second vote. Mario decided to have the vote taken again, and again it was fourteen to fourteen. He then cast his deciding vote for Dom.

There was no real contest for the other offices. Carlo, Salvy, Chichi, and Joe were elected vice-president, secretary, assistant secretary, and treasurer, respectively.

The presidential election was nothing but a count of the voting strength of the two cliques. Carlo later commented to me:

Dom is a good boy. He should be all right. The only reason I wanted to win was to break up that clique. A big clique like that sticking together is bad for the club. No, there's only a few fellows I can really count on—Dodo, Guy, Chichi, Lefty, and Joe the Barber. Yes, Marco would back me up too. I couldn't count on Chris. He just goes for the right point. I only had a few with me, and they had a big clique, but still it was a tie.

Dom said to me:

You know, that office was thrown at me. I didn't want to be president, but Salvy says to me, "We want to make you president to break up that clique."

The accompanying chart presents a picture of the informal or-ganization of the club at the time of the election. We find Carlo definitely in control of the barbershop gang but still unable to con-trol the lunchroom boys.

To Carlo, defeat in the presidential election proved only a tem-porary setback. Within a short time he was in a stronger position than ever before. In the first meeting following the election, he proposed that a recently elected "general purposes committee" of Chris and Ted (a new member) be expanded to include Gus and me. We were elected without opposition.

Several years earlier Gus had been president of a small club whose membership had included Chris and Babe. By the time

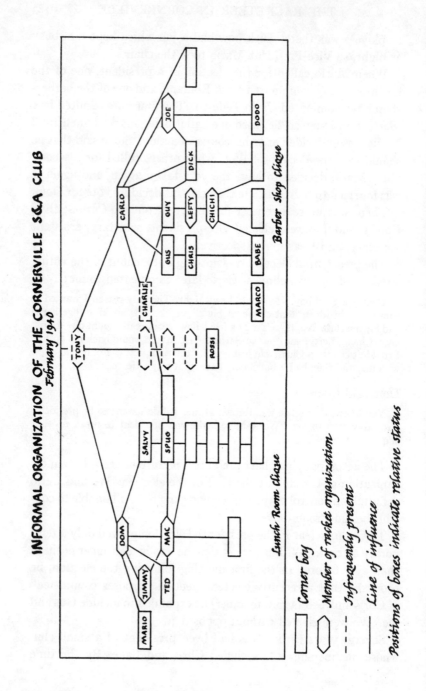

INFORMAL ORGANIZATION OF THE CORNERVILLE S&A CLUB
February 1940

☐ Corner boy

◇ Member of racket organization

- - - Infrequently present

—— Line of influence

Positions of boxes indicate relative status

Lunch Room Clique

Barber Shop Clique

that the Cornerville S. and A. was organized, Chris and Babe had definitely aligned themselves with the barbershop gang, but Gus remained uncommitted. He sided vigorously with the lunchroom boys on the janitorial issue and dropped out of the club when this vote went against him. Carlo had persuaded him to rejoin following the political controversy.

Having proposed Gus for the committee, Carlo subsequently conferred with him on various plans for the club, and Gus definitely aligned himself with Carlo. I had little time for committee or club meetings, and I told Carlo that whatever he decided was all right with me. Since Chris was a follower of Gus and since Ted had little interest in the committee, the reorganization placed Carlo in a position to determine what that body should do, although he was not a committee member at this time.

In the April meeting Carlo proposed that the committee be given greatly increased powers, so that it might make expenditures on behalf of the club without prior authorization and accept new members provisionally until they were voted upon in a meeting. This provoked a heated discussion. Carlo argued that there were many developments which could not wait upon a monthly meeting: sometimes a man applied for membership but lost interest when he found that he could not be admitted for several weeks; and sometimes the club had a chance to buy useful things only if it acted quickly. He said that the committee would always be careful to sound out the sentiment of the members before making a purchase or accepting a new member and that its actions would be subject to review at every club meeting. Finally, his arguments prevailed, and, at the same time, he was voted onto the committee. Carlo told me afterward that he tried to decline the election but the members thought that, since he had asked for the new powers and no one else knew what they were for, he should be put in a position to use them. He agreed to serve for one month.

Carlo's first move on the committee was to buy a set of balls for the Italian game of Bocce, an outdoor bowling game. From the time of their purchase the balls were in use in the late afternoon and early evening nearly every day. Nonmembers joined with members in playing, and, since the game was always played for beer sold by the club, it provided a means of enriching the treasury. Before purchase of the Bocce set, revenues from beer sales had been little more than enough to pay the costs of keeping the beverage on ice. In the first month of Bocce playing the net profits on beer amounted to over nineteen dollars.

The committee's next move was to arrange the first annual outing of the Cornerville S. and A. Club. After consulting with some of the members who had previous experience in outings, Carlo made all the arrangements, and it proved a social and financial success.

Carlo undertook to see what he could do about getting the club a charter. In the June meeting he reported that he had persuaded former Representative Art Porcella to obtain the charter for a charge of only twenty-five dollars—the fee required by the state. He said:

> You'll want to know what I had to promise him. Nothing! I just said, "If you're running for any office, or if you're interested in any candidate, we'll be glad to let you come in our club and talk to the boys. If you can convince them, good luck to you."

Carlo also reported that he had received a contribution of five dollars toward the charter from State Senator George Ravello. While this effort to get the charter subsequently fell through, Carlo gave the impression that he was accomplishing things for the club.

The proceedings of the last meeting I attended provided ample evidence of the change in Carlo's position. The agenda of the meeting included reports on the buying of the Bocce set, the charter, the outing, and the admission of new members. President Dom Romano called on Carlo to speak for the committee on all these subjects. Since there was little else to be considered, Carlo was on his feet reporting or answering questions most of the time. There was no serious opposition to any of his reports. Occasionally, one of the boys made a half-serious gibe at Carlo, but always he was ably defended. It was interesting to observe from which quarters the defense came. Once Salvy spoke in his favor, and several times Dom supported him. The most direct challenge came from Mike, who had recently been readmitted to the club.

Carlo and Mike were no longer friends, and when Mike had expressed a desire to rejoin, Carlo had presented his name to the meeting without comment. Mike claimed that Carlo had promised to resign from the committee position after serving for a month but had refused to do so and was now trying to run the club. Carlo did not defend himself. Dom said that, while he continued to do such a good job, he could hold that position as long as he wished.

In the course of the spring and early summer the gap between the barbershop and the lunchroom had narrowed, the Cornerville Social and Athletic Club had become a closer-knit and more smoothly functioning organization, and Carlo, having had a prominent part in these developments, had taken control. No longer was he simply the leader of one clique; he had become the head man in the club—if we do not count Tony Cataldo. In the meantime Tony had made few appearances in the club, but he had been active behind the scenes. In the course of the spring his partner, Sully Defeo, and four more of his employees were admitted to membership. Counting only members of their organization, Tony and Sully had unchallenged control over a bloc of ten votes. Few of these men attended meetings, but their dues were paid regularly so that they could be present to vote at any time.

I asked Carlo why he did not take action to keep Tony's employees out of the club. He said that he knew what was going on and that he would find a way of meeting the situation. From the beginning it had been the aim of the boys to bring in as many members as possible in order to enrich the treasury and to improve the club's political position. Even one who had made himself as unpopular as Mike was voted in on two occasions. Under these circumstances Carlo could not suddenly draw the line against Tony's friends.

In the June meeting the names of ten prospective members were brought up. Seven of these had already been provisionally accepted by the committee. Carlo said to me that they were all good friends of his and added, "I'm getting my own gang in here." The increased strength of Carlo's position is indicated in the accompanying simplified chart.

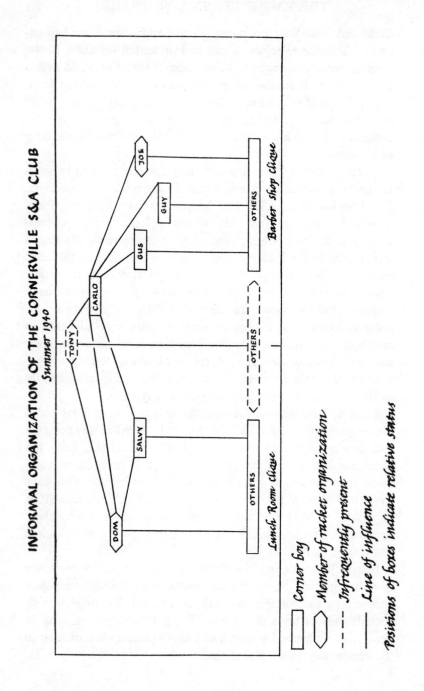

INFORMAL ORGANIZATION OF THE CORNERVILLE S&A CLUB
Summer 1940

JOE

GUY

GUS

CARLO

TONY

DOM

SALVY

OTHERS

OTHERS

OTHERS

Barber shop Clique

Lunch Room Clique

☐ Corner boy

⬦ Member of racket organization

⟨⟩ Infrequently present

--- Line of influence

—— Line of influence

Positions of boxes indicate relative status

I left Cornerville in July, 1940, but when I returned in May, 1941, for a visit the stories I heard indicated that the trend toward unification in the club and toward increasing power for Carlo had continued. In the fall of 1940, Carlo and Tony were once again at odds over the indorsement of candidates for political office. This time Carlo had both cliques behind him, and he did not have to argue alone against Tony. Spug said to Tony's face, "We don't want to go for the racketeer."

Tony had his following, but the indorsement went decisively against him. Carlo commented to me, "The boys seen that they didn't get nothing out of the last election."

In the February election of 1941 Carlo became president of the club and Salvy became vice-president. Shortly after this Salvy was drafted and appeared in Cornerville only occasionally. Even if he had continued to be active in the club, it is unlikely that he would have opposed Carlo's leadership, for the relations between the two men had changed. When I looked for Salvy and Carlo on my visit to Cornerville, I was told that Salvy was spending Sunday morning at Carlo's house. When I saw Carlo later, I asked if he and Salvy still had disagreements. He said: "We understand each other now. Of course, we have fights, but that's just for old time's sake." Spug, who had also become a close friend of Carlo, corroborated this story.

Tony Cataldo was still the biggest man on Shelby Street, but the Cornerville S. and A. had become Carlo Tedesco's club.

8. CARLO AND TONY

The detailed history of the Cornerville Social and Athletic Club indicates that events in the club are to be explained in terms of the rise of Carlo Tedesco and the ups and downs in the power of Tony Cataldo. A review of these developments will place the events in a clearer perspective.

Carlo lost out to Mike in the founding of the club, but, when the boys became dissatisfied with Mike's leadership and his power began to decline, Carlo took the lead in reorganizing the club. He forced Joe and Chichi to desert Mike in the furniture controversy and acted so effectively that he was able to speak for them and for Mike too.

In committing the club to Fiumara without a formal vote of indorsement, Mike took action which was indefensible from a constitutional standpoint. The lunchroom boys felt that he was simply looking after his own interests. While he insisted that he would get nothing out of the commitment and would intercede for them with Fiumara, this would have meant subordinating themselves to Mike, which none of them was prepared to do.

Although he had little time to spend in the club, Tony had maintained his position by occasional visits and by financial favors. When he was called in to settle the furniture controversy, his position was strengthened. He seized the initiative from Mike in the political issue and shrewdly exploited the divisions within the club. By taking the attitude that he was prepared to accept what had been done, so long as Mike acknowledged his mistake, he provided the lunchroom boys with ammunition to use in an attack upon Mike. Tony was not content simply with persuading the boys to accept his views. He wanted to obligate them to him by convincing them that he was doing them a favor in introducing them to Kelly and in getting them jobs at the polls.

The political issue, capped by Fiumara's election, nearly shattered the club. Many members wondered whether it was worth while to try to continue. Carlo decided that it was and took action to have the committee of five chosen. While the committee did not succeed in having most of its policies accepted, it would be a mistake to conclude, therefore, that it was of small significance. The club's equivocal election stand was recognized as a great mistake. Nothing could be done to wipe out that mistake, and yet everyone felt that something must be done. If the members had simply waited for another great issue to arise, the club would have died in the meantime. The main necessity was that there be activity—lots of activity—in the club. The policy finally adopted was not so important as the activity which went along with the adoption of a policy. This gave the boys the impression that their club, after all, was still functioning. In the midst of this activity the crisis simply passed away.

Carlo had been defeated by Tony, but Fiumara's election had increased his prestige at Tony's expense. He took advantage of this situation to improve his position. At every opportunity he showed the members of the lunchroom clique that he had been right and they had been wrong. By these tactics he undermined Salvy's position. He carried his attack to Tony and received recognition of his leading position among the boys. The committee of five served as an important vehicle for Carlo. It provided authorized channels through which he could carry on his activity and initiate action for the members.

Tony's reaction to this situation is revealing. When Carlo charged him with sacrificing the club's interests and tricked him into explaining why he had supported Kelly, Tony responded each time by spending money on Carlo and his friends. For Tony, this was characteristic. Whenever he was opposed, he attempted to act in such a manner as to place his opponents under obligations to him.

It was in the midst of the political controversy that Tony recognized Carlo as the key man in the club. By then it was too late to win him over on the election issue, but, when Fiumara's victory magnified Carlo's importance, it was all the more necessary for Tony to make terms with him. From election day on, Tony dealt with the club through Carlo, decided on club policy with Carlo, acted according to Carlo's suggestions in meetings, and exerted himself socially and financially in Carlo's behalf.

Tony could not have maintained his position through occasional personal appearances. After suffering the effects of taking his advice, the boys, if left to themselves, might have found that they could get along without him. By plunging actively into club affairs, Tony gave them no opportunity to make such a discovery. For six weeks following the election, he had a part in every discussion and in every plan for club action. He was so successful in re-establishing his position that, through Carlo, he was able to arrange a large club excursion to his Beano game. Then, after having some of his employees voted into the club, Tony turned his attention to other matters.

Not having access to Tony's mind, I cannot say to what extent his actions were based upon calculations of personal obligations and to what extent they were unplanned responses to the given situation. No doubt both factors were present in varying degrees, but it is not important to determine Tony's motives. It is sufficient to observe that he customarily acted in a manner which tended to obligate the corner boys to him, and, when these obligations broke down, he acted in the same manner but with greater frequency, thus tending to re-establish the obligations.

When the election of officers approached, Salvy found his own position so insecure that he had no chance for the presidency, and he persuaded Dom to be the candidate of the lunchroom clique. Dom had been taking an increasingly active part in club affairs, and he was popular with the boys. He was intelligent and rather independent in his thoughts and actions, although he could not afford to go too far in antagonizing Tony Cataldo. While his nomination was engineered by Salvy, the history prior to the election indicates that Dom did not take orders from Salvy. Under these circumstances one might have expected Dom to take the leadership away from Carlo. Instead, Carlo continued to initiate action for the members, and with greater and greater frequency. As his actions brought the desired results, each successive initiation strengthened his position until his dominance over both cliques became firmly established.

Since the story of the Cornerville S. and A. has two leading characters, it is natural to compare them with each other. Carlo and Tony had two different sorts of power. Carlo was a corner boy who spent all his time with the corner boys. He was constantly in a position to initiate action for his friends. The activities which gave Tony his superior position in Cornerville made it impossible for him to spend much time with any one group of corner boys. He made frequent appearances in the club only when developments there affected his interests. When both Tony and Carlo were active in the club after the election of Fiumara, it would have been impossible to tell which man held the superior position in Cornerville simply by observing their actions. Tony initiated action for Carlo, but just as frequently Carlo initiated action for Tony. However, when Carlo tried to get Tony to act in the Community Fund drive, he was unsuccessful. In club affairs Carlo could initiate action for Tony; outside the club he was not able to do so. Carlo initiated action in a small sphere of Tony's activities. Tony initiated action in the main area of Carlo's activities. Outside the club Tony initiated action for a large number of men upon whom Carlo could not act, and Tony had "connections" with people in superior positions who were out of Carlo's reach.

When the Cornerville S. and A. was divided, Tony could play upon factional rivalries and upon the obligations owed him by individual members in order to lead the club. When the club was unified under Carlo, Tony could get his way only by dealing personally with Carlo. This he did quite successfully when he was spending time in the club, but when he was busy elsewhere, he could not be sure of Carlo's support. Carlo took care to maintain his independence. He once said to me:

> You go up to Tony and ask him for a couple of bucks, and he's only too glad to give it to you. But he'll expect two hundred back from you, not in money but in favors. He won't care if you give him the deuce back or not. He'll take it if you give it to him, but he don't care. That's the way he buys people..... When Mike is broke, he goes up and borrows from Tony. The same way with a lot of the boys. But I won't do that. Never! And I don't care how bad I need the money, I'll get it from somebody else, not from him. He would be only too glad to give it to me, but I wouldn't give him the chance.

Tony had connections but lacked intimacy with the boys. Furthermore, his business required him to try to persuade them to adopt policies from which they had nothing to gain. Carlo had the intimate corner-boy contacts but lacked important political connections. He realized the limitations of his position but was unwilling to let Tony dominate the club. He said to me:

> Suppose Tony was the boss of that club. Around election time he could go up to Mike Kelly and say, "Mike, there's seventy-five members in my club, that's two-three hundred votes. Now I got ten boys pinched for selling numbers, that's fifty dollars fine each. Can you fix it up?" So Mike Kelly fixes it up. And after, one of the boys in the club goes up to Kelly for a favor, and he gets a big smile, and Kelly tells him, "Why didn't you come up sooner, I just took care of ten of the boys. I'm sorry I can't do nothing for you right now." Then Kelly goes up to Tony and says, "Tony, don't let them boys come up to me. I just took care of ten for you. I can't do everything." That's what would happen. Tony gets the protection for his business, and we don't get nothing.

CHAPTER VI

POLITICS AND THE SOCIAL STRUCTURE

1. THE CHANGING NATURE OF POLITICAL ORGANIZATION

WHEN Boss Joseph Maloney lost his campaign for alderman in 1939, his Cleveland Club lost its last hold upon Cornerville, the South Side, and Welport. The power of the organization had been wasting away for years, and, when the final collapse came, there was nothing that Maloney could do except look back upon the happier days from the 1890's through the 1920's, when the Cleveland Club, under its founder, Matt Kelliher, had dominated Ward 4. He told me the story of the club in this way:

We had a captain in every precinct. He was a man who knew everybody in his precinct and could tell how just about all of them would vote. We had quite a variety of precincts. Over beyond ———— Street was a pretty high-class precinct. You had to have an educated man in charge there. Then we had another precinct where most of the freight handlers lived. That was a different kind of job.

When people wanted help from the organization, they would come right up here to the office [of the club]. Matt would be in here every morning from nine to eleven, and if you couldn't see him then, you could find him in the ward almost any other time. If a man came in to ask Matt for a job, Matt would listen to him and then tell him he'd see what he could do; he should come back in a couple of days. That would give Matt time to get in touch with the precinct captain and find out all about the man. If he didn't vote in the last election, he was out. Matt wouldn't do anything for him—that is, unless he could show that he was so sick he couldn't get to the polls. When Matt heard what kind of a fellow the man was, he could make up his mind about trying to do something for him.

When a man got a job through our influence, he would keep on paying his dues, and around election time we would expect him to make some kind of contribution to support the campaign. We never accepted money to indorse any candidate. In that way we kept our independence. . . . . When I first ran for representative—I didn't want to run; I was selected by the organization—I contributed $150 toward the expenses, and the organization paid the rest.

In those days we held political office in order to be of service to the people. Of course, if Kelliher thought the city was going to buy a certain piece of property, and he had a chance to get it first, all well and good. He was in the real estate business, and there was a lot of money in that business when the city was expanding. But, with him, service to the people always came first. He never took a cent for the favors he was able to do. Matt and I never sold our jobs or charged for a favor.

In those days we really controlled. We could tell within fifty votes how the ward would go in any election. One time we changed the ward from Democratic to Republican overnight. That was in the mayoralty contest of 1905. There was a meeting in the club till three in the morning right before the election. We printed the slate we were backing and circulated it around as much as we had time for. When the people came to the polls, the captain would ask them, "Do you have the slate?" If they didn't, he would give it to them, and they would go in and vote it. When the votes were counted, we had carried the ward for the Republicans just like we carried it for the Democrats. One time a fellow says to Matt, "I'm not going to vote the ticket this time." There were thirteen votes against us in his precinct, and Matt would have given anything to know who the other twelve were.

Maloney explained the breakdown of the organization in terms of the shifting population, the New Deal, and the rise of "the racket element":

Today everything has changed. We've got a floating population in the South Side now. People are moving out all the time. You can't expect a precinct captain to know everybody any more. It's only in Cornerville that people stay in the same place.

Then the Italians will always vote for one of their own. We recognized them when we didn't need to. They didn't have many votes, and we could have licked them every time, but we gave them Italian representatives. We did it for the sake of the organization. But they wouldn't stick by us. The Italian people are very undependable. You can't trust them at all. They play a dirty game too. I estimate that now there are between eight hundred and a thousand repeaters in Cornerville every election. I've tried to stop that, but you can't do it. You can't tell one Italian from another.

In speaking of the disloyalty of the Italians, Maloney referred actually to a conflict of loyalties. From the time that the Italian immigrants got into street fights with their Irish predecessors, there was bitter feeling between the races. Since the Irish controlled the ward politically, the Italians, as long as they were in the minority, had to follow the Cleveland Club in order to gain any political benefits. In recent years Italians who had the political support of the club were looked upon by Cornerville people as disloyal—traitors to the cause of Italian unity. As the proportion of Italian votes in the ward grew steadily, it was to be expected that the Italians would break away from the Cleveland Club.

To Maloney's charge about "repeating" in Cornerville, which is exaggerated but not otherwise untrue, Cornerville people reply with charges that the Cleveland Club would have fallen years earlier if it had permitted honest elections. My own observations and the unanimous testimony of Cornerville people indicate that the club used repeaters whenever needed. Maloney freely admitted that many of his voters lived outside the ward. "A man has a constitutional right to choose his own domicile. As long as he isn't registered in two places, it's all right." He continued his story:

In the old days it was different. The New Deal has changed politics altogether. With home relief and the W.P.A., the politician isn't needed any more in a district like this. Years ago a man out of work would come to us to see what we could do for him. Now he goes on home relief and then he can get on the W.P.A. That's all he wants. This relief is a terrible racket.

I asked whether a man did not need political backing to get on the W.P.A., and Maloney said it could be accomplished without such aid. I took this question up with Carrie Ravello, the wife of the state senator, and she gave me this answer:

That's right. If you're qualified, you can get on without going to a politician. But it will be four weeks before you get certified, and I can push things through so that you get on in a week. And I can see that you get a better job—if you're qualified. If you want to be a supervisor on a contracting job, I can't tell them, "Make Billy Whyte a supervisor," because you're not qualified for that job. You don't have the experience. I can only do something for you if you're qualified.

The corner boys corroborated some of these statements but added that many unqualified men with strong political backing had been able to get good W.P.A. jobs.

There were many politicians in Eastern City. The important question is: Whose political support was important in dealing with the W.P.A.? I asked Mrs. Ravello how she was able to help her constituents in this field. She explained:

I know Dave Collins. He is the state administrator, head of all the projects in the state. I can go right into his office. He knows my connections with [United States] Senator Corcoran.

I asked how Collins had attained his position.

He was appointed six months ago by the regional administrator. The regional administrator appointed him because he had the support of Senator

Corcoran. Billy, I don't care what you say, these days it isn't what you know, it's who you know that counts.

She added that the most important connection one could have for the W.P.A. was the one with Senator Corcoran. Next in importance were connections with Representatives in Congress.

There were important changes in the federal administration of relief after the early days of the New Deal. In the beginning there was a tremendous demand for jobs, and there was no recognized means of distributing them except through the usual political channels. Paul Ferrante, the state senator's secretary, told me that the Ravellos obtained a number of work-assignment slips from a high state official so that, whenever they wished to place a man on a project, they had simply to fill out a slip. As the federal relief setup developed and became established on a permanent basis, the powers of local politicians in dealing with relief were progressively curtailed.

This does not mean that relief was taken out of politics. It means that the pressure had to come from higher up in the political hierarchy. As Carrie Ravello pointed out, she was able to deal effectively with the W.P.A. administration because of her connection with United States Senator Corcoran. If she had not such connections, she could have accomplished very little. This was substantiated by the stories of many other Cornerville people. They did not speak of going to see Senator Corcoran. From the view of the corner boys, his position was so high as to be out of sight. They did speak of soliciting the aid of Congressman Branagan. The congressman had several secretaries, one of whom was a young Italian who lived in the ward. Through him many Cornerville people were able to get W.P.A. work assignments.

There was no state boss to whom Senator Corcoran was responsible. On a smaller scale, Branagan had a similar standing. He had his own organization, and, since he represented several wards in Congress, he was not subject to any one politician in any one of the wards. There was no longer a ward boss in the Matt Kelliher sense in any of these wards. This did not mean that Corcoran and Branagan were independent of all other politicians. They had to perform services for and make informal alliances with

other politicians in order to perpetuate their power. The important point is that they dealt with other politicians in their own
right and were not subject to dictation from anyone in the areas
they represented. With the immense power of federal patronage
in their hands, they had achieved such a commanding position
that other politicians had to come to them in order to secure their
constituents a share in the benefits of the New Deal. With only
his own organization behind him, the ward politician had scant
power, as the story of Joseph Maloney indicates. He had to subordinate himself to his congressman or United States senator in
order to meet the demands of his constituents.

Thus it appears that the New Deal helped to bring about a
political reorganization whereby the localized organizations of
ward bosses were to a great extent supplanted by a more central-
ized political organization headed by the United States senator,
with the congressman next in line, and the ward politicians assuming more subordinate positions.

Maloney concluded his story with a discussion of the racket
element:

Kelliher would never have anything to do with prostitution or with them
fellows. . . . . During prohibition, the bootleggers didn't mix in politics so
much. Yes, they had to have protection, but they minded their own business more. Then, after repeal, the same people that had been bootlegging
got the liquor licenses and when legalized horse and dog racing came along,
they got into that. They've been spreading out all the time, and they've
been trying to take over political control. It was in 1933 that I first realized
how strong they really were. They got a lot of votes against me at that time.
You see, men like Bob Madigan and Red O'Donnell can buy a lot of votes.
Madigan runs that liquor place on ——— Street, and O'Donnell controls a
lot of horse rooms in this ward and has some liquor places too. They have a
lot of fellows hanging around them, and they pass out a lot of free liquor,
especially around election time. Then those number-pool fellows go right
into people's houses, and they get quite a hold on the people. They've been
spreading propaganda about me. Say an agent keeps his numbers and does-
n't want to pay off on a hit. He tells the person, "I'm sorry, Joe Maloney
had me pinched and the cops took all the slips off me, so I can't pay you."
The people hold it against me, but it isn't true. I keep my hands off their
business.

That crowd had been after me for a long time. They've been keeping
their liquor places open after hours, and I didn't like that. And I don't
think it's right to have them open on the Lord's Day either. And I knew
that people were getting robbed in the ——— Cafe, and I complained to

the police about it. You see, the heart of the city is right in this ward. You'll find everything going on at night right down here.

They want to get me out of here. I've been threatened with a gun three times right in this office, and once a fellow pulled a knife on me. T. S. wanted to run me out of politics.

We might still be strong today if we hadn't picked up the wrong men. We elected Art Porcella representative, and he turned against us and went in with that racket crowd. Mike Kelly—he was my mistake. I really took him in against the majority of the organization. He had run for office three times, and he didn't get anywhere. Sometimes when a man ran against us, we recognized him and took him into the organization. Sometimes that policy worked out and sometimes it didn't. Mulrooney [a club member] was friendly with Kelly, and he says to me, "Why don't you give Kelly a chance?" So we talked to Kelly, and he promised he would be faithful to the organization. We indorsed him, but then when the campaign got under way, we began to hear disturbing reports that he was a weak candidate. We sent out our men to investigate, and we found that the reports were true. It looked like two Italian candidates were going to be elected. To prevent that, we had to do something we never did before, indorse just one candidate. That's the way we put Kelly across, and he just made it.

When he went to the legislature, Kelly didn't want to have anything to do with committees dealing especially with the affairs of the city. He wanted to get on the legal affairs committee, and through my influence I got him there. That was at a time when all this new legislation on liquor licenses and horse- and dog-racing was coming through before that committee. Through that position he built up his law practice and got himself made counsel for the Liquor Dealers' Association. He caught me napping. While the racket element was fighting us from the outside, he was boring from within, and he did a lot of damage to the organization. . . . .

Kelly fits right in with that element. That's why I had the police all against me in this last fight.

The Cleveland Club was organized primarily to provide political jobs and favors for its members, but its success depended also upon its relations with legitimate business interests and upon the business activities of its leading figures. Both Matt Kelliher and Joseph Maloney supported themselves through real estate transactions. This meant that neither man was financially dependent upon any group of constituents or any local business interest. When the city ceased to grow and the depression came, this source of income dried up. Maloney was not immediately threatened, since he had made himself a wealthy man in the earlier period, but the change in the situation meant that it would no longer be possible to build or maintain a political organization upon the same foundations that had served the Cleveland Club.

When Matt Kelliher was at the height of his power, industries in the state were expanding rapidly. The public utilities were particularly dependent upon franchises and other grants of power from the city and the state. When Kelliher sought to place some of his constituents in the employ of the railroads or the telephone company, they could not afford to turn him down. The old ward boss owed much of his power to his ability to place men in private industry as well as in government jobs.

The situation then completely changed. Business was no longer seeking new privileges; it was concerned primarily with holding its position. When politicians introduced legislation to deprive business of certain privileges, the businessmen had to defend their interests; but they could offer more money when new opportunities for profit were to be won than when an established position was to be maintained, and in a time of depression few jobs were available for any purpose. George Ravello was elected to the state senate in 1932. His wife told me that neither she nor her husband had ever obtained jobs for their constituents with the public utilities or with other large businesses. She said, "They are not obligated to me. Why should they do me a favor?" The businessman is no longer so intimately concerned with state and local politics. Today when he speaks of government he means the federal government.

The racketeers made money right through the depression and expanded their activities while business was retrenching. In the prohibition era the bootleggers had needed political and police connections, but their problems were relatively simple. A bootleg liquor shipment either went through or was stopped. It was not subject to all sorts of regulations. When a large part of their activities had been legalized, the racketeers needed to apply to the state and city governments for the privilege of carrying on and expanding their operations, just as the legitimate businessmen had done, and they developed an efficient monopoly organization to promote their interests. The rackets took the place of legitimate business in relation to politics.

The Cleveland Club was unable to make an adjustment to the substitution. Joseph Maloney had no scruples against gambling or racketeers as such. Speaking before his club on the eve of the 1939 aldermanic election, he said:

Politics is a business. You have to maintain the organization. Whenever a man has been friendly with the organization, I try to help him. I don't care if he sells numbers or lottery tickets as long as he pays the people when they win. Nobody can say they ever paid tribute to me to do business in this ward. As long as you mind your own business and keep your nose clean, I won't bother you. Of course, if they are friendly with the organization, we will try to help them out. But we don't believe in violence, stickups, and that kind of thing. We want law and order in the ward.

The Cleveland Club was organized to serve its members and could not cater primarily to the interests of another local organization without destroying its own foundations. Consequently, Maloney fought against the extending political power of the racketeers. And he fought in vain.

The young Cornerville politician has grown up along with the expansion of racket activity. The Cornerville lawyer who goes into politics has not been able to afford the best legal education and has not made the social connections required for the practice of corporation law. He finds criminal law the most profitable field in Cornerville and the racket cases the most profitable sector of that field. Even the racket cases do not provide a lucrative income, for a small politician is given only small cases. To finance his campaigns, he needs the help of his business clients, and, among these, the racketeers are most willing to help.

If the young politician had a profitable business, he might be able to support his own campaigns, but success in most businesses seems to draw a man away from a political career. There appears to be only one business which fits well with politics in Eastern City. That is the undertaking business. Senator Ravello and Alderman Fiumara were undertakers.

In the Italian community people generally have an undertaker of "their own kind," a man from the same part of Italy. In and around Cornerville there is at least one undertaker for each section from which many have emigrated. The undertaker must maintain active social relations and establish himself as a prominent figure especially among his *paesani*. The Italian funeral is an elaborate pageant participated in by all relatives and friends

of the family. The undertaker's part in arranging and handling
this occasion strengthens his position in the society.

If he has an established funeral business, the undertaker will
be well known and well supplied with personal contacts before
he enters politics. He counts on his own kind as a nucleus for
political support. As undertaker and as politician, he wants to
broaden his contacts, and the two activities reinforce each other.
A political campaign advertises the funeral business, and the funeral business widens political contacts. Those who are not committed to a particular undertaker are inclined to give a family funeral to a politician in order to establish a connection with him.
Having done the politician a favor by bringing him business, a
man is in a position to ask a favor in return. If some people cannot afford his charges, the politician may bury their relatives for
nothing. The dead man does not vote, but his relatives and
friends do.

While some politicians are more dependent upon him, even the
undertaker-politician must make an adjustment to the power of
the racketeer. There is no one way in which this adjustment must
be made. In Cornerville there is a wide variety in the relations
between politicians and racketeers, as several examples will indicate.

Tom Marino, boss of the Taylor Club, was a 50 per cent man
in the numbers long before he entered politics. He ran for representative twice and continued his numbers business in his corner store at the same time. He was a figure of moderate importance both in politics and in the rackets. Marino was the only
racketeer in Cornerville who had actually run for office, until
Sully Defeo entered politics.

One local politician was known as the racketeer's candidate,
since he owed his election to their support. He served the racketeers loyally in connection with all liquor and racing legislation
and was rewarded with financial support and a number of jobs at
the race track for his constituents. I have heard corner boys
complain that the only way to get anything out of this politician
was to approach him with the support of some prominent member

of the T. S. racket organization, and in one campaign I had an opportunity to observe him taking his orders from the racket boss.

Eastern City newspaper stories about George Ravello presented the picture of a politician completely identified with racket interests. That was inaccurate, and yet it is easy to see how the impression arose. When Joe Kenney, a prominent and colorful Welport racketeer, was shot, Ravello rushed to his deathbed. The newspapers headlined his visit. Two days later Carrie Ravello had this to say to me about Kenney and her husband:

> I liked Joe Kenney because he was so regular. There was a lot of class to him. He was always helping out the poor people in his district. If you were down and out, you could go up to him and say, "Are you Joe Kenney? I hear you're a regular fellow." And he would give you something and tell you not to worry. He was very popular down in Welport. He could get all them bums and drunks out any time. You just go up to a house and knock on the door and say, "Joe Kenney sent me," and the man will get dressed and come with you to vote and repeat for Joe Kenney. There was a lot of class to Joe Kenney. He was a regular fellow. He knew his place in society.
>
> It was a great shock to me when I heard he was killed. I really liked him. I won't deny it. When he was dying, George was the only politician that was with him. . . . . They [several prominent politicians] all ought to have gone to him in his hour of need. But they was all afraid to except George. George says to me, "I don't care what they say about him, he was always all right with me."

Shortly after the repeal of prohibition, Kenney had asked Ravello to try to secure for him a night-club liquor license. Ravello was new in office and was unable to do it. Kenney managed to get his license through someone who had better connections, but he knew that Ravello had done his best, and they were friends from that time on. Kenney supported Ravello in his political campaigns. Ravello enjoyed the company of tough guys, and he appreciated their political support.

While Ravello had done favors for Cornerville racketeers, he was never known as their particular candidate. With one exception, T. S. opposed Ravello in all his campaigns. Ravello was on a level with the racket boss and did not take his orders. He had nothing against racketeers, but he was not dependent upon them for financial support, and he refused to accept money from them or from anybody else in payment for favors.

Andy Cotillo had to fight against the influence of the racketeers in order to get his start in politics. Art Porcella was his strongest Italian rival and once defeated him in a very close election by means of racketeer support and the votes of repeaters. Cotillo set out to organize the district against this control at the same time that he fought against the Cleveland Club. He and his organization indorsed a dark-horse candidate for mayor when all other political organizations in Cornerville were supporting other men. On the day of that election Cotillo got into an argument with Len Cardullo, a prominent racketeer who was a close friend of Porcella. Cotillo said that if his candidate for mayor was elected, he would put the Cornerville racketeers right out of business. Cardullo answered him with a slap in the face. Cotillo was much bigger and stronger than Cardullo, but he was discreet enough to refrain from returning the blow. The story of this encounter was all over the district within a few hours after it took place.

Cotillo's candidate won the election, and Cotillo became the only Cornerville politician who had a connection with the new mayor. Immediately new members began to join his Victory Club, and within a few months Cotillo had the largest political organization in Cornerville. He himself got a job in the mayor's office. Just a year after his clash with Cardullo, he had his club indorse one of its members, Al Macarella, for representative, and he managed to secure the candidate's indorsement from a number of other clubs, so that he had an excellent chance of winning. Up until this time, Cotillo had complained about the elections that had been stolen from him. Now he let it be known that, through his connections with the mayor and the board of elections, he would have his men in control inside the Cornerville polling places. Still he needed more votes. He got together with Len Cardullo and made a deal. Cardullo's men were instructed to vote for Macarella for representative, and Cotillo's men were instructed to vote for Cardullo's candidate for the state senate.

Although Cotillo started his campaigns with the explicit purpose of overthrowing the political power of the racketeers and of the Cleveland Club, he had to make an agreement with one group in order to defeat the other. The agreement was a matter of temporary mutual advantage and did not necessarily mean that Cotillo would be unable to maintain a position of relative independence.

I have never heard of any Cornerville politician, except Andy Cotillo, delivering a direct challenge to the racketeers. Cotillo has never repeated his challenge. Whether he likes it or not, the politician must take into account the social position of the racketeer, which is in many respects similar to his own. The politician and the racketeer grow up in similar environments, have influence over the same groups or the same sorts of groups, are expected to perform some of the same functions, and have many interests in common. Between them, co-operative relations, of varying degrees of intimacy, are bound to develop. Carrie Ravello summed it up in this way: "Let's not kid ourselves, Bill; when we want to win, we go to the racketeers—all of us." Here she mentioned three of the most prominent and respected politicians in the state. "They do it, and the rest of them—we all do it."

2. THE POLITICAL CAREER

A Cornerville man can get ahead either in Republican or in Democratic politics. The nature of his activity will depend upon which route he chooses, for there is a fundamental difference between the two careers.

The Republican politician gets ahead by drawing himself to the attention of the upper-class people who control the party in the state, and, in so doing, he draws himself away from Cornerville. The career of Judge Gennelli provides an outstanding example of such behavior. He was born in Cornerville of a poor Italian family. He sold papers and shined shoes when he was a boy. He put himself through law school, became active in Republican politics, and won a minor judiciary appointment. Becoming more successful in his law business, he set up offices in the center of the Eastern City business district and hired girls of native American background as secretaries. Some time later he was given a better appointment on the bench. Quite early in his career he had moved out of Cornerville to a fashionable suburb. He won his party's nomination for attorney-general and waged a vigorous campaign to win the Italian vote. In this he failed. The Republicans lost and Gennelli ran behind his ticket. He fared little better in Cornerville than the other Republican candidates. Upper-class people looked upon him as an excellent judge and felt that his career testified to the vitality of American democracy. Cornerville people looked upon him as a high-class lawyer who was not concerned with helping them out of trouble. However, his inability to swing the Italian vote did not prevent Gennelli from rising. A later Republican administration promoted him to the highest court in the state.

Chick Morelli may never rise so high, but he is proceeding step by step along the route taken by Judge Gennelli—and every step takes him further away from Cornerville.

The Democratic politician gains his strength from the support of Cornerville people. His success depends upon his ability to deal with groups of people inside his district. Therefore, in order to understand his career, it is necessary to have some general knowledge of the nature of these groupings.

Corner gangs, such as the Nortons, or corner boys' clubs, such as the Cornerville S. and A., are to be found throughout the district. They function as independent units, and at the same time some of the smaller ones fit in as parts of larger organizations.

In Cornerville there are a number of political clubs, each one started by a politician and built around him. Such a club is organized for the purpose of electing its boss (or one selected by him) to public office and of providing him with the voting strength necessary in order to make good political connections. In return, the boss is expected to advance the interests of the members. The members are pledged to support all candidates indorsed by the club. In practice, the boss decides which candidates are to be indorsed. When the club boss runs for office, he can generally count on the active support of most of his members; but often the club is united only nominally in other contests. The political club is made up of a number of corner gangs. (The boss and some members may be above the corner-boy level, but the bulk of the members consider themselves corner boys and are so looked upon by others.) The boss's own clique, with which he started his club, can be relied upon to support his decisions, but the other cliques maintain their informal associations and a considerable independence of action. Unless the boss takes pains to tie the cliques in closely with the nucleus of the club through consulting their leaders on matters of policy and giving recognition to the informal clique organization in prestige and favors, the club may break up. This has happened in a number of instances.

Each of the Italian Catholic churches has a large and active Holy Name Society. Officially, they have nothing to do with politics and do not indorse candidates, but in them one can readily observe certain major divisions in terms of political allegiance. For example, one of the societies was divided fairly evenly between supporters of Art Porcella's Washington Club and Andy Cotillo's Victory Club. Within these major divisions were various corner-boy cliques. Doc of the Nortons told me this story:

Joe wanted me to join the Holy Name Society. I stalled him off. I said, "I hear you've got a lot of cliques in there."

Joe said, "No, there's no cliques. Why don't you come in some night and see for yourself?"

So I did. I had to laugh when I came in that night. There were ten tables in that big room, and there were ten cliques. At one table was the A Street crowd. At another I saw the boys from X corner. It was that way all around the room. One fellow called me over to sit with his boys. Then Joe called me over to sit with his clique. . . . . . I said to him, "What do you mean, there are no cliques here?"

He said, "Well, we get along pretty good just the same."

The mutual aid societies of the first-generation Italians participate in politics, and each politician seeks to gain the support of his *paesani*. However, the societies are not so influential in politics as the number of their members would indicate, for many of the members are aliens. It is the young men who are most active in politics, and it is generally they who mobilize the support of the older groups.

The local divisions of the Knights of Columbus and the Sons of Italy are important to the politician primarily for providing opportunities for making valuable contacts. Since these organizations include men from all parts of the district, a number of whom have considerable influence over groups of Cornerville people, it is advantageous for the politician to become prominent in their activities. While the local council of the Knights of Columbus is wholly Italian in membership, the prominent council official has opportunities to make contacts with Irish Knights of Columbus leaders, who have important political positions or connections.

It is commonly assumed that the family is the most important social unit in ward politics. Since the first and second generations have drifted apart in Cornerville, the family seems to be less significant for politics than the informal clique, and yet its importance should not be underestimated. In spite of the weakening of his family ties, the Italian's network of family obligations extends far beyond that which is experienced by the middle-class native American. Relatives are expected to help one another and to act in concert when it is in the interest of the family. Thus the politician must reckon with the family group in his campaigns. The women, who have no equivalent to the corner gang, tend to be particularly influenced by their family connections.

A man who is part of a large family and can "swing" its vote to one candidate or another becomes thereby a political figure of some consequence. Such a man will probably be a leader or close to the top in his informal group associations, in which case the groupings will all support the same politician. It is the man who is not a leader in one or both groups who faces a possible conflict. If his family supports one candidate and "the boys" support another, he must choose between his loyalties. That situation accounts for the defection of many men from either the family policy or the policy of the informal group.

Another break in the united group front results when the group is committed to Politician A but one of its members is committed to Politician B because he has received some specific favor. In this case the other members will recognize that this man is "doing the right thing" in discharging his obligations, and they will not put pressure on him to support Politician A.

The *paesani* tend to settle in one area, and those who are members of the same family usually live close together. The informal corner groups are also strictly localized. And each Cornerville politician has an area, generally where he grew up, which he considers his stronghold. Thus, if a man lives with his family on A

Street, hangs on a corner of A Street, and A Street comes within the orbit of one particular politician, no conflict is likely to arise.

The politician does not build his organization out of an undifferentiated mass of people. He grows up in a society which is complexly organized. To be successful in his career, he must be familiar with its ramifications and know how to win the support of the groups which make it up.

No politician in Cornerville can be successful without the support of corner boys, and many corner-boy leaders enter politics. The corner-boy leader performs some of the politician's functions for his followers. He looks after their interests and speaks for them in contacts with outsiders. Yet there are a number of things he cannot do. He cannot get them political jobs or favors unless he subordinates himself and his group to some politician. It frequently occurs to him and his followers to ask themselves why the leader should have to subordinate himself. He feels that the politicians have neglected the people's interests. His friends try to persuade him to enter the contest. If he has any capacity for public speaking, their urgings will be hard to resist. He will begin to extend his contacts so that he moves in wider and more influential social circles.

In his first campaign he simply tries to prove that he has enough support to be taken seriously. When he has shown his strength, he is in a position to stage a more vigorous campaign or to make terms with his rivals. If he becomes an important figure, he will be offered money or perhaps even a political job if he will drop out of the contest and support another politician. If he accepts, his followers feel that he has "sold out," and it is difficult for him to continue as a political figure of any prominence. He may be able to retain some personal following if he is able to do favors for the boys, but he will no longer have a chance to win an election.

If he refuses to compromise himself and continues to run for office, the politician must find a way of financing his campaigns. Furthermore, he is required by the nature of his position to spend a great deal of money that he need not spend as a private citizen. Whenever a local organization gives any sort of entertainment, he is expected to contribute an advertisement for the program book or to buy a number of tickets. People know that the politician cannot afford to turn them down, and they put him at the top of the "sucker list." He is also expected to be a free spender in entertaining his friends and acquaintances. His corner boys can contribute little to help finance such political activity. If the politician has built up his own political club, he may obtain a campaign contribution from its treasury, but it is a rare club which has much to spare even for this purpose in the first few years of its existence. Since a man becomes obligated to those who contribute money to his campaign, the high cost of political activity tends to draw Cornerville politicians away from their original group ties.

At every stage in his career, the Cornerville politician is confronted with an actual or potential conflict of loyalties. The conflict develops as he attempts to advance himself politically and at the same time to maintain the support of the friends who were with him at the start of his career.

When the politician is elected—to the office of representative in the state legislature, for example—he carries on his activities at a higher level in the social structure. If he wants simply to make money and jockey himself into a political sinecure when his term is finished, he may do so by making the proper connections; but let us assume that he has a genuine desire to help his constituents and discharge his political obligations to them. He cannot do many favors for them at the beginning of his term. Under a Democratic governor, he will find that he is given one or two jobs to pass out to his constituents. Each representative of the controlling party receives a small share of patronage in return for supporting the governor's policies. If the Republican party is in power, the Democratic representative has little chance of getting any jobs from the administration. When I last inquired, jobs at the tracks for the racing season were handled through political channels under the supervision of the governor. The politician who supported legislation favored by the racing interests was rewarded by a share in this patronage. To get favors for his constituents, the legislator must make connections with the politicians who have power. In order to obtain their help, he must try to do favors in return. As a new man, he has little power to reciprocate and, consequently, has difficulty in obtaining favors.

It is frequently difficult for the politician to reconcile his loyalty to his constituents with the conduct required of him by his political superiors. In explaining why he had not done more for Cornerville, Joseph Maloney spoke in this way to a club of corner boys:

> Sometimes you try to get a man a job through the mayor, and then some issue comes up between you and the mayor. Should you fight him or should you keep quiet? You have to weigh that question carefully. If you fight, you might lose a man a life-job, and he'll always say, "If Joe didn't pick that fight, I would have my job today."

On the other hand, if the politician never fights, his superiors conclude that he is easily brought into line and need be given only the crumbs of political patronage.

The Italian politician faces another difficulty. He wages his campaign locally against the Irish domination of the ward. When he goes up to the capital, he finds the Irish in control there. If they are to help his friends, he must help their friends, so he finds himself doing favors for the Irish. If his Italian constituents discover this, they are likely to conclude that he is betraying their trust.

It has been the experience of certain Italian politicians that the Italians are less appreciative of favors done them by Italians than are the Irish. Italians feel that the racial bond obligates other Italians to help them. Therefore, they expect and demand help. Irishmen do not feel that Italians are obligated to them and therefore make an effort to show their appreciation for every favor received. The Italian politician starts his career with bitter feeling against the Irish. When he gets to know some Irish and has political dealings with them, he finds that they are really quite nice people—in this respect, nicer than his own. If he does not watch his step, his associations with the Irish and his regard for them will cut him off from his Italian constituents.

The ward politician is expected to maintain his position by doing favors, but that alone is not enough. The number of large and small favors within his power is limited, and the manner of distribution has important effects upon his career.

Generally speaking, the importance of the favors done for constituents varies with the importance of their positions in the social structure of the community. That is, the "big shot" who has influence over a number of groups receives more than the corner-boy leader who only influences one, and the corner-boy leader receives more than his followers. Thus, in order to get the maximum results, the man at the bottom level must try to have a man above him take his request to the politician. He then becomes obligated to his superior, and the superior becomes obligated to the politician who does the favor.

Late in the day of the Fiumara-Kelly-Maloney election, I met Mike Giovanni's brother Terry. He was wearing a Fiumara button and had been walking around to see what was going on in the various Cornerville precincts. I asked him who had done the really effective work for Fiumara. He said:

What do you mean? I don't want to favor nobody on that. You might as well say I'm doing the work. I was with the man three years ago when he started—before anybody around here knew him. [Fiumara's home was on the South Side.] If he wins, I'll be in. We'll show them cheap racketeers something. I was offered a lot of money to get out of town during this fight. I refused. Then I heard that I was gonna get beat up election day. Well, here I am, and they ain't touched me yet.

I asked what the racketeers would do if Fiumara were elected. "They'll try to make connections with him. They'll have to come and see me."

Six months later I again met Terry, and I asked him how his friend Fiumara was getting along. He answered, "What friend? To hell with him. Bill, the only good politician is a dead politician." He was uncommunicative about the reasons for his break with Fiumara, but it is clear that his earlier expectations had been bitterly disappointed.

Terry Giovanni had been state middleweight champion, and he was well known and popular on the street corner. He had the most influence around a corner where he had grown up, but he had many contacts among the corner boys throughout Cornerville and in other parts of the ward. He had been making a precarious living conducting a crap game and taking bets on horses. As his words indicate, he was an independent in action and did not consider himself part of the racket organization. I learned from other sources that he had given me a fairly accurate account of his services to Fiumara. He supported the politician at the very outset and was always a tireless and loyal worker. He persuaded his friends to take an active part in the campaign, but, after all, he was just a corner boy. He did not have a position in the community which would have made it natural for the racketeers to come to see him when they wished to approach the politician. Since his conception of the size of the favors owed him by Fiumara was much bigger than his position in the social structure warranted, he was disappointed.

The politician must take the social organization of the neighborhood into account. Within the limitations it imposes, he may do favors for his old friends and for the rank and file of the people, and, if he refrains from taking all the cream for himself and his family, he may satisfy some of the corner boys. Yet there will always be a large number of the boys who will consider him disloyal because he gives the more important things to the more important people. The corner boys look upon politics as "a racket" and consider politicians double-crossers.

If an important man who influences many votes feels that a politician is untrustworthy, the politician is gravely handicapped. If some of the corner boys feel that he is untrustworthy, the handicap is not nearly so great. It is therefore not necessary for the politician to be trusted by people at all levels in his society. In fact, it is almost impossible for him to enjoy such general confidence. When he begins his career, his closest friends are little people like himself. Naturally, he promises them that they will receive the major benefits of his political activity. If he concentrates upon serving his own group, he will never win widespread support. In order to win support, he must deal with important people who influence other groups. When he has to make a choice, he must keep his promises to the big shots even at the expense of breaking those made to his friends. As long as he keeps his promises to the important people and they allow some political benefits to filter down to the men below them and so retain their positions in the social structure, the politician can be confident of retaining his popular support. Some corner boys will turn against him, but other groups of corner boys can be brought into line to take their places.

The process whereby the politician moves up in his career can be described in terms of frequency of interaction with groups at different levels in society. As leader of a corner-boy group, the future politician has a high rate of interaction with his followers. He interacts more frequently with members of other groups than do his followers, but his corner gang is the center of his activities. When he enters politics, he increases his rate of interaction with other corner groups and, necessarily, decreases his rate of interaction with his original group. As he advances further, he begins interacting with men higher in the social structure. As he increases his rate of interaction with his "connections" and interacts with higher and higher connections, the frequency of his contacts with his original group is still further diminished. If some of the members of this group have been able to move up with him and mix in the same circles, the politician can maintain a high rate of interaction with them, but, as he rises in position, he loses touch with the day-to-day activities of the boys. He is no longer the leader of a corner-boy group in the sense that he once was. As the politician ceases to participate actively in the group, someone else must become its leader and take over the direction of its activities —assuming that the group remains a unit. In order to hold the support of his original group, the politician must maintain cordial relations with the new leader (involving a higher rate of interaction with him than with his followers). If, in the opinion of the leader and his group, the politician does not meet his obligations to them, the breakdown of their social relations may be observed in the sudden or gradual diminishing of the rate of interaction between the politician and the corner-boy leader.

3. ORGANIZING THE CAMPAIGN

If he is to have any prospect of success, the politician must have a section of the community predisposed to support him before he begins to campaign. He may have his own political club, though the case of Senator Ravello indicates that that is not always essential to success.

Such assured support provides the candidate with a foundation of political strength. It convinces the uncommitted that he has a chance of winning and that, whatever the outcome, he is important enough to be able to get them favors. It also provides him with a number of willing political workers.

The purpose of the campaign is to add new blocs of voters to the nucleus of assured support. In order to do so, the politician attempts to win over men strategically placed in the social organization.

He begins upon certain big shots who have widespread personal influence. In Cornerville and adjoining sections of the city, most of these big shots will be politicians and racketeers.

When George Ravello decided to run for Congress in the fall of 1937, he first sought and won the support of Ed Murphy and John Feeney. Murphy was a former governor, whose campaigns Ravello had always supported, and the two men were good friends. Ravello had supported Feeney in his successful campaign for attorney-general. Since the congressional district included Wards 4, 5, 6, and 7 and the cities of Maxton and Belfry, whereas up to this time Ravello had only campaigned in Wards 4, 5, and 6, it was important for him to be supported by men who had influence where he was relatively unknown. Jack Flanagan, a popular politician in Ward 7 (Ansbury), had been appointed to public office by Murphy and supported Ravello out of loyalty to his superior. Tom Foley was a popular figure in Ward 6, and Murphy had appointed him to a prominent position in the state administration. Foley had been a close friend of Ravello for years, and his support was assured at the outset. Joe Kenney, the Welport racketeer who was later murdered, pledged his support to the campaign. The Cleveland Club had always opposed Ravello in the past, but lengthy conferences between Ravello and Joseph Maloney finally won the club's support.

Representative Art Porcella, former Representative DiAngelis, and former Ward 5 Alderman Capizza had all filed nomination papers. If Ravello was to defeat the most powerful Irish candidate, these men had to be removed from the competition. Capizza was persuaded to withdraw when Ravello undertook (unsuccessfully) to get him a job on the staff of the federal attorney-general. A conference was then held in one of Eastern City's largest hotels for the purpose of "promoting the cause of Italian unity." Six men attended. They were Ravello, Porcella, DiAngelis, T. S. (the Cornerville racket boss), Al Dantone (the Ward 5 racket boss), and Municipal Court Judge Frangello. DiAngelis steadfastly refused to withdraw, but the conferees were able to bring about an agreement whereby Porcella withdrew in favor of Ravello, and Ravello promised to support Porcella in his contest for state senator the following year. This was a historic conference, since it not only brought about an agreement between two bitter political rivals but also won Ravello the support of T. S. for the first time in his career.

It is important that the big shots be won over, but they cannot be counted on to deliver the vote. It is well known that a politician can get more votes for himself than he can deliver to someone else. When a politician runs for a ward office himself, he establishes direct contact with the groups whose support he seeks. He becomes obligated to them, and they expect to call upon him for favors to discharge that obligation. When the same politician calls upon these groups to support another man, the boys are one step further removed from the source of favors. When they seek a favor, they must go to the politician who directly solicited their support, and he is expected to carry the request to the man that he supported.

There is a further difficulty in that one politician may support another for reasons which are of no particular concern to the corner boys. In the aldermanic campaign of 1939 George Ravello supported Joseph Maloney "because I owe him a debt of gratitude —because he supported me when I ran for Congress." It was generally felt that Ravello was under a personal obligation to Maloney, but only those who were most closely bound to Ravello's cause felt themselves obligated to vote for his candidate.

The Kelly-Maloney-Fiumara campaign also indicated that,

when an Italian politician or racketeer sought to mobilize support for an Irishman, the strength of racial feeling cut his influence to a minimum. How many votes a man can influence depends upon the nature of the situation as well as upon his position in society.

There are a number of men known as "fakers" or "phonies," who claim to control large blocs of votes and are willing to deliver them in return for a money payment or for favors done in advance. Since there are over 17,000 votes in the ward, even the experienced politician cannot be sure in every case whether a man is a faker or whether he actually does influence a moderate number of votes. The faker is most successful in dealing with politicians from outside the ward who need votes in Cornerville but lack the support of local politicians.

In a ward contest the politician seeks to contact directly as many clubs or groups as he can. It is his business to know the people in his district and to know something about the relative position of men in their groups. He implicitly recognizes that there is in every such group a man who customarily leads his fellows in their activities. He attempts to win over the leader and induce him to mobilize his followers for political action. In a contest covering a wide area the politician must delegate a large part of the work at this level to subordinates.

The politician can offer the corner-boy leader money as a personal gift or to be spent at the leader's discretion in support of the campaign. He can promise favors to the leader and his followers. And he can give the leader the opportunity of achieving some small prominence by allowing him to speak to other groups in the politician's behalf and to become personally identified with the politician before the public.

Frequently, the politician gives a club enough money to pay the rent on its rooms for several months, secures it a charter from the state, or makes it some other gift. In this case the leader has secured a benefit for his boys and his position with them is strengthened. If the boys find that the leader alone is benefiting in receiving money or favors, that is, if they find that he has violated his obligations to them in order to advance himself, he will lose his position and influence in the group. There is ample evidence to indicate that this has happened to many corner-boy leaders. It is recognized as one of the risks of political activity. I have heard men say that they steer clear of politics because on past occasions when they supported a politician, some thought that they were doing it exclusively for their own benefit, and this suspicion damaged their standing in the neighborhood. It is common for a corner-boy leader who loses his support in this way to continue to be active in politics as a faker.

When the politician feels that he has a real chance of winning the election, he faces a new problem. In every campaign there are a number of men who file nomination papers simply in order to damage the cause of the leading candidates. For many years the Cleveland Club maintained political supremacy in the ward by placing Italian "stooges" in the contest to split the Italian vote. The Boss would pick out a young Italian who had a following in Cornerville and who perhaps had run for office before. The Italian would be offered political favors, perhaps a job, and payment of his campaign expenses. Such arrangements would be kept as secret as possible, and the Italian stooge would publicly denounce the domination of the Cleveland Club just as vigorously as any of his rivals.

Such stooges are not to be confused with the Italian Cleveland Club members who were sometimes indorsed and elected to office by the organization. Since they were responsible to the club, this was a means of satisfying the racial feeling of the Italians without allowing control to slip from the hands of the organization. Sometimes the club placed a stooge in the field as well as its regularly indorsed Italian candidate. The stooge was selected for the purpose of taking votes away from the strongest independent candidate.

In one of George Ravello's campaigns for the state senate, he placed an Irish stooge in the field. This may be done more frequently in the future, but until now the Irish have been in superior positions politically and have had more to offer to stooges.

Some Italians file nomination papers in order to seek the best bargain available. They find out how much the Irish politicians will offer them to remain in the contest and how much the Italian

politician will offer for their withdrawal. Few such political extortionists influence more than a hundred votes, in spite of grandiose claims, but a small bloc of votes may have a large nuisance
value.

George Ravello, in addressing a political rally, had this to say
about one of his successful campaigns for state senator: "The
last time there were twelve Italians in the race. Six of them got
out. But they didn't get out for nothing. I fixed them up. . . . ."

In talking with members of the Italian Community Club,
Ravello said that he had spent six hundred dollars for this purpose. A suit or a suit, hat, and overcoat seem to be the most common prices paid for such withdrawals.

When the active campaigning begins, the candidate calls a
campaign committee meeting. Those who worked for him in past
campaigns plus new converts who promise to have neighborhood
influence are summoned to the headquarters. The most influential supporters do not appear at such a meeting. The candidate
confers with them privately.

About thirty men and several women attended the first congressional campaign workers' meeting for George Ravello. All
were Italians except two representatives of Syrian clubs.

The meeting was called to order by Chairman Leo Fatalo, who
was prominent in a large Italian club on the South Side. Tom
Bongiorno, who was campaign manager, Al Deleo, Ravello's
former secretary, who had been appointed to a secure political
position through Ravello, and Paul Ferrante, Ravello's secretary,
were active behind the scenes. The senator could not be present
himself, but Carrie Ravello welcomed his supporters and reviewed
the political situation for them. She said that the purpose of the
meeting was to get all the workers together and organized as
committees of one to get others to work for them in their precincts. She concluded with these words:

> In these years our office and our home has always been open to you,
> whenever you have needed our help. And I don't need to tell you that when
> George goes to Washington, I will still be here, and our door will be open to
> you just like it always was. I will see the people in the various city depart-
> ments, the departments of the state, and the welfare just like I have done in
> the past. I'm doing this not because I have to do it, but because I love to

do it. Even if my health can't stand it, I would be lost if I didn't do these things.

When Leo Fatalo declared the meeting open to anyone who had suggestions about the conduct of the campaign, about twenty of the workers made brief speeches.

If they had supported Ravello in previous campaigns, they said that they had always been "on the firing line" or had always "gone down the line" for him. They then spoke of the services that the candidate had performed for the poor people of his district and the benefits he had won for his people through breaking down the barrier of discrimination which had prevented Italians from winning public office. They spoke of the work they had been doing in the campaign and predicted that their particular sections would be stronger for George Ravello this time than ever before.

Several suggestions on campaign strategy were made, but I could not see that they received any attention beyond polite recognition at the moment. Paul Ferrante told me that the purpose of the meeting was simply to arouse enthusiasm among the workers.

At the second meeting of the campaign workers the following week, there was one suggestion made which aroused general interest and discussion. A representative of a Syrian organization suggested that a captain be appointed for each precinct and that five or six people be assigned to work under him to canvass the voters. A representative of an Italian club replied: "Somebody said we should have captains in each precinct. Why captains? We're all equal. Why should one man have a better position than the next?" He added that the precinct-captain system would make for hard feelings and suggested instead that every man should constitute himself a committee of one, as Mrs. Ravello had said.

These two points of view are significant for an explanation of the organization of Ravello's campaign in relation to the social structure of the district. George Ravello had founded no political club through which he distributed favors and upon which he relied in his campaigns. He prided himself on not placing any organization between himself and the man or woman who sought his aid. He said that anyone could come to see him personally about anything, and this was a fact. He or his wife spent part of every morning in his office seeing all the people who asked their attention. During the rest of the day, when the legislature was not in session, they went about to see various politicians seeking favors for their constituents. Whenever they were at home, their constituents might drop in to seek a favor or just to sit around and talk and have a drink or perhaps a plate of spaghetti. The Ravellos were on call at any hour of the day or night. They were much more accessible to the common man than most other politicians in the district.

In campaigns George Ravello relied upon his direct personal contacts. He knew a number of men in each precinct who had some influence with their fellows. If he had singled out one man as captain, he might have alienated the others. He had not officially set up a hierarchy such as exists in political clubs, and the candidates for the job of precinct captain were not so related to one another in the social structure that one of them was accustomed to telling the others what to do.

Of course, a hierarchy on an informal basis actually did exist. At the top were former Governor Murphy and Attorney-General Feeney. On a level with the candidate were politicians Joseph Maloney, Tom Foley, and Jack Flanagan and racketeers T. S., Joe Kenney, and Al Dantone. Below Ravello was Frank Capizza, who was in charge of the campaign in Westland (Ward 5). Representative Art Porcella was in charge of part of the Cornerville campaign. Immediately below Capizza were Al Deleo, Leo Fatalo, Tom Bongiorno, and Paul Ferrante. Below these four were the corner-boy leaders and followers (see the accompanying chart).

Although Bongiorno was campaign manager, George Ravello organized his own campaign except for the sections covered by the men at his own level in the hierarchy. He gave all the orders and made (and frequently changed) all arrangements. Tom had nothing to do but hang around and perform such minor assignments as the candidate gave him.

In his desire to avoid setting up a hierarchy, Ravello neglected

RAVELLO CAMPAIGN ORGANIZATION

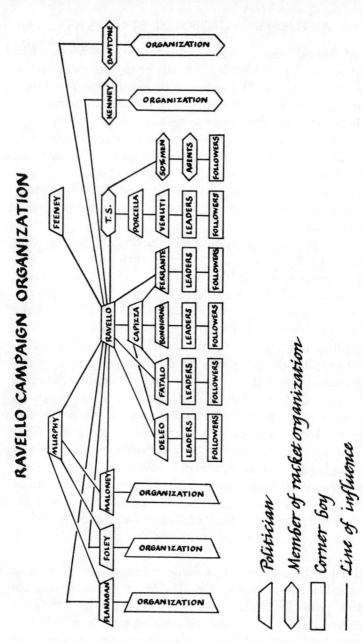

Politician

Member of racket organization

Corner boy

Line of influence

Positions of boxes indicate relative status

to apportion authority and responsibility among his underlings. There was no system by which the functions of Tom, Paul, Al, or Leo were determined. Since they had no understanding among themselves, each one tried to claim the attention of the candidate and play a leading role. They spent many hours hanging around the political office or the Ravello home so that they would not miss anything that went on at headquarters. A number of the corner-boy leaders simply took to following the candidate around wherever they could and neglected the work of canvassing voters in their sections. Those who did work hard were afraid that their efforts would go unrecognized because they did not spend their time telling the candidate what they were doing. Paul tried to deal with this situation whenever he saw the workers by saying to them: "I hear you're doing wonderful work over in ———. Keep it up. I'll speak to George about it." But Paul's standing was not good enough to give these words much weight. The corner-boy leaders regarded his efforts as unwarranted interference in the relations between themselves and their candidate. By organizing the campaign without precinct captains, Ravello avoided some difficulties but ran into others.

The manner of organizing a campaign depends to a large extent upon the office at stake and the size of the district which is to vote for that office. The case of Sam Venuti provides an example of campaign organization for a contest for representative for Ward 4. Sam was secretary of the Washington Club, of which Art Porcella was president and founder. In this campaign Art was running for state senator. While the club indorsed both men, the major effort was made in Art's behalf, and Sam had to build up his campaign largely through his own efforts.

Two weeks before election, when he had organized his more important supporters, Sam called into his office fifteen of his closest friends among the club members. He said that, since he was confident of his Cornerville support, the major effort would have to be made in other parts of the ward. He asked those present to undertake to make a house-to-house canvass of the South Side, where he had virtually no support. They were to say that Sam Venuti was a friend of theirs, that he had always worked hard for community improvements, that he had achieved recognition in various civic movements, and that he was capable of filling the office. The community improvements of particular interest to that section were to be mentioned. Then the workers would ask whether the voter would vote for Venuti. By keeping track of the number who agreed to do so, they would be able to keep Sam informed as to the progress of the campaign. Sam impressed upon them that this work was to be carried out secretly so that no other candidates would attempt to counteract it. He said that he realized he was asking the boys to do a difficult job, which would take up every night for almost two weeks, but they could do nothing which would make him more grateful to them.

This intensive campaign was carried through faithfully, and the workers reported that a thousand people had pledged their votes to Sam Venuti. However, on election day Sam received only three hundred votes outside of Cornerville in the entire ward, and only a part of these could be attributed to the canvass. It appears that, while his workers may have been very persuasive, they did not have connections with the people they were canvassing, and promises without such a foundation in the social structure proved to be of little value.

As a campaign proceeds, the district becomes flooded with political advertising. Each candidate has a squad of workers to hang posters. Cards with his picture on one side and his qualifications (education, business and political experience, civic activity) on the other are printed for distribution at political rallies. Sound trucks circulate through the streets proclaiming the virtues of the candidate and announcing the rallies.

In Cornerville very little campaign literature is distributed. The Cleveland Club always printed a one-page appeal to the voters, but this was not mailed to Cornerville people until Joseph Maloney had begun to lose his hold on the ward.

Politicians do not expect to influence many votes by such advertising. They feel that it is necessary to keep their names always before the people. If it is known that a particular candidate is spending a great deal of money on his campaign, many feel that there is something to be gained from being associated with him.

The advertising seems to build up a picture of a powerful, affluent, and possibly successful candidate, and to that extent it may place the voter in a receptive mood for his appeal.

4. POLITICAL RALLIES

The last weeks of the political campaign are crowded with rallies for all the candidates. Individual rallies are held for the candidates for minor offices such as representative or alderman only when the major offices are not being contested at the same time. When there is a mayoralty or gubernatorial campaign under way, the major candidates have their local committees working in the district, and each committee stages at least one rally for its candidate. The major candidate usually does not appear until well on in the evening, as he has a number of other rallies at which he must speak. To start the program, the chairman (a leading Cornerville supporter of the major candidate) announces that his campaign committee is glad to give the local candidates who are competing for minor offices an opportunity to speak to the crowd. There will be several of them already sitting on the stage, waiting to be called upon. When they finish speaking, they leave the hall and proceed to a rally elsewhere in the ward, while those who have attended other rallies come in in the course of the evening and await their turns. Sometimes there is entertainment, popular songs, or jokes.

If the main speaker is delayed in making his appearance, as he usually is, and the crowd becomes restless, the chairman announces that the candidate has just left a previous rally and is due any minute. Finally, there is noise of honking cars outside, and word comes from the back of the hall that he has arrived. A moment later the candidate strides down the center aisle followed by a mobile column of supporters who accompany him from rally to rally. The minor candidate who happens to be speaking at the time must wait while the crowd cheers, the big man marches ahead, acknowledging the reception, and his hangers-on push down the aisle as fast as possible so that they may be seen in close proximity to him. Then, while his followers stand in the aisle, the major candidate climbs onto the stage, shakes hands with the chairman and with all the minor candidates, and sits down. The chairman calls on the man who was interrupted to finish his speech, and, if he is wise, he will be brief. Before introducing the main speakers, the chairman announces that other minor candidates are awaiting their turn and asks the audience to remain to the end of the program. Then comes the main speech, and, after its conclusion, the candidate strides up the aisle surrounded by his hangers-on. Most of the crowd leaves with him.

Most people who attend rallies are not committed just to one candidate. They may be interested in a candidate for governor, one for state senator, and one for Representative. However, the seats in the hall tend to be divided informally on neighborhood geographic and political lines. Men from one street corner who are supporting their local candidate take up positions in one part of the hall. The corner crowd supporting another politician is seated elsewhere. While the older men and women do not congregate in such compact groups, one who is familiar with the corners of Cornerville and their political allegiances could draw a map of the seating positions on this basis with very little difficulty.

Sometimes the supporters of rival minor candidates are for the same major candidate, but usually both divisions fall along the same lines. If Club A and Club B are rivals in ward politics and Club A has established close relations with one candidate for mayor, then Club B has little to gain from supporting the same man, since, if he wins, Club A will have the inside track for patronage in the district.

The nature of the appeal made at such a rally depends upon the office for which the candidate is running and upon his contacts with local people. At one of Ravello's congressional campaign rallies, the important speeches were given by Jack Flanagan and the candidate. Since this was a special election for Congress and since no other offices were being contested, the talk was all about Ravello.

Chairman Frank Capizza introduced the Irish politician as "that militant Democrat, that fighting Democrat, the great clerk of the court in Ansbury—Jack Flanagan!" Flanagan spoke in this way:

Maybe I'm the only Irishman here, but this is not a racial contest. You don't select your man because of his race. There are too many who cry him down because of that. But these people that sit behind closed doors and discriminate against a man because of his race have no place in American life. George Ravello may not be everything we seek in public life. No man is perfect. But one thing I know, George Ravello never asked a man's race, creed, or color when the man called on him for help. I've known him before he ever held public office. I have always respected him for his love of the masses of the working class. He never dodged the issue. He never deserted the plain people. He has the character that fights. He may not always use the proper grammar, but—George Ravello is a man of action for those who can't speak for themselves. When he goes to Washington, he will ask those officers of departments in the federal government, "What about the people of my district?" When others are tired, George Ravello will speak for the plain people, for the people who know him and love him.

This district don't house men and women that vote only because of their racial strain. For the immigrants of your race and my race, I have no apology. In the time of need, we answered the call of our country. One of the largest quotas of men was sent out from this district. At that time there was no discrimination because of a man's race, there was no turning men back for that reason. We sent out boys by the thousands in order that we might enjoy the blessings of free government. Here we never turn down a man because of his race or creed. We are true American citizens, and we glory in that fact.

George Ravello is not a wealthy man, but he has a heart of gold. He answers the call of the downtrodden. We need a man who will demand of government and individuals the right to work and maintain a home. We need a man who will cry out and demand these things as only he can. We don't ask for much. All we seek is the right to work. We don't ask for charity. George Ravello will get action from those government offices.

It is wonderful to see the unity that is displayed in this district. All the factional leaders have shown the unity among the Italian people. Some have gone elsewhere, but they are generals without an army. In Cornerville, all through Ward 4, there is unity. There is only one grand character missing, and it would be to her everlasting glory if she could continue the work she has been doing. [Carrie Ravello's health broke down in the midst of the campaign.] But now she is laying on her bed of pain in the hospital. I can hear Carrie Ravello cry out about all those unfortunates, the poor people that toil for a living. When she met the President and his wife, she told them that her people were the best in the land. And now that she is laying on that bed of pain in the hospital, she is wondering what her people will do for her.

Flanagan's speech was greeted with great enthusiasm.

Chairman Capizza stepped forward to read a telegram from Mrs. Ravello. He said:

You all know how Carrie Ravello has worked for you. She has been an angel of mercy, a merchant of good deeds. Now she is laying in bed, praying for the success of her husband. I know that when you cast your vote to-morrow, you will have in your minds the picture of that angel of mercy, Carrie Ravello.

The telegram read:

To my people of Cornerville:
This is the saddest day of my life because I can't be with you tonight. You have never failed me before, and I know you won't fail me now. Thank you for what you have done in the past. CARRIE RAVELLO.

There were cheers, and then Capizza continued:

The doctor has given her medicine, but I know that the one thing that will give her courage to get well and carry on in the same charitable manner as before will be the election of her husband, George Ravello.

A man in the rear of the hall stood up and moved that Carrie be sent a telegram wishing her a speedy recovery and expressing confidence in her husband's election. The motion was carried with cheers.

Following Flanagan's speech, George Ravello arrived at the hall and took his place on the stage, as the crowd gave him an enthusiastic reception. Chairman Capizza made this introduction.

George Ravello is here, and he's nervous and raring to go. In all the forty-eight states there is only one Italian in Congress. This is the time and the opportunity. He is the only man that can win. Politically, we have been going downhill. Let's put on the brakes and unite on the only man that can win. The LaGuardia of Eastern City, a man of proven ability, a diamond in the rough, a fighter who has a heart bigger than the inflated heads of his opponents.

As Ravello stepped forward, somebody shouted, "Give it to 'em, George," and he called back, "I can give it to 'em." There were cheers. He reviewed his past campaign and spoke of his vote-getting ability. He sized up the present campaign in this way:

I just came from a big rally in Maxton. Joe Brennan, president of the Maxton City Council for twenty-five years spoke for George Ravello tonight. There are 1,100 Italian votes in Maxton. I'll get 1,000 of them and another 1,000 from the Portuguese, the Lithuanians, and the Irish. I'm gonna win this contest. For the first time in the history of Ward 4, Art Porcella, Mike Kelly, Andy Cotillo, and everybody was on the platform for George Ravello. For the first time in the history of Democratic politics the Cleveland Club is supporting an Italian for Congress. In Ward 6, Tom Foley is out for George Ravello.

He reviewed his earlier campaigns and spoke about his experiences when he was first elected to the Senate.

> They asked, "How is this fellow?" Somebody told them, "He's pretty fresh." They said they would give me six months. I've been there nearly six years. They said, "He can't speak so good, we'll talk him to death." I wounded up by talking them to death.
>
> They ask me how I win. I'll tell you how. Because I always been on the level. I stand four square for the people. I always take care of my people. If I can do a favor for you, I don't ask what district you come from.
>
> When I'm in Washington, I'll be down there looking for jobs for the working people. I won't sell out to the big corporations. They say Ravello talks too much. Well, I don't know. I speak when I have to speak, and I fight when I have to fight. I can talk because nobody ever gave me a dollar and a half to keep quiet. If you don't take their dollar and a half to shut up, you can say two-fifty worth.

In expressing his appreciation for the large crowd that had turned out to hear him, Ravello said:

> There's only one missing that I want here. That is my good wife. You know the work she used to do in Cornerville. I want to thank you for this demonstration by the friends of my wife, and I'm bringing to you a message from her. She says, "Words can't express how I feel now, but I know if every Italian goes to the polls tomorrow and votes like they always vote, we can all celebrate."

As he started the next sentence, somebody on the platform came forward to readjust the Italian flag, which had come loose in its stand beside the American flag. Ravello told him to leave it alone. George pulled the flag loose and waved it at the people, to the accompaniment of enthusiastic cheering. He carried the flag on his shoulder for a while as he continued his speech and then laid it on a table.

Ravello asked how many in his audience worked for the post office. There was no response. He asked how many had any sort of federal government job. After a pause, one man stood up. Ravello asked the man to come forward to the platform. He asked him how long he had been in his present job and what kind of work he did. He took the man's name and said, waving him to a seat on the stage, "All right, sit down. I'll promote you next week." There was laughter and applause. The man started back to his former seat, but Ravello waved him again to a seat on the stage, as he came to the conclusion of his talk:

Vote for me. . . . . Elect me your congressman, and I'll leave home and business behind me for three years. And then I'll come back, and I'll be the first Italian-American mayor of this city. (*Cheers.*) And when I'm mayor, this flag of ours will wave from the front of the City Hall.

He received an ovation as he finished.

Political speeches in Cornerville cover five main points: the racial appeal, the class appeal, the personal appeal, a statement of qualifications for office, and the statement of the candidate's political strength.

In making the racial appeal, the local candidate tells his people that they are discriminated against because of their race. They must "stick together" and elect an Italian who will fight to break down this barrier, to increase the prestige of his people, and to broaden their opportunities.

This appeal arouses more enthusiasm in an Italian audience than any other. Politicians make frequent references to the great accomplishments of Italians in order to show that their people are just as good as any other race—if not better.

The non-Italian politician tries to establish a sympathetic bond by stressing his high regard for the Italian people. He says he comes from a large family like a good Italian, that he grew up in Cornerville or in a similar district—or that he likes Italian cooking.

In the pre-war days non-Italian politicians frequently appealed for votes with praise of Mussolini. In 1938 I heard one of the outstanding Irish politicians in the state refer to the dictator as "the most potential force for peace in Europe and the world."

The significance of race in Cornerville politics was illustrated most strikingly in the presidential election of 1940. In his first two campaigns Roosevelt had been tremendously popular in Cornerville, running considerably ahead of the state Democratic ticket. At this time Roosevelt and democracy did not conflict with Mussolini and fascism in the minds of Cornerville people. They would say, "Mussolini for Italy; Roosevelt for the United States." The President created that conflict when he attacked Mussolini with the Charlottesville "stab-in-the-back" speech. An avowedly anti-Fascist policy such as the government followed was bound to

alienate some Italian voters, but this effect could have been minimized had the President not phrased his attack to strike Cornerville in such a sensitive spot. The Italian immigrants have for
years been trying to live down the reputation of being people who
are inclined to stick knives into the backs of their enemies.
Roosevelt's phrase opened an old wound. Willkie was also outspoken in his opposition to fascism, but he did not use such a telling phrase. Republican politicians and some Democrats took up
the cry. From April to November the people were constantly reminded of "the stab in the back," and all my informants agreed
that this was the most effective weapon used in the Cornerville
presidential campaign. Its effect can be roughly measured by the
following comparison in the percentages of Roosevelt and Republican votes in Cornerville in the elections of 1936 and 1940:

1936 Election

Roosevelt............................ 89

Landon.............................. 11

1940 Election

Roosevelt............................ 51

Willkie 49

In 1936 Roosevelt carried the district by 3,278 votes; in 1940 his
margin was 117 votes. While the Democratic candidate for governor ran behind the local showing of the state ticket in other years,
he was able to poll 63 per cent of the Cornerville vote.

The appeal to racial feeling logically conflicts with another sentiment which is widely held in Cornerville and elsewhere: that
the politician should serve all his constituents without regard to
their racial background. However, this does not prevent the
speakers from appealing to both sentiments in the same speech,
and most political speeches do just this.

The racial bond is of little help to the politician unless he can
also establish a connection with the class of people whose support
he seeks. This was illustrated when Judge Gennelli ran for attorney-general. Carrie Ravello told me that Gennelli was just as easy
for local Democratic politicians to contend with as any High
Street Republican candidate. She commented: "Gennelli was a
big lawyer. You go up to his office for something, and he would

charge you a lot of money. He was born down here, but he moved out long ago. He had nothing to do with the people here, and they had nothing to do with him." Gennelli's supporters complained that "the trouble with the Italian people is that they won't stick together."

The class appeal is closely related to the racial appeal. The local candidate dwells upon the similarity of his background to that of his constituents. The outsider attempts to establish the same bond. The cause of the working people is felt to be particularly worthy. The phrase "God's own poor" was heard frequently in the Ravello campaign. One of the common arguments against an opponent is that he is moving in higher social circles and has lost his regard for the working people.

It is not enough for the candidate simply to avow his interest in the Italian working people. He tries to reach them with a personal appeal. He says that he is always ready to help the poor, and he speaks in general of the favors he has done in the past.

The frequent references to the illness of Ravello's wife provide a particular example of the personal appeal. It would have made little difference to the voters that Carrie Ravello was ill if they had not had a personal regard for her and for her husband. She had established thousands of personal contacts throughout the senatorial district, and many people felt a strong bond of loyalty to her.

In speaking of his qualifications for public office, the candidate must bear two considerations in mind. He tries to convince his listeners that he is so well qualified by education and experience that he will be able to meet the "big shots" of politics on an even footing, but at the same time he points out that he is still of the common people and will be loyal to them no matter how far he advances. The most important qualification a politician can claim is that he has been and will always be loyal to his old friends, to his class, and to his race. He is expected to better his personal position only in order to be able to serve his people.

Each candidate tries to convince his audience that he is going to win. He speaks of the organizations and prominent people who are behind him. It is in the interest of groups that are not already committed to support the winning candidate so that they can establish relations with him before the favors are passed out. Most candidates predict that they will win, though at the same time they seek to show people that they have such good connections that they will be able to do favors, win or lose.

Those who seek the more important offices must deal with special topics. For example, candidates for district attorney or sheriff stress their "humane" policies when they talk in Cornerville, although they stress law enforcement in middle- and upper-class districts.

Rallies provide politicians with opportunities for making public appearances and advertising themselves and allow prominent supporters of the candidate to become more prominent and thus to increase their devotion to his cause. Without close personal ties, a politician has no chance of success. But, given certain contacts to start with, he finds public appearances useful in extending them. His name becomes known throughout the district, and people with whom he has had no previous contact come to seek his help. If he can do favors for them, he extends his sphere of influence.

The main purpose of the rally, as recognized by local politicians, is to arouse the enthusiasm of their followers. When Doc was being pressed by his friends to run for office, he said to me, "They just want to have somebody to cheer for." The politician who is to speak at a particular rally passes the word around among his followers, who attend in large numbers. Their politician is their champion. They enjoy great vicarious satisfaction from his prominent position before the public. When their man is called upon to speak, they give him an ovation. At appropriate times during the speech they clap and cheer. When he finishes, they shout and cheer again.

Most of those who attend Cornerville rallies are already committed to a candidate. As Sam Venuti said to his campaign committee:

As far as Cornerville is concerned, all the people who will vote for me are already convinced of the way they'll vote. I'll go to the rallies in Cornerville, but rallies are just for blowing off steam. I go to them just to keep up with the times, so to speak. The same people attend them. Just the hangers-on.

In Cornerville rallies the politician speaks primarily to his own supporters. This explains the course of the local contest for representative, which otherwise appears quite anomolous. Since the voters may check two candidates for this office, it is in the interest of each politician to avoid antagonizing the supporters of his opponents so that he may win their second votes. In the early period of the campaign the candidates minimize attacks upon one another and concentrate upon their own qualifications, but, as rally follows rally, they assail one another with ever increasing vehemence. Each candidate spares certain of his opponents to concentrate his attack upon one or two men. This conduct cannot fail to antagonize some of the people who are counted upon to deliver their second vote, and yet the politician is driven to it by the requirements of his supporters. They become bored with repetitious statements of their candidate's qualifications, and their enthusiasm feeds upon such attacks. The candidate must not only arouse his followers but he must keep them aroused; the statement which stirred them yesterday must be surpassed today.

The words used by the politician furnish ammunition to his supporters. While a personal obligation is recognized as sufficient reason for supporting a candidate, it cannot be used effectively as an argument to persuade those who are not obligated. The candidate must be best qualified, most sincere, and most loyal to his friends. Opposing candidates must have shown their incompetence or disloyalty. The candidate himself is expected to take the lead in furnishing such arguments.

On one occasion when Art Porcella and George Ravello were running against each other for the state senate, both spoke at a rally in Westland. The following morning Porcella told a number of his supporters what had gone on. He described Ravello's speech briefly and then went over his own at some length to show how he had "made Ravello look bad." Later in the morning, X, who had been present neither at the rally nor to hear Porcella's description, met Y, who had just come from the politician's office. X said that he couldn't arouse much enthusiasm for his work for

Porcella because he had been hearing that "Ravello made Art look bad" at the rally. Y assured X that quite the opposite was true and advised him to go to Porcella to hear the real story. X joined a group in the office to hear Art go through his version again. When X left the office, his enthusiasm was rekindled, and he went about telling others what (according to Porcella) had really happened.

Cornerville people value fluent and forceful expression very highly, and yet they do not simply elect the most eloquent man. Some years ago Tony Cardio's eldest brother ran for representative. Doc told me that his corner boys came away from all the rallies with the highest praise for Cardio's speaking ability. They thought him easily the most eloquent of all candidates, yet none of them voted for him because, from their contacts with Cardio, they were convinced that he considered himself socially superior.

Speeches may persuade more people in campaigns for higher offices in which the candidates cannot have personal contacts with many Cornerville people. This is a partial explanation of the destructive effect of Roosevelt's Charlottesville speech. However, even such a telling phrase did not directly activate the masses of Cornerville voters. It influenced certain people who in turn influenced others. There was a long process of fermentation in which people interacted to bring about this change of allegiance. Even the biggest men in state politics try to work through local leaders who line up support through personal contacts, and they recognize that without the personal contacts they will not get this support.

It is not the purpose of the Cornerville politician in addressing rallies to make a reasoned argument designed to persuade the unpersuaded. He makes an emotional appeal which is expected to activate those who are already partly or fully persuaded, so that they will work to extend the network of human relations necessary for a successful political organization.

5. ELECTION DAY

All elections in Eastern City are held under the authority of the board of elections. The members of the board are appointed by the mayor. Two must be Democrats and two Republicans. The board appoints all precinct election officials. A warden is placed in charge of each polling place. Under him are a clerk and two inspectors. These appointments must be evenly divided between the two major parties.

Having announced his name and address to the inspector at the entrance gate, the voter receives a ballot, retires to one of the booths, and marks his choices. At the exit gate an inspector checks his name again before allowing the vote to drop into the box and the voter to leave the inclosure. A police officer is stationed in each polling place.

On election day each candidate has a number of his supporters working at the polls. They stand on the sidewalk (at least 50 feet from the entrance to the polling place, as required by law), wearing buttons or ribbons which bear their candidate's name. As the voters pass by, they say, "Don't forget, vote for ———," and pass out small cards which carry the same instructions. For this work the candidate tries to select men who are well known in the precinct.

Not even the poll workers believe that they win many votes. One of them said to me:

> You don't influence nobody. People already got their minds made up. Now if I come up to you three or four weeks before election, and I say, "Bill, I'm interested in this candidate. If you ain't tied up, can you give him a vote?" Nine times out of ten you'll say, "Why the hell not?" But on election day it's different. You don't change no votes this way.

One function of the poll workers is to see that the supporters of opposing candidates do not gain an undue advantage. In past years there were frequent attempts to intimidate voters, and fights were likely to break out between opposing poll workers. While I was observing Cornerville elections, I frequently heard that trouble was expected at the polls, but except for one or two small altercations the voting proceeded quietly.

Each contesting political organization is equipped with an official list of the names and addresses of all the voters, precinct by precinct. These names are gone over before the election, those who are certain to be committed to an opposing candidate are left out, but all others are supposed to be canvassed in advance, and all who would like to be driven to the polls are checked so that cars may be provided on election day.

At an earlier period each candidate was allowed to have one of his workers inside each precinct polling place in order to protect his interests. Such men had the official list of all voters in the precinct for reference, and they could check each voter who came in and challenge any suspicious characters. From time to time, they could step outside and pass the names of those who had not voted to their associates, so that the organization could make an effort to "get out the vote."

Claiming that the men inside the polling places gave out information which enabled their associates to send in "repeaters" to vote under the names of people who had not yet voted, the board of elections ruled that only appointed officials could be allowed inside the polling places. The effect of this ruling was to transfer the checking by the political workers from inside to outside. The man with the voting list stands on the sidewalk near the polling place and checks off the names of voters as they go by. Since he cannot be present when they announce their names and addresses to the election officials, he has a more difficult job; but, if he knows his precinct well, he is able to keep a fairly accurate record.

In Ward 4 and elsewhere in Eastern City a fairly large proportion of the vote was cast by repeaters or by people who lived outside the ward. Many men who had become indebted to the Cleveland Club through obtaining a political job or other favors had moved out to more socially desirable sections. In order to continue giving their votes to the organization, they made arrangements with the keepers of rooming-houses and hotels so that, when the police officer came to check the names of those residing in each building on January 1, their names were given him. Officers on this assignment rarely made any effort to check the information given them. Some voters sought to stay inside the law technically by spending the night of January 1 at the address from which they were registered. In that way many people remained on the voting list long after they had ceased to live in the district. They were known as "mattress voters."

If a mattress voter is voting under his own name, which is included in the list of registered voters, he cannot be successfully challenged at the polls. As Joseph Maloney explained: "If you're going to challenge that registration, you have to do it at least 14 days before the election. We put that law through so that the citizens couldn't be intimidated by challenges without cause."

The club had a number of repeaters who voted many times during the day, giving each time the name of a voter who was out of town or had not yet voted. In this way the organization could be sure that all its members and many more had voted or had been voted.

While the Cleveland Club had a tremendous head start in this field, Italian political organizations recently have been able to pad the voting lists in their own interests. Not being able to call upon so many loyal supporters who had moved out of the district, the Italians had the more difficult task of registering fictitious names. One of the first powerful independent Italian politicians arranged to have his club members give the additional names to the officers making up the list of residents. During the time for registration of voters, certain of his supporters were told to register themselves under these names. They were instructed to appear before a particular window in the office of the board of elections, where the politician had evidently made arrangements with the clerk in charge. On election day the names were voted by the club's repeaters.

Widespread repeating is impossible without the co-operation of the board of elections. A position on the board is an attractive political plum, for the members receive a comfortable salary, have little work to do, and gain positions of strategic importance. In order to secure the political support of a prominent ward politician, the mayor may appoint one of his men to a vacancy on the board. That member will then see to it that the politician to whom he is responsible gets a large number of his own organization members into the polling places of his ward as inspectors, clerks, and wardens. The requirement that these appointees be evenly divided between the major parties is an inconsequential obstacle to unified control over the Ward 4 polling places. It is the practice to appoint residents of the ward to the positions. The few Republicans are dependent upon the Democratic politician for appointment in their ward and therefore are likely to make little trouble for him. It is not necessary for the ward politician to have his men in charge of all polling places at all times. If he has control of a certain number, he will be able to organize large-scale repeating.

Since political workers have been excluded from the polling places, it has become easier to organize repeating. In the earlier period one organization would have its own men appointed to the official positions in the polling place and would pay off the officer in charge, but there would still be the workers of opposing candidates to contend with. If these men continually protested, the policeman and the officials would have to challenge the voters, if only to protect themselves, and the system would break down. It would then be necessary to pay off the opposing political workers or to threaten them with violence when they stepped outside the building.

Now it is only necessary to have the election officials, particularly the warden, and the policeman in the polling place on the side of the organization which promotes the repeating. If the legally registered voter comes in later to find that his name has already been voted under, this does not concern the organization. If the man takes the trouble of appearing before the board of elections and proves his identity, he will be allowed to vote, but that cannot affect the first vote cast under his name.

In the congressional campaign Joseph Maloney had control of the precincts in Ravello's home ward, and repeaters operated throughout the ward in the late afternoon and evening. However, Branagan, Ravello's principal opponent, had control of the Ward 6 precincts, and, according to reports from Ravello's observers, he had fifty cabs from the city's largest taxi company carrying repeaters and other voters to all precincts in that ward. There were said to be over fifty repeaters operating with these motorized units, and each man voted twice in each of the twenty-odd precincts. This would account for a bloc of over two thousand votes. Branagan's repeating, being much larger in volume, added to his margin of victory, but repeating in itself did not decide this particular election, for Branagan had a clear margin of legitimate votes.

In Cornerville it is generally conceded that repeating is "wrong." The justification is that if you don't steal the election, somebody else will. The opposing political organizations are built out of groups which have sharp rivalries, and there is bitter feeling between them. An election is not looked upon as an opportunity for the people to make a free choice. It is considered a struggle for power and prestige, in which victory is to be won at all costs.

The election-day organization reveals a social differentiation among those participating, according to the jobs assigned them. The poll workers and repeaters are corner boys or older men of comparable social standing. The repeaters are a specialized group, since not all poll workers are willing to repeat. They run generally to the "tough guys" at the bottom level of society. At the next level in the structure are the men who drive voters or repeaters to the polls. Above them are the men who are in charge of the work at particular precincts. Even in the Ravello campaign of 1937, when it was agreed that there were to be no precinct captains, certain men were assigned to take informal charge of most of the precincts. Above the precinct captains there is generally a man in charge of a district or a number of precincts. At the top of the organization are the candidate himself, or the boss of his organization, and certain powerful allies. They cover the whole of the district and drive around supervising all operations.

6. THE NATURE OF POLITICAL OBLIGATIONS

The Cornerville political organization can best be described as a system of reciprocal personal obligations. The nature of the obligations may be understood by observing the situations in which they arise, the actions which create them, and the actions which are required to discharge them.

Everyone recognizes that when a politician does a favor for a constituent, the constituent becomes obligated to the politician. Depending upon the importance of the favor, the obligation may be discharged by voting for the politician or by performing more important services for him. The politician need not bring the whole weight of his personal influence to bear in obtaining each favor for his constituents. When dealing with authorities, the person who speaks English poorly or not at all has an obvious need for an interpreter, and even the corner boy who has grown up speaking English tends to be inarticulate when he is out of his own sphere. Besides, the uninitiated do not understand the complex organization of government and do not know how to find the channels through which they can obtain action. In some cases the constituent has an undeniable claim to a certain benefit and may secure it simply by appearing before the proper authority and stating his case. Nevertheless, the person who does not know where to go or how to speak for himself must ask for a guide and spokesman, and the politician who serves in that capacity performs a real service, which results in the creation of an obligation.

The politician becomes obligated to those who support his campaign, and the high cost of political activity tends to put a premium on financial support. The more the politician can contribute to the support of his own political activity, the freer he will be from this particular type of obligation. This may account for the fact that the undertaker-politician is less closely tied to the racketeers than is the lawyer-politician, for whom the racketeers are the most important clients as well as the largest campaign contributors.

Discussion of the campaign indicates the different ways in which money may be spent but does not show how the politician decides into which particular channels to pour his funds. In practice the politician spends most of his money in areas where he lacks popular support.

Fiumara's campaign of 1937 provides an illustration of this sort of behavior. For years Joseph Maloney had been so firmly intrenched as alderman that most Italian politicians concentrated their attention upon other offices. At this time Fiumara was just another undertaker to the voters of the ward. When he opened his campaign, he set about winning over the various Italian and other non-Irish groups. He paid clubs for their indorsements and in addition financed election parties in their quarters. He gave

out money to be spent in his interest. His expenditure, locally reported as $6,400, was unparalleled in the history of Ward 4 alder-
manic contests, and some of it may have been wasted, but it
served to establish Fiumara as Boss Maloney's chief rival for the
office. In his first campaign Fiumara polled over three thousand
votes and ran second to Maloney. Without such lavish financing,
Fiumara would have been only one more minor competitor, and
he would have had no chance to defeat the Cleveland Club boss in
1939.

Even so free a spender as Fiumara does not spread his money
evenly. He tries to win as much Italian support as he can without
spending money. In the election of 1939 most of the Fiumara poll
workers in Cornerville served as volunteers. Maloney and Kelly,
who had little support in Cornerville, paid five dollars each to
their poll workers in that section. That is the situation in general.
Where a politician has established a chain of personal obligations,
he spends little, and where he lacks such a chain he concentrates
his funds.

The politician who must pay cash for a large proportion of his
support may offset this by charging his constituents for favors.
This practice has become increasingly common.

In order to get a job, to have a case fixed, or to obtain some
other favor, one is required to pay a sum of money which varies
with the importance of the favor. The ward politician does not
keep all this himself. He must pay someone who has the power to
grant the favor. If it is an important favor which must be performed by a man near the top of the political hierarchy, the money passes through an intermediary. The ward politician pays the
"bag man," who turns the money over to the "big shot." All important politicians who operate according to this system have
trusted friends who serve as graft collectors in order to protect
their superiors from prosecution. It is understood in Cornerville
that the constituent's money is not paid in full to the big shot.
The ward politician takes his "cut" and the bag man does likewise. If the favor is performed, the constituent is not expected to
interest himself in the fate of his money. Not all Ward 4 politi-

cians work on this basis. There are some, like George Ravello, who refuse to accept cash payment for their political services.

The nature of the obligations existing between politicians and their constituents depends upon whether the services performed on either side are paid for or furnished free of charge. The constituent who pays for a favor feels less obligated than the one who is not charged. Money need not entirely destroy the basis of personal obligation. That depends to a certain extent upon the size of the payment and the importance of the favor. The constituent may say to himself: "I paid the politician for getting me a job, but, still, jobs are in demand; there are plenty of others who would have paid what I did and more for this job; the politician was a good fellow to do this for me, and I'll be with him at the next election." Nevertheless, the obligation is not so secure when money passes from constituent to politician.

As Joseph Maloney expressed it in attacking his rival, Mike Kelly, in the campaign of 1939:

> There is one candidate that has promised at least two hundred jobs. How is he going to deliver them? He's got men with him, yes, they've all got their price, but they should realize that when they get their price the obligation is discharged.

One of the corner boys expressed his opinion in this way:

> Sometimes them politicians want to give you money if you work for them. Then when you come up to them after for a job, they say, "What's the matter, didn't I pay you?" . . . . If you're smart, you don't take the money, and then maybe you got a chance to get something.

Many take the opposite view. Tony Cataldo, Carlo, and several other members of the Cornerville S. and A. held that the corner boys should recognize that they were not going to get anything after the election anyway and that therefore they should demand cash in advance. The politician would then not be obligated to them for their support, but, if they had received the money, they would be satisfied.

If the politician uses money to secure a large part of his support, he frees himself from his obligations to those constituents. Lacking strong personal ties, they may turn against him after the election, but in the next campaign he can win them over with money once more, or, if they desert him permanently, he can find other groups which will respond to the same incentive.

The effectiveness of cash payments in securing votes should not be overemphasized. The corner boys' attitude toward money in politics is something like this: Politics is a racket; the politician is just trying to use us to get something for himself; we might as well promise him anything and get all we can out of him; then we'll do what we want to do anyway. In this connection it is pertinent to recall the speech made in the Cornerville S. and A. Club by the Fiumara supporter who advised the boys: "Don't be chumps. Take their dough. You can use it, but then go in and vote for Fiumara." The political obligation depends not alone upon a favor done by the politician but upon the personal contacts between the politician and his constituents. Where these are lacking, money cannot fill the gap.

This discussion should not give the impression that the politician is free to select his course of action. If he has not been able to establish a sufficiently extensive network of obligations before the campaign, he will have to use money freely in order to win support. If, when elected, he cannot raise sufficient funds in other ways, he may have to take money for the favors he does. Since many of his superiors operate on a cash basis, he may be forced to do likewise. One of the reasons given for George Ravello's failure to secure more jobs and favors for his constituents was his unwillingness to arrange for their purchase. In his first term he asked certain big shots for favors and was told that they could be had for a price. When word got around that Ravello would not pay, the big shots simply told him that the favors could not be done.

This does not mean that all important favors must be paid for. The relations between politicians, like those between the politician and his constituents, are based upon personal nonfinancial obligations as well as upon cash payments. By refusing to pay cash, the politician cuts himself off from some but not all the available favors.

According to Cornerville standards, the politician who does a favor for friendship is considered morally superior to one who does it for money. Similarly, the constituent who shows his devotion to the candidate's cause by contributing freely to his campaign fund is superior to the man who tries to buy a specific favor. Favors should be reciprocated out of personal loyalty, as they are in the corner gang.

Although political organizations have changed profoundly in recent years, most Cornerville people continue to believe in these standards. Still, cash in advance has a powerful appeal, and people do not always support the candidate for whom they have the most respect. Since more and more of the ward candidates have taken to a cash basis, their constituents have less choice in the matter of obtaining favors. They feel that it is better to pay for a favor than to get no favor at all.

So far, obligations and favors have been discussed in personal terms. It is believed in Cornerville as well as elsewhere that the politician has an obligation to his community to secure parks, playgrounds, and other improvements contributing to the general welfare. Cornerville people complain bitterly that their representatives have failed to meet this obligation. Brief inspection is all that is needed to convince one that the district has fared worse than others in obtaining such improvements.

Cornerville people have a variety of explanations for this condition. They say that the politicians sell them out, that the politicians are not interested in improving the district, or that they do not want to do too much for fear that the people will be able to get along without them. These expressions of sentiment throw little light upon the question. We should not expect a politician who sincerely desires to obtain improvements to lose interest in this goal as soon as he is elected. Even if he were only interested in graft, there can be more graft in a public improvement project than in anything else.

Evidently, the explanation must be made in different terms. The politician-constituent and politician-politician personal relations provide a clue.

It would be pleasing to people in general to have public improvements, but the political structure is not based upon people in general. The politician has obligations to particular people, and he maintains his organization by discharging a certain number of these obligations.

The politician must concentrate his efforts where there are the most pressing demands. If a man wants three things—to keep out of jail, to get a job, and to have new play space for his children—he will not ask for them all at once. First, he wants to secure his freedom and then a means of obtaining money. If the politician can do these favors for him, he will be satisfied and probably will not mention the park at all, for the constituents realize that what they can ask from a politician depends upon what they can do for him.

The constituents feel that people in general have a right to community improvements and therefore they do not look upon them as personal favors. The man who has a job and has no trouble with the law does not make the effort to establish close personal relations with the politician in order to obtain community improvements.

When he is asked to fix a pinch for a corner boy or to use his influence to protect the racketeers, the politician must make the connections with the police and the district attorney which such action requires. The closest possible connections with these people will not aid him toward obtaining community improvements because they have no jurisdiction in such matters. When he is asked to get a man on the relief rolls, he must make connections with the authorities who handle such matters, and they also have nothing to do with initiating community improvements. When he is asked to get a man a political job, he must try to make connections with the important figures in the administration, and there he comes into contact with the people who have power over improvements. But he cannot ask for everything. It is well understood in politics that one politician cannot ask a great deal of another unless he can perform important services in return. If he asks too much, the connection breaks down, and he can get nothing.

The interactions necessary in the hierarchy in order to obtain community improvements differ from those which are required for personal favors. Several examples will show the nature of these interactions.

A man is arrested by a patrolman or a sergeant. He gets in touch with one of the ward politicians. The politician speaks to the captain, who is the superior of the arresting officer. The captain asks the officer to forget the charge. The officer does so, and the man is released. While the captain is in charge of his division, he has deputy superintendents, a superintendent, and the police chief above him in the hierarchy. In this case, as in most such cases, the interactions do not need to reach above the level of the captain.

A man is taken to court for some petty crime. He asks the help of a ward politician. The judges of the lowest court are men who have recently been active in politics and have secured their positions by means of this activity. The ward politician speaks to the judge, and the judge agrees to be lenient. To deal with higher courts, more important connections are needed, but cases at the bottom level can be handled as personal matters without reaching above this level in the hierarchy.

A man is to be prosecuted by one of the assistant district attorneys. He speaks to a ward politician. If he has made connections at such a level in the hierarchy, the politician speaks directly to the district attorney, and the district attorney tells his assistant to drop the case. Otherwise it is frequently possible to secure results without taking the case up to the district attorney. His subordinates are susceptible to certain sorts of political pressure.

A different course of action is required in order to secure a general community improvement. The following story will serve as an illustration.

Some corner boys were playing softball in a small park. Some of the more powerful hitters occasionally drove the ball over the wall bounding the lot and against the building across the street. Several windows had been broken. The building was owned by the Eastern City Bank and Trust Co. The caretaker complained to the real estate division of the bank, and an official there got in touch with the park commissioner. The park commissioner ruled that no boys over sixteen should be allowed to play softball in this lot and asked the Cornerville police captain to take action. The captain spoke to the sergeant, and the sergeant broke up a hotly contested game one Sunday afternoon.

Sam Franco, the leader of one of the corner gangs, had been organizing a softball league, which was to include sixteen teams. The commissioner's ruling only served to intensify interest in softball, and Sam sought some means of gaining the use of the park. He talked with an older man who had met the park commissioner. The commissioner attended a near-by church. Sam and his friend waited for him outside and asked if his department could erect a wire-netting extension to the wall so that the building would be protected. He said that he had no appropriation for such a purpose and could do nothing for them. A few days later they sought to talk with him again, but he said, "I don't want to have anything to do with you," and brushed past them.

Having made his acquaintance through Doc's recreation center, Sam now consulted Mr. Kendall, head of boys' work at the Cornerville House. Mr. Kendall told Sam to continue with his plans for the league and arranged for the captains of all the teams to meet once every two weeks so that they could follow developments and discuss plans.

Mr. Kendall talked to the man in charge of the bank's Cornerville properties, who expressed his sympathy with the corner boys but said that he could do nothing. He did not offer to take the case to higher authorities in the bank's hierarchy. Mr. Kendall then talked with Sam Venuti, a local politician who had had some contact with the park commissioner. The politician went to see the commissioner but was not able to accomplish anything.

Meanwhile the corner boys had been holding meetings, and Sam told Mr. Kendall that, unless something was accomplished soon, they would lose interest and the organization would break up. Mr. Kendall telephoned both Alderman Fiumara and Andy Cotillo, one of the mayor's secretaries, and each agreed to see what he could do. Ten days later he again telephoned Fiumara. The alderman had forgotten the matter. Sensing that the politician did not see the potential voting strength involved in the softball organization, Mr. Kendall took some of the team captains to see Fiumara in person.

At this point things began to happen fast. Fiumara promised to introduce a bill calling for a fence appropriation and to see the mayor about it. Andy Cotillo sprang into action at the same time. Both men had several conferences with the mayor. Mr. Kendall was notified of the results after each one. Cotillo would call and say, "I've just seen the mayor, and he says everything is going to be all right." Five minutes later Fiumara would telephone the same message. Neither man mentioned the other, though they had obviously been together in the executive offices. Within a short time the money was appropriated. The league's opening game was scheduled before the fence was to go up, and the softball diamond was shifted in direction, which hampered the game but protected the windows. At least a thousand people turned out for this game, and Fiumara was there. After the game, the captains of the teams met in the Cornerville House with Mr. Kendall and Fiumara to decide whether the league should continue on its newly arranged diamond or wait for the fence. Sam argued that the city would require at least a month to get around to erecting the fence. Fiumara said he would see the mayor the following morning and try to press matters. That afternoon the mayor came to inspect the park lot with a city engineer, and within a week the fence was erected and two softball games were being held each night.

Many people were surprised at these results. This was said to be the first time in years that Cornerville had obtained an appropriation for new construction in the park department budget. The speed with which the plan was put into effect, when once the right channels had been struck, was also impressive.

To understand what transpired, it is necessary to make a distinction between the legislative and executive branches of government. The executive branch has its own hierarchies in the administrative departments, like the park department. They are subject to pressure from the legislators, but to a certain extent they must resist pressure, for they develop their own channels of interaction and standards of procedure in carrying out the re-

quirements of their jobs. A new plan of action involving an administrative hierarchy cannot be introduced on the initiative of
constituents unless the pressure on the legislative side is carried up
to a person in a position to give an order to the head of a department. If the demand for action comes from the bottom of the society, there must be organization and co-ordination of effort at
every level in order to make the pressure effective at the top of the
legislative hierarchy.

MAKING & FIXING A PINCH

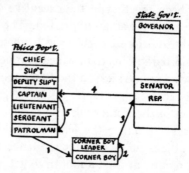

Arrows indicate direction & sequence of interactions
Positions of boxes indicate relative status

In this case the corner boys were not able to deal directly with
the park commissioner. There was too big a gap between their
positions. Sam Venuti could talk with the commissioner, but he
could not give him an order. Angelo Fiumara was not interested
in acting for Mr.Kendall until he realized that the social worker
was part of a well-knit organization, which in this case included
Sam Franco, sixteen corner-boy leaders, and all their followers.
Then he and Andy Cotillo acted upon the mayor. Cotillo was in
the mayor's office, and Fiumara had made his connections
through Cotillo. Both men were in a position to exert pressure
upon the top point in this legislative hierarchy, and, when they
did, the course of action initiated by Sam Franco was brought to
a successful conclusion.

OBTAINING THE PARK FENCE

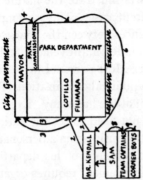

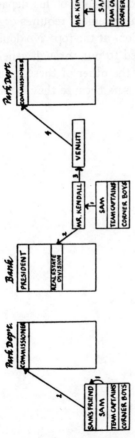

Arrows indicate direction & sequence of interactions

Positions of boxes indicate relative status

The accompanying charts illustrate the nature of the actions involved in the two different cases. These examples show that there are important differences between the course of interactions required to secure a community improvement and that required to secure a personal favor. Most personal favors do not require reaching up to the top of a political organization. The action may take place near the bottom of the hierarchy. Even if the top man must be reached, he does not need to set the entire hierarchy in motion. He can transact the business on a personal basis without disturbing the established relations of his department. The securing of a community improvement requires organization at the bottom and good connections at the top. No doubt many Cornerville politicians have failed to put through general measures because they lacked one or the other of these requirements. They are considered double-crossers because they cannot do the things that are expected of them.

PART III
CONCLUSION

CONCLUSION

1. THE GANG AND THE INDIVIDUAL

THE corner-gang structure arises out of the habitual association of the members over a long period of time. The nuclei of most gangs can be traced back to early boyhood, when living close together provided the first opportunities for social contacts. School years modified the original pattern somewhat, but I know of no corner gangs which arose through classroom or school-playground association. The gangs grew up on the corner and remained there with remarkable persistence from early boyhood until the members reached their late twenties or early thirties. In the course of years some groups were broken up by the movement of families away from Cornerville, and the remaining members merged with gangs on near-by corners; but frequently movement out of the district does not take the corner boy away from his corner. On any evening on almost any corner one finds corner boys who have come in from other parts of the city or from suburbs to be with their old friends. The residence of the corner boy may also change within the district, but nearly always he retains his allegiance to his original corner.

Home plays a very small role in the group activities of the corner boy. Except when he eats, sleeps, or is sick, he is rarely at home, and his friends always go to his corner first when they want to find him. Even the corner boy's name indicates the dominant importance of the gang in his activities. It is possible to associate with a group of men for months and never discover the family names of more than a few of them. Most are known by nicknames attached to them by the group. Furthermore, it is easy to overlook the distinction between married and single men. The married man regularly sets aside one evening a week to take out his wife. There are other occasions when they go out together and entertain together, and some corner boys devote more attention to their wives than others, but, married or single, the corner boy can be found on his corner almost every night of the week.

His social activities away from the corner are organized with similar regularity. Many corner gangs set aside the same night each week for some special activity, such as bowling. With the Nortons this habit was so strong that it persisted for some of the members long after the original group had broken up.

Most groups have a regular evening meeting-place aside from the corner. Nearly every night at about the same time the gang gathers for "coffee-and" in its favorite cafeteria or for beer in the corner tavern. When some other activity occupies the evening, the boys meet at the cafeteria or tavern before returning to the corner or going home. Positions at the tables are fixed by custom. Night after night each group gathers around the same tables. The right to these positions is recognized by other Cornerville groups. When strangers are found at the accustomed places, the necessity of finding other chairs is a matter of some annoyance, especially if no near-by location is available. However, most groups gather after nine in the evening when few are present except the regular customers who are familiar with the established procedure.

The life of the corner boy proceeds along regular and narrowly circumscribed channels. As Doc said to me:

> Fellows around here don't know what to do except within a radius of about three hundred yards. That's the truth, Bill. They come home from work, hang on the corner, go up to eat, back on the corner, up a show, and they come back to hang on the corner. If they're not on the corner, it's likely the boys there will know where you can find them. Most of them stick to one corner. It's only rarely that a fellow will change his corner.

The stable composition of the group and the lack of social assurance on the part of its members contribute toward producing a very high rate of social interaction within the group. The group structure is a product of these interactions.

Out of such interaction there arises a system of mutual obligations which is fundamental to group cohesion. If the men are to carry on their activities as a unit, there are many occasions when they must do favors for one another. The code of the corner boy requires him to help his friends when he can and to refrain from doing anything to harm them. When life in the group runs smoothly, the obligations binding members to one another are not explicitly recognized. Once Doc asked me to do something for him, and I said that he had done so much for me that I welcomed the chance to reciprocate. He objected: "I don't want it that way. I want you to do this for me because you're my friend. That's all."

It is only when the relationship breaks down that the underlying obligations are brought to light. While Alec and Frank were friends, I never heard either one of them discuss the services he was performing for the other, but when they had a falling-out over the group activities with the Aphrodite Club, each man complained to Doc that the other was not acting as he should in view of the services that had been done him. In other words, actions which were performed explicitly for the sake of friendship were revealed as being part of a system of mutual obligations.

Not all the corner boys live up to their obligations equally well, and this factor partly accounts for the differentiation in status among them. The man with a low status may violate his obligations without much change in his position. His fellows know that he has failed to discharge certain obligations in the past, and his position reflects his past performances. On the other hand, the leader is depended upon by all the members to meet his personal obligations. He cannot fail to do so without causing confusion and endangering his position.

The relationship of status to the system of mutual obligations is most clearly revealed when one observes the use of money. During the time that I knew a corner gang called the Millers, Sam Franco, the leader, was out of work except for an occasional odd job; yet, whenever he had a little money, he spent it on Joe and Chichi, his closest friends, who were next to him in the structure of the group. When Joe or Chichi had money, which was less frequent, they reciprocated. Sam frequently paid for two members who stood close to the bottom of his group and occasionally for others. The two men who held positions immediately below Joe and Chichi were considered very well off according to Cornerville standards. Sam said that he occasionally borrowed money from them, but never more than fifty cents at a time. Such loans he repaid at the earliest possible moment. There were four other members with lower positions in the group, who nearly always had more money than Sam. He did not recall ever having borrowed from them. He said that the only time he had obtained a substantial sum from anyone around his corner was when he borrowed eleven dollars from a friend who was the *leader* of another corner gang.

The situation was the same among the Nortons. Doc did not hesitate to accept money from Danny, but he avoided taking any from the followers.

The leader spends more money on his followers than they on him. The farther down in the structure one looks, the fewer are the financial relations which tend to obligate the leader to a follower. This does not mean that the leader has more money than others or even that he necessarily spends more—though he must always be a free spender. It means that the financial relations must be explained in social terms. Unconsciously, and in some cases consciously, the leader refrains from putting himself under obligations to those with low status in the group.

The leader is the focal point for the organization of his group. In his absence, the members of the gang are divided into a number of small groups. There is no common activity or general conversation. When the leader appears, the situation changes strikingly. The small units form into one large group. The conversation becomes general, and unified action frequently follows. The leader becomes the central point in the discussion. A follower starts to say something, pauses when he notices that the leader is not listening, and begins again when he has the leader's attention. When the leader leaves the group, unity gives way to the divisions that existed before his appearance.

The members do not feel that the gang is really gathered until the leader appears. They recognize an obligation to wait for him before beginning any group activity, and when he is present they expect him to make their decisions. One night when the Nortons had a bowling match, Long John had no money to put up as his side bet, and he agreed that Chick Morelli should bowl in his place. After the match Danny said to Doc, "You should never have put Chick in there."

Doc replied with some annoyance, "Listen, Danny, you yourself suggested that Chick should bowl instead of Long John."

Danny said, "I know, but you shouldn't have let it go."

The leader is the man who acts when the situation requires action. He is more resourceful than his followers. Past events have shown that his ideas were right. In this sense "right" simply means satisfactory to the members. He is the most independent in judgment. While his followers are undecided as to a course of action or upon the character of a newcomer, the leader makes up his mind.

When he gives his word to one of his boys, he keeps it. The followers look to him for advice and encouragement, and he receives more of their confidences than any other man. Consequently, he knows more about what is going on in the group than anyone else. Whenever there is a quarrel among the boys, he hears of it almost as soon as it happens. Each party to the quarrel may appeal to him to work out a solution; and, even when the men do not want to compose their differences, each one takes his side of the story to the leader at the first opportunity. A man's standing depends partly upon the leader's belief that he has been conducting himself properly.

The leader is respected for his fair-mindedness. Whereas there may be hard feelings among some of the followers, the leader cannot bear a grudge against any man in the group. He has close friends (men who stand next to him in position), and he is indifferent to some of the members; but, if he is to retain his reputation for impartiality, he cannot allow personal animus to override his judgment.

The leader need not be the best baseball player, bowler, or fighter, but he must have some skill in whatever pursuits are of particular interest to the group. It is natural for him to promote activities in which he excels and to discourage those in which he is not skilful; and, in so far as he is thus able to influence the group, his competent performance is a natural consequence of his position. At the same time his performance supports his position.

The leader is better known and more respected outside his group than are any of his followers. His capacity for social movement is greater. One of the most important functions he performs is that of relating his group to other groups in the district. Whether the relationship is one of conflict, competition, or cooperation, he is expected to represent the interests of his fellows. The politician and the racketeer must deal with the leader in order to win the support of his followers. The leader's reputation outside the group tends to support his standing within the group, and his position in the group supports his reputation among outsiders.

The leader does not deal with his followers as an undifferentiated group. Doc explained:

On any corner you would find not only a leader but probably a couple of lieutenants. They could be leaders themselves, but they let the man lead them. You would say, "They let him lead because they like the way he does things." Sure, but he leans upon them for his authority. Many times you find fellows on a corner that stay in the background until some situation comes up, and then they will take over and call the shots. Things like that can change fast sometimes.

The leader mobilizes the group by dealing first with his lieutenants. It was customary for the Millers to go bowling every Saturday night. One Saturday Sam had no money, so he set out to persuade the boys to do something else. Later he explained to me how he had been able to change the established social routine of the group. He said:

I had to show the boys that it would be in their own interests to come with me—that each one of them would benefit. But I knew I only had to convince two of the fellows. If they start to do something, the other boys will say to themselves, "If Joe does it—or if Chichi does it—it must be a good thing for us too." I told Joe and Chichi what the idea was, and I got them to come with me. I didn't pay no attention to the others. When Joe and Chichi came, all the other boys came along too.

Another example from the Millers indicates what happens when the leader and his lieutenant disagree upon group policy. This is Sam talking again:

One time we had a raffle to raise money to build a camp on Lake Blank [on property lent them by a local businessman]. We had collected $54, and Joe and I were holding the money. That week I knew Joe was playing pool, and he lost three or four dollars gambling. When Saturday came, I says to the boys, "Come on, we go out to Lake Blank. We're gonna build that camp on the hill."

Right away, Joe said, "If yuz are gonna build the camp on the hill, I don't come. I want it on the other side."

All the time I knew he had lost the money, and he was only making up excuses so he wouldn't have to let anybody know. Now the hill was really the place to build that camp. On the other side, the ground was swampy. That would have been a stupid place. But I knew that if I tried to make them go through with it now, the group would split up into two cliques. Some would come with me, and some would go with Joe. So I let the whole thing drop for a while. After, I got Joe alone, and I says to him, "Joe, I know you lost some of that money, but that's all right. You can pay up when you have it and nobody will say nothin'. But, Joe, you know we shouldn't have the camp on the other side of the hill because the land is not good there. We should build it on the hill."

So he said, "All right," and we got all the boys together, and we went out to build the camp.

Disagreements are not always worked out so amicably. I once asked Doc and Sam to tell me who was the leader of a corner gang that was familiar to both of them. Sam commented:

Doc picked out Carmen. He picked out the wrong man. I told him why he was wrong—that Dominic was the leader. But that very same night, there was almost a fight between the two of them, Dominic and Carmen. And now the group is split up into two gangs.

Doc said:

Sometimes you can't pick out one leader. The leadership may be in doubt. Maybe there are a couple of boys vying for the honors. But you can find that out.

The leadership is changed not through an uprising of the bottom men but by a shift in the relations between men at the top of the structure. When a gang breaks into two parts, the explanation is to be found in a conflict between the leader and one of his former lieutenants.

This discussion should not give the impression that the leader is the only man who proposes a course of action. Other men frequently have ideas, but their suggestions must go through the proper channels if they are to go into effect.

In one meeting of the Cornerville S. and A., Dodo, who held a bottom ranking, proposed that he be allowed to handle the sale of beer in the clubrooms in return for 75 per cent of the profits. Tony spoke in favor of Dodo's suggestion but proposed giving him a somewhat smaller percentage. Dodo agreed. Then Carlo proposed to have Dodo handle the beer in quite a different way, and Tony agreed. Tony made the motion, and it was carried unanimously. In this case Dodo's proposal was carried through, after substantial modifications, upon the actions of Tony and Carlo.

In another meeting Dodo said that he had two motions to make: that the club's funds be deposited in a bank and that no officer be allowed to serve two consecutive terms. Tony was not present at this time. Dom, the president, said that only one motion should be made at a time and that, furthermore, Dodo should not make any motions until there had been opportunity for discussion. Dodo agreed. Dom then commented that it would be foolish to deposit the funds when the club had so little to deposit. Carlo expressed his agreement. The meeting passed on to other things without action upon the first motion and without even a word of discussion on the second one. In the same meeting, Chris, who held a middle position, moved that a member must be in the club for a year before being allowed to hold office. Carlo said that it was a good idea, he seconded the motion, and it carried unanimously.

The actions of the leader can be characterized in terms of the origination of action in pair and set events. A pair event is one which takes place between two people. A set event is one in which one man originates action for two or more others. The leader frequently originates action for the group without waiting for the suggestions of his followers. A follower may originate action for the leader in a pair event, but he does not originate action for the leader and other followers at the same time—that is, he does not originate action in a set event which includes the leader. Of course, when the leader is not present, parts of the group are mobilized when men lower in the structure originate action in set events. It is through observation of such set events when the top men are not present that it is possible to determine the relative positions of the men who are neither leaders nor lieutenants.

Each member of the corner gang has his own position in the gang structure. Although the positions may remain unchanged over long periods of time, they should not be conceived in static terms. To have a position means that the individual has a customary way of interacting with other members of the group. When the pattern of interactions changes, the positions change. The positions of the members are interdependent, and one position cannot change without causing some adjustments in the other positions. Since the group is organized around the men with the top positions, some of the men with low standing may change positions or drop out without upsetting the balance of the group. For example, when Lou Danaro and Fred Mackey stopped participating in the activities of the Nortons, those activities continued to be organized in much the same manner as before, but when Doc and Danny dropped out, the Nortons disintegrated, and the patterns of interaction had to be reorganized along different lines.

One may generalize upon these processes in terms of group equilibrium. The group may be said to be in equilibrium when the interactions of its members fall into the customary pattern through which group activities are and have been organized. The pattern of interactions may undergo certain modifications without upsetting the group equilibrium, but abrupt and drastic changes destroy the equilibrium.

The actions of the individual member may also be conceived in terms of equilibrium. Each individual has his own characteristic way of interacting with other individuals. This is probably fixed within wide limits by his native endowment, but it develops and takes its individual form through the experiences of the individual in interacting with others throughout the course of his life. Twentieth-century American life demands a high degree of flexibility of action from the individual, and the normal person learns to adjust within certain limits to changes in the frequency and type of his interactions with others. This flexibility can be developed only through experiencing a wide variety of situations which require adjustment to different patterns of interaction. The more limited the individual's experience, the more rigid his manner of interacting, and the more difficult his adjustment when changes are forced upon him.

This conclusion has important implications for the understanding of the problems of the corner boy. As we have seen, gang activities proceed from day to day in a remarkably fixed pattern. The members come together every day and interact with a very high frequency. Whether he is at the top and originates action for the group in set events, is in the middle and follows the origination of the leader and originates for those below him, or is at the bottom of the group and always follows in set events, the individual member has a way of interaction which remains stable and fixed through continual group activity over a long period of time. His mental well-being requires continuance of his way of interacting. He needs the customary channels for his activity, and, when they are lacking, he is disturbed.

Doc told me this story:

One night Angelo and Phil went to the Tivoli to see a picture. They didn't have enough money for Frank, so they had to leave him behind. You should have seen him. It's a terrible thing to be left behind by the boys. You would have thought Frank was in a cage. I sat next to him by the playground. Danny was holding the crap game in the playground. Frank said to me, "Do you think Danny would have a quarter for me?"

I said, "I don't know. Ask him if you want to."

But Frank didn't want to ask him. He asked me, "Do you think Long John has a quarter?"

I said, "No, I know that Long John is clean." Frank didn't know what to do. If he had got the nerve up to ask Danny for the quarter right away, he could have run after the boys and caught up with them before they reached the theater. I knew that he would run if he had the money. But he waited too long so he wouldn't be able to catch up with them. It was nine-thirty when the crap game broke up. Frank went into the playground with me. He wanted me to ask Danny for something, but I told him to ask himself. He didn't want to. He said he thought he would go home, and he started, but then he came back. He asked us when we were going down to Jennings. I told him ten o'clock. We always go at ten now. He said that was too long to wait so he went home. Danny, Long John, and I went down to Jennings. We had been there about fifteen minutes when in walks Frank, and he sits down at a table next to us and starts reading the paper. Danny says, "What's the matter, Frank, no coffee?"

Frank says, "That's all right. I don't feel like it."

Danny says, "Go ahead, get your coffee." So Frank got coffee. We were ready to go before Angelo and Phil had come in. I could see that Frank didn't want to leave, but he had to because you're supposed to go out with the man that takes care of your check. He walked home with us, and then I guess he went back to Jennings' to meet Angelo and Phil.

Frank had a very high regard for Danny and Doc, and at an earlier period he would have been perfectly happy in their company, but since Angelo had become the leader of the group he had seldom interacted with them and he had been interacting regularly and frequently with Angelo and Phil. When he was deprived of their company, the resulting disturbance was strikingly apparent.

A man with a low position in the group is less flexible in his adjustments than the leader, who customarily deals with groups outside of his own. This may explain why Frank was so upset by events of only a few hours' duration. However, no matter what the corner boy's position, he suffers when the manner of his interaction must undergo drastic changes. This is clearly illustrated in the cases of Long John's nightmares and Doc's dizzy spells.

Long John had had this trouble on certain previous occasions, but then the fear of death had gone, and he had been able to sleep without difficulty. He had not been troubled for a long period up to the time that he experienced his latest attack. I do not know the circumstances surrounding the earlier attacks, but on this occasion Long John's social situation seemed clearly to explain his plight. He had become adjusted to a very high rate of interaction with Doc and Danny. While he did not have great influence among the followers in the Nortons, they did not originate action for him in set events, and he occasionally originated action for them. When the Nortons broke up and Doc and Danny went into Spongi's inner circle, Long John was left stranded. He could no longer interact with Doc and Danny with the same frequency. When he went over to Norton Street, he found the followers building up their own organization under the leadership of Angelo. If he was to participate in their activities, he had to become a follower in set events originated by Angelo. The members who had been below him in the Nortons were constantly trying to originate action for him. When his relationship with Doc and Danny broke down, he had no defense against these aggressions.

Doc brought about the cure by changing Long John's social situation. By bringing him into Spongi's inner circle, Doc reestablished the close relationship between Long John, Danny, and himself. In so doing, he protected Long John from the aggressions of the former followers. When Long John was once more inter-acting with Doc and Danny with great frequency, his mental dif-ficulties disappeared, and he began acting with the same assurance that had previously characterized his behavior.

Doc's dizzy spells came upon him when he was unemployed and had no spending money. He considered his unemployment the cause of his difficulties, and, in a sense, it was, but in order to un-derstand the case it is necessary to inquire into the changes which unemployment necessitated in the activity of the individual. While no one enjoys being unemployed and without money, there are many Cornerville men who could adjust themselves to that situation without serious difficulties. Why was Doc so different? To say that he was a particularly sensitive person simply gives a name to the phenomenon and provides no answer. The observa-tion of interactions provides the answer. Doc was accustomed to a high frequency of interaction with the members of his group and to frequent contacts with members of other groups. While he sometimes directly originated action in set events for the group, it was customary for one of the other members to originate action for him in a pair event, and then he would originate action in a set event. That is, someone would suggest a course of action, and then Doc would get the boys together and organize group activity. The events of Doc's political campaign indicate that this pattern had broken down. Mike was continually telling Doc what to do about the campaign, and I was telling him what to do about see-ing Mr. Smith and others to get a job. While we originated action for him with increasing frequency, he was not able to originate action in set events. Lacking money, he could not participate in group activities without accepting the support of others and let-ting them determine his course of action. Therefore, on many oc-casions he avoided associating with his friends—that is, his fre-quency of interaction was drastically reduced. At a time when he should have been going out to make contacts with other groups, he was unable to act according to the political pattern even with the groups that he knew, and he saw less and less of those outside his circle of closest friends. When he was alone, he did not get dizzy, but, when he was with a group of people and was unable to act in his customary manner, he fell prey to the dizzy spells.

When Doc began his recreation-center job, the spells disappeared. He was once again able to originate action, first for the boys in his center, but also for his own corner boys. Since he now had money, he could again associate with his friends and could also broaden his contacts. When the job and the money ran out, the manner of interaction to which Doc was adjusted was once more upset. He was unemployed from the time that the center closed in the winter of 1939-40 until he got a W.P.A. job in the spring of 1941. The dizzy spells came back, and shortly before he got his job he had what his friends called a nervous breakdown. A doctor who had an excellent reputation in Eastern City examined him and was unable to find any organic causes to account for his condition. When I visited Cornerville in May, 1941, he was once again beginning to overcome the dizzy spells. He discussed his difficulties with me:

When I'm batted out, I'm not on the corner so much. And when I am on the corner, I just stay there. I can't do what I want to do. If the boys want to go to a show or to Jennings or bowling, I have to count my pennies to see if I have enough. If I'm batted out, I have to make some excuse. I tell the boys I don't want to go, and I take a walk by myself. I get bored sometimes hanging in Spongi's, but where can I go? I have to stay there. Danny offers me money, and that's all right, but he's been getting tough breaks. Last week he was complaining he was batted out and a couple of days later he offered me two dollars. I refused. I don't want to ask anybody for anything. Sometimes I say to Danny or Spongi, "Do you want a cigarette?" They say, "No, we've got some," and then I say, "All right, I'll have one of yours." I make a joke out of it, but still it is humiliating. I never do that except when I'm desperate for a cigarette. Danny is the only one that ever gives me money.

Before I got this W.P.A. job, I looked terrible. I eat here at home, but I can't expect them to buy clothes for me. I had one suit, and that was through at the elbow, and the cuffs had more shreds than a chrysanthemum. When I had to go places, I kept my overcoat on, or else I carried it over my arm to hide the hole in the elbow. And I was literally walking on the soles of my feet. You think I like to go around like that?

Lou Danaro has been after me to go out with him. He's got a new Buick—a brand-new Buick. That's pretty nice, you know. He wants me to get a girl, and we'll go out together. But I won't go. I'd have to play a secondary role. No, that's what you want me to say. I mean, I wouldn't be able to do what I want to do.

Last summer, they asked me to be chairman of the Norton Street Settlement outing. I worked with the committee, and all that, but the night before the outing the whole committee was supposed to go out to the camp and spend the night there. That was a big time. But I didn't go. I didn't have any money. Next morning I saw them off on the bus, and I said I would be out later. I went around and bummed a couple of bucks and drove up with one of the boys. I stayed a couple of hours, and then I came home. The chairman is expected to be active at one of those affairs. He is supposed to treat people—things like that. They think I'm shirking my responsibilities, but it isn't true. It's the money.

I have thought it all over, and I know I only have these spells when I'm batted out. I'm sorry you didn't know me when I was really active around here. I was a different man then. I was always taking the girls out. I lent plenty of money. I spent my money. I was always thinking of things to do and places to go.

Doc showed that he was well aware of the nature of his difficulties, but understanding was not enough to cure him. He needed an opportunity to act in the manner to which he had grown accustomed. When that was lacking, he was socially maladjusted. If he had been a man with low standing in the group and had customarily been dependent upon others to originate action for him in set events, the dependence which resulted from having no money would have fitted in with the pattern of his behavior in the group. Since he had held the leading position among his corner boys, there was an unavoidable conflict between the behavior required by that position and the behavior necessitated by his penniless condition.

The type of explanation suggested to account for the difficulties of Long John and Doc has the advantage that it rests upon the objective study of actions. A man's attitudes cannot be observed but instead must be inferred from his behavior. Since actions are directly subject to observation and may be recorded like other scientific data, it seems wise to try to understand man through studying his actions. This approach not only provides information upon the nature of informal group relations but it also offers a framework for the understanding of the individual's adjustment to his society.

2. THE SOCIAL STRUCTURE

The story of Cornerville has been told in terms of its organization, for that is the way Cornerville appears to the people who live and act there. They conceive society as a closely knit hierarchical organization in which people's positions and obligations to one another are defined and recognized. This view includes not only the world of Cornerville but also the world of the supernatural. The picture becomes clear when one observes the way in which people symbolically represent their world to themselves.

The annual *Festa* of the patron saint reveals not only the nature of religious beliefs and practices but also the outlines of the social organization. Until the summer of 1940 the *paesani* of each town which had a sufficient population in and about Cornerville banded together for this celebration. Each *Festa* committee set aside a particular week end every year and selected a location for the construction of a street altar and poles to hold strings of colored lights over the surrounding area.

There were band concerts on Friday and Saturday nights, but Sunday was the day of the real celebration. In the morning the *paesani* attended a special Mass in honor of their patron.

The Mass represented the only direct connection of the church with the *Festa*. While it formed a part of the general religious life, the *Festa* was entirely a people's ceremonial.

Early Sunday afternoon all those who wished to participate in the procession—and anyone could take part—assembled before the altar. The committee accepted contributions from those members who sought the privilege of carrying the statue of the saint through the streets. In some of the larger processions several hundred people marched with the saint. There was the children's band and the fife-and-drum corps of one or of both Italian churches, in addition to one or two professional bands. Little children, dressed as angels, carried bouquets of flowers. A few of the men and many of the women marched carrying lighted candles. Some, particularly the older women, marched without shoes or even without stockings.

To the canopy above the statue of the saint were attached

streamers on which contributions of money were pinned. Several of the women carried a large flag or sheet stretched between them to catch change thrown from windows. Others circulated through the crowd lining the streets to solicit donations. In recognition of the larger contributions, the professional band faced the house of the contributor and played the Italian national anthem. Upon passing each of the churches, the procession halted and the statue was turned toward the church, but no ceremonial followed.

The return of the saint to the altar climaxed the procession. The bands played, a string was pulled to release streamers and pigeons which had been imprisoned in a decorated box suspended over the center of the street. There was usually some declamation upon the life of the saint and his connection with the townspeople before the statue was replaced.

Sunday evening there was a final band concert, there were brief speeches by certain members of the committee, and usually a prominent politician expressed his respect for the religious devotions of the Italian people.

The *Festa* furnished the occasion for a great reunion of the *paesani* who had moved to other cities and even to other states. Thousands of people milled about the streets in the evenings. Vendors of ice-cream and other confections did a thriving business. The local barrooms and restaurants were filled with friends and relatives celebrating the occasion. All members of a family gathered in one house to eat and drink together. The *Festa* was a religious and social ceremonial and a sort of carnival at the same time. It was an elaborate affair entailing an expense up to $2,500 and receipts of a comparable amount.

I talked with members of the committees of various *Festas* to get an explanation of what it meant to them. One of my informants expressed it in this way:

The reason for the feasts is this. We want to renew and reinforce the faith of the people in God. We want to make ourselves disciples of Christ among the people. In this way we set a good example for the young. The child sees the *Festa* when he is growing up, and later he passes it on to his own children in the same way that it came to him. In that way we help to preserve our religion and keep it strong. Protestants pray directly to God. They say, "God knows us, he knows everything we do. Why should we not pray to him?"

Yes, God knows everything, but we are weak sinners. Why should he grant us the favors that we ask? Instead we pray to some saint—to a person once a human being like ourselves, whose holiness and sanctity have been proven in order to make him a saint. We pray to this saint who is without sins: who has led such a pure life that he can take some of our sins off of our shoulders. We ask the saint to intercede for us and be our advocate before God. We are poor, little people. If we celebrated the feast of our saint once every twenty or thirty years, the saint would ask, "Who are these people that are calling upon me?" No, we set aside a day each year for our saint, and every year we celebrate the feast on that day so that the saint will come to know us as his people and will try to help us when we pray for his aid.

Some ignorant people think that the saint can perform miracles. That is not true. The saint can only ask God to perform the miracles. God is a God of Mercy. If the sinner prays to the saint, the saint stands in right with God, and God takes pity upon the sinner and forgives him his sins. That is the spiritual world. It is the same way in the material world except that here we are dealing with material things. If you drive a car, and the policeman stops you for speeding and gives you a ticket, you don't wait till you go before the judge. You go to the sergeant, the lieutenant, or the captain—some person of influence—and perhaps the captain knows your brother or some friend of yours. Out of friendship he will forgive you for what you did and let you go. If the captain won't listen to you, you talk to the sergeant or the lieutenant, and he will speak to the captain for you.

I inquired whether paying the captain to drop the matter was the same thing as giving money to the saint in the procession.

No, that's different. When you give money to the saint, you do it because you want to make the feast a success. You want to show your devotion to the saint. You make a vow that you will give a certain amount of money to the saint, or you will walk barefoot in the procession, or that you will carry the saint. You do that to show your faith. You cannot buy a favor from God. God is not influenced by money. You give that money to maintain your religious institutions. Of course, there are people that will not do things for you just for friendship. They are just after the material things.

It is true that the *Festas* are largely activities of the older generation, but nevertheless the view of society that they represent is fundamentally the same as that of the younger generation. According to Cornerville people, society is made up of big people and little people—with intermediaries serving to bridge the gaps between them. The masses of Cornerville people are little people. They cannot approach the big people directly but must have an intermediary to intercede for them. They gain this intercession by establishing connections with the intermediary, by performing services for him, and thus making him obligated to them. The intermediary performs the same functions for the big man. The interactions of big shots, intermediaries, and little guys build up a hierarchy of personal relations based upon a system of reciprocal obligations.

Corner gangs such as the Nortons and the cliques of the Cornerville Social and Athletic Club fit in at the bottom of the hierarchy, although certain social distinctions are made between them. Corner-boy leaders like Doc, Dom Romano, and Carlo Tedesco served as intermediaries, representing the interests of their followers to the higher-ups. Chick and his college boys ranked above the corner boys, but they stood at the bottom of another hierarchy, which was controlled from outside the district. There are, of course, wide differences in rank between big shots. Viewed from the street corner of Shelby Street, Tony Cataldo was a big shot, and the relations of the corner-boy followers to him were regulated by their leaders. On the other hand, he served as an intermediary, dealing with big shots for the corner boys and trying to control the corner boys for the big shots. T. S., the racket boss, and George Ravello, the state senator, were the biggest men in Cornerville. T. S. handled those below him through his immediate subordinates. While Ravello refused to allow any formal distinctions to come between himself and the corner boys, the man at the bottom fared better when he approached the politician through an intermediary who had a connection than when he tried to bridge the gap alone.

The corner gang, the racket and police organizations, the political organization, and now the social structure have all been described and analyzed in terms of a hierarchy of personal relations based upon a system of reciprocal obligations. These are the fundamental elements out of which all Cornerville institutions are constructed.

3. THE PROBLEM OF CORNERVILLE

The trouble with the slum district, some say, is that it is a disorganized community. In the case of Cornerville such a diagnosis is extremely misleading. Of course, there are conflicts within Cornerville. Corner boys and college boys have different standards of behavior and do not understand each other. There is a clash between generations, and, as one generation succeeds another, the society is in a state of flux—but even that flux is organized.

Cornerville's problem is not lack of organization but failure of its own social organization to mesh with the structure of the society around it. This accounts for the development of the local political and racket organizations and also for the loyalty people bear toward their race and toward Italy. This becomes apparent when one examines the channels through which the Cornerville man may gain advancement and recognition in his own district or in the society at large.

Our society places a high value upon social mobility. According to tradition, the workingman starts in at the bottom and by means of intelligence and hard work climbs the ladder of success. It is difficult for the Cornerville man to get onto the ladder, even on the bottom rung. His district has become popularly known as a disordered and lawless community. He is an Italian, and the Italians are looked upon by upper-class people as among the least desirable of the immigrant peoples. This attitude has been accentuated by the war. Even if the man can get a grip on the bottom rung, he finds the same factors prejudicing his advancement. Consequently, one does not find Italian names among the leading officers of the old established business of Eastern City. The Italians have had to build up their own business hierarchies, and, when the prosperity of the twenties came to an end, it became increasingly difficult for the newcomer to advance in this way.

To get ahead, the Cornerville man must move either in the world of business and Republican politics or in the world of Democratic politics and the rackets. He cannot move in both worlds at once; they are so far apart that there is hardly any connection between them. If he advances in the first world, he is recognized by society at large as a successful man, but he is recognized in Cornerville only as an alien to the district. If he advances in the second world, he achieves recognition in Cornerville but becomes a social outcast to respectable people elsewhere. The entire course of the corner boy's training in the social life of his district prepares him for a career in the rackets or in Democratic politics. If he moves in the other direction, he must take pains to break away from most of the ties that hold him to Cornerville. In effect, the society at large puts a premium on disloyalty to Cornerville and penalizes those who are best adjusted to the life of the district. At the same time the society holds out attractive rewards in terms of money and material possessions to the "successful" man. For most Cornerville people these rewards are available only through advancement in the world of rackets and politics.

Similarly, society rewards those who can slough off all characteristics that are regarded as distinctively Italian and penalizes those who are not fully Americanized. Some ask, "Why can't those people stop being Italians and become Americans like the rest of us?" The answer is that they are blocked in two ways: by their own organized society and by the outside world. Cornerville people want to be good American citizens. I have never heard such moving expressions of love for this country as I have heard in Cornerville. Nevertheless, an organized way of life cannot be changed overnight. As the study of the corner gang shows, people become dependent upon certain routines of action. If they broke away abruptly from these routines, they would feel themselves disloyal and would be left helpless, without support. And, if a man wants to forget that he is an Italian, the society around him does not let him forget it. He is marked as an inferior person—like all other Italians. To bolster his own self-respect he must tell himself and tell others that the Italians are a great people, that their culture is second to none, and that their great men are unsurpassed. It is in this connection that Mussolini became important to Cornerville people. Chick Morelli expressed a very common sentiment when he addressed these words to his Italian Community Club:

> Whatever you fellows may think of Mussolini, you've got to admit one thing. He has done more to get respect for the Italian people than anybody else. The Italians get a lot more respect now than when I started going to school. And you can thank Mussolini for that.

It is a question whether Mussolini actually did cause native Americans to have more respect for Italians (before the war). However, in so far as Cornerville people felt that Mussolini had won them more respect, their own self-respect was increased. This was an important support to the morale of the people.

If the racket-political structure and the symbolic attachment to Italy are aspects of a fundamental lack of adjustment between Cornerville and the larger American society, then it is evident that they cannot be changed by preaching. The adjustment must be made in terms of actions. Cornerville people will fit in better with the society around them when they gain more opportunities to participate in that society. This involves providing them greater economic opportunity and also giving them greater responsibility to guide their own destinies. The general economic situation of the Cornerville population is a subject so large that brief comments would be worse than useless.

One example, the Cornerville House recreation-center project, will suggest the possibilities in encouraging local responsibility. The center project constituted one of the rare attempts made by social workers to deal with Cornerville society in its own terms. It was aimed to reach the corner gangs as they were then constituted. The lesson which came out of the project was that it is possible to deal with the corner boys by recognizing their leaders and giving them responsibility for action.

The social workers frequently talk about leaders and leadership, but those words have a special meaning for them. "Leader" is simply a synonym for group worker. One of the main purposes of the group worker is to develop leadership among the people with whom he deals. As a matter of fact, every group, formal or informal, which has been associated together for any period of time, has developed its own leadership, but this is seldom recognized by the social workers. They do not see it because they are not looking for it. They do not think of what leadership is; instead they think of what it should be. To outsiders, the leading men of the community are the respectable business and professional men—people who have attained middle-class standing. These men, who have been moving up and out of Cornerville, actually have little local influence. The community cannot be moved through such "leaders." Not until outsiders are prepared to recognize some of the same men that Cornerville people recognize as leaders will they be able to deal with the actual social structure and bring about significant changes in Cornerville life.

So far this discussion sounds much like the anthropologist's prescription to the colonial administrator: respect the native culture and deal with the society through its leaders. That is certainly a minimum requirement for dealing effectively with Cornerville, but is it a sufficient requirement? Can any program be effective if all the top positions of formal authority are held by people who are aliens to Cornerville? What is the effect upon the individual when he has to subordinate himself to people that he recognizes are different from his own?

Doc once said to me:

You don't know how it feels to grow up in a district like this. You go to the first grade—Miss O'Rourke. Second grade—Miss Casey. Third grade—Miss Chalmers. Fourth grade—Miss Mooney. And so on. At the fire station it is the same. None of them are Italians. The police lieutenant is an Italian, and there are a couple of Italian sergeants, but they have never made an Italian captain in Cornerville. In the settlement houses, none of the people with authority are Italians.

Now you must know that the old-timers here have a great respect for schoolteachers and anybody like that. When the Italian boy sees that none of his own people have the good jobs, why should he think he is as good as the Irish or the Yankees? It makes him feel inferior.

If I had my way, I would have half the schoolteachers Italians and three-quarters of the people in the settlement. Let the other quarter be there just to show that we're in America.

Bill, those settlement houses were necessary at first. When our parents landed here, they didn't know where to go or what to do. They needed the social workers for intermediaries. They did a fine job then, but now the second generation is growing up, and we're beginning to sprout wings. They should take that net off and let us fly.

APPENDIX

ON THE EVOLUTION OF *STREET CORNER SOCIETY*

In the years since completing *Street Corner Society* I have several times sought to teach students the research methods needed for field studies of communities or organizations. Like other instructors in this field, I have been severely handicapped by the paucity of reading matter that I can assign to students.

There are now many good published studies of communities or organizations, but generally the published report gives little attention to the actual process whereby the research was carried out. There have also been some useful statements on methods of research, but, with a few exceptions, they place the discussion entirely on a logical-intellectual basis. They fail to note that the researcher, like his informants, is a social animal. He has a role to play, and he has his own personality needs that must be met in some degree if he is to function successfully. Where the researcher operates out of a university, just going into the field for a few hours at a time, he can keep his personal social life separate from field activity. His problem of role is not quite so complicated. If, on the other hand, the researcher is living for an extended period in the community he is studying, his personal life is inextricably mixed with his research. A real explanation, then, of how the research was done necessarily involves a rather personal account of how the researcher lived during the period of study.

This account of living in the community may help also to explain the process of analysis of the data. The ideas that we have in research are only in part a logical product growing out of a careful weighing of evidence. We do not generally think problems through in a straight line. Often we have the experience of being immersed in a mass of confusing data. We study the data carefully, bringing all our powers of logical analysis to bear upon them. We come up with an idea or two. But still the data do not fall in any coherent pattern. Then we go on living with the data—and with the people—until perhaps some chance occurrence casts a totally different light upon the data, and we begin to see a pattern that we have not seen before. This pattern is not purely an artistic creation. Once we think we see it, we must re-examine our notes and perhaps set out to gather new data in order to determine whether the pattern adequately represents the life we are observing or is simply a product of our imagination. Logic, then, plays an important part. But I am convinced that the actual evolution of research ideas does not take place in accord with the formal statements we read on research methods. The ideas grow up in part out of our immersion in the data and out of the whole process of living. Since so much of this process of analysis proceeds on the unconscious level, I am sure that we can never present a full account of it. However, an account of the way the research was done may help to explain how the pattern of *Street Corner Society* gradually emerged.

I am not suggesting that my approach to *Street Corner Society* should be followed by other researchers. To some extent my approach must be unique to myself, to the particular situation, and to the state of knowledge existing when I began research. On the other hand, there must be some common elements of the field research process. Only as we accumulate a series of accounts of how research was actually done will we be able to go beyond the logical-intellectual picture and learn to describe the actual research process. What follows, then, is simply one contribution toward that end.

1. PERSONAL BACKGROUND

I come from a very consistent upper-middle-class background. One grandfather was a doctor; the other, a superintendent of schools. My father was a college professor. My upbringing, therefore, was very far removed from the life I have described in Cornerville.

At Swarthmore College I had two strong interests: economics (mixed with social reform) and writing. In college I wrote a number of short stories and one-act plays. During the summer after college I made an attempt at a novel. This writing was valuable to me largely in what it taught me about myself. Several of the stories appeared in the college literary magazine, and one was accepted for publication (but never published) in *Story* magazine. Three of the one-act plays were produced at Swarthmore in the annual one-act playwriting contest. Not a bad start for someone who had hopes, as I did then, for a writing career. But yet I felt uneasy and dissatisfied. The plays and stories were all fictionalized accounts of events and situations I had experienced or observed myself. When I attempted to go beyond my experience and tackle a novel on a political theme, the result was a complete bust. Even as I wrote the concluding chapters, I realized that the manuscript was worthless. I finished it, I suppose, just so that I could say to myself that I had written a novel.

Now I had read the often-given advice to young writers that they should write out of their own experience, so I had no reason to be ashamed of this limitation. On the other hand, it was when I reflected upon my experience that I became uneasy and dissatisfied. My home life had been very happy and intellectually stimulating—but without adventure. I had never had to struggle over anything. I knew lots of nice people, but almost all of them came from good, solid middle-class backgrounds like my own. In college, of course, I was associating with middle-class students and middle-class professors. I knew nothing about the slums (or the gold coast for that matter). I knew nothing about life in the factories, fields, or mines—except what I had gotten out of books. So I came to feel that I was a pretty dull fellow. At times this sense of dulness became so oppressive that I simply could not think of any stories to write. I began to feel that, if I were really going to write anything worth while, I would somehow have to get beyond the narrow social borders of my existence up to that time.

My interest in economics and social reform also led in the direction of *Street Corner Society*. One of my most vivid college memories is of a day spent with a group of students in visiting the slums of Philadelphia. I remember it not only for the images of dilapidated buildings and crowded people but also for the sense of embarrassment I felt as a tourist in the district. I had the common young man's urge to do good to these people, and yet I knew then that the situation was so far beyond anything I could realistically attempt at the time that I felt like an insincere dabbler even to be there. I began to think sometimes about going back to such a district and really learning to know the people and the conditions of their lives.

My social reform urges came out in other forms on the campus. In my sophomore year I was one of a group of fifteen men who resigned from their fraternities amid a good deal of fanfare. This was an exciting time on the campus, and some of the solid fraternity men were fearful lest the structure would crumble under their feet. They should not have worried. Fraternities went right along without us. In my senior year I became involved in another effort at campus reform. This time we were aiming at nothing less than a reorganization of the whole social life of the campus. The movement got off to a promising start but then quickly petered out.

These abortive reform efforts had one great value to me. I saw that reform was not so easy. I recognized that I had made a number of mistakes. I also came to the realization that some of the people who had fought against me the hardest were really pretty nice fellows. I did not conclude from this that they were right and I was wrong, but I came to recognize how little I really knew about the forces that move people to action. Out of my own reflections about the failures of my campus reform efforts grew a keener interest in understanding other people.

There was also a book that I had read, which weighed most heavily with me at this time. It was the *Autobiography of Lincoln Steffens*. I got my hands on it during the year I spent in Germany between high school and college. In my efforts to master German, this was the only thing written in English that I read for some time, so perhaps it weighed more heavily with me than it otherwise would. In any case, I was fascinated by it and read it through several times. Steffens had begun as a reformer, and he never abandoned this urge to change things. Yet he had such an unending curiosity about the world around him that he became more and more interested in discovering how society actually functioned. He demonstrated that a man of a background similar to my own could step out of his own usual walks of life and gain an intimate knowledge of individuals and groups whose activities and beliefs were far different from his own. So you could actually get these "corrupt politicians" to talk to you. This I needed to know. It helped me sometimes when I had the feeling that the people I was interviewing would much rather have me get out of there altogether.

2. FINDING CORNERVILLE

When I was graduated from Swarthmore in 1936, I received a fellowship from the Society of Fellows at Harvard. This provided me with a unique sort of opportunity—three years of support for any line of research I wished to pursue. The only restriction was that I was not allowed to accumulate credits toward a Ph.D. degree. I am grateful now for this restriction. If I had been allowed to work for the Ph.D., I suppose I should have felt that I must take advantage of the time and the opportunity. With this avenue cut off, I was forced to do what I wanted to do, regardless of academic credits.

I began with a vague idea that I wanted to study a slum district. Eastern City provided several possible choices. In the early weeks of my Harvard fellowship I spent some of my time talking up and down the streets of the various slum districts of Eastern City and talking with people in social agencies about these districts.

I made my choice on very unscientific grounds: Cornerville best fitted my.picture of what a slum district should look like. Somehow I had developed a picture of run-down three- to five-story buildings crowded in together. The dilapidated wooden-frame buildings of some other parts of the city did not look quite genuine to me. To be sure, Cornerville did have one characteristic that recommended it on a little more objective basis. It had more people per acre living in it than any other section of the city. If a slum meant overcrowding, this was certainly it.

3. PLANNING THE STUDY

As soon as I had found my slum district, I set about planning my study. It was not enough for me at the time to plan for myself alone. I had begun reading in the sociological literature and thinking along the lines of the Lynds' *Middletown*. Gradually I came to think of myself as a sociologist or a social anthropologist instead of an economist. I found that, while slums had been given much attention in the sociological literature, there existed no real community study of such a district. So I set out to organize a community study for Cornerville. This was clearly a big job. My early outline of the study pointed to special researches in the history of the district, in economics (living standards, housing, marketing, distribution, and employment), politics (the structure of the political organization and its relation to the rackets and the police), patterns of education and recreation, the church, public health, and—of all things—social attitudes. Obviously, this was more than a one-man job, so I designed it for about ten men.

With this project statement in hand I approached L. J. Henderson, an eminent biochemist who was secretary of the Society of Fellows.

We spent an hour together, and I came away with my plans very much in a state of flux. As I wrote to a friend at this time: "Henderson poured cold water on the mammoth beginning, told me that I should not cast such grandiose plans when I had done hardly any work in the field myself. It would be much sounder to get in the field and try to build up a staff slowly as I went along. If I should get a ten-man project going by fall, the responsibility for the direction and co-ordination of it would inevitably fall upon me, since I would have started it. How could I direct ten people in a field that was unfamiliar to me? Henderson said that, if I did manage to get a ten-man project going, it would be the ruination of me, he thought. Now, the way he put all this it sounded quite sensible and reasonable."

This last sentence must have been written after I had had time to recover from the interview, because I remember it as being a crushing experience. I suppose good advice is just as hard to take as poor advice, and yet in a very short time I realized that Henderson was right, and I abandoned the grandiose plan I had made. Since people who offer painful but good advice so seldom get any thanks for it, I shall always be glad that I went to see Henderson again shortly before his death and told him that I had come to feel that he had been absolutely right.

While I abandoned the ten-man project, I was reluctant to come down to earth altogether. It seemed to me that, in view of the magnitude of the task I was undertaking, I must have at least one collaborator, and I began to cast about for means of getting a college friend of mine to join me in the field. There followed through the winter of 1936–37 several revisions of my outline of the community study and numerous interviews with Harvard professors who might help me to get the necessary backing.

As I read over these various research outlines, it seems to me that the most impressive thing about them is their remoteness from the actual study I carried on. As I went along, the outlines became gradually more sociological, so that I wound up this phase planning to devote major emphasis to a sort of sociometric study of the friendship patterns of people. I would start with one family and ask them who their friends were and who the people were that they were more or less hostile to. Then I would go to these friends and get the list of their friends and learn in the process something of their activities together. In this way, I was to chart the social structure of at least some of the community. Even this, of course, I did not do, for I came to find that you could examine social structure directly through observing people in action.

When, a year later in the fall of 1937, John Howard, also a Harvard junior fellow, changed his field from physical chemistry to sociology, I invited him to join me in the Cornerville study. We worked together for two years, with Howard particularly concentrating on one of the churches and its Holy Name Society. The discussions between us helped immensely in clarifying my ideas. But only a few months after I had begun Cornerville field work, I had completely abandoned the thought of building up a Cornerville staff. I suppose that I found Cornerville life so interesting and rewarding that I no longer felt a need to think in large-scale terms.

Although I was completely at sea in planning the study, at least I had valuable help in developing the field research methods which were eventually to lead to a study plan as well as to the data here reported.

It is hard to realize now how rapid has been the development of sociological and anthropological studies of communities and organizations since 1936, when I began my work in Cornerville. At that time nothing had yet been published on W. Lloyd Warner's "Yankee City" study. I had read the Lynds' *Middletown* and Carolyn Ware's *Greenwich Village* with interest and profit, and yet I began to realize, more and more as I went along, that I was not making a community study along those lines. Much of the other sociological literature then available tended to look upon communities in terms of social problems so that the community as an organized social system simply did not exist.

I spent my first summer following the launching of the study in reading some of the writings of Durkheim and Pareto's *The Mind and Society* (for a seminar with L. J. Henderson, which I was to take in the fall of 1937). I had a feeling that these writings were helpful but still only in a general way. Then I began reading in the social anthropological literature, beginning with Malinowski, and this seemed closer to what I wanted to do even though the researchers were studying primitive tribes and I was in the middle of a great city district.

If there was then little to guide me in the literature, I needed that much more urgently to have the help of people more skilled and experienced than I in the work I was undertaking. Here I was extraordinarily fortunate in meeting Conrad M. Arensberg at the very outset of my Harvard appointment. He also was a junior fellow, so that we naturally saw much of each other. After having worked for some months with W. Lloyd Warner in the Yankee City study, he had gone with Solon Kimball to make a study of a small community in Ireland. When I met him, he had just returned from this field trip and was beginning to write up his data. With Eliot Chapple, he was also in the process of working out a new approach to the analysis of social organization. The two men had been casting about together for ways of establishing such social research on a more scientific basis. Going over the Yankee City data and the Irish study, also, they had set up five different theoretical schemes. One after the other each of the first four schemes fell to the ground under their own searching criticism or under the prods of Henderson or Elton Mayo or others whom they consulted. At last they began to develop a theory of interaction. They felt that, whatever else might be subjective in social research, one could establish objectively the pattern of interaction among people: how often A contacts B, how long they spend together, who originates action when A, B, and C are together, and so on. Careful observation of such interpersonal events might then provide reliable data upon the social organization of a community. At least this was the assumption. Since the theory grew out of research already done, it was natural that these previous studies did not contain as much of the quantitative data as the theory would have required. So it seemed that I might be one of the first to take the theory out into the field.

Arensberg and I had endless discussions of the theory, and in some of these Eliot Chapple participated. At first it seemed very confusing to me—I am not sure I have it all clear yet—but I had a growing feeling that here was something solid that I could build upon.

Arensberg also worked with me on field research methods, emphasizing the importance of observing people in action and getting down a detailed report of actual behavior completely divorced from moral judgments. In my second semester at Harvard, I took a course given by Arensberg and Chapple concerning social anthropological community studies. While this was helpful, I owed much more to the long personal conversations I had with Arensberg throughout the Cornerville research, particularly in its early stages.

In the fall of 1937 I took a small seminar with Elton Mayo. This involved particularly readings from the works of Pierre Janet, and it included also some practice in interviewing psychoneurotics in an Eastern City hospital. This experience was too brief to carry me beyond the amateur stage, but it was helpful in developing my interviewing methods.

L. J. Henderson provided a less specific but nevertheless pervasive influence in the development of my methods and theories. As chairman of the Society of Fellows, he presided over our Monday-night dinners like a patriarch in his own household. Even though the group included A. Lawrence Lowell, Alfred North Whitehead, John Livingston Lowes, Samuel Eliot Morrison, and Arthur Darby Nock, it was Henderson who was easily the most imposing figure for the junior fellows. He seemed particularly to enjoy baiting the young social scientists. He took me on at my first Monday-night dinner and undertook to show me that all my ideas about society were based upon softheaded sentimentality. While I often resented Henderson's sharp criticisms, I was all the more determined to make my field research stand up against anything he could say.

4. FIRST EFFORTS

When I began my work, I had had no training in sociology or anthropology. I thought of myself as an economist and naturally looked first toward the matters that we had taken up in economics courses, such as economics of slum housing. At the time I was sitting in on a course in slums and housing in the Sociology Department at Harvard. As a term project I took on a study of one block in Cornerville. To legitimize this effort, I got in touch with a private agency that concerned itself in housing matters and offered to turn over to them the results of my survey. With that backing, I began knocking on doors, looking into flats, and talking to the tenants about the living conditions. This brought me into contact with Cornerville people, but it would be hard now to devise a more inappropriate way of beginning a study such as I was eventually to make. I felt ill at ease at this intrusion, and I am sure so did the people. I wound up the block study as rapidly as I could and wrote it off as a total loss as far as gaining a real entry into the district.

Shortly thereafter I made another false start—if so tentative an effort may even be called a start. At the time I was completely baffled at the problem of finding my way into the district. Cornerville was right before me and yet so far away. I could walk freely up and down its streets, and I had even made my way into some of the flats, and yet I was still a stranger in a world completely unknown to me.

At this time I met a young economics instructor at Harvard who impressed me with his self-assurance and his knowledge of Eastern City. He had once been attached to a settlement house, and he talked glibly about his associations with the tough young men and women of the district. He also described how he would occasionally drop in on some drinking place in the area and strike up an acquaintance with a girl, buy her a drink, and then encourage her to tell him her life-story. He claimed that the women so encountered were appreciative of this opportunity and that it involved no further obligaion.

This approach seemed at least as plausible as anything I had been able to think of. I resolved to try it out. I picked on the Regal Hotel, which was on the edge of Cornerville. With some trepidation I climbed the stairs to the bar and entertainment area and looked around. There I encountered a situation for which my adviser had not prepared me. There were women present all right, but none of them was alone. Some were there in couples, and there were two or three pairs of women together. I pondered this situation briefly. I had little confidence in my skill at picking up one female, and it seemed inadvisable to tackle two at the same time. Still, I was determined not to admit defeat without a struggle. I looked around me again and now noticed a threesome: one man and two women. It occurred to me that here was a maldistribution of females which I might be able to rectify. I approached the group and opened with something like this: "Pardon me. Would you mind if I joined you?" There was a moment of silence while the man stared at me. He then offered to throw me downstairs. I assured him that this would not be necessary and demonstrated as much by walking right out of there without any assistance.

I subsequently learned that hardly anyone from Cornerville ever went into the Regal Hotel. If my efforts there had been crowned with success, they would no doubt have led somewhere but certainly not to Cornerville.

For my next effort I sought out the local settlement houses. They were open to the public. You could walk right into them, and—though I would not have phrased it this way at the time— they were manned by middle-class people like myself. I realized even then that to study Cornerville I would have to go well beyond the settlement house, but perhaps the social workers could help me to get started.

As I look back on it now, the settlement house also seems a very unpromising place from which to begin such a study. If I had it to do over again, I would probably make my first approach through a local politician or perhaps through the Catholic church, although I am not myself Catholic. John Howard, who worked with me later, made his entry very successfully through the church, and he, too, was not a Catholic—although his wife was.

However that may be, the settlement house proved the right place for me at this time, for it was here that I met Doc. I had talked to a number of the social workers about my plans and hopes to get acquainted with the people and study the district. They listened with varying degrees of interest. If they had suggestions to make, I have forgotten them now except for one. Somehow, in spite of the vagueness of my own explanations, the head of girls' work in the Norton Street House understood what I needed. She began describing Doc to me. He was, she said, a very intelligent and talented person who had at one time been fairly active in the house but had dropped out, so that he hardly ever came in any more. Perhaps he could understand what I wanted, and he must have the contacts that I needed. She said she frequently encountered him as she walked to and from the house and sometimes stopped to chat with him. If I wished, she would make an appointment for me to see him in the house one evening. This at last seemed right. I jumped at the chance. As I came into the district that evening, it was with a feeling that here

I had my big chance to get started. Somehow Doc must accept me and be willing to work with me.

In a sense, my study began on the evening of February 4, 1937, when the social worker called me in to meet Doc. She showed us into her office and then left so that we could talk. Doc waited quietly for me to begin, as he sank down into a chair. I found him a man of medium height and spare build. His hair was a light brown, quite a contrast to the more typical black Italian hair. It was thinning around the temples. His cheeks were sunken. His eyes were a light blue and seemed to have a penetrating gaze.

I began by asking him if the social worker had told him about what I was trying to do.

"No, she just told me that you wanted to meet me and that I should like to meet you."

Then I went into a long explanation which, unfortunately, I omitted from my notes. As I remember it, I said that I had been interested in congested city districts in my college study but had felt very remote from them. I hoped to study the problems in such a district. I felt I could do very little as an outsider. Only if I could get to know the people and learn their problems first hand would I be able to gain the understanding I needed.

Doc heard me out without any change of expression, so that I had no way of predicting his reaction. When I was finished, he asked: "Do you want to see the high life or the low life?"

"I want to see all that I can. I want to get as complete a picture of the community as possible."

"Well, any nights you want to see anything, I'll take you around. I can take you to the joints—gambling joints—I can take you around to the street corners. Just remember that you're my friend. That's all they need to know. I know these places, and, if I tell them that you're my friend, nobody will bother you. You just tell me what you want to see, and we'll arrange it."

The proposal was so perfect that I was at a loss for a moment as to how to respond to it. We talked a while longer, as I sought to get some pointers as to how I should behave in his company. He warned me that I might have to take the risk of getting arrested in a raid on a gambling joint but added that this was not serious. I only had to give a false name and then would get bailed out by the man that ran the place, paying only a five-dollar fine. I agreed to take this chance. I asked him whether I should gamble with the others in the gambling joints. He said it was unnecessary and, for a greenhorn like myself, very inadvisable.

At last I was able to express my appreciation. "You know, the first steps of getting to know a community are the hardest. I could see things going with you that I wouldn't see for years otherwise."

"That's right. You tell me what you want to see, and we'll arrange it. When you want some information, I'll ask for it, and you listen. When you want to find out their philosophy of life, I'll start an argument and get it for you. If there's something else you want to get, I'll stage an act for you. Not a scrap, you know, but just tell me what you want, and I'll get it for you."

"That's swell. I couldn't ask for anything. better. Now I'm going to try to fit in all right, but, if at any time you see I'm getting off on the wrong foot, I want you to tell me about it."

"Now we're being too dramatic. You won't have any trouble. You come in as my friend. When you come in like that, at first everybody will treat you with respect. You can take a lot of liberties, and nobody will kick. After a while when they get to know you they will treat you like anybody else—you know, they say familiarity breeds contempt. But you'll never have any trouble. There's just one thing to watch out for. Don't spring [treat] people. Don't be too free with your money."

"You mean they'll think I'm a sucker?"

"Yes, and you don't want to buy your way in."

We talked a little about how and when we might get together. Then he asked me a question. "You want to write something about this?"

"Yes, eventually."

"Do you want to change things?"

"Well—yes. I don't see how anybody could come down here where it is so crowded, people haven't got any money or any work to do, and not want to have some things changed. But I think a fellow should do the thing he is best fitted for. I don't want to be a reformer, and I'm not cut out to be a politician. I just want to understand these things as best I can and write them up, and if that has any influence. . . ."

"I think you can change things that way. Mostly that is the way things are changed, by writing about them."

That was our beginning. At the time I found it hard to believe that I could move in as easily as Doc had said with his sponsorship. But that indeed was the way it turned out.

While I was taking my first steps with Doc, I was also finding a place to live in Cornerville. My fellowship provided a very comfortable bedroom, living-room, and bath at Harvard. I had been attempting to commute from these quarters to my Cornerville study. Technically that was possible, but socially I became more and more convinced that it was impossible. I realized that I would always be a stranger to the community if I did not live there. Then, also, I found myself having difficulty putting in the time that I knew was required to establish close relations in Cornerville. Life in Cornerville did not proceed on the basis of formal appointments. To meet people, to get to know them, to fit into their activities, required spending time with them—a lot of time day after day. Commuting to Cornerville, you might come in on a particular afternoon and evening only to discover that the people you intended to see did not happen to be around at the time. Or, even if you did see them, you might find the time passing entirely uneventfully. You might just be standing around with people whose only occupation was talking or walking about to try to keep themselves from being bored.

On several afternoons and evenings at Harvard, I found myself considering a trip to Cornerville and then rationalizing my way out of it. How did I know I would find the people whom I meant to see? Even if I did so, how could I be sure that I would learn anything today? Instead of going off on a wild-goose chase to Cornerville, I could profitably spend my time reading books and articles to fill in my woeful ignorance of sociology and social anthropology. Then, too, I had to admit that I felt more com-

fortable among these familiar surroundings than I did wander-
ing around Cornerville and spending time with people in whose
presence I felt distinctly uncomfortable at first.

When I found myself rationalizing in this way, I realized that
I would have to make the break. Only if I lived in Cornerville
would I ever be able to understand it and be accepted by it.
Finding a place, however, was not easy. In such an overcrowded
district a spare room was practically nonexistent. I might have
been able to take a room in the Norton Street Settlement House,
but I realized that I must do better than this if possible.

I got my best lead from the editor of a weekly English-language
newspaper published for the Italian-American colony. I had
talked to him before about my study and had found him sympathetic. Now I came to ask him for help in finding a room. He
directed me to the Martinis, a family which operated a small
restaurant. I went there for lunch and later consulted the son
of the family. He was sympathetic but said that they had no
place for any additional person. Still, I liked the place and enjoyed the food. I came back several times just to eat. On one
occasion I met the editor, and he invited me to his table. At
first he asked me some searching questions about my study:
what I was after, what my connection with Harvard was, what
they had expected to get out of this, and so on. After I had
answered him in a manner that I unfortunately failed to record
in my notes, he told me that he was satisfied and, in fact, had
already spoken in my behalf to people who were suspicious that
I might be coming in to "criticize our people."

We discussed my rooming problem again. I mentioned the
possibility of living at the Norton Street House. He nodded but
added: "It would be much better if you could be in a family.
You would pick up the language much quicker, and you would
get to know the people. But you want a nice family, an educated family. You don't want to get in with any low types.
You want a real good family."

At this he turned to the son of the family with whom I had
spoken and asked: "Can't you make some place for Mr. Whyte
in the house here?"

Al Martini paused a moment and then said: "Maybe we can fix it up. I'll talk to Mama again."

So he did talk to Mama again, and they did find a place. In fact, he turned over to me his own room and moved in to share a double bed with the son of the cook. I protested mildly at this imposition, but everything had been decided—except for the money. They did not know what to charge me, and I did not know what to offer. Finally, after some fencing, I offered fifteen dollars a month, and they settled for twelve.

The room was simple but adequate to my purposes. It was not heated, but, when I began to type my notes there, I got myself a small oil-burner. There was no bathtub in the house, but I had to go out to Harvard now and then anyway, so I used the facilities of the great university (the room of my friend, Henry Guerlac) for an occasional tub or shower.

Physically, the place was livable, and it provided me with more than just a physical base. I had been with the Martinis for only a week when I discovered that I was much more than a roomer to them. I had been taking many of my meals in the restaurant and sometimes stopping in to chat with the family before I went to bed at night. Then one afternoon I was out at Harvard and found myself coming down with a bad cold. Since I still had my Harvard room, it seemed the sensible thing to do to stay overnight there. I did not think to tell the Martinis of my plan.

The next day when I was back in the restaurant for lunch, Al Martini greeted me warmly and then said that they had all been worried when I did not come home the night before. Mama had stayed up until two o'clock waiting for me. As I was just a young stranger in the city, she could visualize all sorts of things happening to me. Al told me that Mama had come to look upon me as one of the family. I was free to come and go as I pleased, but she wouldn't worry so much if she knew of my plans.

I was very touched by this plea and resolved thereafter to be as good a son as I could to the Martinis.

At first I communicated with Mama and Papa primarily in smiles and gestures. Papa knew no English at all, and Mama's knowledge was limited to one sentence which she would use when some of the young boys on the street were making noise below her window when she was trying to get her afternoon nap. She would then poke her head out of the window and shout: "Goddam-sonumabitcha! Geroutahere!"

Some weeks earlier, in anticipation of moving into the district, I had begun working on the Italian language myself with the aid of a Linguaphone. One morning now Papa Martini came by when I was talking to the phonograph record. He listened for a few moments in the hall trying to make sense out of this peculiar conversation. Then he burst in upon me with fascinated exclamations. We sat down together while I demonstrated the machine and the method to him. After that he delighted in working with me, and I called him my language professor. In a short time we reached a stage where I could carry on simple conversations, and, thanks to the Linguaphone and Papa Martini, the Italian that came out apparently sounded authentic. He liked to try to pass me off to his friends as *paesano mio*—a man from his own home town in Italy. When I was careful to keep my remarks within the limits of my vocabulary, I could sometimes pass as an immigrant from the village of Viareggio in the province of Tuscany.

Since my research developed so that I was concentrating almost exclusively upon the younger, English-speaking generation, my knowledge of Italian proved unnecessary for research purposes. Nevertheless, I feel certain that it was important in establishing my social position in Cornerville—even with that younger generation. There were schoolteachers and social workers who had worked in Cornerville for as much as twenty years and yet had made no effort to learn Italian. My effort to learn the language probably did more to establish the sincerity of my interest in the people than anything I could have told them of myself and my work. How could a researcher be planning to "criticize our people" if he went to the lengths of learning the language? With language comes understanding, and surely it is easier to criticize people if you do not understand them.

My days with the Martinis would pass in this manner. I would get up in the morning around nine o'clock and go out to break-fast. Al Martini told me I could have breakfast in the restaurant, but, for all my desire to fit in, I never could take their breakfast of coffee with milk and a crust of bread.

After breakfast, I returned to my room and spent the rest of the morning, or most of it, typing up my notes regarding the previous day's events. I had lunch in the restaurant and then set out for the street corner. Usually I was back for dinner in the restaurant and then out again for the evening.

Usually I came home again between eleven and twelve o'clock, at a time when the restaurant was empty except perhaps for a few family friends. Then I might join Papa in the kitchen to talk as I helped him dry the dishes, or pull up a chair into a family conversation around one of the tables next to the kitchen. There I had a glass of wine to sip, and I could sit back and mostly listen but occasionally try out my growing Italian on them.

The pattern was different on Sunday, when the restaurant was closed at two o'clock, and Al's two brothers and his sister and the wives, husband, and children would come in for a big Sunday dinner. They insisted that I eat with them at this time and as a member of the family, not paying for my meal. It was always more than I could eat, but it was delicious, and I washed it down with two tumblers of Zinfandel wine. Whatever strain there had been in my work in the preceding week would pass away now as I ate and drank and then went to my room for an after-noon nap of an hour or two that brought me back completely refreshed and ready to set forth again for the corners of Corner-ville.

Though I made several useful contacts in the restaurant or through the family, it was not for this that the Martinis were important to me. There is a strain to doing such field work. The strain is greatest when you are a stranger and are constantly wondering whether people are going to accept you. But, much as you enjoy your work, as long as you are observing and inter-viewing, you have a role to play, and you are not completely relaxed. It was a wonderful feeling at the end of a day's work to be able to come home to relax and enjoy myself with the family.

Probably it would have been impossible for me to carry on such a concentrated study of Cornerville if I had not had such a home from which to go out and to which I might return.

5. BEGINNING WITH DOC

I can still remember my first outing with Doc. We met one evening at the Norton Street House and set out from there to a gambling place a couple of blocks away. I followed Doc anxiously down the long, dark hallway at the back of a tenement building. I was not worried about the possibility of a police raid. I was thinking about how I would fit in and be accepted. The door opened into a small kitchen almost bare of furnishings and with the paint peeling off the walls. As soon as we went in the door, I took off my hat and began looking around for a place to hang it. There was no place. I looked around, and here I learned my first lesson in participant observation in Cornerville: Don't take off your hat in the house—at least not when you are among men. It may be permissible, but certainly not required, to take your hat off when women are around.

Doc introduced me as "my friend Bill" to Chichi, who ran the place, and to Chichi's friends and customers. I stayed there with Doc part of the time in the kitchen, where several men would sit around and talk, and part of the time in the other room watching the crap game.

There was talk about gambling, horse races, sex, and other matters. Mostly I just listened and tried to act friendly and interested. We had wine and coffee with anisette in it, with the fellows chipping in to pay for the refreshments. (Doc would not let me pay my share on this first occasion.) As Doc had predicted, no one asked me about myself, but he told me later that, when I went to the toilet, there was an excited burst of conversation in Italian and that he had to assure them that I was not a G-man. He said he told them flatly that I was a friend of his, and they agreed to let it go at that.

We went several more times together to Chichi's gambling joint, and then the time came when I dared to go in alone. When

I was greeted in a natural and friendly manner, I felt that I was now beginning to find a place for myself in Cornerville.

When Doc did not go off to the gambling joint, he spent his time hanging around Norton Street, and I began hanging with him. At first, Norton Street meant only a place to wait until I could go somewhere else. Gradually, as I got to know the men better, I found myself becoming one of the Norton Street gang.

Then the Italian Community Club was formed in the Norton Street Settlement, and Doc was invited to be a member. Doc maneuvered to get me into the club, and I was glad to join, as I could see that it represented something distinctly different from the corner gangs I was meeting.

As I began to meet the men of Cornerville, I also met a few of the girls. One girl I took to a church dance. The next morning the fellows on the street corner were asking me: "How's your steady girl?" This brought me up short. I learned that going to the girl's house was something that you just did not do unless you hoped to marry her. Fortunately, the girl and her family knew that I did not know the local customs, so they did not assume that I was thus committed. However, this was a useful warning. After this time, even though I found some Cornerville girls exceedingly attractive, I never went out with them except on a group basis, and I did not make any more home visits either.

As I went along, I found that life in Cornerville was not nearly so interesting and pleasant for the girls as it was for the men. A young man had complete freedom to wander and hang around. The girls could not hang on street corners. They had to divide their time between their own homes, the homes of girl friends and relatives, and a job, if they had one. Many of them had a dream that went like this: some young man, from outside of Cornerville, with a little money, a good job, and a good education would come and woo them and take them out of the district. I could hardly afford to fill this role.

6. TRAINING IN PARTICIPANT OBSERVATION

The spring of 1937 provided me with an intensive course in participant observation. I was learning how to conduct myself, and I learned from various groups but particularly from the Nortons.

As I began hanging about Cornerville, I found that I needed an explanation for myself and for my study. As long as I was with Doc and vouched for by him, no one asked me who I was or what I was doing. When I circulated in other groups or even among the Nortons without him, it was obvious that they were curious about me.

I began with a rather elaborate explanation. I was studying the social history of Cornerville—but I had a new angle. Instead of working from the past up to the present, I was seeking to get a thorough knowledge of present conditions and then work from present to past. I was quite pleased with this explanation at the time, but nobody else seemed to care for it. I gave the explanation on only two occasions, and each time, when I had finished, there was an awkward silence. No one, myself included, knew what to say.

While this explanation had at least the virtue of covering everything that I might eventually want to do in the district, it was apparently too involved to mean anything to Cornerville people.

I soon found that people were developing their own explanation about me: I was writing a book about Cornerville. This might seem entirely too vague an explanation, and yet it sufficed. I found that my acceptance in the district depended on the personal relationships I developed far more than upon any explanations I might give. Whether it was a good thing to write a book about Cornerville depended entirely on people's opinions of me personally. If I was all right, then my project was all right; if I was no good, then no amount of explanation could convince them that the book was a good idea.

Of course people did not satisfy their curiosity about me simply by questions that they addressed to me directly. They turned to Doc, for example, and asked him about me. Doc then answered the questions and provided any reassurance that was needed.

I learned early in my Cornerville period the crucial importance of having the support of the key individuals in any groups or organizations I was studying. Instead of trying to explain myself to everyone, I found I was providing far more information about myself and my study to leaders such as Doc than I volunteered to the average corner boy. I always tried to give the impression that I was willing and eager to tell just as much about my study as anyone wished to know, but it was only with group leaders that I made a particular effort to provide really full information.

My relationship with Doc changed rapidly in this early Cornerville period. At first he was simply a key informant—and also my sponsor. As we spent more time together, I ceased to treat him as a passive informant. I discussed with him quite frankly what I was trying to do, what problems were puzzling me, and so on. Much of our time was spent in this discussion of ideas and observations, so that Doc became, in a very real sense, a collaborator in the research.

This full awareness of the nature of my study stimulated Doc to look for and point out to me the sorts of observations that I was interested in. Often when I picked him up at the flat where he lived with his sister and brother-in-law, he said to me: "Bill, you should have been around last night. You would have been interested in this." And then he would go on to tell me what had happened. Such accounts were always interesting and relevant to my study.

Doc found this experience of working with me interesting and enjoyable, and yet the relationship had its drawbacks. He once commented: "You've slowed me up plenty since you've been down here. Now, when I do something, I have to think what Bill Whyte would want to know about it and how I can explain it. Before, I used to do things by instinct."

However, Doc did not seem to consider this a serious handicap. Actually, without any training he was such a perceptive observer that it only needed a little stimulus to help him to make explicit much of the dynamics of the social organization of Cornerville. Some of the interpretations I have made are his more than mine, although it is now impossible to disentangle them.

While I worked more closely with Doc than with any other individual, I always sought out the leader in whatever group I was studying. I wanted not only sponsorship from him but also more active collaboration with the study. Since these leaders had the sort of position in the community that enabled them to observe much better than the followers what was going on and since they were in general more skilful observers than the followers, I found that I had much to learn from a more active collaboration with them.

In my interviewing methods I had been instructed not to argue with people or pass moral judgments upon them. This fell in with my own inclinations. I was glad to accept the people and to be accepted by them. However, this attitude did not come out so much in interviewing, for I did little formal interviewing. I sought to show this interested acceptance of the people and the community in my everyday participation.

I learned to take part in the street corner discussions on baseball and sex. This required no special training, since the topics seemed to be matters of almost universal interest. I was not able to participate so actively in discussions of horse-racing. I did begin to follow the races in a rather general and amateur way. I am sure it would have paid me to devote more study to the *Morning Telegraph* and other racing sheets, but my knowledge of baseball at least insured that I would not be left out of the street corner conversations.

While I avoided expressing opinions on sensitive topics, I found that arguing on some matters was simply part of the social pattern and that one could hardly participate without joining in the argument. I often found myself involved in heated but good-natured arguments about the relative merits of certain major-league ball players and managers. Whenever a girl or a group of girls would walk down the street, the fellows on the corner would make mental notes and later would discuss their evaluations of the females. These evaluations would run largely in terms of shape, and here I was glad to argue that Mary had a better "build" than Anna, or vice versa. Of course, if any of the men on the corner happened to be personally attached to Mary or Anna, no searching comments would be made, and I, too, would avoid this topic.

Sometimes I wondered whether just hanging on the street corner was an active enough process to be dignified by the term "research." Perhaps I should be asking these men questions. However, one has to learn when to question and when not to question as well as what questions to ask.

I learned this lesson one night in the early months when I was with Doc in Chichi's gambling joint. A man from another part of the city was regaling us with a tale of the organization of gambling activity. I had been told that he had once been a very big gambling operator, and he talked knowingly about many interesting matters. He did most of the talking, but the others asked questions and threw in comments, so at length I began to feel that I must say something in order to be part of the group. I said: "I suppose the cops were all paid off?"

The gambler's jaw dropped. He glared at me. Then he denied vehemently that any policemen had been paid off and immediately switched the conversation to another subject. For the rest of that evening I felt very uncomfortable.

The next day Doc explained the lesson of the previous evening. "Go easy on that 'who,' 'what,' 'why,' 'when,' 'where' stuff, Bill. You ask those questions, and people will clam up on you. If people accept you, you can just hang around, and you'll learn the answers in the long run without even having to ask the questions."

I found that this was true. As I sat and listened, I learned the answers to questions that I would not even have had the sense to ask if I had been getting my information solely on an interviewing basis. I did not abandon questioning altogether, of course. I simply learned to judge the sensitiveness of the question and my relationship to the people so that I only asked a question in a sensitive area when I was sure that my relationship to the people involved was very solid.

When I had established my position on the street corner, the data simply came to me without very active efforts on my part. It was only now and then, when I was concerned with a particular problem and felt I needed more information from a certain individual, that I would seek an opportunity to get the man alone and carry on a more formal interview.

At first I concentrated upon fitting into Cornerville, but a little later I had to face the question of how far I was to immerse myself in the life of the district. I bumped into that problem one evening as I was walking down the street with the Nortons. Trying to enter into the spirit of the small talk, I cut loose with a string of obscenities and profanity. The walk came to a momentary halt as they all stopped to look at me in surprise. Doc shook his head and said: "Bill, you're not supposed to talk like that. That doesn't sound like you."

I tried to explain that I was only using terms that were common on the street corner. Doc insisted, however, that I was different and that they wanted me to be that way.

This lesson went far beyond the use of obscenity and profanity. I learned that people did not expect me to be just like them; in fact, they were interested and pleased to find me different, just so long as I took a friendly interest in them. Therefore, I abandoned my efforts at complete immersion. My behavior was nevertheless affected by street corner life. When John Howard first came down from Harvard to join me in the Cornerville study, he noticed at once that I talked in Cornerville in a manner far different from that which I used at Harvard. This was not a matter of the use of profanity or obscenity, nor did I affect the use of ungrammatical expressions. I talked in the way that seemed natural to me, but what was natural in Cornerville was different from what was natural at Harvard. In Cornerville, I found myself putting much more animation into my speech, dropping terminal g's, and using gestures much more actively. (There was also, of course, the difference in the vocabulary that I used. When I was most deeply involved in Cornerville, I found myself rather tongue-tied in my visits to Harvard. I simply could not keep up with the discussions of international relations, of the nature of science, and so on, in which I had once been more or less at home.)

As I became accepted by the Nortons and by several other groups, I tried to make myself pleasant enough so that people would be glad to have me around. And, at the same time, I tried to avoid influencing the group, because I wanted to study the situation as unaffected by my presence as possible. Thus, throughout my Cornerville stay, I avoided accepting office or leadership positions in any of the groups with a single exception. At one time I was nominated as secretary of the Italian Community Club. My first impulse was to decline the nomination, but then I reflected that the secretary's job is normally considered simply a matter of dirty work—writing the minutes and handling the correspondence. I accepted and found that I could write a very full account of the progress of the meeting as it went on under the pretext of keeping notes for the minutes.

While I sought to avoid influencing individuals or groups, I tried to be helpful in the way a friend is expected to help in Cornerville. When one of the boys had to go downtown on an errand and wanted company, I went along with him. When somebody was trying to get a job and had to write a letter about himself, I helped him to compose it, and so on. This sort of behavior presented no problem, but, when it came to the matter of handling money, it was not at all clear just how I should behave. Of course, I sought to spend money on my friends just as they did on me. But what about lending money? It is expected in such a district that a man will help out his friends whenever he can, and often the help needed is financial. I lent money on several occasions, but I always felt uneasy about it. Naturally, a man appreciates it at the time you lend him the money, but how does he feel later when the time has come to pay, and he is not able to do so? Perhaps he is embarrassed and tries to avoid your company. On such occasions I tried to reassure the individual and tell him that I knew he did not have it just then and that I was not worried about it. Or I even told him to forget about the debt altogether. But that did not wipe it off the books; the uneasiness remained. I learned that it is possible to do a favor for a friend and cause a strain in the relationship in the process.

I know no easy solution to this problem. I am sure there will be times when the researcher would be extremely ill advised to refuse to make a personal loan. On the other hand, I am convinced that, whatever his financial resources, he should not look for opportunities to lend money and should avoid doing so whenever he gracefully can.

If the researcher is trying to fit into more than one group, his field work becomes more complicated. There may be times when the groups come into conflict with each other, and he will be expected to take a stand. There was a time in the spring of 1937 when the boys arranged a bowling match between the Nortons and the Italian Community Club. Doc bowled for the Nortons, of course. Fortunately, my bowling at this time had not advanced to a point where I was in demand for either team, and I was able to sit on the sidelines. From there I tried to applaud impartially the good shots of both teams, although I am afraid it was evident that I was getting more enthusiasm into my cheers for the Nortons.

When I was with members of the Italian Community Club, I did not feel at all called upon to defend the corner boys against disparaging remarks. However, there was one awkward occasion when I was with the corner boys and one of the college boys stopped to talk with me. In the course of the discussion he said: "Bill, these fellows wouldn't understand what I mean, but I am sure that you understand my point." There I thought I had to say something. I told him that he greatly underestimated the boys and that college men were not the only smart ones.

While the remark fitted in with my natural inclinations, I am sure it was justified from a strictly practical standpoint. My answer did not shake the feelings of superiority of the college boy, nor did it disrupt our personal relationship. On the other hand, as soon as he left, it became evident how deeply the corner boys felt about his statement. They spent some time giving explosive expressions to their opinion of him, and then they told me that I was different and that they appreciated it and that I knew much more than this fellow and yet I did not show it.

My first spring in Cornerville served to establish for me a firm position in the life of the district. I had only been there several weeks when Doc said to me: "You're just as much of a fixture around this street corner as that lamppost." Perhaps the greatest event signalizing my acceptance on Norton Street was the baseball game that Mike Giovanni organized against the group of Norton Street boys in their late teens. It was the old men who had won glorious victories in the past against the rising youngsters. Mike assigned me to a regular position on the team, not a key position perhaps (I was stationed in right field), but at least I was there. When it was my turn to bat in the last half of the ninth inning, the score was tied, there were two outs, and the bases were loaded. As I reached down to pick up my bat, I heard some of the fellows suggesting to Mike that he ought to put in a pinch-hitter. Mike answered them in a loud voice that must have been meant for me: "No, I've got confidence in Bill Whyte. He'll come through in the clutch." So, with Mike's confidence to buck me up, I went up there, missed two swings, and then banged a hard grounder through the hole between second and short. At least that is where they told me it went. I was so busy getting down to first base that I did not know afterward whether I had reached there on an error or a base hit.

That night, when we went down for coffee, Danny presented me with a ring for being a regular fellow and a pretty good ball player. I was particularly impressed by the ring, for it had been made by hand. Danny had started with a clear amber die discarded from his crap game and over long hours had used his lighted cigarette to burn a hole through it and to round the corners so that it came out a heart shape on top. I assured the fellows that I would always treasure the ring.

Perhaps I should add that my game-winning base hit made the score 18–17, so it is evident that I was not the only one who had been hitting the ball. Still, it was a wonderful feeling to come through when they were counting on me, and it made me feel still more that I belonged on Norton Street.

As I gathered my early research data, I had to decide how I was to organize the written notes. In the very early stage of exploration, I simply put all the notes, in chronological order, in a single folder. As I was to go on to study a number of different groups and problems, it was obvious that this was no solution at all.

I had to subdivide the notes. There seemed to be two main

possibilities. I could organize the notes topically, with folders for politics, rackets, the church, the family, and so on. Or I could organize the notes in terms of the groups on which they were based, which would mean having folders on the Nortons, the Italian Community Club, and so on. Without really thinking the problem through, I began filing material on the group basis, reasoning that I could later redivide it on a topical basis when I had a better knowledge of what the relevant topics should be.

As the material in the folders piled up, I came to realize that the organization of notes by social groups fitted in with the way in which my study was developing. For example, we have a college-boy member of the Italian Community Club saying: "These racketeers give our district a bad name. They should really be cleaned out of here." And we have a member of the Nortons saying: "These racketeers are really all right. When you need help, they'll give it to you. The legitimate businessman— he won't even give you the time of day." Should these quotes be filed under "Racketeers, attitudes toward"? If so, they would only show that there are conflicting attitudes toward racketeers in Cornerville. Only a questionnaire (which is hardly feasible for such a topic) would show the distribution of attitudes in the district. Furthermore, how important would it be to know how many people felt one way or another on this topic? It seemed to me of much greater scientific interest to be able to relate the attitude to the *group* in which the individual participated. This shows why two individuals could be expected to have quite different attitudes on a given topic.

As time went on, even the notes in one folder grew beyond the point where my memory would allow me to locate any given item rapidly. Then I devised a rudimentary indexing system: a page in three columns containing, for each interview or observation report, the date, the person or people interviewed or observed, and a brief summary of the interview or observation record. Such an index would cover from three to eight pages. When it came time to review the notes or to write from them, a five- to ten-minute perusal of the index was enough to give me a reasonably full picture of what I had and of where any given item could be located.

7. VENTURE INTO POLITICS

July and August, 1937, I spent away from Cornerville with my parents. Perhaps I was just too accustomed to the family summer vacation to remain in Cornerville, but at least I rationalized that I needed some time to get away and do some reading and get some perspective upon my study. The perspective was not easy to come by at that time. I still did not see the connecting link between a broad study of the life of the community and intensive studies of groups.

I came back feeling that I must somehow broaden my study. That might have meant dropping my contacts with the Nortons and the Italian Community Club in order to participate more heavily in other areas. Perhaps that would have been the logical decision in terms of the way I saw my Cornerville study at the time. Fortunately, I did not act that way. The club took only one evening a week, so there was no great pressure to drop that. The Nortons took much more time, and yet it meant something important to me to have a corner and a group where I was at home in Cornerville. At the time I did not clearly see that there was much more to a study of a group than an examination of its activities and personal relationships at a particular point in time. Only as I began to see changes in these groups did I realize how extremely important it is to observe a group over an extended period of time.

While I wandered along with the Nortons and the Italian Community Club more or less by a process of inertia, I decided I should expand the study by getting a broader and deeper view of the political life of the community. Street corner activities and politics in Cornerville were inextricably intertwined. There were several political organizations seeking to build up rival candidates. I felt that I could best gain an inside view of politics if I aligned myself actively with one political organization, yet I was afraid this might so label me that I would have difficulty with my study afterward in relation to people who were against this particular politician.

The problem solved itself for me. In the fall of 1937 there was a mayoralty contest. An Irish politician who had formerly been mayor and governor of the state was running again. Among the good Yankees, Murphy's name was the personification of corruption. However, in Cornerville, he had a reputation for being a friend of the poor man and of the Italian people. Most of the Cornerville politicians were for him, and he was expected to carry the district by a tremendous majority. I therefore decided that it would be a good thing for my study if I could get my start in politics working for this man. (Among my Harvard associates, this new political allegiance led to some raised eyebrows, but I rationalized that a complete novice could hardly be of any influence in securing the election of the notorious politician.)

In order to enlist in the campaign, I had to have some sort of local connection. I found this with George Ravello, state senator representing our ward and two others. At the restaurant where I lived, I met Paul Ferrante, who was Ravello's secretary and also a friend of the Martini family. Ferrante's services to Ravello were entirely on a volunteer basis. Paul was unemployed at the time and was working for the politician in hopes that he would some day get a political job out of it.

After a little preliminary discussion, I enlisted as the unpaid secretary of the unpaid secretary of the state senator for the duration of the mayoralty campaign. When that election was over, I re-enlisted, for there was a special election for a vacant seat in Congress, and George Ravello was running for that office. Fortunately for my study, all the other Cornerville politicians were at least officially for Ravello, since he was running against several Irishmen. I therefore felt that I could be active in his campaign without creating barriers for myself anywhere else in the district.

As a campaign worker for the state senator, I was a complete anomaly. Most workers in such campaigns can at least claim to be able to deliver substantial numbers of votes; I could not pledge anything but my own. It was hard for the organization to get used to this. On one occasion, George Ravello gave me a ride up to the State House, in the course of which he wanted to know when I was going to deliver him the indorsement of the Italian Community Club. This was quite a touchy topic within the club at the time. On the one hand, all the members were interested in seeing an Italian-American advance to higher office, and yet they were embarrassed by being identified with George Ravello. The language he used in public was hardly refined, and he had gained publicity that had embarrassed the young men on several occasions. There was, for example, the time when a woman was testifying against a bill introduced into the senate by Ravello. Ravello got angry in the midst of the hearing and threatened to throw the good woman off the wharf and into the harbor if she ever set foot in his district. On another occasion, the newspapers carried a picture of Ravello with a black eye, which he had received in a fight with a member of the State Parole Board.

I explained to Ravello that it was against the policy of the club to indorse candidates for any public office. While this happened to be true, it was hardly a satisfactory explanation to the Senator. Still, he did not press the matter further, perhaps recognizing that the support of the Italian Community Club did not count for very much anyway.

Not being able to deliver votes, I sought to make myself useful by running errands and doing various odd jobs, such as nailing up Ravello posters in various parts of the district.

I am sure no one thought I was any real help to the Senator's campaign, but neither did I appear to be doing any harm, so I was allowed to hang around in the quarters which served as a combination political office and funeral parlor.

I found this one of the more unpleasant places to hang around, because I never was able to gain complete scientific detachment regarding funeral parlors. One of my most vivid and unpleasant memories of Cornerville stems from this period. One of the Senator's constituents had died. The stairs to his flat being too narrow to accommodate the casket, the deceased was laid out for friends and family in the back room of the funeral parlor. Unfortunately, he was laid out in two pieces, since he had had his leg amputated shortly before his death. The rest of his body had been embalmed, but I was told that there was no way of embalming a detached leg. The gangrenous leg gave off a most sickening odor. While family and friends came in to pay their last respects, we political workers sat in the front part of the office trying to keep our attention on politics. Now and then Paul Ferrante went about the room spraying perfume. The combination of perfume with the gangrenous stench was hardly an improvement. I stayed at my post through the day but finished up a trifle nauseated.

Since the politicians did not know what to do with my services and yet were willing to have me hang around, I found that I could develop my own job description. Before one of the meetings of the political workers, I suggested to Carrie Ravello—the candidate's wife and the real brains of the family—that I serve as secretary for such meetings. I then took notes while the meeting proceeded and typed her out a summary for later use. (The invention of carbon paper enabled me to retain my own copy of all the records.)

Actually, it was of no importance for the organization to have such a record. Although they were officially considered meetings to discuss political strategy and tactics, they were only pep rallies for the second string of political powers supporting Ravello. I never did get in on the top-level political discussions where the real decisions were made. However, my note-taking at these political meetings did give me a fully documented record of one area of activity. From here I went on to the large-scale political rally, where I sought to record on the spot the speeches and other activities of the leading Ravello supporters.

When election day came, I voted as the polls opened and then reported for duty at the candidate's headquarters. There I found I had been assigned to work with Ravello's secretary in another ward. I spent the first part of election day outside of Cornerville following Ferrante around and being of no real use to myself or to the organization. I did not worry about my contribution, because I was getting a growing impression that a lot of what passed under the name of political activity was simply a waste of time. On election-day morning we stopped in to chat with a number of friends of Paul Ferrante and had a drink or a cup of coffee here and there. Then we drove around to offer voters transportation to the polls, which in such a crowded district would be just around the corner. We made about thirty stops and took one voter to the polls, and she said she had been going to walk down in five minutes anyway. The others were either not home or told us they were going to walk down later.

At two o'clock I asked if it would be all right for me to leave and return to my ward. This was readily granted, so I was able to spend the rest of the day in Cornerville.

When I got home, I began hearing alarming reports from the home ward of the Irish politician who was Ravello's chief rival. He was said to have a fleet of taxicabs cruising about his ward so that each of his repeaters would be able to vote in every precinct of the ward. It became clear that, if we did not steal the election ourselves, this low character would steal it from us.

Around five o'clock one of the senator's chief lieutenants rushed up to a group of us who were hanging on the corner across the street from my home polling place. He told us that Joseph Maloney's section of our ward was wide open for repeaters, that the cars were ready to transport them, and that all he needed were a few men to get to work. At the moment the organization was handicapped by a shortage of manpower to accomplish this important task. The senator's lieutenant did not ask for volunteers; he simply directed us to get into the cars to go to the polling places where the work could be done. I hesitated a moment, but I did not refuse.

Before the polls had closed that night, I had voted three more times for George Ravello—really not much of a feat, since another novice who had started off at the same time as I managed to produce nine votes in the same period of time. Two of my votes were cast in Joseph Maloney's end of the ward; the third was registered in my home polling place.

I was standing on the corner when one of the politician's henchmen came up to me with the voting list to ask me to go in. I explained that this was my home polling place and that I had already voted under my own name. When they learned that this had been when the polls opened, they told me that I had nothing to worry about and that a new shift was now on duty. They had the name of Frank Petrillo picked out for me. They told me that Petrillo was a Sicilian fisherman who was out to sea on election day, so we were exercising his democratic rights for him. I looked at the voting list to discover that Petrillo was forty-five years old and stood five feet nine. Since I was twenty-three and six feet three, this seemed implausible to me, and I raised a question. I was assured that this made no difference at all, since the people inside the polling place were Joe Maloney's people. I was not completely reassured by this, but, nevertheless, I got in line to wait my new turn in the rush of the hour before the polls closed.

I gave my name, and the woman at the gate checked me in, I picked up my ballot, went back to the booth, and marked it for George Ravello. As I was about to put the ballot into the box, this woman looked me over and asked me how old I was. Suddenly the ridiculousness of my masquerade struck home to me. I knew I was supposed to say forty-five, but I could not voice such an absurd lie. Instead, I compromised on twenty-nine. She asked how tall I was, and again I compromised, giving the figure as six feet. They had me all right, but still the questioning went on. The woman asked me how I spelled my name. In the excitement I spelled it wrong. The other woman checker now came over and asked me about my sisters. I thought I had recalled seeing the names of some female Petrillos on the list, and, in any case, if I invented names that did not appear, they could be names of women who were not registered. I said, "Yes, I have two sisters." She asked their names. I said, "Celia and Florence."

She leered at me and asked, "What about this Marie Petrillo?"

I took a deep breath and said, "She's my cousin."

They said they would have to challenge my vote. They called for the warden in charge of the polling place.

I had a minute to wait before he stepped forward, and that was plenty of time to mull over my future. I could see before my eyes large headlines on the front pages of Eastern City's tab-loids—HARVARD FELLOW ARRESTED FOR REPEATING. Why wouldn't they play it up? Indeed, this was an ideal man-bites-dog news-paper story. In that moment I resolved that at least I would not mention my connection with Harvard or my Cornerville study when I was arrested.

The warden now stepped up, said he would have to challenge my vote, and asked me to write my name on the back of the ballot. I went over to the booth. But, by this time, I was so nerv-ous that I forgot what my first name was supposed to be and put down "Paul." The warden took my ballot and looked at the back of it. He had me swear that this was my name and that I had not voted before. I did so. I went through the gate. He told me to stop. As I looked over the crowd coming in, I thought of trying to run for it, but I did not break away. I came back. He looked at the book of registered voters. He turned back to the booth, and for a moment his back was to me. Then I saw him scratch out the name I had written on the back of the ballot. He put the ballot into the box, and it registered with a ring of the bell. He told me I could go out, and I did, trying to walk in a calm and leisurely manner.

When I was out on the street, I told the politician's lieutenant that my vote had been challenged. "Well, what do you care? We didn't lose anything by it." Then I told him that the vote had finally gone through. "Well, so much the better. Listen, what could they have done to you? If the cops had taken you in, they wouldn't hold you. We would fix you up."

I did not eat well that night. Curiously enough, I did not feel nearly so guilty over what I had done until I had thought that I was going to be arrested. Up to that point, I had just gone numbly along. After supper, I went out to look up Tony Cardio of the Italian Community Club. As I had walked into his home precinct to repeat, I encountered him coming out of the polling place. As we passed, he grinned at me and said: "They're working you pretty hard today, aren't they?" I immediately jumped to the conclusion that he must know that I was going in to repeat. Now I felt that I must see him as soon as possible to explain in the best way that I could what I had been doing and why. For-tunately for me, Tony was not home that night. As my anxiety subsided, I recognized that, simply because I knew my own guilt, it did not necessarily follow that everybody else and Tony knew what I had done. I confirmed this indirectly when I had a conversation with Tony later about the election. He raised no question concerning my voting activities.

That was my performance on election day. What did I gain from it? I had seen through firsthand personal experience how repeating was accomplished. But this was really of very little value, for I had been observing these activities at quite close range before, and I could have had all the data without taking any risk. Actually, I learned nothing of research value from the experience, and I took a chance of jeopardizing my whole study. While I escaped arrest, these things are not always fixed as firmly as the politician's henchman think they are. A year later, when I was out of town at election time, somebody was actually arrested for voting in *my* name.

Even apart from the risk of arrest, I faced other possible losses. While repeating was fairly common in our ward, there were only relatively few people who engaged in it, and they were generally looked down upon as the fellows who did the dirty work. Had the word got around about me, my own standing in the district would have suffered considerable damage. So far as I know, my repeating never did become known beyond some of the key people in Ravello's organization. Most of my repeating had been done outside of Cornerville, and my Norton Street friends did not vote in the same precinct where I put in my second Cornerville vote. I had not been observed by anyone whose opinion could damage me. Furthermore, I was just plain lucky that I did not reveal myself to Tony Cardio; in fact, I was lucky at every point.

The experience posed problems that transcended expediency. I had been brought up as a respectable, law-abiding, middle-class citizen. When I discovered that I was a repeater, I found my conscience giving me serious trouble. This was not like the picture of myself that I had been trying to build up. I could not laugh it off simply as a necessary part of the field work. I knew that it was not necessary; at the point where I began to repeat, I could have refused. There were others who did refuse to do it. I had simply got myself involved in the swing of the campaign and let myself be carried along. I had to learn that, in order to be accepted by the people in a district, you do not have to do everything just as they do it. In fact, in a district where there are different groupings with different standards of behavior, it may be a matter of very serious consequence to conform to the standards of one particular group.

I also had to learn that the field worker cannot afford to think only of learning to live with others in the field. He has to continue living with himself. If the participant observer finds himself engaging in behavior that he has learned to think of as immoral, then he is likely to begin to wonder what sort of a person he is after all. Unless the field worker can carry with him a reasonably consistent picture of himself, he is likely to run into difficulties.

8. BACK ON NORTON STREET

When the campaign was over, I went back to Norton Street, I did not sever my ties with the Ravello organization altogether. For this there were two reasons: I wanted to maintain my connections for possible further research in politics; but then also I did not want them to think of me as just another of those "phonies" who made a fuss over the politician when he seemed to have a chance to win and abandoned him when he lost. Still, I had no strong personal tie to hold me to the organization. Carrie Ravello I liked and respected; the Senator puzzled and interested me, but I never felt that I got to know him. His one-time secretary just dropped out of sight for a while after the election—still owing me ten dollars. The others did not really matter to me personally. And, as I review my notes today, even their names have little meaning.

As I became more active once again on Norton Street, the local world began to look different. The world I was observing was in a process of change. I saw some of the members of the Italian Community Club establishing contacts with the upper world of Yankee control as I followed them to All-American Night at the Women's Republican Club. I saw the stresses and strains within the Nortons growing out of contacts with the Aphrodite Club and the Italian Community Club. I watched Doc, completely without scientific detachment, as he prepared for his doomed effort to run for public office.

Then in April, 1938, one Saturday night I stumbled upon one of my most exciting research experiences in Cornerville. It was the night when the Nortons were to bowl for the prize money; the biggest bowling night of the whole season. I recall standing on the corner with the boys while they discussed the coming contest. I listened to Doc, Mike, and Danny making their predictions as to the order in which the men would finish. At first, this made no particular impression upon me, as my own unexpressed predictions were exactly along the same lines. Then, as the men joked and argued, I suddenly began to question and take a new look at the whole situation. I was convinced that Doc, Mike, and Danny were basically correct in their predictions, and yet why should the scores approximate the structure of the gang? Were these top men simply better natural athletes than the rest? That made no sense, for here was Frank Bonnelli, who was a good enough athlete to win the promise of a tryout with a major-league baseball team. Why should not Frank outdo us all at the bowling alley? Then I remembered the baseball game we had had a year earlier against the younger crowd on Norton Street. I could see the man who was by common consent the best baseball player of us all striking out with long, graceful swings and letting the grounders bounce through his legs. And then I remembered that neither I nor anyone else seemed to have been surprised at Frank's performance in this game. Even Frank himself was not surprised, as he explained: "I can't seem to play ball when I'm playing with fellows I know like that bunch."

I went down to the alleys that night fascinated and just a bit awed by what I was about to witness. Here was the social structure in action right on the bowling alleys. It held the individual members in their places—and I along with them. I did not stop to reason then that, as a close friend of Doc, Danny, and Mike, I held a position close to the top of the gang and therefore should be expected to excel on this great occasion. I simply felt myself buoyed up by the situation. I felt my friends were for me, had confidence in me, wanted me to bowl well. As my turn came and I stepped up to bowl, I felt supremely confident that I was going to hit the pins that I was aiming at. I have never felt quite that way before—or since. Here at the bowling alley I was experiencing subjectively the impact of the group structure upon the individual. It was a strange feeling, as if something larger than myself was controlling the ball as I went through my swing and released it toward the pins.

When it was all over, I looked at the scores of all the other men. I was still somewhat bemused by my own experience, and now I was excited to discover that the men had actually finished in the predicted order with only two exceptions that could readily be explained in terms of the group structure.

As I later thought over the bowling-alley contest, two things stood out in my mind. In the first place, I was convinced that now I had something important: the relationship between individual performance and group structure, even though at this time I still did not see how such observation would fit in with the over-all pattern of the Cornerville study. I believed then (and still believe now) that this sort of relationship may be observed in other group activities everywhere. As an avid baseball fan, I had often been puzzled by the records of some athletes who seemed to be able to hit and throw and field with superb technical qualifications and yet were unable to make the major-league teams. I had also been puzzled by cases where men who had played well at one time suddenly failed badly, whereas other men seemed to make tremendous improvements that could not be explained simply on the basis of increasing experience. I suspect that a systematic study of the social structure of a baseball team, for example, will explain some of these otherwise mysterious phenomena. The other point that impressed me involved field research methods. Here I had the scores of the men on that final night at the bowling alleys. This one set of figures was certainly important, for it represented the performance of the men in the event that they all looked upon as the climax of the year. However, this same group had been bowling every Saturday night for many months, and some of the members had bowled on other nights in between. It would have been a ridiculously simple task for me to have kept a record for every string bowled by every man on every Saturday night of that season and on such other evenings as I bowled with the men. This would have produced a set of statistics that would have been the envy of some of my highly quantitative friends. I kept no record of these scores, because at this time I saw no point to it. I had been looking upon Saturday night at the bowling alleys as simply recreation for myself and my friends. I found myself enjoying the bowling so much that now and then I felt a bit guilty about neglecting my research. I was bowling with the men in order to establish a social position that would enable me to interview them and observe important things. But what were these important things? Only after I passed up this statistical gold mine did I suddenly realize that the behavior of the men in the regular bowling-alley sessions was the perfect example of what I should be observing. Instead of bowling in order to be able to observe something else, I should have been bowling in order to observe bowling. I learned then that the day-to-day routine activities of these men constituted the basic data of my study.

9. REPLANNING THE RESEARCH

The late spring and summer of 1938 brought some important changes into my research.

On May 28, I was married to Kathleen King, and three weeks later we returned to Cornerville together. Kathleen had visited me at the restaurant and had met some of my friends. Even as a married man, I did not want to move out of the district, and Kathleen, fortunately, was eager to move in. This presented problems, because, while we were not asking for everything, we did hope to find an apartment with a toilet and bathtub inside it. We looked at various gloomy possibilities until at last we found a building that was being remodeled on Shelby Street. Some of my Norton Street friends warned us against the neighborhood, saying that the place was full of Sicilians who were a very cutthroat crowd. Still, the apartment had the bathtub and toilet and was clean and relatively airy. It had no central heating, but we could be reasonably comfortable with the kitchen stove.

Now that we were two, we could enter into new types of social activites, and Kathleen could learn to know some of the women as I had become acquainted with the men. However, these new directions of social activity were something for the future. My problem now was to find where I was and where I was going. This was a period of stocktaking.

In describing my Cornerville study, I have often said I was eighteen months in the field before I knew where my research was going. In a sense, this is literally true. I began with the general idea of making a community study. I felt that I had to establish myself as a participant observer in order to make such a study. In the early months in Cornerville I went through the process that sociologist Robert Johnson has described in his own field work. I began as a nonparticipating observer. As I became accepted into the community, I found myself becoming almost a nonobserving participant. I got the feel of life in Cornerville, but that meant that I got to take for granted the same things that my Cornerville friends took for granted. I was immersed in it, but I could as yet make little sense out of it. I had a feeling that I was doing something important, but I had yet to explain to myself what it was.

Fortunately, at this point I faced a very practical problem. My three-year fellowship would run out in the summer of 1939. The fellowship could be renewed for a period up to three years. Applications for renewal were due in the early spring of 1939.

I was enjoying Cornerville, and I felt that I was getting somewhere, yet at the same time I felt that I needed at least three more years. I realized that so far I had little to show for the time I had spent. When I submitted my application for renewal, I must also submit some evidence that I had acquitted myself well in the first three-year period. I would have to write something. I had several months in which to do the writing, but the task at first appalled me. I sat down to ask myself what it was in Cornerville upon which I had reasonably good data. Was there anything ready to be written up? I pondered this and talked it over with Kathleen and with John Howard, who was working with me in the district.

Still thinking in terms of a community study, I recognized that I knew very little about family life in Cornerville, and my data were very thin upon the church, although John Howard was beginning to work on this area. I had been living with the restaurant family in a room that overlooked the corner where T. S., the most prominent Cornerville racketeer, sometimes was seen with his followers. I had looked down upon the group many times from my window, and yet I had never met the men. Racketeering was of obvious importance in the district, yet all I knew about it was the gossip I picked up from men who were only a little closer to it than I. I had much more information regarding political life and organization, but even here I felt that there were so many gaps that I could not yet put the pieces together.

If these larger areas were yet to be filled in, what on earth did I have to present? As I thumbed through the various folders, it was obvious that the Norton and Community Club folders were fatter than the rest. If I knew anything about Cornerville, I must know it about the Nortons and the Italian Community Club. Perhaps, if I wrote up these two stories, I would begin to see some pattern in what I was doing in Cornerville.

As I wrote the case studies of the Nortons and of the Italian Community, a pattern for my research gradually emerged in my mind.

I realized at last that I was not writing a community study in the usual sense of that term. The reader who examines *Middletown* will note that it is written about people in general in that community. Individuals or groups do not figure in the story except as they illustrate the points that the authors are making (the sequel, *Middletown in Transition*, presents one exception to this description with a chapter on the leading family of the community). The reader will further note that *Middletown* is organized in terms of such topics as getting a living, making a home, training the young, and using leisure.

The Lynds accomplished admirably the task they set out to

accomplish. I simply came to realize that my task was different. I was dealing with particular individuals and with particular groups.

I realized also that there was another difference that I had stumbled upon. I had assumed that a sociological study should present a description and analysis of a community at one particular point in time, supported of course by some historical background. I now came to realize that *time* itself was one of the key elements in my study. I was observing, describing, and analyzing groups as they evolved and changed through time. It seemed to me that I could explain much more effectively the behavior of men when I observed them over time than would have been the case if I had got them at one point in time. In other words, I was taking a moving picture instead of a still photograph.

But, if this was a study of particular individuals and there were more than twenty thousand people in the district, how could I say anything significant about Cornerville on this individual and group basis? I came to realize that I could only do so if I saw individuals and groups in terms of their positions in the social structure. I also must assume that, whatever the individual and group differences were, there were basic similarities to be found. Thus I would not have to study every corner gang in order to make meaningful statements about corner gangs in Cornerville. A study of one corner gang was not enough, to be sure, but, if an examination of several more showed up the uniformities that I expected to find, then this part of the task became manageable.

On the Italian Community Club, I felt that I needed no additional data. There were few enough college men in Cornerville at the time, so that this one group represented a large sample of people in this category. It also seemed to me that they represented significant points in the social structure and in the social mobility process. There would certainly be others like them coming along after they had left the district, even as the Sunset Dramatic Club had gone before them. Furthermore, examination of their activities showed up important links with Republican politics and with the settlement house.

I now began to see the connection between my political study and the case study of the corner gang. The politician did not seek to influence separate individuals in Cornerville; consciously or unconsciously he sought out group leaders. So it was men like Doc who were the connecting links between their groups and the larger political organization. I could now begin writing my study by examining particular groups in detail, and then I could go on to relate them to the larger structures of the community. With this pattern in mind, I came to realize that I had much more data on politics than I had thought.

There were sill important gaps in my study. My knowledge of the role of the church in the community was fragmentary, and this I hoped to fill in. I had done no systematic work upon the family. On the one hand, it seemed inconceivable that one could write a study of Cornerville without discussing the family; yet, at the same time, I was at a loss as to how to proceed in tying family studies into the organization of the book as it was emerging in my mind. I must confess also that for quite unscientific reasons I have always found politics, rackets, and gangs more interesting than the basic unit of human society.

The gap that worried me most was in the area of the rackets and the police. I had a general knowledge of how the rackets functioned, but nothing to compare with the detailed interpersonal data I had upon the corner gang. As my book was evolving, it seemed to me that this was the gap that simply must be filled, although at the time I had no idea how I would get the inside picture that was necessary.

I finished the writing of my first two case studies and submitted them in support of my application for a renewal of the fellowship. Some weeks later I received my answer. The fellowship had been renewed for one year instead of the three for which I had been hoping. At first, I was bitterly disappointed. As I was just beginning to get my bearings, I did not see how it would be possible to finish an adequate study in the eighteen months that then remained.

I am now inclined to believe that this one year cut-off was a very good thing for me and my research. In a sense, the study of a community or an organization has no logical end point. The more you learn, the more you see that there is to learn. If I had had three years instead of one, my study would have taken longer to complete. Perhaps it might have been a better study. On the other hand, when I knew I had just eighteen months to go, I had to settle down and think through my plans more thoroughly and push ahead with the research and writing much more purposefully.

10. AGAIN THE CORNER GANG

The most important steps I took in broadening my study of street corner gangs grew out of Doc's recreation center project, although at first I had some other interests in mind. It began with one of my periodic efforts to get Doc a job. When I heard that the Cornerville House had finally been successful in getting its grant to open three store-front recreation centers, I sought to persuade Mr. Smith, the director, to man them with local men who, like Doc, were leaders in their groups. I found that he had planned to man them with social workers trained in group work. When I realized that it was hopeless to get him to select three local men, I tried to urge at least Doc upon him. I could see that Mr. Smith was tempted by the idea and afraid of it at the same time. When I brought Doc in to meet him, I found that I lost ground instead of gaining it, for, as Doc told me later, he had got a dizzy spell there in the settlement-house office, and he had been in no condition to make a favorable personal impression. If Doc and I had figured out correctly the underlying causes for his dizzy spells, then a steady job and the money that would enable him to resume his customary pattern of social activity would cure these neurotic symptoms. On the other hand, I could hardly explain this to Mr. Smith. I was afraid that it appeared that I was simly trying to do a favor for a friend. As my last effort in this direction, I turned over to Mr. Smith a copy of my case study of the Nortons—and asked him please to keep it confidential, since I was not ready to publish.

This made the difference. Mr. Smith agreed to hire Doc.

As the preliminary activities of setting up the recreation centers got under way, I began to worry about my confident predictions of Doc's success. In the preliminary meetings to discuss plans for the centers, Doc was passive and apparently apathetic. Nevertheless, almost from the moment that Doc's center opened, it became apparent that it was to be a success.

On one of my early visits to Doc's center, he introduced me to Sam Franco, who was to play a far more important part in my study than brief mentions of him in the book indicate. Doc met Sam the night his center opened. Sam's gang was hanging around outside of the center looking the place over. Sam came in as the emissary of his group—a move which immediately identified him as the leader to Doc. The two men discussed the center briefly, and then Sam went out and brought his gang in. By the second night of the center, Sam had become Doc's lieutenant in its administration. Doc knew a few people in this part of the district, but Sam knew everybody.

Doc knew that I was trying to extend my corner gang study, and he suggested that Sam might be the man to help me. Doc had already learned that Sam had been keeping a scrapbook with newspaper accounts of Cornerville activities and some personal material on his own group.

I invited Sam and his scrapbook up to our apartment. There I learned that Sam had got started on his scrapbook after an experience on a National Youth Administration Project, where he had been working for a man who was writing a study of the problems of youth in this region. The scrapbook was completely miscellaneous and undirected, but it did have one part that particularly interested me. Sam had a section for his own gang with one page for each member. At the top of the page was a line drawing (from memory) of the individual, and then he wrote in such points as age, address, education, job, and ambition. (Usually he had written "none" opposite the heading, "ambition.")

My task was now to persuade Sam that, while it was fine to look upon these men as individuals, it was even better to look upon them in terms of their relations with each other. I had only begun my explanation when Sam got the point and accepted it with enthusiasm. Of course, this was the sort of thing he knew; he had so taken it for granted that it had not occurred to him how important it might be. From this point on until the end of my study Sam Franco was my research assistant. I even managed to get Harvard to pay a hundred dollars for his services.

We began with an analysis of Sam's own gang, the Millers. We also looked at other gangs that came into Doc's recreation center. Here we had the great advantage of having two sharp observers checking each other on the same groups. I was reassured to find that they were in complete agreement on the top-leadership structure of every gang—with one exception. This one exception did trouble me until the explanation presented itself.

I had spent part of one afternoon listening to Doc and Sam argue over the leadership of one gang. Doc claimed that Carl was the man; Sam argued that it was Tommy. Each man presented incidents that he had observed in support of his point of view. The following morning Sam rushed up to my house with this bulletin: "You know what happened last night? Carl and Tommy nearly had it out. They got into a big argument, and now the gang is split into two parts with some of them going with Carl and the rest going with Tommy." So their conflicting views turned out to be an accurate representation of what was taking place in the gang.

As I worked on these other gang studies, I assumed that I had finished my research on the Nortons. Still, I kept in close touch with Doc, and, just for recreation, I continued to bowl with the remnants of the Nortons on some Saturday nights.

With my attention directed elsewhere, I failed to see what was happening among the Nortons right before my eyes. I knew Long John was not bowling as he had in previous years, and I also knew that he was not as close to Doc, Danny, and Mike as he had been. I had noticed that, when Long John was on Norton Street, the followers badgered him more aggressively than they ever had before. I must have assumed some connection among these phenomena, and yet I did not make much of the situation until Doc came to me and told me of Long John's psychological difficulties.

It was as if this information set off a flash bulb in my head. Suddenly all the pieces of the puzzle fell together. The previous season, I had stumbled upon the relationship between position in the group and performance at the bowling alleys. I now saw the three-way connection between group position, performance, and mental health. And not only for Long John. Doc's dizzy spells seemed to have precisely the same explanation.

We could put it more generally in this way. The individual becomes accustomed to a certain pattern of interaction. If this pattern is subject to a drastic change, then the individual can be expected to experience mental health difficulties. That is a very crude statement. Much further research would be needed before we could determine the degree of change necessary, the possibilities of compensating with interactions in other social areas, and so on. But here at least was one way of tying together human relations and psychological adjustment.

Furthermore, here was an opportunity to experiment in therapy. If my diagnosis was correct, then the line of treatment was clear: re-establish something like Long John's pre-existing pattern of interaction, and the neurotic symptoms should disappear. This was the first real opportunity to test my conclusions on group structure. I embraced it with real enthusiasm.

Convinced as I was of the outcome that should follow, I must confess that I was somewhat awestruck when, under Doc's skilfully executed therapy program, Long John not only lost his neurotic symptoms but also closed out the season by winning the prize money in the final bowling contest. Of course, this victory was not necessary to establish the soundness of the diagnosis. It would have been enough for Long John to have re-established himself *among* the top bowlers. His five-dollar prize was just a nice bonus for interaction theory.

11. STUDYING RACKETEERING

My meeting with Tony Cataldo, the prominent Cornerville racketeer, came about almost by chance. I dropped in one afternoon at the restaurant where I had first lived in Cornerville. Ed Martini, Al's older brother, was there at the time. He was grumbling about a pair of banquet tickets he had had to buy from a local policeman. He said that his wife did not want to go to banquets; perhaps I might like to accompany him.

I asked what the occasion was. He told me that the banquet was in honor of the son of the local police lieutenant. The young man had just passed his bar examinations and was starting out on his legal career. I thought a moment. It was perfectly obvious what sorts of people would be present at the banquet: mainly policemen, politicians, and racketeers. I decided that this might be an opportunity for me.

At the banquet hall, Ed and I took up our position in the lounge outside the men's room. Here we encountered Tony Cataldo and one of his employees, Rico Deleo. It turned out that Ed Martini knew Tony slightly and that Rico lived right across the street from me. Rico asked what I was doing, and I said something about writing a book on Cornerville. Tony said he had seen me around taking photographs of the *feste* that had been staged on Shelby Street the previous summer. This proved to be a fortunate association in his mind, since I could talk quite freely about what I had been trying to learn of the *feste*—which were actually just a minor interest in the research.

The four of us went up to a banquet table together, where we had to wait more than an hour for our food. We munched on olives and celery and sympathized with one another over the poor service. After the dinner we stepped downstairs and bowled three strings together. By this time, Tony was quite friendly and invited me to stop in at his store any time.

I paid several visits to the back room of the store from which Tony operated some of his business. A week after we had met, Tony invited Kathleen and me to dinner at his home. His wife, an attractive young girl, told us later that he had spoken of us as a Harvard professor and a commercial artist. She was very upset that he gave her only one day's notice for the dinner when she felt she needed at least a week to prepare for such important personages. The food was nevertheless quite elaborate, and each course seemed like a whole meal. After dinner, Tony drove us out to meet some of his relatives in one of the suburbs. Then we all went bowling together.

We had dinner twice at their home, and they came to ours twice. On each occasion, apart from the small talk, the research pattern was similar. We talked some about the *feste*, about the club life of the *paesani* from the old country, and about such things which Tony associated with my study. Then, I gradually eased him into a discussion of his business. The discussion seemed to move naturally in this direction. It was just like a friend asking a legitimate businessman about the progress he was making and the problems he was meeting. Tony seemed glad to unburden himself.

I now felt optimistic about my future in racketeering. We seemed to be getting along very well with the Cataldos, and I was ready to follow Tony into the new field. However, after the first exchanges of sociability, Tony seemed to lose interest in us.

I was puzzled by this sudden cooling-off. I am not sure I have the full explanation, but I think there were at least two parts of it.

In the first place, Tony ran into a business crisis at about this time. Some men broke into his horse room one afternoon, held it up, and took all the money from the customers and from Tony. In order to maintain good relations with his customers, Tony had to reimburse them for the robbery, so that afternoon was doubly costly. It was also most frustrating, because, as the men were making their getaway, Tony could look out of the window and see them running right beneath him. He had a clear shot at them, yet he could not shoot, because he knew that a shooting would close down gambling in Cornerville like nothing else. As long as these things were done quietly, the "heat" was not so likely to be on.

This might have accounted for an interruption in our social life together but hardly for a complete cessation. It seems to me that the other factor was a problem in social status and mobility. At first, Tony had built me up to his wife—and probably to friends and relatives also—as a Harvard professor. Both the Cataldos were highly status-conscious. They did not allow their young son to play with the local riffraff. They explained that they only lived in the district because it was necessary for business reasons and that they still hoped to move out. When we were their guests, they introduced us to their friends and relatives who lived in more fashionable parts of the city.

On the other hand, when the Cataldos came to our house for dinner they just met with us and nobody else. Furthermore, Tony was now seeing me associating with the men on Shelby Street who were distinctly small fry to him. At first, he had thought that his contact with me was something important; now, perhaps, he considered it insignificant.

To some extent, I was aware of this risk and thought of the possibility of having Harvard friends in to dinner with the Cataldos. I had been keeping the two worlds apart. One Harvard friend, a symbolic logician, had once asked me to introduce him to a crap game. He explained that he had figured out mathematically how to win in a crap game. I explained that my crap-shooting friends had reached the same mathematical conclusion by their rule-of-thumb method, and I begged off from this adventure. On another occasion, we had the wife of one of my Harvard associates visiting us when one of the local men dropped in. Sizing up his new audience, he began regaling her with accounts of famous murders that had taken place in Cornerville in recent years. She listened with eyes wide open. At the end of one particularly hair-raising story she asked, "Who killed him?"

Our Cornerville friend shook his head and said: "Lady! Lady! Around here you don't ask them things."

That incident did us no damage, for the man knew us well enough to take it all as a joke. Still, I was hesitant about mixing Harvard and Cornerville. I did not worry about what Cornerville would do to Harvard, but I did worry lest some Harvard friend would unintentionally make a blunder that would make things awkward for me or would act in such a way as to make the local people ill at ease. For that reason, I kept the two worlds separate, but that meant that Tony could not improve his social standing through associating with us.

When it became evident that I was at a dead end with Tony, I cast about for other avenues leading to a study of racketeering.

Two possibilities seemed open. Tony had an older brother who worked for him. I reasoned that, since the two men were brothers and worked so closely together, Henry would know almost as much about racket developments as Tony. I already had seen something of Henry, and I set about building the relationship further. This went along smoothly with visits back and forth from house to house as well as conversations in the back room of the store. (This indicates that Tony did not drop us out of suspicion, for in that case he could have seen to it that we did not take up with his brother.)

This led to a good deal of discussion of Tony's racket organization, which was exceedingly valuable to me. Still, I had an uneasy feeling that I was not getting what I needed. I was not yet ready to give up the possibility of getting close to Tony and of observing him in action. I understood that he was a member of the Cornerville Social and Athletic Club, which was located right across the street from our apartment. I joined the club then in order to renew my pursuit of Tony Cataldo.

At first I was disappointed in the fruits of my decision. While officially a member, Tony was rarely in the clubroom. In a few weeks it became evident that I was not going to cement relations with him in this area. What next? I considered dropping out of the club. Perhaps I would have done so if there had been other research openings then demanding my attention. Since I had planned to concentrate upon the role of the racketeer and had no other plans at the time, I rationalized that I should stay with the club. I did not record the reasons for my decision at the time. Perhaps I had a hunch that interesting things would break here. Or perhaps I was just lucky.

At least, I recognized that the club presented some new angles in research. It was far larger than any corner gang I had studied. Here was an opportunity to carry further the observational methods I had used on the Nortons.

When I wrote my first draft of this present statement, I described how I developed these new methods to a point where I had systematic knowledge of the structure of the club *before* the election crisis. In other words, when Tony entered and sought to manipulate the club, I already had a full picture of the structure he was attempting to manipulate. I must now admit, following a review of my notes, that this is a retrospective falsification. What I first wrote was what I *should* have done. Actually, I began my systematic observations of the club several weeks before the election. When the crisis arrived, I had only an impressionistic picture of group structure. The notes I had then justified no systematic conclusions.

There were two factors that propelled me into more systematic efforts at charting the organizational structure. In the first place, when I began spending time in the club, I also began looking around for *the* leader. Naturally, I did not find *him*. If Tony was not around much, then somebody must take over in his absence. The club had a president, but he was just an indecisive nice guy who obviously did not amount to much. Of course, I did not find *the* leader because the club consisted of two factions with two leaders and—just to make matters more confusing for me—Carlo Tedesco, the leader of one faction, was not even a member of the club when I began my observations. Since I was completely confused in my crude efforts to map the structure, it followed that I must get at the data more systematically.

Then the political crisis underlined the necessity of pushing ahead with such observations. I had to learn more about the structure that Tony was seeking to manipulate.

Here I had a more complicated task than any I had faced before. The club had fifty members. Fortunately, only about thirty of them were frequent attenders, so that I could concentrate on that smaller number, but even that number presented a formidable problem.

I felt I would have to develop more formal and systematic procedures than I had used when I had been hanging on a street corner with a much smaller group of men. I began with positional mapmaking. Assuming that the men who associated together most closely socially would also be those who lined up together on the same side when decisions were to be made, I set about making a record of the groupings I observed each evening in the club. To some extent, I could do this from the front window of our apartment. I simply adjusted the venetian blind so that I was hidden from view and so that I could look down and into the store-front club. Unfortunately, however, our flat was two flights up, and the angle of vision was such that I could not see past the middle of the clubroom. To get the full picture, I had to go across the street and be with the men.

When evening activities were going full blast, I looked around the room to see which people were talking together, playing cards together, or otherwise interacting. I counted the number of men in the room, so as to know how many I would have to account for. Since I was familiar with the main physical objects of the clubroom, it was not difficult to get a mental picture of the men in relation to tables, chairs, couches, radio, and so on. When individuals moved about or when there was some interaction between these groupings, I sought to retain that in mind. In the course of an evening, there might be a general reshuffling of positions, I was not able to remember every movement, but I tried to observe with which members the movements began. And when another spatial arrangement developed, I went through the same mental process as I had with the first.

I managed to make a few notes on trips to the men's room, but most of the mapping was done from memory after I had gone home. At first, I went home once or twice for mapmaking during the evening, but, with practice, I got so that I could retain at least two positional arrangements in memory and could do all of my notes at the end of the evening.

I found this an extremely rewarding method, which well compensated me for the boring routines of endless mapping. As I piled up these maps, it became evident just what the major social groupings were and what people fluctuated between the two factions of the club. As issues arose within the club, I could predict who would stand, where.

In the course of my observations I recorded 106 groupings. Upon inspecting the data, I divided the club tentatively into the two factions I thought I was observing. Then, when I re-examined the data, I found that only 40, or 37.7 per cent, of the groupings observed contained members of both factions. I found further that only 10 out of these 40 groupings contained two or more members of each faction. The other 30 were cases where a single individual of the other faction joined in the card game or conversation. I then divided the groupings into two columns, placing in one column those which were predominantly of one faction and in the other column those which were predominantly of the other faction. Then I underlined in red those names which did not "belong" in the column where I found them. Out of a total of 462 names, 75, or approximately 16 per cent, were underlined in red. Of course, we would not expect a pure separation of two cliques in any club, but the figures, crude as they were, seemed to demonstrate that the two factions were real entities which would be important in understanding any decisions made by the club.

This observation of groupings did not, in itself, point out the influential people in the club. For that purpose, I tried to pay particular attention to events in which an individual originated activity for one or more others—where a proposal, suggestion, or request was followed by a positive response. Over a period of six months, in my notes I tabulated every observed incident where A had originated activity for B. The result of this for pair events (events involving only two people) was entirely negative. While I might have the impression that, in the relationship between A and B, B was definitely the subordinate individual, the tabulation might show that B originated for A approximately as much as A for B. However, when I tabulated the set events (those involving three or more people), the hierarchical structure of the organization clearly emerged.

As this phase of the research proceeded, I saw more clearly how to relate together the large racket organization and the street corner gang or club. In fact, the study of the role of Tony Cataldo in this setting provided the necessary link, and the observational methods here described provided the data for the analysis of this linkage.

While I was working up these research methods, I committed a serious blunder. It happened during the political crisis. Tony had been trying to persuade the club to invite his candidate in to address us, although nearly all the members were disposed to support Fiumara. At this crucial point, I participated actively, saying that, while we were all for Fiumara, I thought it was a good idea to hear what other politicians had to say. The vote was taken shortly after I spoke, and it went for Tony against Carlo. That led to the rally for Mike Kelly in our clubroom and to the most serious dissension within the club.

Here I violated a cardinal rule of participant observation. I sought actively to influence events. In a close and confused contest such as this, it is quite likely that my indorsement of Tony's position was a decisive factor. Why did I so intervene?

At the time, I was still hoping to re-establish close relations with Tony Cataldo, and I wanted to make some move that would build in that direction. So I sought to do the impossible: to take a stand which would not antagonize Carlo and his boys but would be appreciated by Tony. It was a foolish and misguided attempt. I did antagonize Carlo, and he forgave me only on the assumption that I was ignorant of the situation in which I was acting. Ignorance being preferable to treachery, I accepted this excuse.

Ironically enough, my effort to win favor with Tony was a complete failure. Before the political crisis, he had hardly known Carlo and had not recognized his leadership position in the club. When Carlo opposed him so vigorously and effectively, Tony immediately recognized Carlo's position and made every effort to establish closer relations with him. As I had taken a position on his side in the crisis, Tony needed to make no efforts to establish closer relations with me.

I did not have to speak in this situation at all. If I had spoken against Tony, it seems likely that this would have done more to re-establish our close relations than what I actually did.

As I thought over this event later, I came to the conclusion that my action had not only been unwise from a practical research standpoint; it had also been a violation of professional ethics. It is not fair to the people who accept the participant observer for him to seek to manipulate them to their possible disadvantage simply in order to seek to strengthen his social position in one area of participation. Furthermore, while the researcher may consciously and explicitly engage in influencing action with the full knowledge of the people with whom he is participating, it is certainly a highly questionable procedure for the researcher to establish his social position on the assumption that he is not seeking to lead anyone anywhere and then suddenly throw his weight to one side in a conflict situation.

12. MARCHING ON CITY HALL

I suppose no one goes to live in a slum district for three and a half years unless he is concerned about the problems facing the people there. In that case it is difficult to remain solely a passive observer. One time I gave in to the urge to do something. I tried to tell myself that I was simply testing out some of the things I had learned about the structure of corner gangs, but I knew really that this was not the main purpose.

In all my time in Cornerville I had heard again and again about how the district was forgotten by the politicians, how no improvements were ever made, how the politicians just tried to get themselves and their friends ahead. I heard a good deal about the sporadic garbage collections, but perhaps the bitterest complaint concerned the public bathhouse, where in the summer of 1939 as well as in several earlier summers there was no hot water available. In a district where only 12 per cent of the flats had bathtubs, this was a matter of serious moment.

People complained to each other about these matters, but apparently it did no good to try to work through the local politicians, who were primarily concerned about doing favors for friends and potential friends. If you could not go through the local politicians, why not go direct to the mayor—and on a mass basis? If, as I assumed, the corner gang leaders were able to mobilize their gangs for action in various directions, then it should be possible through working with a small number of individuals to organize a large demonstration.

I talked this over with Sam Franco, who was enthusiastic and ready to act at once. He promised me the support of his section of Cornerville. For the Norton Street area I called on Doc. For the area around George Ravello's headquarters, I picked one of the local leaders. With my new acquaintances on Shelby Street, I was able to cover that end of the district.

Then began the complicated task of organizing the various groups, bringing them together, and getting them ready to march at the same time. And who was going to lead this demonstration? Since I was the connecting link among most of these corner gang leaders and since I had begun the organizing activity, I was the logical man to take over. But I was not then prepared to depart so far from my observer's role. I agreed with the others that I would serve on the organizing committee, but we would have to have a different chairman. I proposed Doc, and all the others agreed to this. But, as I talked with Doc, I found that, while he was happy to go along with us, he was not prepared to accept the leadership responsibility. I then proposed Mike Giovanni, and he too was acceptable to the small group with whom I was working in preparing the demonstration. Mike said that he would conduct a public meeting in Cornerville in getting people together for the march, but he thought that the chairman from that point on should be elected by the representatives of the different corners who were there assembled. We agreed on this.

But then we had a misunderstanding as to the composition of this public meeting. Sam Franco brought just several representatives from his end of the district, while a large part of the Shelby section marched en masse down to the meeting. Thus, when there were nominations for chairman, a man from Shelby Street who had previously taken no part in the planning was nominated and elected. Sam Franco's friends were considerably annoyed by this, for they felt they could have elected one of their candidates if they had simply brought their boys along. Sam and several of the other men also suspected our chairman's motives. They were convinced that he would try to turn the demonstration to his personal advantage, and I had to concede that there was a good possibility of this. From this point on, part of the efforts of our committee were to hem in the chairman so that he would have no opportunity to go off on his own tangent.

In this election meeting we had been misled by our own conception of democratic processes. It makes sense to elect a chairman only from a regularly constituted group or constituency. In this case the election had turned out quite fortuitously because of the overrepresentation of Shelby Street.

We next had difficulty with the date on which we were to march. It had been set about a week from the election meeting, but now the men on Shelby Street were telling me that their people were all steamed up and wanted to march much sooner. I consulted Sam Franco and one or two other members of the committee but was not able to get all the committee together. In spite of this, I told them that maybe we should move the march up a couple of days. We then scheduled a meeting of the full committee to take place the night before the march. When the committee began assembling, it became evident that some of them were annoyed that they had been bypassed, and I realized that I had made a serious blunder. Fortunately, at this point one of the local politicians came in and tried to argue against the march. This was a great morale booster. Instead of arguing with each other as to how we had been handling the plan, we got all our aggressions off against the politician.

The next morning we assembled in the playground in front of the bathhouse. We had had mimeographed handbills distributed through the neighborhood the day before; the newspapers had been notified. We had our committee ready to lead the march, and we had the playground pretty well filled. Some of the older generation were there lining the sides of the playground. I assumed they would be marching with us, but, significantly enough, they did not. We should have realized that, if we wanted to get the older generation, we had to work through their leadership too. As the march got under way, young boys from all over the district thronged in among us carrying their home-made banners. And so we set off for city hall right through the center of the business district. We had the satisfaction of stopping traffic all along the route, but it was not for long, since the parade moved very fast. We had made the mistake of having all our committee up in front, and it seemed that everybody behind us was trying to get to the front, so that we leaders were almost stampeded. And some of the women pushing baby carriages were unable to keep up.

We had no opposition from the police, who were only concerned with an orderly demonstration as we assembled in the courtyard below the city hall. Then the ten committee members went up to see the mayor, while the rest of the marchers sang "God Bless America" and other songs to the accompaniment of an improvised band. We had known that the mayor was out of town, but our demonstration could not wait, so we talked to the acting mayor. He got our names and a list of our grievances, treating us seriously and respectfully. As our committee members began to speak, I heard Sam saying behind me in a low voice: "Get out of here, you cheap racketeer." I turned to see the local politician, Angelo Fiumara, elbowing his way in. Fiumara stood his ground and spoke up at the first opportunity: "I would like to add my voice to the protest as a private citizen. . . ." Sam interrupted, calling out: "He's got nuttin' to do with us. He's just trying to chisel in." Mike Giovanni reiterated Sam's remarks, and the acting mayor ruled that he would not hear Fiumara at that time. While the speaking was going on, I distributed a prepared statement to the reporters. At the end of our session the acting mayor promised that all our protests would be seriously considered and that any possible action would be taken.

We then marched to the bathhouse playground, where we told our followers what had taken place in the mayor's office. Here again, Angelo Fiumara tried to address the crowd, and we elbowed him out. The next day's newspapers carried big stories with pictures of our demonstration. We were given credit for having three hundred to fifteen hundred marchers with us in the various papers. The fellows happily accepted the figure of fifteen hundred, but I suspect three hundred was closer to the truth. The day after the demonstration, engineers were examining the boilers in the bathhouse, and in less than a week we had hot water. The street-cleaning and the garbage collections also seemed to be pepped up, for at least a short time. For all the mistakes we had made, it was evident that the demonstration had brought results.

But now the problem was: What next? We had got an organization together, and we had staged a demonstration. Somehow, we must keep Cornerville working together.

In this effort we were completely unsuccessful. Several committee meetings petered out without any agreements on concerted action. I think there were several difficulties here. In the first place, the committee members were not accustomed to meeting together or working together personally. There was nothing to bring them together except the formal business of the meeting. Their ties were on their various street corners. In the second place, we had started off with such a sensational performance that anything else would be anticlimax. It seemed hard to get up enthusiasm for any activity that would be dwarfed beside our protest march.

I came to realize that any over-all street corner organization would have to be built around some sort of continuing activity. The softball league developed the following spring and met this need to some extent. In fact, I worked with the same men in setting up the league, so in a sense the march on city hall did have continuing consequences, though they fell far short of our fond hopes.

13. FAREWELL TO CORNERVILLE

Through the spring and summer of 1940, most of my time was spent in writing the first draft of *Street Corner Society*. I already had the case studies of the Nortons and the Italian Community Club. I followed these with three manuscripts which I then called "Politics and the Social Structure," "The Racketeer in the Cornerville S. and A. Club," and "The Social Structure of Racketeering."

As I wrote, I showed the various parts to Doc and went over them with him in detail. His criticisms were invaluable in my revision. At times, when I was dealing with him and his gang, he would smile and say: "This will embarrass me, but this is the way it was, so go ahead with it."

When I left Cornerville in midsummer of 1940, the Cornerville S. and A. Club had a farewell beer party for me. We sang "God

Bless America" three times and the "Beer Barrel Polka" six times. I have moved around many times in my life, and yet I have never felt so much as though I were leaving home. The only thing that was missing was a farewell from the Nortons, and that was impossible, for the Nortons were no more by this time.

14. CORNERVILLE REVISITED

Compared to the anthropologist who studies a primitive tribe in a remote part of the world, the student of a modern American community faces distinctly different problems. In the first place, he is dealing with a literate people. It is certain that some of these people, and perhaps many of them, will read his research report. If he disguises the name of the district as I have done, many outsiders apparently will not discover where the study was actually located. I am still surprised to encounter people who locate Cornerville some hundreds of miles from its actual locale. The people in the district, of course, know it is about them, and even the changed names do not disguise the individuals for them. They remember the researcher and know the people with whom he associated and know enough about the various groups to place the individuals with little chance of error.

In such a situation the researcher carries a heavy responsibility. He would like his book to be of some help to the people in the district; at least, he wants to take steps to minimize the chances of it doing any harm, fully recognizing the possibility that certain individuals may suffer through the publication.

I cannot write a sequel entitled "Cornerville in Transition," for my visits back to the district have been infrequent and of short duration. However, I can provide a little information on what has happened to some of the chief people in the book in the intervening years and as to what effect, if any, the book has had on them and the district.

It took Doc a long time to find a secure place upon the economic ladder. He had no steady job until the war boom got well under way. Then at last he caught on and was doing very well until the postwar cutback came. People were then laid off according to their seniority, and Doc was out of work once more.

At last he did get a job in an electronics plant. At the time of my last visit (December, 1953) I found that he had worked his way up to a position as assistant supervisor in the production planning department of the factory. Such a department is a nerve center for the factory, for it handles the scheduling of the orders through every department of the plant.

Doc has achieved some success in attaining this position, but he tends to minimize his accomplishments. He explains, "On the technical side, I stink. The only place I really shine is where I have to go around and talk the foreman into running a new order ahead of the one he was planning to run. I can do that without getting him upset." So Doc is applying some of the social skill he displayed in Cornerville in this new factory world. However, he is working in an industry of very advanced technical development, so that his lack of knowledge in this field will probably set a ceiling upon his advancement.

Doc got married shortly after he got his first steady job in World War II. His wife was an attractive Cornerville girl, a very intelligent and able person who had developed a small clothing store of her own.

I had one visit with Doc about five years after the book was published. Doc's reaction at the time seemed a combination of pride and embarrassment.

I asked Doc for the reaction of the members of his own gang. He said that Mike (to whom I had sent a copy) had seemed to like the book. Danny's only comment was: "Jesus, you're really a hell of a guy. If I was a dame, I'd marry you." The other members of the gang? So far as Doc knew, they had never read it. The question had come up all right. One night on the corner, one of the fellows said to Doc: "Say, I hear Bill Whyte's book is out. Maybe we should go up to the library and read it." Doc steered them off. "No, you wouldn't be interested, just a lot of big words. That's for the professors."

On another occasion, Doc was talking to the editor of the English-language weekly newspaper dealing with the Italian colony. The editor was thinking of publishing an article about the book. Doc discouraged him, and no such notice appeared.

I assume that in his quiet way Doc did everything he could to discourage the local reading of the book for the possible embarrassment it might cause a number of individuals, including himself. For example, it could hardly be pleasant reading for the low-ranking members of the Nortons to see it pointed out how low they ranked and what sort of difficulties they got into. Therefore, I have every sympathy with Doc's efforts in limiting the circulation of the book.

Mike Giovanni moved on from Cornerville to become a labor-union leader. It began with a job in a rapidly expanding war industry. Mike had no sooner been hired than he began looking around to organize a union. Shortly after this, he was fired. He took his case to the appropriate government agency, charging that he was fired for union activities. The company was ordered to put Mike back to work. He wrote me that, when he reappeared on the job, the situation seemed to change suddenly and dramatically. The other workers had thought they had seen the last of him. Now that he showed what could be done, they began signing up. For some months Mike was at the plant gate for half an hour before the shift came on and half an hour after his shift went home, distributing pledge cards. And he personally signed up fifteen hundred members. When the union was recognized, Mike became its vice-president. He also wrote a weekly column in the union paper under the heading of "Mr. CIO." The column was written in a colorful style and must have commanded a good deal of attention in the local.

At the next union election, Mike ran for president. He wrote me that his opponent was a man who had had very little to do with organizing the union. But he was a popular fellow—and he was an Irishman. Mike lost. Shortly after this time, the company began large-scale layoffs following the end of the war. Without a union office, Mike's seniority did not protect him, and he dropped out of his job.

All I know about Danny is that he finally got married to the pious girl who had always loved him in spite of his gambling and other activities. At last reports he is still working in Spong's horse room.

George and Carrie Ravello have been out of politics for a long time, but George has a fancy new funeral parlor.

What has happened to Chick Morelli? I was particularly anxious to answer that question, and yet I hesitated to go out for the answer. I debated the question with myself. I finally decided that Chick could be the individual whom I had hurt. I must find out what the book had done to him.

I telephoned Chick to ask if I could see him. At first he missed my name, but then he replied quite cordially. Still I was wondering what would happen when we sat down to talk.

I found that he had moved out of Cornerville, but, paradoxically enough, he still lived in the same ward inside the city. Doc, the old corner boy, had moved to the suburbs, and Chick, the man who was on his way up, had stayed in the center of the city.

Chick introduced me to his wife, an attractive and pleasant girl, who neither came from Cornerville nor was of Italian extraction. We sat in the living-room of an apartment that, with its furniture, books, curtains, and so on, looked distinctly middle class. For a few minutes we skirted about the subject that we all knew we were going to discuss. Then I asked Chick to tell me frankly his reactions to my book.

Chick began by saying that there were just two main criticisms as far as he was concerned. In the first place, he said that he did not think I distinguished his own way of speaking sufficiently from that of the corner boys when I quoted him. "You made me talk too rough, just like a gangster."

I expressed surprise at this, and here his wife joined in with the comment that she thought that I had made Chick look like a snob. Chick agreed that he had got that picture too. His wife pulled the book down from the shelf and reread the passage where I quote Doc on the occasion of a political meeting in which Chick is on and off the stage seven times in order to take the tickets that he is going to sell for the candidate. They both laughed at this, and Chick commented that he would never do a thing like that any more. She said that Chick had told her before they got married that he had once had a book written about him.

But she added that he didn't give her the book to read until after they had been married.

Chick laughed at this, and then he went on to his second criticism. "Bill, everything you described about what we did is true all right, but you should have pointed out that we were just young then. That was a stage that we were going through. I've changed a lot since that time."

Chick expressed concern over the reactions of other people to my book. "You know, after the book was out a while, I ran into Doc, and he was really upset about it. He said to me, 'Can you imagine that! After all I did for Bill Whyte, the things he put in the book about me. You know that thing about when I said you would step on the neck of your best friend just to get ahead. Well, now, maybe I said that, but I didn't really mean it. I was just sore at the time.' "

Chick seemed really concerned about what the book had done to my relationship with Doc. I did not tell him that Doc had read every page of the original manuscript, nor did I give my interpretation that Doc was simply going around repairing his fences after some of these intimate reactions had been exposed.

Chick assured me that he was not the hard character that the book seemed to make him. "Really, I'm a soft touch." And he gave me instances where he had helped out his friends at no advantage to himself.

As I was getting ready to leave, I asked Chick if he had anything more to say about the book.

"Well, I wonder if you couldn't have been more constructive, Bill. You think publishing something like this really does any good?"

I asked what he meant. Then he mentioned my pointing out (as he had told me himself) that he had difficulty with his *th* sound. I had also discussed the commotion the fellows sometimes caused in the theaters, the fact that they sometimes went to dances without ties, and so on—all points that make Cornerville look like a rather uncouth district. (I am unable to locate any references in the book to commotion in the theaters or men at dances without ties.)

"The trouble is, Bill, you caught the people with their hair down. It's a true picture, yes; but people feel it's a little too personal."

As he walked with me to the subway station, we got to talking about his political career. I had been quite astounded to hear that he had missed being elected to the Board of Aldermen by a scant three votes. The Chick Morelli whom I had known never could have come so close. Without expressing my surprise, I tried to get him to talk about this.

"You know, the funny thing is, Bill, I didn't get many votes from Cornerville. The people that you grow up with, it seems, are jealous of anybody that is getting ahead. Where I got my support was right around here where I live now. I know these fellows on the street corner, and I really fit with them."

As if to demonstrate for me, he nodded and waved cordially at several corner groups as we walked by. In a later visit to Cornerville, I learned that Chick Morelli had at last been elected to office.

Chick left me with a good deal to think over. In the first place, it is hard to describe the sense of relief I felt after seeing him. Although it must have hurt him at the time to read the book, he had been able to take it in stride, and he was now even able to laugh at himself in that earlier period. As I discussed these things later with Doc, I began to wonder whether the book might perhaps even have helped Chick. It was Doc who presented this theory. He argued that not many people have an opportunity to see themselves as other people see them. Perhaps the reading of the book enabled Chick to get valuable perspective on himself and even enabled him to change his behavior. Certainly, Doc argued, Chick had changed a good deal. He was still working hard to get ahead, but he seemed no longer the self-centered, insensitive person that he had earlier appeared to be. Chick certainly had to change in order to have any hopes of getting ahead in Democratic politics—and somehow, for reasons that I cannot now explain, Chick had decided that his future lay with the Democrats rather than with the Republicans, in whose direction he seemed to be moving as I left Cornerville. So, at least, the book had not hurt Chick, and it seemed just possible that it had helped him.

I was also pleased to find that basically Chick accepted the book. This, of course, pleased me as a writer, but it also spoke well of Chick. I suspect that the man who can accept such a portrait of himself is also the man who can change the behavior described.

Chick's objections to the book seemed quite interesting to me. As to the way I had quoted him in the book, I felt on very firm ground. He did talk differently from the corner boys, but not quite as differently as he had imagined. If a quotation from him contained an ungrammatical expression or some typical corner-boy phrase, I am reasonably sure that that part of it is authentic. I was so sensitive to the differences between Chick and the corner boys that I would have been unlikely to imagine any expressions that made them appear more alike. The criticism seemed to say more about Chick's status and aspirations than it did about my research methods.

Perhaps, indeed, I should have pointed out that Chick and his friends were young and were just going through a stage of development. But youth, in itself, does not seem to be a full explanation. These men were not adolescents; they were at least in their mid-twenties. I think that the important fact is that they had not yet secured any firm foothold in society. They were young men who had left home and had not yet arrived anywhere. I am inclined to agree that this is an important factor in explaining the aggressiveness, the self-centeredness, and so on, that appear in Chick and some of his friends at that period. Later on, when Chick had found something of a place for himself, he could relax and be more concerned with other people. Is this just a phenomenon of social mobility out of the slums and into middle-class status? As I think back upon my own career, I can recall with a trace of embarrassment some of the things that I said and did in the early stages when I was struggling to gain a good foothold on the academic ladder. It is easy to be modest and unassuming once you have achieved a fairly secure position and won a certain amount of recognition.

I had no quarrel with Chick's point that I had caught people with their hair down, and yet I could sympathize with the people who felt that way. If you are going to be interviewed for the newspaper, you put on your good suit and your best tie, make sure that the kitchen dishes are cleaned up, and in general take all the steps you associate with making a public appearance. You appear before the public in the role that you would like to play before the public. You cannot do this with a social researcher who comes in and lives with you. I do not see any way of getting around this difficulty. I suppose there must always be aspects of our reports that will give a certain amount of embarrassment to the people we have been studying. At least I was reassured to find that the reaction in this case had not been nearly so serious as I had feared.

While we can only speculate about the impact of the book upon Doc and Chick and many others, there is one man upon whom it has had a profound effect—and I was not always sure that the effect would be constructive. Working with me made Sam Franco, who had only a high-school education, want to be a human relations research man.

When the war broke out, Sam enlisted in the Marine Corps. I wrote to him around the time that *Street Corner Society* was to be published, asking whether I should send a copy to him. He wrote to say that his unit was about to be shipped overseas, that where he was going he would be able to carry nothing extra, and that I should send the book to his wife in Cornerville. Some months later I again heard from him. He had fought through three island landings. On the third, his closest friend in the service was killed beside him, and he was knocked unconscious by the concussion. He came to on a hospital ship heading back to San Diego. His first letter to me from the hospital seemed somewhat discouraged and disorganized, as is natural for a man who has gone through such experiences. A week later he wrote me again, full of enthusiasm. He had called for his wife to send the book as soon as he had returned to this country, and now he had read it. He wanted me to know that he believed in the book, and he believed in this sort of work. He was going back to Cornerville to carry on himself.

He even enrolled in a correspondence course in sociology, but this he abandoned after a while. He wrote me that somehow it did not seem the sort of thing that he and I had been doing in Cornerville.

After returning to Eastern City, he got himself a very good job with a firm that handled window decorations for department stores, and he was making money on the side with floats for parades and various odd jobs in the artistic line. Still, he had not abandoned the idea that he wanted to do social research. He even worked at it in the Marine Corps Reserve, where he was first a corporal and then a sergeant. (He had been offered a chance to go to OCS during his basic training but had turned it down.) The reserve unit had one evening of training each week, and after each session Sam would pound out a record of what had taken place on his typewriter. He not only observed; he also experimented on the informal group structure. He picked out a task that would call for four or five men. He picked out one individual and told him to get three or four others of his own choosing and then do the job. Then Sam observed which individuals the man chose and how effectively the job was done. He picked out men whom he considered followers in the informal structure, and observed the inefficiencies and inco-ordinations that developed as they sought to get the group working with them. He also picked out individuals he had tabbed as leaders and observed the marked contrast in the effectiveness of the performance. Of course, the freedom that he gave the individual to pick his own work associates helped Sam to delineate the natural groupings.

Sam went through this process, obsessed with the idea that even the Marine Corps (for which he had the typical Marine Corps loyalty) could be a much more effective organization if officers and non-coms had a better understanding of informal group structures.

As best I could, operating from a great distance, I tried to get Sam the help that he needed. First, George Homans took an interest in his field work and got him in touch with a Marine Corps officer who was then attached to Harvard. On his own, Sam managed to interest his superior officers of the Marine Corps Reserve in his group observations.

Sam wrote that he was quite prepared to drop his decorating job and re-enlist in the Marine Corps if he could have some assurance that he would be able to pursue the sort of human relations research upon which he was embarked. We found, however, that the Marine Corps had no provision for any such activity. There were some people within the Corps who thought so well of Sam and his ideas that they even sought to get a special classification set up for him, but that was too much to expect. So Sam continued researching on his own, torn between his job and the work he wanted to do.

The Korean War changed all this. We visited Sam and his family several weeks after the outbreak of hostilities. At the time he had already received his call to go back into the service, and he was a very discouraged and disgruntled man. There was, of course, the question of survival. When a Marine goes into battle, he told me, he does not expect to come through it alive. In fact, his whole training conditions him to accepting death on the battlefield. If, by some remarkable good fortune, he does escape, he feels that he has more than used up his chances of survival. If he should go into combat again, death would be an absolute certainty. And now he had a family to think of, and he had got used to peacetime pursuits. He and the other men in his reserve unit would go back when they were called, of course, but they all felt that they had done as much as should be asked of them.

There was something more than physical survival at stake. For years Sam had been struggling to do research on human relations. Perhaps it was a foolish and vain hope, but he hated to give it up. And going back to combat duty certainly meant giving it up.

I said it was too bad that Sam was in the Marine Corps, for that was the one branch of the services that presented the very least opportunity to develop the work in which he was interested. If he were in the Air Force or in the Navy or even in the Army, there might be some chance of his fitting into a research program.

It was then that he told me that there was some chance of being assigned to "detached duty," that, as a Marine, he could be assigned to one of the other services if a special request came through and was accepted by the Marine Corps. Without any real hope of success, I told him I would work on this.

I wrote to a man I knew who was in charge of a research program in the Air Force. I gave a full account of Sam's work with me and of what I thought he could do—if he were working under professional supervision. I got back a noncommittal letter indicating that something might possibly be done. A few weeks later, to my surprise, I learned that the wheels were actually turning. The research unit of the Air Force had made an official request that Sam Franco be assigned to it. The papers were on their way up the line in the Air Force, and strong recommendations for Sam from his superior officers in the Marine Corps were also going up through channels. At last I heard that the request had been turned down, and this looked final, even though Sam told me that there was one loophole remaining. Meanwhile, Sam was back in training and awaiting shipment overseas. Toward the end of December, 1950, he called me long distance. "Bill, it's just like in the movies. Yesterday I received my orders to ship out for Korea, and today the papers came through for the assignment with the Air Force."

Sam has been with the Air Force for about three years now, for the first two on detached duty and finally as an Air Force master sergeant as the result of a transfer that had to be approved by the commanding generals of both the Marine Corps and the Air Force. So, at last, he has been able to get into research full time. He has been operating in an atmosphere where questionnaires are the accepted method and where the professional research men readily admit that they cannot utilize Sam as he should be utilized. Nevertheless, he has been out on several brief organizational studies and has shown that he can get data that are generally unavailable to the civilians with the research unit. How far he can go, no one can yet say, but he is in the field where he wants to be and is working at writing up his observations on discipline and leadership in military organizations.

So the story has a happy ending—so far. But it was only by an extraordinary chance that Sam was able to pursue the work that he wanted to do. Had the chance not come, his association with me might simply have served to frustrate him with ambitions that he could never expect to gratify.

How widely has the book been read in Eastern City and in Cornerville in particular? Here I had one of my great surprises at the very outset. The publisher sent review copies to the major newspapers in the largest cities in the country. I did not expect to get very many such newspaper reviews, but I assumed at least that the book would get some attention in the Eastern City papers. I was sure that no one who was really familiar with the life of the city could read the book without knowing he was reading of his own city or without identifying the particular section of it. This local angle would naturally bring the book a good deal more attention. What effect this would have—other than selling copies—I did not stop to imagine.

Curiously enough, while the book did receive full-column reviews in several large metropolitan newspapers, not a single one of the Eastern City dailies gave it any attention whatsoever. Just why this was, I am still unable to conjecture. The nearest I got to a local review was one which appeared in the nearest major city, but there the reviewer shrewdly guessed that the locale of my study had been in a city a thousand miles away.

Even without newspaper fanfare, the book naturally attracted some attention in Cornerville. Kathleen's book jacket (a street corner scene) was posted on the bulletin board for "recent books of interest" in the Cornerville branch library for at least five years after publication. It proved popular enough, so that the library had to buy a second copy, and then someone did me the compliment of stealing a copy. Sam Franco, however, reports after a visit with a member of the local library staff: "When she told me that the book was very popular, I said that it did not tie in with what I had found out. When I mentioned your book, most of them knew of it. When I pinpointed them into telling me something about the book, they would in all cases tell me they had never read it. . . . Still, it is my strong opinion that your book was intensively read by the settlement houses, social workers, and all those involved in your book." Even here, we must have our reservations, for, according to Doc, most of the Nortons had not read the book.

I seem to be looked upon by the social workers, at Norton Street at least, as a man who turned against his own people. One of my informants passed on this reaction from the settlement, after talking with one of the social workers. He said that they felt that "they had taken you in good faith, but you gave them the business. He went on to say that you only gave one side of the story in order to make sensational reading, that you were immature, that your 'sophomoric attitude' hurt them. I asked him to explain how the book hurt them. He didn't know what to say and then said that the book didn't really hurt them but that many social workers and all the people at Harvard read the book, and that's what he said was 'hurting.' "

What has been happening to social work in Cornerville? Today the Cornerville House has two full-time workers of Italian extraction (but not from Cornerville) on its staff. The Norton Street House has a full-time man, born and reared in Cornerville, on its staff for work with young boys. I believe that all three of these people have had college educations and professional training beyond that.

On my latest visit to Cornerville I had a long talk with Mr. Kendall, who was head of boys' work in the period of my study and is now head of the Cornerville House.

He began by recognizing that the settlements do not generally reach the corner boys with whom I was dealing. However, he said that some people questioned whether this group should be reached by a settlement. The parents like to look upon the settlement as a place where their children are in a wholesome environment. If the typical corner group were taken in, its very presence might drive out those whom the settlements have been successful in reaching.

I acknowledged this possibility, but further discussion brought out an interesting contradiction within the experience of Mr.

Kendall and his Cornerville House. In the late stages of World War II, Kendall became concerned that the house gymnasium was getting very little use. He hired a returning war hero and corner-boy leader to do "outside work" in organizing a basketball league. Within several weeks he had organized *forty-two* teams into several basketball leagues. In the succeeding months the house was seething with basketball excitement, and everyone seems now to look back upon this period as one of the highpoints in the history of the house. Mr. Kendall mentioned no cases of groups dropping out because various roughnecks were using the gym. (After this one season the emergency funds that had made the position possible were no longer available, and the very successful organizer was not retained on the staff.)

There was also a dancing class that brought in first a few and then large numbers of adolescent girls and boys. The boys, from all I could learn, seemed to be authentic corner boys. At first there was some horseplay, but the teacher, a very capable Italian-American woman, soon got things organized in real ballroom style.

Apparently a settlement house can take in a broader range of groups than may be commonly supposed—given always the limitation that a corner gang wants a meeting place for every night of the week and that no settlement can provide such space.

What are the prospects for hiring local men who have not had college or social work training? The answer seems to be: Not very good. The heads of the institutions who would make such appointments are under pressure to move in quite a different direction. The schools of social work have for years been trying to get social work recognized as a profession. How can it become a profession if the young man who got his basic training on the street corner is accepted? The standards must be raised. That means a college degree *and* an M.A. in social work.

No one is threatened that his funds will be cut off if he hires other than M.A.'s in social work. But the head worker is asked how many people on his staff have this degree, and he hears references to other institutions which are not "measuring up."

Upon inquiry, he learns that the institutions that are not measuring up" are those which persist in hiring people who do not have
their social work M.A.'s.

A similar pressure affects even the summer camping activities.
No one can require that all the counselors be social work M.A.'s,
but it seems to be desirable that they be *college boys*. The agency
that evaluates summer camps circulates a questionnaire which
asks how many college boys and how many noncollege boys
are to serve as counselors. It is evident what the right answer is
on this point. On this question, the better the settlement-house
camp, the fewer local men it will have as counselors. (Of course,
there will be a few local college men available, but the pressure
toward hiring college men will inevitably lead the institution to
look outside the district.)

So there seems to be little chance that future corner-boy leaders will play a greater role in organizing settlement-house activities. Perhaps it is only through reaching social work students
that *Street Corner Society* could have any impact upon social work.

15. REFLECTIONS ON FIELD RESEARCH

As I carried through the Cornerville study, I was also learning
how to do field research. I learned from the mistakes I made. The
most important of these I have described fully. I learned from
the successes that I had, but these were less spectacular and more
difficult to describe. It may therefore be worth while to try to
summarize the main characteristics of the research.

Of course, I am not claiming that there is a one best way to do
field research. The methods used should depend upon the nature
of the field situation and of the research problem. I am simply
trying to fit together the findings of the study and the methods
required to arrive at such findings.

In the first place, the study took a long time. This was due
in part to the fact that I had had no previous field experience
and very little educational background that was directly relevant
to my problem. But that was not all. It took a long time because
the parts of the study that interest me most depended upon an

intimate familiarity with people and situations. Furthermore, I learned to understand a group only through observing how it changed *through time*.

This familiarity gave rise to the basic ideas in this book. I did not develop these ideas by any strictly logical process. They dawned on me out of what I was seeing, hearing, doing—and feeling. They grew out of an effort to organize a confusing welter of experience.

I had to balance familiarity with detachment, or else no insights would have come. There were fallow periods when I seemed to be just marking time. Whenever life flowed so smoothly that I was taking it for granted, I had to try to get outside of my participating self and struggle again to explain the things that seemed obvious.

This explains why my research plans underwent such drastic changes in the course of the study. I was on an exploration into unknown territory. Worse than unknown, indeed, because the then existing literature on slum districts was highly misleading. It would have been impossible to map out at the beginning the sort of study I eventually found myself doing.

This is not an argument against initial planning of research. If his study grows out of a body of soundly executed research, then the student can and should plan much more rigorously than I did. But, even so, I suspect that he will miss important data unless he is flexible enough to modify his plans as he goes along. The apparent "tangent" often turns out to be the main line of future research.

Street Corner Society is about particular people and situations and events. I wanted to write about Cornerville. I found that I could not write about Cornerville in general without discarding most of the data I had upon individuals and groups. It was a long time before I realized that I could explain Cornerville better through telling the stories of those individuals and groups than I could in any other way.

Instead of studying the general characteristics of classes of people, I was looking at Doc, Chick, Tony Cataldo, George

Ravello, and others. Instead of getting a cross-sectional picture of the community at a particular point in time, I was dealing with a time sequence of interpersonal events.

Although I could not cover all Cornerville, I was building up the structure and functioning of the community through intensive examination of some of its parts—*in action*. I was relating the parts together through observing events between groups and between group leaders and the members of the larger institutional structures (of politics and the rackets). I was seeking to build a sociology based upon observed interpersonal events. That, to me, is the chief methodological and theoretical meaning of *Street Corner Society*.

INDEX